DATABANKS
in a Free Society

Computers, Record-Keeping and Privacy

DATABANKS
in a Free Society

Computers, Record-Keeping and Privacy

ALAN F. WESTIN: Project Director
MICHAEL A. BAKER: Assistant Project Director

Report of the Project on Computer Databanks
of the
Computer Science and Engineering Board
National Academy of Sciences, Washington, D.C. Project
on Computer Databanks.

This study was supported by a grant
from Russell Sage Foundation

Quadrangle Books
A New York Times Company

Notice

The study reported herein was undertaken under the aegis of the National Research Council with the express approval of the Governing Board of the NRC. Such approval indicated that the Board considered that the problem is of national significance, that elucidation of the problem required scientific or technical competence, and that the resources of NRC were particularly suitable to the conduct of the project. The institutional responsibilities of the NRC were then discharged in the following manner:

The members of the study committee were selected for their individual scholarly competence and judgment with due consideration for the balance and breadth of disciplines. Responsibility for all aspects of this report rests with the study committee, to whom sincere appreciation is expressed.

Although the reports of study committees are not submitted for approval to the Academy membership or to the Council, each report is reviewed by a second group of appropriately qualified individuals according to procedures established and monitored by the Academy's Report Review Committee. Such reviews are intended to determine, *inter alia*, whether the major questions and relevant points of view have been addressed and whether the reported findings, conclusions, and recommendations arose from the available data and information. Distribution of the report is approved, by the president, only after satisfactory completion of this review process.

This study was undertaken with the support of Russell Sage Foundation, which is not to be construed as implying approval by the foundation, its trustees, or its staff with the contents of this report. The National Academy of Sciences is grateful for the support of the foundation.

Acknowledgement gratefully given to Alfred A. Knopf, Inc. for permission to print a portion of *The Trial*, by Franz Kafka, pages 198-199. Copyright © 1937 and renewed 1965 by Alfred A. Knopf, Inc.

Library of Congress Card Number: 75-183193

International Standard Book Number 0-8129-0292-0

The Project on Computer Databanks

Director

Alan F. Westin, Professor of Public Law and Government, Columbia University

Assistant Director

Michael A. Baker, Instructor in Sociology, Brooklyn College of the City University of New York

---

*Staff Associates**

Robert F. Boruch, Assistant Professor of Psychology, Northwestern University

Howard Campaigne, Professor of Mathematics, Slippery Rock State College

Gerald L. Grotta, Associate Professor of Journalism, Southern Illinois University

Lance J. Hoffman, Assistant Professor of Electrical Engineering and Computer Sciences, University of California, Berkeley

Charles Lister, Attorney at Law, Washington, D.C.

Consultant

Joel E. Cohen, Assistant Professor, Department of Biology and School of Public Health, Harvard University

Research Assistants

Robert Belaire, Columbia University Law School

J. Paul Blum, Department of History, Columbia University

Jerrold Kamensky, George Washington University Law School

Linda Lorenzetti, Program Librarian, Computation Group, Stanford Linear Accelerator Center

Administrative Assistants
Madelyn Miller
Lorene Cox

Administrative Secretaries
Barbara Arenson
Bernice Holmes

---

*Oliver Eugene Dial, then Chairman of the Political Science Department of Baruch College, City University of New York, served as a staff associate until September 1970, when other commitments required him to withdraw.

In addition, Messrs. Ray Debuse, Tom Headrick, Kenneth Laudon, and Phil Lochner aided the project by participating in particular site visits and contributing reports to the staff.

National Advisory Group

Contents

Foreword   *xiii*

Preface   *xix*

I   Records, Computers, and Civil Liberties:
    The Setting of the Issues   **1**

II   Profiles from the World of
    Computerizing Organizations   **21**

Government Organizations:
The Federal Level   *29*

   The Social Security Administration—31
   The Federal Bureau of Investigation's
     National Crime Information Center—47
   New York State Department of
     Motor Vehicles—66
   Kansas City, Missouri, Police Department—77
   New Haven, Connecticut—89
   Santa Clara County, California—101

Commercial Organizations   *111*

   The Bank of America—113
   TRW-Credit Data Corporation—132
   Mutual of Omaha—143
   R. L. Polk and Company—156

Nonprofit Organizations   *168*

   The Massachusetts Institute of Technology—169
   The American Council on Education—183

The Church of the Latter-day Saints—194
The Kaiser-Permanente Medical Care Program—205

III   Site-Visit Findings from 55 Advanced Systems   **215**

Trends in Computerization
   of Personal Records   *217*
Effects on Privacy, Confidentiality,
   and Due Process   *241*
Effects on Record-Keeping   *280*

IV   Future Directions in Computer
      Technology   **317**

Elements of a Technological Forecast   *319*

V   Implications for Public Policy   **337**

The Broad Significance of Our Findings   *341*

Areas of Priority for Public Policy   *355*

Appendix A   *407*

   *Report on a Survey of Managerial Opinion
   on the Impact of Computers in Record-
   Keeping*

Appendix B   *463*

   *Public Opinion Surveys on Computers,
   Privacy, and Record-Keeping*

Appendix C   *487*

   Databank Developments in Other Nations

Appendix D   *495*

   Site-Visit Letters

Index   *503*

Foreword

In the fall of 1968, when Alan Westin of The Computer Science and Engineering Board first proposed to Russell Sage Foundation a study of computerized databanks in American society, it was evident at once that here was a great opportunity for a private foundation to contribute to the public good. During the decade of the 1960s a number of popular books were published in the United States on the issue of individual privacy. These stimulated a great deal of public discussion, and several subsequent congressional committee hearings have focused on the problem. But there were few reasoned inquiries or balanced analyses of the fundamental conflict between the individual's right to privacy and society's right to know. Of these, Dr. Westin's earlier book, *Privacy and Freedom*, is the best. The opportunity to assist Dr. Westin, a longtime friend of the foundation, and the National Academy of Sciences, with whom the foundation already had worked very successfully on other studies, to carry out a definitive analysis of the role of databanks in modern society was a rare and happy occasion.

Support of this study continued Russell Sage Foundation's long-standing concern with the issue of privacy. The foundation's entry into this area began in 1961 when it launched a program of research on the consequences of standardized ability testing in the United States. Studies[1] on the use of standardized ability tests examined American attitudes toward and beliefs about intelligence testing, and set forth the implications for school policies in the dissemination of ability test scores. One important outcome was

---

[1]David A. Goslin, *The Search for Ability: Standardized Testing in Social Perspective*. New York: Russell Sage Foundation, 1963; Orville G. Brim, Jr., David C. Glass, John Neulinger, and Ira Firestone, *American Beliefs and Attitudes about Intelligence*. New York: Russell Sage Foundation, 1969.

the identification of an important set of issues relating to the collection and use by school personnel of data about pupils and their families, including standardized test scores. Despite efforts to decentralize some school systems, the persistent trend toward larger administrative units in public education results in the adoption of more formalized record-keeping systems. Virtually all school systems now maintain extensive records containing, in addition to a pupil's attendance and achievement record, standardized test scores, personality data, information on family background and current status, health data, teacher and counselor observations, and anecdotal records. Foundation-supported studies clearly indicated the lack of uniformity—or even existence—of school policy for using information about pupils for determining the conditions under which information might be collected, and for regulating access to the data. A subsequent foundation-sponsored conference on ethical and legal aspects of school record-keeping resulted in the development of a set of guidelines[2] for the management of school records. This report, distributed to more than 100,000 educational leaders and school policymakers in this country, has led to widespread deliberations on policies regarding educational records at the local level. Currently this mode of analysis is being extended to student record-keeping in institutions of higher education in the United States.

These studies of the educational institution led to the support of a number of other projects dealing with the balance between personal privacy and institutional record-keeping. One of the central issues in contemporary American society concerns the power of organizations over their individual members. The increased bureaucratization of modern society has led to a natural growth of record-keeping systems, and the possible misuse of such systems has emerged as a social problem. As concerned individuals began speculating on the appropriate balance between the need for information and the possibility of its misuse, it became apparent how little is really known about the way in which organizations use their records. Stanton Wheeler of the foundation staff and the Yale University Law School brought together a number of original papers by experts in the various sectors of institutional record-keeping that analyzed the way in which organizations handle such information. This study[3] included reports on record-keeping in

---

[2] *Guidelines for the Collection, Maintenance, and Dissemination of Pupil Records.* New York: Russell Sage Foundation, 1970.

[3] Stanton Wheeler (ed.), *On Record: Files and Dossiers in American Life.* New York: Russell Sage Foundation, 1970.

educational and professional institutions, in business, in government, and in welfare systems.

In 1964, the foundation became concerned with a second aspect of the problem of privacy, that of human experimentation. As one of the major private foundations supporting applied social science research, it sought to develop guidelines for experimentation on human subjects. An influential study[4] by the chairman of the board of trustees of the foundation, Oscar M. Ruebhausen, and the president, set forth the guidelines for social research that would be followed by the foundation in subsequent years. These guidelines found their way into the official statements on human experimentation by the Department of Health, Education, and Welfare, and into the codes of ethics being developed by social science professional associations.

The foundation subsequently encouraged several major inquiries into the question of human experimentation. While scientific research on human beings has a long history, during this decade there was a distinct increase in human experimentation. One aspect was specifically associated with a need to test new drugs and related therapeutic procedures before releasing them for public consumption. Bernard Barber of Columbia University examined the review and approval committees of peers that exercise control over human experimentation in universities and other research institutions; he included a study of socialization of researchers into the ethics of using human subjects, and the ways in which informal and formal research associations influence ethical behavior of the researchers.[5] Jay Katz of the Yale University Law School completed a casebook dealing with the subject of human experimentation and its effect on national life.[6] The latter volume represents the most comprehensive effort to date to provide casebook materials on the problem of human experimentation. In utilizing studies from medicine, biology, psychology, sociology, and law, it examines the problems raised from a vantage point of each of its major participants—investigator, subjects, professions, and the state.

A third concern over individual privacy developed a half

---

[4] Oscar M. Ruebhausen and Orville G. Brim, Jr., "Privacy and Behavioral Research," *Columbia Law Review*, Vol. 65 (November 1965), pp. 1184-1211.

[5] Bernard A. Barber, *Experimenting with Humans*. New York: Russell Sage Foundation, 1972.

[6] Jay Katz, *Experimentation with Human Beings: The Authority of the Investigator, Subject, Profession, and State in the Human Experimentation Process*. New York: Russell Sage Foundation, 1972.

dozen years ago when Russell Sage Foundation moved to provide national leadership in the development of social indicators for our country. On the premise that intelligent formulation of public policy requires greater knowledge and understanding of the social and economic forces that shaped our future, and in recognition of the rapid pace of change in the structure of American society, a major part of foundation activity was devoted to improving the measurement of social change through the development of social indicators. Two influential foundation studies[7] resulted—one dealing with the development of indicators of changes in institutions and social processes, such as the family, health, and social mobility, and the other concerned with social psychological changes in the American population, including beliefs about the quality of life, the suitability of housing, and trust in political representatives. In the past few years the concept of indicators itself, and research in the area, have risen to national and international prominence. Official cognizance of the potential impact of measures of change is exemplified by a number of developments. There is a recent report of the White House National Goals Research Staff. The United Nations Commission on Social Development has called for the preparation of social indicators. National and international meetings of various professional, academic, and governmental agencies provide program sessions for the discussion of such measures and their utilization. American federal statistical agencies are planning the periodic release of data on social trends. In the process of consolidating the foundation's work in this area, its staff has participated in most of these activities.

The very process of establishing a system for monitoring social change demands the collection and analysis of statistical data from the various segments of the nation's population. The fact that a wide variety of information may be obtained for the purpose of social planning in conjunction with already existent data available from tens of millions of Americans gives substance to fears concerning the invasion of privacy. Consequently, there is a severe challenge for those who compile and use data for the public welfare and also recognize legitimate claims to individual privacy.

---

[7] Eleanor Bernert Sheldon and Wilbert E. Moore (eds.), *Indicators of Social Change: Concepts and Measurements.* New York: Russell Sage Foundation, 1968; Angus Campbell and Philip E. Converse (eds.), *The Human Meaning of Social Change.* New York: Russell Sage Foundation, 1972.

There has been, and still is, much confused thinking about databanks in our society. We have our doomsday prophets crying out about national data centers, our widely shared anecdotes about credit-card society and tattooed Social Security numbers, and plenty of wild and misinformed testimony at congressional hearings. Alan Westin and the Computer Science and Engineering Board of the National Academy of Sciences are to be congratulated for this most important contribution to the analysis of the enduring problem of balancing the rights of the individual and the rights of society.

Orville G. Brim, Jr.
President
Russell Sage Foundation

Preface

Due process and privacy have long been matters of fundamental importance to all Americans. At its inception in July 1968, the Computer Science and Engineering Board of the National Academy of Sciences invited one of its members, Alan F. Westin, Professor of Public Law and Government at Columbia University, to discuss issues of due process and of privacy in the context of trends toward increasing computerization of personal records. Because of the sparseness of information, the board concluded that the public interest would be served by searching out and publishing a comprehensive body of facts about the actual effects that computers, communications, and allied information technologies have had on creating, sharing, and using files on individuals.

This goal was to be reached through firsthand studies in depth of as broad a cross-section of private and public files as resources would permit. In keeping with the board's policy, commitment to this goal implied looking not merely at file technology, but also at the nontechnical factors shaping its use; it implied estimating technological trends and developing the future implications of these trends for individual and public policy choices on matters of due process and of privacy. Including classified government files in the study was precluded by legal limitations on access to these files and, when access is granted, on freedom to publish findings. Attempting, as an alternative, to develop implications for public policy choices from the fragmented and unverifiable information publicly available seemed unwise.

Professor Westin, with Dr. Launor Carter, Vice-president and Manager of the Public Systems Division of the Systems Development Corporation; Dr. John R. Meyer, President of the National

Bureau of Economic Research and Professor of Economics at Yale University; Dr. John R. Pierce, then Executive Director of the Research Communications Sciences Division at Bell Laboratories and now Professor of Engineering at the California Institute of Technology; and Dr. J. Barkley Rosser, Professor of Mathematics and Director of the Mathematics Research Center at the University of Wisconsin, developed a study plan for review and approval by the board.

Sharing as they do the board's interest in the interrelation of law, the behavioral sciences, and technology, Russell Sage Foundation and its President, Orville G. Brim, Jr., were receptive to our plan. In February 1969, Russell Sage Foundation accepted a formal study proposal submitted by the Computer Science and Engineering Board and approved by the President and Council of the National Academy of Sciences. Named Project Director, Alan Westin, with the advice of the board, assembled a staff well versed in computer science, economics, journalism, law, political science, psychology, and sociology. Based on the contributions and critical comments of the entire project staff, the final report was written by Alan F. Westin and Michael A. Baker.

To assure that major viewpoints and contrasting positions on basic issues involved in databanks would influence the planning, research, and reporting of the project, the board appointed a National Advisory Group to the project. With the understanding that their role was advisory and that responsibility for this report rests with the authors, the Computer Science and Engineering Board and the National Academy of Sciences, these people gave fully and freely of their advice and their criticism at several stages of the work. This report owes much to their probing and their prodding.

A distinguishing mark of this report is its fascinating first-hand accounts of 14 out of over 50 site visits made by the project director and his staff to public and private organizations whose files on people are in transition from manual to computer technology. The staff was welcomed with courtesy over extended and, occasionally, repeated visits. To each organization and to every individual in it who met with the staff and answered their questions, the board expresses its thanks.

Those who answered the questionnaires used in the study were pledged anonymity. In their privacy, they too have our thanks, along with the anonymous reviewers of this report selected by the National Academy of Sciences' Report Review Committee.

The board closely supervised the study throughout its course. Alan Westin and his staff gave of themselves unstintingly in developing the factual base for their findings and analyses. The board deeply appreciates their efforts and is pleased to commend this report to all Americans.

Computer Science and Engineering Board

By _____

Anthony G. Oettinger
Chairman

Part I

Records, Computers, and
Civil Liberties:
The Setting of the Issues

In Greek mythology, the course of each man's destiny in life was set by three sisters known as the Fates, daughters of the god Zeus. Clotho spun the thread of life; Lachesis measured its length; and Atropos cut it. Those whom the Fates smiled upon were given a long and bright thread; those whom the Fates did not favor learned to their anguish that no effort on their part could reverse the "implacable decree" of the Three Sisters. A friendly god might be able to help an individual "cheat the Fates" temporarily, as by diverting the attention of a god who was watching a battle to see that the apportioned judgment took place. But the Greeks accepted the idea that each individual's progress in life unfolded as the Fates had determined it.

In modern society, of course, we live by different myths. But as Americans entered the post-World War II era, it seemed as though the role of the Three Fates might be reappearing in modern dress. The life thread of each man was now spun in the formal records that gatekeeper organizations began to keep about him at birth. He was measured at each step of his growth according to the information woven into these proliferating files. And when critical decisions affecting his adult life were made by managers of the government agencies, commercial enterprises, and private institutions which controlled the destiny of individuals in industrial civilization, the individual's personal record was perhaps the most important single resource used to make those judgments. The Three Sisters with shuttle and shears had been replaced by the record-weaving looms of large organizations.

Then, in the 1960s, another symbolic image began to take shape. The record-keeping looms were automated. With the advent of electronic data processing and the rapid adoption of this technology by large organizations, information about individuals moved from the filing cabinet to the computer. For the supporters of high-technology society, the power of computer systems was welcome, since it promised to enable organizational evaluators to obtain the timely and complete information with which to make truly informed decisions about individuals. But to other observers, and to major sectors of public opinion, computerization of personal records promised something else as well.

The tremendous speed of processing, the large storage capacities, and the rapid data communication that computer systems made possible could, they feared, dramatically increase the amount of information collected, consolidated, and exchanged about individuals. Such a trend was seen as threatening the boundaries of personal privacy and confidentiality that had evolved out of a combination of technological limitations and civil-liberties rules in precomputer America. At the same time, it was feared that many vital judgments about people might no longer be made by clerks and managers but instead would be determined in rigid fashion through the cold calculations of computer systems. If the Three Fates symbolized the caprice of the ancient gods, and the organizational record-keeping of the welfare state represented the essence of modern bureaucracy, the arrival of computerization in record-keeping evoked for many Americans the disturbing spectre of "all-knowing" machines sitting in judgment on men.

To move from symbolic to real events, the 1960s witnessed wide public anxiety over what has come to be called the "databank issue"—an amalgam of concerns about the extent and uses of record-keeping by organizations, their move to computers, and possible effects of computerization on rights of personal privacy. Books such as Vance Packard's *The Naked Society* and Myron Brenton's *The Privacy Invaders* appeared in the mid-1960s. National television programs warned about the dangers to civil liberties presented by the marvels of new surveillance technology, including computers. During 1966 and 1967, congressional hearings were held into two areas where the use of personal data and the move to computers raised serious questions of privacy: the operations of commercial credit bureaus and proposals to create a National Data Center for statistical research. By the late 1960s, the "databank issue" had become one of the most widely discussed and emotionally laden civil-liberties questions facing American society.

For all the attention that the issue received, however, one vital ingredient was lacking in American society's consideration of the databank problem—a sound factual knowledge of what was actually taking place as organizations moved to computerize their records. Many public commentators focused on technological possibilities, assuming that what could be done in a laboratory or in the environment of a special project would inevitably, and soon, become widespread organizational practice. Other commentators relied on the long-range system plans and project proposals of organizations, assuming that the goals and timetables portrayed there would be achieved as stated. With a sense of such rapidly accelerating change, legislators and judges began to wonder how they could intervene to bring this mushrooming technology under legal and administrative controls.

It was in this context, as Professor Oettinger notes in his Preface, that the Computer Science and Engineering Board decided to commission a national study of computer databanks and civil liberties. The critical need, the board felt, was to gather empirical data about what was actually happening in the world of computers and organizations, and to explore the implications of these facts for public policy.

Events since the launching of this project in 1969 show that there has been no slackening of public anxieties over the databank issue. Many new books, articles, and television programs have dealt with computers and privacy; disclosure of the U.S. Army's surveillance of political dissidents in the late 1960s increased the levels of public concern; and Sen. Sam Ervin's hearings in 1971 into "Federal Data Banks, Computers, and the Bill of Rights" revealed deep congressional uneasiness about the impact computerization was having on constitutional rights.

An Outline of the Report

The report of our study will proceed as follows. In the rest of this Introduction, we describe some fundamentals of electronic data processing and civil liberties for readers who may want an orienting discussion about these central topics of our study. In part two, we present profiles of 14 governmental, commercial, and private organizations that are leaders in their fields in the use of computers for record-keeping. Based on detailed on-site visits and followup contacts made by our project staff to 55 leading organizations between 1970 and 1972, these profiles illustrate the motives, programs, problems, and civil-liberties issues to be found in the real world of computerizing organizations during the past decade and today.

Following these profiles, part three of the report offers our principal findings, organized into three chapters. The first is a general overview of computer uses in the organizations we visited. The second describes changes in organizational record-keeping patterns and civil-liberties protections that many commentators believed to be taking place but which we did *not* find to be happening as yet among the organizations we studied. The final chapter in part three discusses changes that we *did* observe taking place, together with our findings about accuracy and security problems in computerized record systems.

Part four is a forecast of the directions in which computer technology is likely to move in the remaining years of the 1970s, to provide public policymakers with a picture of likely trends for use in their consideration of current policy choices.

Finally, part five turns to analysis of policy implications. We first consider the meaning of our empirical findings in terms of the sociopolitical context of American life, focusing specifically on the moment in our national history at which computers arrived and were taken up by large organizations. Then, the last section sets out a general framework for considering issues of record-keeping, computers, and civil liberties, and discusses six major areas of priority for public policy in dealing with these problems.

There are three substantive appendixes to our report. In the winter and spring of 1971, we conducted exploratory surveys in 14 different fields, probing managerial opinion about the computer's impact on record-keeping. While the site visits focused upon organizations which are advanced in their computerization of personal records, the 1,500 survey respondents were drawn for the most part from a wide range of organizations in each of these fields. Appendix A, covering the results of these surveys, treats the computer's impact on data gathering, sharing, and use; managerial awareness of civil-liberties complaints from record subjects; and managers' opinions about the need for new technological, administrative, and legal safeguards for civil liberties in record systems.

Appendix B covers recent literature on general public opinion about privacy issues, analyzing available survey data on how the American public reacts to invasion of privacy as a general issue; how people balance individual claims to privacy and due process against organizational claims about the necessity for data collection and the use of closed administrative procedures; and how the American public views the computer as a source of privacy and record-keeping problems.

While the full discussions of managerial and general public opinion on computers and privacy are presented in these Appendixes, conclusions from this material are used in our presentations of site-visit findings and public policy choices.

Appendix C contains a survey of databank developments and policy responses in foreign nations, based on studies of the 23 industrialized countries making up the Organization for Economic Co-operation and Development (OECD).

Rather than present a long methodological discussion in this Introduction, we will reserve our discussion of research objectives and procedures for the points at which they are relevant to a substantive discussion in the report. The conduct of our site visits is described at the opening of part two, the methods used to derive our site-visit findings are described at the opening of part three, procedures for our survey of managers are related in the first section of Appendix A, and so forth.

We now turn to the discussion of some basic concepts concerning computers and civil liberties. Readers already knowledgeable on these topics may want to skip to part two, though they may wish to read our presentation of basic concepts to see the perceptions with which we have gone forward in the project.

Fundamentals of Computer Technology

The history of technology has seen the introduction of many devices which served to augment human capabilities—extending the muscles, transcending the limits of human senses, and moving beyond the limits of the human voice for the transmission of information through space. But aside from advances in communication technology and the development of some devices for counting, the computer is the first technology developed to *use* information, not only by following preset instructions automatically but also taking into account the results of its own operations. The computer, more than any other technological development, extends some functions of the human brain, expanding in crude but important ways some of man's abilities to reason and to remember.

The analogy to the human brain may be quite misleading, however, for computers approximate only the very simplest of human memory and reasoning functions. Using a carefully explicit set of human instructions, computers are capable of performing relatively simple comparing and calculating tasks, repetitively and with high reliability, at speeds heretofore incredible. Huge files can be searched literally in an instant, and complex calculations, broken down into a series of relatively simple steps, are completed so fast that they appear to have taken no time at all. Yet even though the computer may do in a second calculations which could require a lifetime of effort on the part of a single human, it has no capability for handling in any period of time the reasoning and learning tasks characteristic of even a young child. Thinking which involves substantial relational analysis is not among the computer's capabilities, at least not on any level that would support an analogy to the brain. Even relatively simple recognition processes—such as distinguishing among the letters of the alphabet in a handwritten message—have proved very difficult to achieve on the computer. This is because humans often accomplish such tasks as much by the sense of what they are reading as by having learned what the different letters look like. Still more complex recognition tasks—such as distinguishing between laughter and hysteria, or between bland phrases and writing that is heavy with irony—are even further from the computer's grasp at present.

Though it is not the "thinking machine" sometimes envisaged in popular literature, the computer does promise to reshape the processing and use of information in society. To see how this is being done, let us note the main devices associated with computerized information processing.

Input

Ultimately, all the information stored and processed in computer systems—even narrative text—must be reduced to some combination of ones and zeros. This is because digital computers are designed around binary (as opposed to decimal or alphabetic) electronic devices. On magnetic computer tape (which works in principle like the tape in a cassette recorder) information is represented by the presence (one) or absence (zero) of a magnetic field in a given location on the tape. In a computer's internal memory, magnetic cores perform the same function but can be "read" or "written into" at very high electronic speeds. These cores are doughnut-shaped and the direction of magnetization, clockwise or counterclockwise, presents a "one" or a "zero." An individual's name, for instance, may be written into the computer's memory as a unique sequence of several ones and zeros. The computer reads this name out of memory by examining the magnetic field direction in each of a sequence of magnetic cores at the location where the name had previously been written.

Once the information has been coded appropriately it has to be put into "computer-readable" form. Sometimes access to the computer's memory is directly from a terminal keyboard device which automatically translates the numbers or letters into the appropriate sequence of ones and zeros. More often, however, an entry is made on magnetic tape, either directly through an electronic device or indirectly as the holes in punched cards are read by a device that translates them into magnetic entries on tapes.

Storage

Information can be stored in computer-readable form on reels of magnetic tape, on disks or drums (with surfaces made of material similar to that used for tape) and in the magnetic core memory of the central processing unit of the computer. In almost all cases, however, the only information stored permanently within the central processing unit concerns basic operating programs of the computer.[1]

A computer user rarely, if ever, needs to think about the zeros and ones used to represent, say, an individual's name in storage devices. In the areas of concern to us, it has proved convenient instead to think of a *field* of information (the blank for name and address on a form or space allocated for this purpose in a punched card) incorporated into a *record* (the payroll record of the named individual) grouped with similar records into a *file* (the payroll file for an organization).

In general, a record is a set of facts or attributes about a particular individual retrievable by his name or some other personal identifying label (e.g., his Society Security number). Each fact or attribute is usually contained in a field; the collection of fields makes up the record. A file is a set of records about various individuals in a particular class—employee personnel files; police files of arrested persons; a file of persons making claims for insurance payments, etc.

Manual record systems are based on written or printed records and on mainly hand-operated files. Computer record systems may require some conversion of written input records into ma-

---

[1] The popular term "databank" is used without much precision to mean a collection of information about individuals assembled in one place for easy access by a number of users. In part three below, we will look at what organizations have said they wanted to build along such lines and what they have actually achieved, and at that point offer some definitions of different kinds of databanks.

chine-readable form, but transaction records are then searched and read electronically.

Processing

For our purposes here, it is not necessary to understand the electronics of computer processing. It is enough simply to treat the computer in this respect as a "black box," the capacities of which we know even if the details of its internal workings remain a mystery. The central processing unit of the computer consists of two parts, a control unit and a calculating unit. The former controls the flow and sequencing of the work which the latter unit performs. The processing unit takes substantive data (e.g., identifying information, monthly hours, and pay rates) which are fed into its electronic memory and, according to sets of instructions called *programs*, performs calculations on or makes comparisons among the data (e.g., computes payroll deductions on the gross amount of each check and figures the net amount of the check). The processing unit itself works at extremely high speed, so fast in fact that for most processing operations far more time is spent putting in the information to be processed, "calling up" the right programs, and printing out the results than it takes the central processing unit to perform its scanning or calculating operations.

It is important for our purposes to note the difference between two types of computer processing. *Batch processing* involves gathering a number of transactions which need to be accomplished (say, a day's worth of new lab reports that need to be entered into appropriate patient medical records), putting them in the proper sequence (e.g., alphabetically by name), and having the computer perform the transactions with a single pass through the entire file. This mode of processing is often associated with systems in which information is stored on magnetic tape. Reading a tape file from beginning to end takes minutes, but each transaction (entering each lab test result) may take as little as a few billionths of a second. Handling all of the transactions with a single pass through each tape is done for the sake of efficiency. Systems designed for batch-processing discourage ad hoc transactions (e.g., entering the lab results for one patient record at a time) since making an entry in a single file might entail locating the appropriate programs and file tapes, mounting them on the equipment, searching the entire length of the file tape for the right record, making the transaction, rewinding and restoring the tapes, etc., a series of steps which, if they had to be done for each transaction, would defeat the efficiency goals set for the computer system.

On-line processing usually involves individual transactions which can be keyed directly into the computer (as in the case of a flight reservation inquiry in an airlines reservation system). It is usually associated with the presence of information stored on *random-access* devices, in which it is possible to reach every record (every flight passenger list) with the same speed—virtually instantaneously. On-line systems are used for the most part where continuous access to a file or files is needed (for making and checking reservations as they come in, 24 hours a day), as opposed to situations where only periodic access to the file is required (e.g., once a week for payroll processing).

Output

A number of different devices are used for the output of information from the computer, ranging from printers—which do just what their name implies, producing what looks like typed copy— to cathode-ray-tube devices which work on the same principle as a TV screen, and microfilm, prepared when information is displayed as visual images on a screen and then photographed. Information can also be recorded on magnetic tape or punched cards and then copied from either of these media onto others.

It is important to note that input or output transactions can be accomplished from terminals located far from the central processing unit. Information is transmitted over phone lines, through space via radio waves, and by other means. Tapes and other storage media can also be transported physically from one place to another—in most cases far more easily than the equivalent amount of data in the form of manual records.

Programming

Programming is specialized work which covers such things as writing codes by which eye-readable data are converted into machine-readable form; preparing sets of instructions for the specific operations of the computer, using one of many available programming "languages"; and writing programs to tell the central processing unit how to use its time most effectively. The various general and specific sets of instructions for the computer are together called *software*, in contrast to the electronic central processing unit and peripheral equipment, which are called *hardware*.

What computer systems have to offer, then, is processing speed and convenient storage for masses of data. For some organizations, this represents the possibility of stabilizing costs (as when a bank computerizes its checking-account files); for others it is the possibility of improving services (as in a law-enforcement agency which wants to reduce the amount of time it takes a patrol officer to check a car against a file of stolen vehicles).

Computers are owned or rented under a number of different arrangements. Departments within an organization may have their own computer; central data processing units may be set up to serve several departments; and commercial service bureaus may sell computer time and programming assistance. Today, computers range in price from a few thousand dollars (those purchased for under $50,000 are often called "minicomputers") to as much as $25 million for the largest single machine in use.

A Brief History of Electronic Data Processing

It is also important for understanding computerization and record-keeping to look at the stages of development that computer technology has undergone during the past two decades. Computerization in organizations has advanced in step with the rapid development of computer technology since 1954, when electronic data processing (EDP) machines first appeared on the commercial market alongside the electronic accounting machines (EAM) of the precomputer era. EAM equipment simply combined rudimentary electronic calculating devices with the punched-card accounting machines that had evolved since Herman Hollerith developed the first of these for tabulating the 1890 census. EDP machines, on the other hand, offered major new capabilities. Most significant among these was the ability to follow automatically complex sequences of instructions inserted into their memory devices. A large repertoire of instructions, including some for selecting subsequent programs according to the results produced by preceding ones, enabled EDP systems to deal with problems of much greater scope and complexity than EAM machines could handle.

Advances in the aspirations of computerizing organizations since 1954 coincide with the appearance on the market of three successive generations of EDP machines. These generations can be distinguished by advances both in hardware aspects of computer technology, such as operating speed and memory size, and in software aspects, such as the ease of writing programs. Since the precomputer era, operating speed has jumped impressively from a few instructions carried out per second to nearly one hundred million per second. The size and variety of available memories have also increased dramatically. Advances in software technology, although significant, have been comparatively modest to date.

The *first generation* of EDP hardware appeared on the market in the early fifties; it was based on vacuum-tube computing elements that were expensive and unreliable by today's standards. The memory technologies then available limited the amount of data that could be stored internal to the computer and retrieved at electronic speeds to one-thousandth of today's capacities. As a result, most programs had to be built with the most elementary instructions as building blocks.

Files such as payroll records would not fit into the fast internal memories of the central processing unit, but were typically stored on magnetic tape. Using these files efficiently required the batch processing of transactions.

Transactions generally could not be individually keyed directly into the computer, in the on-line mode we have already described; they were transcribed off-line from handwritten or printed documents into punched cards and later batched for computer processing. Both the files and the volume of transactions that could be handled effectively by first-generation equipment were therefore small by today's standards.

Newly invented transistors replaced vacuum tubes in the *second-generation* machines that appeared in the late fifties. Operating speed and reliability increased; the cost of basic computing elements decreased. Improved magnetic-core technology provided internal memories faster and larger than those of the first-generation equipment. The greater storage density and the ability to read these at higher speeds permitted the automation of larger files and the processing of more transactions than with the first generation. Instruction repertoires better tailored to user needs became available as software tools were developed to shift much of the burden of programming detail from the programmer to the computer.

During this period magnetic drum and disk memories (small by today's standard) began to appear in significant numbers. With such random-access devices, it became possible to reach every record in a file with equal speed, in contrast to the interval of minutes between access to the first and last records on a tape file. While this new capability was used typically to increase the efficiency of programs for batch processing, it lent itself also to experiments foreshadowing significant new capabilities of third-generation equipment. The need for multiple simultaneous accesses to memory and to other resources from many widespread terminals stimulated the development of resource-sharing and tele-communications capabilities.

Random-access memories big enough to hold major files, built-in hardware and software mechanisms for sharing resources among several simultaneous users, and telecommunications facilities for linking terminals and computers into networks are hall-marks of the *third generation* of EDP systems. These systems, which came on the market in the early '60s, are also based on new integrated-circuit technology that once again had marked advantages in speed, reliability, and cost over its predecessors. Software tools, by now the products of investments often bigger than those in the hardware, shifted still more routine burden from programming and operating personnel to the computer system itself. (Although the term "fourth generation" has been used to describe EDP systems of the early 1970s, these are really more in the nature of improved third-generation systems, and we will therefore be talking of progress through third-generation systems in our report.)

Although different aspects of computer systems have developed unevenly, the ratio of one hundred million-to-one in computing speed epitomizes the range of technological capacity for record-keeping from the pre-computer era to the early '70s. This is the backdrop against which the effect of computerized record-keeping on due process and civil liberties will be analyzed.

Civil Liberties and Record-Keeping

Record-keeping is one of man's oldest activities. In this perspective, computerization of personal records represents the latest stage in a procession of techniques that has developed over the past 4,000 years from clay tablet and papyrus scroll to typewriter, teletype, and Xerox copier. As we noted in the beginning of this Introduction, widespread reliance on formal record-keeping about individuals had already become a hallmark of American society before computers began to enter organizational life. At that point, there were two major constitutional principles—the right to privacy and the right to receive due process of law—that provided a basic legal and public policy framework for questions about what personal information should be put into records, with whom it should be shared, and what individuals were entitled to know and contest about their records when these were used to make judgments affecting their rights and opportunities. We begin, therefore, by describing the concepts of due process and privacy, and outlining how these had been applied to various types of record-keeping and fields of organizational activity as of the middle and late 1960s, when computer usage was spreading through the organizational world.

Due Process and Record Systems

Due process is probably the most valued traditional concept in Anglo-American law; as Justice Felix Frankfurter once observed, the history of liberty itself is very largely the history of observing due process. As the Supreme Court held in a 1959 case, "Certain principles have remained relatively immutable in our jurisprudence. One of these is that where government action seriously injures an individual and the reasonableness of the action depends on fact findings, the evidence used to prove the Government's case must be disclosed to the individual so that he has an opportunity to show that it is untrue. . . This Court has been zealous to protect these rights . . . not only in criminal cases . . . but also in all types of cases where administrative and regulatory actions were under scrutiny."[2]

In its essentials, due process involves three major elements: that the rules of conduct set by authorities be specified in advance and communicated to those affected by them; that a fair hearing be given to every individual before he is penalized for violation of the rules; and that some appeal to higher authority be available to afford a review of the initial proceedings. The procedural guarantees that due process has been held to require, such as the individual's right to know the evidence being used against him, to confront his accusers, and to have the right to counsel, have been found over centuries of experience to be indispensable for the exposure of error and bias in adjudications; simply put, they offer

[2]*Greene* v. *McElroy*, 360 U.S. 474 (1959).

the best chance for adjudications to arrive at truth. Other due-process rights, such as the privilege against self-incrimination, affirm a constitutional society's commitment to the dignity of the individual, even when he stands officially accused of misconduct against society. Guarantees of public trial, habeas corpus, and a jury of one's peers are fundamental tools for controlling the exercise of arbitrary power by the state. Under American law, the most rigorous forms of due process have been required in criminal proceedings where a person's life or liberty are at stake. Less complete or different notions of due process are involved where proceedings are administrative or involve legislative fact finding.

During the 1960s, the Supreme Court considerably widened the definition of proceedings and personal interests that require due process; for example, the determination of welfare eligibility and access to public housing have been held to require due-process protections.

However, while the requirement of due process means that government must bring forward the evidence it relies on in both criminal and administrative proceedings, producing records where those were essential, American constitutional law did not give individuals any due-process right to inspect their records when these were simply being held in government files. To obtain such a right of access, individuals had to rely either on legislation that stipulated such access in a particular record system or on the administrative policies of the government agency.

Some additional opportunities for the individual to gain access to his own record came from the operations of common-law rules defining public records. These rules, many of which were updated and codified in twentieth century state and federal free-dom-of-information statutes, were based on the principle that public records in democratic government should generally be open to the press and public, in the interest of keeping government visible and responsible. Where government agencies maintain a public record as a legal duty, it must be open to inspection at reasonable times and places to anyone who displays a legitimate interest (press, researchers, etc.). Certain exceptions were made in such laws for police intelligence records, medical files, and similar records involving aspects of either secrecy for certain government operations or privacy for the sensitive records of individuals in-volved in government programs. While freedom-of-information laws were not conceived in terms of giving individuals a right to see their own record, rulings that a particular file was a public record generally had the effect of allowing the individual access to his own record in that file.

In terms of legal rights, therefore, a considerable number of the records kept about individuals by local, state, or federal agencies were not available for inspection or challenge by the individual on whom they were kept.

Due-process rights in the record systems of private institutions and commercial organizations moved along a very different legal track. Since the Bill of Rights generally applies only to the actions of government and not of private persons or groups, the record-keeping and decision-making procedures of private organizations were traditionally held to be their own internal affairs. However, procedures for hearings and appeals were usually provided by churches, labor unions, private universities, business corporations, sports clubs, and many other private organizations whenever they took serious disciplinary action against their members. This was not required by law or the courts, but responded to public expectations of fair treatment.

In some instances, however, legislatures considered some private organizations to be fulfilling such vital public functions that laws were enacted requiring that certain due-process measures be followed. An example is the federal Landrum-Griffin Act of 1959, providing important procedural rights for members of labor unions.

Despite these exceptions, however, nongovernmental organizations have generally been free from judicial or legislative supervision of their record-keeping procedures. This has included the questions of whether an individual who is the subject of a record must be notified about its maintenance, has a right to inspect its contents, and is given any procedure for challenging its accuracy, completeness, or propriety. It was not until 1970 that a major departure from this laissez-faire tradition took place, with the passage by the federal government and several states of legislation requiring certain due-process safeguards for individuals affected by the operations of commercial reporting agencies. This change will be discussed in several of the profiles and in parts three and five.

The Right to Privacy

Privacy—the "right to be let alone"—has been called by Justice Louis Brandeis the "right most valued by civilized men." While there is no doubt that claims to individual and group privacy have been part of the American civil-liberties tradition throughout our history,[3] legal definition of the right to privacy has been less firmly developed than due process. At the constitutional level, the Bill of Rights contains no mention of the term "privacy." However, in the course of protecting some explicitly stated constitutional rights, the Supreme Court has given protection over the past decades to many important "components" of the right to privacy.

Thus, much of the protection for privacy against improper government seizure of documents and goods or physical monitoring of conversations or acts has been rested on the Fourth Amendment's guarantee against unreasonable searches and seizures. The Fifth Amendment's protection against self-incrimination has been used to curtail physical or psychological intrusions into a person's mind or body. The Court has also used the First Amendment's guarantees of free speech and association to protect anonymity of expression (in leafleting cases); privacy of association (to forbid compulsory disclosure of membership lists of political organizations where the courts find no compelling government need for them); and "political privacy" (in protecting individual beliefs and associations from compulsory disclosure to legislative investigating committees or state bar examining committees). The Court has also threaded together the main amendments of the Bill of Rights, including the Ninth Amendment's declaration of rights reserved to the people, to strike down birth-control laws that intruded into "marital privacy," and has stated that a person has a right to read even obscene literature in the privacy of his home.[4] The courts have also declared that a woman's decision to have an abortion is part of her "constitutional right to privacy."[5]

---

[3] For a detailed treatment of privacy in its historical, legal, political, and sociological aspects, readers may consult Alan F. Westin, *Privacy and Freedom.* New York: Atheneum, 1967.

[4] Discussions of these doctrines and the cases developing them can be found in Westin, *op. cit.*, chapters 13 and 14; and Arthur R. Miller, *The Assault on Privacy: Computers, Data Banks and Dossiers.* Ann Arbor: University of Michigan Press, 1971, chapters 5 and 6.

[5] See, for example, *People v. Belous*, 71 Cal. 2d 854 (1969); *U.S.* v. *Vuitch*, 402 U.S. 62 (1970); and *Doe* v. *Scott*, 321 F. Supp. 1385 (N. D. Ill., 1971). In 1972, the U.S. Supreme Court struck down a Massachusetts statute under which a lecturer had been convicted for dispensing contraceptive foam to a young woman attending his lecture on birth control. "If the right of privacy means anything," the Court stated, "it is the right of the *individual*, married or single, to be free from unwarranted governmental intrusion into matters so fundamentally affecting a person as the decision whether to bear or beget a child." *Eisenstadt* v. *Baird*, 31 L. Ed. 362 (1972).

At the time computers became available for organizational record-keeping, these aspects of constitutional protection for personal privacy had been applied to the record-keeping area in only a few cases. During the 1950s and 1960s, there were no Supreme Court cases upholding plaintiffs who claimed that executive agencies should not be allowed to collect information directly from individuals for use in a government program because that would violate the individual's right to privacy. Instead, the federal and state courts in these years consistently upheld the constitutionality both of requiring information from the citizen for major government programs (as with the decennial census),[6] and allowing wide-ranging personal information to be collected *about* him (as with law-enforcement investigative files).[7]

In private law, the majority of American states, either by statute or judicial decision, recognize what is known as the common-law right to privacy. This gives the individual legal redress (such as damages or injunctive relief) if things are done such as appropriating his name and likeness for advertising purposes without his consent or intruding into his solitude. For the most part, however, the common law right to privacy did not play a role in the record-keeping area. The courts had not held that individuals could invoke the common-law right to prevent the recording of personal information about themselves by a government agency or private organization.

Despite the absence of "hard" constitutional law on the individual's right to privacy, certain traditions respecting the privacy of the citizen were part of American legislative and administrative approaches to the collection and storing of information by government agencies. The civil-liberties tradition was that government should not compel the disclosure of information at all about certain aspects of the individual's private life, such as his religion or his voting choices, or where confidential relations were involved, as between lawyer and client or doctor and patient. It was also a general principle that sensitive personal information collected by government agencies for a specific purpose mandated by law should not be given to other agencies or individuals. As a result, some statutes provided that information gathered for a particular governmental activity (such as taxation, public health, or juvenile

---

[6] *U.S.* v. *Rickenbacker*, 197 F. Supp. 924 (1961); 309 F. 2d 462 (1962); cert. den. 371 U.S. 962 (1963).

[7] *Anderson* v. *Sills*, 56 N. J. 210, 265 A. 2d 678 (1970).

court proceedings) must be held confidentially, with access either denied to other government agencies entirely or with rules providing for limited data sharing. However, much information about the individual held in government files was not covered by such confidentiality rules. Even where it was covered, an informal exchange system among government and private-organizational officials produced extensive data sharing in particular fields. The issue of confidentiality and its breaches will be a major topic of discussion throughout the profiles in part two and in other parts of this report as well.

As for private organizations, what information should be collected about an individual and with whom it could be shared was generally a matter of custom within each particular field, and varied according to the type of client, customer, or member being served. There were sometimes statutes or judicial decisions defining the obligations of particular types of organizations to hold information in confidence and not to release it without the consent of the individual or under a proper legal order, as in banking or medicine. Such confidentiality law was very limited, however, both in how much of it had been elaborated and in the degree to which it was or could be used by individuals to limit circulation of their records among cooperating private organizations.

As this necessarily brief account indicates, there were some important constitutional rules and traditions of due process and privacy that operated as part of the environment for the conduct of some governmental and private record-keeping. Where certain types of organizational activities or uses of information were involved, statutes and common-law decisions provided for confidentiality or allowed hearings to contest decisions made on the basis of formal records. But the reality of the 1960s was that civil liberties in record-keeping was an underdeveloped area of American law. Thus, computers moved into the world of organizational record-keeping at a time when both American law and public opinion were just beginning to confront the problems of defining more clearly what rights of privacy and due process individuals should have in the various major zones of manual record-keeping that had come to exercise a major effect on the lives of individuals in the post-World War II era.

Part II

Profiles from the World of Computerizing Organizations

In seeking factual information about the significance of computerization for civil liberties, one must investigate those governmental, commercial, and nonprofit enterprises that have had the financial, managerial, and technical resources to apply computer technology to the processing of information about people. For this project, we conducted detailed on-site investigations of 55 such organizations. Our aims were to discover the general extent of EDP applications in record-keeping among computerizing organizations; to identify those developments which are special to each major sphere of record-keeping; and then to gauge the effects of computerization on civil-liberties interests.

We began our site-visit program by collecting system plans and other descriptive materials concerning more than 500 organizations whose computerization activities had generated public attention. By looking at the main types of personal records that individuals generate in their lifetimes (e.g., education, employment, financial, military service, law enforcement), we grouped the organizations having prominent computerization programs into 20 important types of personal record-keeping. We then arranged briefing sessions with "applications" specialists from two major computer manufacturers and three consulting firms in software and systems design, to gain further information about trends in data processing in these fields.

Working from these sources, we selected an initial group of organizations for intensive study, estimating that 10-15 on-site visits would be sufficient. To gain field experience, we conducted three experimental studies in the spring of 1970, visiting an Eastern municipality, a Western county, and a credit reporting agency.

Based on these visits, we drew up a checklist of topics to be investigated at each site. This served also as a format for later staff site-visit reports. The headings from this checklist indicate the kinds of information we sought at each site:

(1) The organization visited: history, function, style, environment;
(2) Data now held about individuals and groups, in manual and automated forms:

(a) Data about its own employees or executives
(b) Data about clients, customers, and subjects
(c) Data about other, "third" persons outside the organization;
(3) The present computer system described;
(4) Comparison of its operation with prior manual systems;
(5) The decision to computerize: why and how made, by whom;
(6) Transitions from initial computerization to the present;
(7) Management perceptions of information needs and data usage;
(8) Data confidentiality and data access: rules, practices, cases, issues;
(9) Management attitudes toward the tension between information needs and civil liberties;
(10) Impact on subjects of data collection;
(11) Future plans for data systems and management expectations for such systems.

The early site visits proved to be as important as we had anticipated. In the course of conducting them, however, we came to feel that there were variations in computer development *within* organizational realms that deserved further investigation. As a result, we decided to expand our coverage; by the close of the project's research phase, we had completed visits to 55 sites. Most took place during the summer and fall of 1970, with a few additional visits made in early 1971. Follow-up contacts were carried on until the final revision of this report in the spring of 1972.

The 55 organizations we selected were clearly among the most organizationally and technologically innovative in their respective fields. Their EDP experiences reflect this, representing activity along the frontiers of computerization during the past 15 years and displaying patterns of development different from the "mainstream" organizations in their field. The computer's impact on record-keeping, we thought, would be clearest among these most advanced organizations. In selecting sites, we also chose those which were pursuing computer applications most germane to civil-liberties issues: "databank" projects, computerization of files containing sensitive personal information, and organizations joining in data-sharing networks through advanced computer-communication systems.

The range and type of systems included are described in table 2-1.

Table 2-1

TOTAL SITE VISITS, 1970-71: 55 ORGANIZATIONS

Governmental Systems (29)		*Private Systems (26)*	
By Jurisdictional Level:		*By Type of Activity:*	
Federal	8	Insurance	3
State	9		
County or Regional	8	Banking	3
Municipal	4	Private university	1
Subject-Area Agencies Covered: *(56)**		Religious body	1
		Airline	1
Law enforcement/public safety	13	Hospital/health service	4
Motor vehicles	2		
Welfare/social security	10	Research project	4
School system/university	5		
Health/hospital	7	Manufacturing corporation personnel system	2
Military record center	1	Newspaper	1
Personnel/civil service	2	Information supplier	4
Taxation/finance/controller	8		
Courts/corrections	3	Computer service bureau	2
Statistical/census	1		
Management services	4		
By Geographic Location:		*By Geographic Location:*	
East Coast	13	East Coast	15
Midwest	4	Midwest	6
West Coast	12	West Coast	5

*This includes separate departments studied as part of what counted as a single visit to a city or county, and therefore totals 56, rather than 29.

The site visits were arranged by a letter describing the National Academy of Sciences' project and expressing our hope that the organization's managers would be willing to cooperate.[1] Only four organizations—three life-insurance companies and one credit-card company—declined to participate. Three cited major data-conversion activity as a reason why a visit at that time would be inconvenient; the fourth gave no reason for declining.

---

[1] The text of the letter used appears in Appendix D.

We promised each cooperating organization that its managers would have an opportunity to examine any identified write-up used in our final report, in order to comment on its factual accuracy and to supply us with additional explanation or commentary if this were desired.

To prepare for the actual site visit, we obtained extensive materials in advance from the organization's officials describing the organization and its computer systems. The first half of the site visits were each conducted by a team of between two and five staff members, representing a mixture of legal, social science, and technical backgrounds. Later visits were conducted by smaller one- or two-man teams, since the record-keeping aspects of the industry or field were by then familiar to us.

At most sites, one to three full days were spent in interviewing an average of ten persons in the organization. Among those included were the top executives, managers of the data-processing unit, heads of principal "user departments," professional staffs in data processing, and legal counsel. Wherever possible, additional written materials were secured from the organization's files to document the accounts of practice and policy given us orally. For example, we compared data collection forms used before and after computerization to assess managerial accounts of how computerization had affected the quantity and quality of information collected for a particular file. We collected manuals of procedures, published regulations, and similar evidence of how rules were communicated through the organization. Follow-up visits or extensive telephone conversations were made when necessary to complete our inquiries or update our files.

In addition to materials drawn directly from each organization, we searched local and national newspapers and other media sources for journalistic commentary on the organization and its field, made extensive use of court briefs and reports from investigative and appropriations hearings, and discussed many of the sites with local "guardian groups" such as labor unions, minority-rights groups, and civil-liberties organizations. In a few cases, we also found it worthwhile to talk with those who were the subjects of data collection at organizations we visited.[2]

---

[2]Early in the project, we rejected the idea of going directly to the subjects of data collection in each organization to learn about the computer's impact on records concerning them. Aside from the difficulty of doing this in a systematic fashion at each site, we knew that one of the important civil liberties problems faced by such individuals is that they do not, in most cases,

We were aware as we visited the organizations that we were asking managers and employees to tell us about aspects of their operations, attitudes, and problems that had rarely been made public, at least not with the detail and candor we sought. By the close of our site visits, we concluded that we had obtained the full range of information we desired in all but three or four cases, where the interviews were more guarded and our inspection of documents and operating systems was limited. Even in those instances, however, we secured enough data from sources inside and outside the organization to use information about these record systems in formulating our general findings. We attribute the generally high level of cooperation and self-revelation to several factors: a favorable estimate of the National Academy of Sciences, as our organizational sponsor; our project's character as an empirically oriented, scholarly study, rather than a legislative or journalistic inquiry; and the basic belief of these managers that they are engaged in legal and proper organizational record-keeping practices which they welcomed a chance to explain.

Based primarily on the site visits, we developed detailed reports and derived a set of basic findings. These are presented in part three. However, to give readers a concrete sense of how computers are being used, and a basis for judging the conclusions we will present, we felt a strong need to convey the experience of real organizations in computerizing their files and to describe the kinds of civil-liberties issues that are being generated by their record-keeping practices. With this in mind, we are presenting "profiles" of 14 of our 55 organizations, identified by name and discussing specific events and issues. These were selected to illustrate major patterns of computerization, different fields of record-keeping, and a variety of civil-liberties problems. Where we could choose from more than one organization in an important area, we chose larger organizations (whose record-keeping activities affect a greater number of individuals), and those with the longest experience with computerization of personal records.

Six government organizations, four commercial firms and four non-profit institutions were selected. The government profiles

---

have a clear picture of the record-keeping policies and practices in organizations which have files on them; nor are they always in a position to know whether or not computers are even used to process and store these records.

The question of managers' perceptions of complaints from record subjects is covered in our discussion of survey responses, Appendix A, pages 446-453 below.

include a federal social service agency, a federal law-enforcement agency, a state motor vehicle department, a city police department, a city government, and a county government. The commercial firms include a large commercial bank, a credit bureau, a health insurance company, and a business services firm involved in direct-mail advertising. The nonprofit institutions include a university, the research arm of a national educational association, a religious body, and a health plan.

To ensure that these profiles present the most accurate and complete descriptions possible, we sent an initial draft back to each organization, inviting managers to inform us of any factual errors and provide additional explanations or comments they might want us to consider. On the basis of their responses and further outside research, revised drafts were written and again sent to the organization for a check of factual accuracy and additional commentary.[3] The organizations were not asked to approve the profiles.

The profiles are presented in a generally descriptive fashion, following the site-visit guide quoted earlier in this introduction. This reserves overall evaluation of the computer's impact on civil liberties for part three. Frequent quotations from organizational spokesmen are used to give readers as authentic a feeling as possible of management attitudes about data collection and civil-liberties issues.

---

[3] Copies of the letters used in this process are in Appendix D.

Government Organizations: The Federal Level

On June 30, 1971 the federal government was operating 5,961 general-purpose computers.[1] Federal EDP costs reached $2.1 billion in 1970, with the accumulated federal hardware inventory valued at some $23.2 billion. Fifty-seven percent of the federal computers are in the Department of Defense. The next largest users are the Atomic Energy Commission and National Aeronautics and Space Administration. Large computer inventories are also found in the Departments of Transportation; Health, Education, and Welfare; Treasury; Veterans Administration; and Interior.

A simple five-year count of the federal computer inventory since 1950 shows the tremendous spurt of growth during the period 1965-70:

Year	Number of Computers
1950	2
1955	45
1960	403
1965	1,826
1970	5,277

Dramatic as these figures are, they *underestimate* the actual growth in *computing power* in this period, since they do not portray the increased storage capacity, speed, and versatility of the computers installed during the last five years.

Computerization in federal agencies has led to the creation of

---

[1] Approximately 70,000 computers were in operation in the United States in 1971, with 90,000 estimated to be in operation at the close of 1972.

automated files or databank collections of personal information within at least a dozen of the major agencies. In the Defense Department alone, these include nonclassified files such as the names of 150,000 persons exposed to radiation; 465,000 persons in a family housing information system; 55,000 persons in a civilian personnel databank; 1.6 million persons in the defense industrial security program; and 1.4 million persons in the navy's manpower and personnel management information system.

In civilian agencies, computerized "people databanks" include a file of pilots and aircraft owners maintained by the Federal Aviation Agency; a "migrant student" record system on 300,000 children, maintained for the U.S. Office of Education; a civil disturbance file on 13,000 persons in the Department of Justice; a file on 200,000 persons held in the organized/crime intelligence unit of the Justice Department; 95,000 persons listed (on an average day) in the FBI's National Crime Information Center; 40 million names in the master index of the Immigration and Naturalization Service; 2.6 million persons in the National Driver Register Service of the National Highway Safety Bureau; 240,000 names of passport applicants "of law-enforcement interest," maintained by the State Department Passport Bureau; a Secret Service list with the names of 50,000 persons considered potentially dangerous to the President; and a computerized checklist of "suspicious" persons against which the FCC checks all license applications.[2]

We treated as separate site visits eight federal bureaus, agencies, or departments, generally those most widely discussed in terms of civil liberties and federal data collection. We will be presenting two of these agencies in profile, one in the social service area and one in law enforcement.

Federal Social Services

A number of federal agencies maintain health or social-service programs and make use of the computer for record-keeping within them, from Agriculture's food stamp and school lunch programs to the extensive health and hospital network operated by the Veterans Administration. However, most of the welfare dollars in

---

[2] For a convenient summary of "databanks" maintained by federal agencies, see *The Congressional Digest* (October 1971), pp. 225-56.

the nation are spent through programs which fall under the administrative umbrella of the Department of Health, Education, and Welfare. With more than 200 different public assistance, insurance, health, vocational education, and other social programs, HEW stands at the top of a social-services pyramid which reaches down through the states to county and city levels.

These "welfare" programs are of two types: (1) those in which individuals receive some kind of assistance out of public funds (money, counseling, medical care, goods), and (2) income and medical-insurance programs in which contributing participants are more like policyholders than recipients of government largesse.

Assistance programs aiding some 13 million persons annually include local, short-term "relief" arrangements which are funded and administered by city or county departments; federal HEW programs such as Aid to the Blind, and Aid to Families with Dependent Children; and supplementary state programs. Computerization efforts vary widely across the departments which handle these programs. Some welfare departments have developed their own applications independently; others are participating in federally assisted statewide plans for developing uniform EDP systems across departments; and still others have computerized their records as part of countywide EDP developments. Most HEW assistance programs are regionalized; as a result, records on individuals are stored in county and state welfare offices, with HEW receiving only statistical reports.

In contrast, most of HEW's income and medical-insurance programs, such as Medicare and Social Security, are centralized, and it is here that we find the largest federally held files and the greatest EDP development. EDP expenditures by the Social Security Administration (SSA), which administers both the Social Security and Medicare programs, represented 80 percent of HEW's total EDP outlay in 1971. Its centralized computer files contain records on more than 150 million citizens, and it is to an examination of SSA that we turn in our first profile.

THE SOCIAL SECURITY ADMINISTRATION

In 1935, with the nation struggling to recover from the Great Depression, Congress passed President Franklin Roosevelt's proposal for a radically new system of federal old-age insurance. Under this plan, each worker covered by the Social Security Act has a portion of his earnings deducted by his employer, who adds a matching "contribution" and forwards the money to the Internal Revenue Service. The taxes so collected are put into a special federal trust fund. When the employee becomes disabled, reaches the official retirement age, or dies, monthly payments are made to him or to his family, with the amount determined in part by his contributions to the trust fund throughout his working lifetime.

Today, as a result of Congress' steady expansion of Social Security coverage, nine out of ten working people in the United States are part of the program. Since 1935, over 200 million individual records have been created by SSA and almost $5 *trillion* has been posted to them.

In 1966, Congress established the Medicare program, under an amendment to the Social Security Act. Part of an increased Social Security tax contribution is now placed in a hospital insurance fund, enabling workers over 65 to meet some of their hospital bills. A voluntary medical-insurance plan was also established to pay some of the doctor bills and other medical expenses of the citizen over 65. More than 19 million persons are enrolled in one or both of these programs.

To manage these activities, SSA maintains a 12-building headquarters complex in Baltimore, Maryland, 900 field offices, and 6 regional payment centers, with 55,000 employees in all. Each month during 1971, SSA mailed 27 million payments to Social Security recipients and beneficiaries, and processed more than $18 million in hospital bills.

Personal Information in SSA Files

Files on an individual are begun when he seeks a Social Security number. He supplies the Administration with his real name, the name he "will use in work or business," date and place of birth, "present age," mother's maiden name, father's name, sex, "color or race," mailing address, and telephone number. With this information, SSA assigns a number for the individual, supplying him with a card on which the number is printed. The Administration thereafter records the individual's earnings on a quarterly basis up to a specified level (currently $7,600 per year).

Except for any changes of name, no additional information is collected about account holders until they apply for benefits, a period of 40 or more years later in most cases. There is no need to know, for instance, the individual's current home mailing address; as a result, SSA files contain address information only on the current *employer*, not the account holder. When an individual becomes disabled, retires, or dies, entitlement information is obtained from him or from his survivors. In the case of disability claims, an extensive set of medical and legal documents may be submitted by the account holder. When insurance payments begin, up-to-date address information is maintained and close track is kept of an individual's earnings; according to law, these cannot exceed a set amount without affecting, dollar for dollar, the level of benefits he will receive.

Applicants for Medicare and supplementary medical insurance supply the Administration with identification and work-history information, in addition to certifying their age. As payments are made to the individual, his physician, or a hospital, SSA keeps a record of claims and gathers information with which to monitor the activities of those providing medical services.

Data Processing within SSA

From its inception, the SSA experienced very rapid and unanticipated growth. Expecting to handle 25 million sets of records when the program began in 1936, SSA wound up accepting 45 million applications in the first year. To manage this volume, the Administration's Records Division used an 8-column summary-of-earnings punch card for each account on which earnings were recorded as they accumulated. These cards were manipulated on a complex array of electric accounting machinery which SSA purchased or helped develop for the task: keypunch machines, card sorters, collators, reproducers, tabulators, and ledger posting machines. By 1943, with files opened on over 100 million individuals, SSA's punch cards filled six and a half acres of storage space.

In 1951, Congress made several changes in coverage and computation of benefits that required the posting of an annual earnings summary for each record. In meeting this requirement, all of the remaining space on each account punch card would have been used up within five years. Starting a second card at that point would have doubled the size of the Social Security account file, creating major problems of storage and handling under the EAM system, and the Records Division knew that a third card would be required in a few additional years.

Fortunately, however, an Administration study of electronic data processing in 1954 concluded that this technology had reached the point where it could be adapted effectively to SSA's record-keeping operations. The Administration's first computer, a first-generation (vacuum-tube) IBM 705, was delivered in 1956. From then to the present, SSA has steadily acquired the latest in second- and third-generation computer systems, until it now maintains the largest civilian computer operation in the United States housed under one roof.

In 1971, the Administration's computer inventory included 52 EDP systems, with an annual equipment cost alone of $19 million. More than 700,000 reels of magnetic tape are used to store basic account data, with a medium-sized computer used to keep track of the tapes themselves. Nine thousand employees work in the Bureau of Data Processing, almost 1,500 of them programmers, systems analysts, and electronic equipment operators. To facilitate rapid transmission of data, the 900 SSA field offices and payment centers are connected through a teletype network maintained by the General Services Administration.

"Today," SSA Commissioner Robert Ball commented, "you couldn't run the Social Security Administration without computers. A completely manual system would require a staff many times larger than we now have. Additionally, the process would be much less accurate and responsive to the individual. In fact, the complexity of the law is such that many provisions could not be consistently applied in a manual system, regardless of the number of people involved." In addition, a basic problem facing SSA is that "the checks must go out"—27 million on the first of each month—and doing this manually would be a staggering job.

Current SSA Files

With the coming of computers to SSA, a mixed system of manual, EAM, and computer processing developed, with information on each number holder contained in three or more separate files. Of the files maintained by the Administration, the following are among the most important:

1. Original applications for a Social Security number and Medicare are stored in manual files.

2. The Social Security number application file, also manual, contains basic participant information, including name, Social Security number, age, sex, race, and address at time of initial registration.[3]

---

[3] The question regarding race came under criticism in the early days of the civil-rights movement, SSA continued to use it, however; Commissioner Ball explained: "SSA feels that it must have data on how the program is working with reference to blacks versus whites in order to find out who is really in need."

3. The National Employee Index is a partly computerized, partly microfilmed file, organized alphabetically and used for cross-referencing.

4. Quarterly earnings reported by employers are kept on microfilm under each individual's account number. Yearly earnings summaries are stored in a computerized master file.

5. A computerized Beneficiary File contains some eligibility information, but is principally a record of payments.

6. The documentary evidence submitted in proof of eligibility is not computerized at all, since this is essentially a file used at one point in time only. More than 32 million such manual files are maintained in SSA Payment Centers and Federal Record Centers. At this time the folders are used as transaction records in some cases; an on-line computer system has been devised for keeping track of them during their short periods of use.

For the Medicare program, the Administration must maintain extensive computerized records on the utilization of medical services. The Master Health Insurance and Entitlement Record of Medicare includes both standard identification data, a record of the participant's health-care premiums and claims for medical or psychiatric care, and notations which permit cross-referencing to other records, including those of dependents. In a related record-keeping activity of massive proportions, Social Security receives 49 million bills from physicians and other health-care providers each year.

EAM equipment is still used extensively within the Administration, with 1,800 machines currently in operation and rental costs of $1.2 million in 1971.

The Computer's Impact at SSA

SSA collects no more information today for its insurance programs than it did in the manual era. In fact, the form for entering data has remained virtually unchanged since 1935. The Medicare program, on the other hand, has dramatically increased the amount of information in SSA files, and was designed for computer processing; however, SSA officials note that the quantity or quality of personal information Medicare added to each individual's file was not a direct result of computer capacity, but of the Administration's need for medical data.

Each increase or expansion of SSA's benefit programs by Congress has placed a premium on the "start-up" capacity of the Administration's computer systems. For example, a recent 5 percent benefit increase in 25 million accounts involved some complex programming changes; so too did a recalculation program, involving a revised formula for computing benefits on earnings accumulated before 1951. All this must be done without disturbing the basic SSA operation. SSA officials also note that computers have made possible automatic recomputation of benefits: this resulted in increases between $1 and $25 monthly for 2 million Social Security recipients in 1970. In SSA's opinion, computerization has enabled them to tailor their benefit programs more closely to the needs and income of different groups of beneficiaries.

SSA officials acknowledge that they do not yet use computers as an aid to management decision making. In their judgment, long-term program development decisions continue to be made esentially as they were in the manual era.

The Confidentiality of Social Security Files

To help secure passage of the Social Security Act, President Roosevelt pledged that the confidentiality of records would be carefully protected by SSA. Workers had expressed fears that communications between the new government agency and their employers would uncover instances where they had lied about their ages or identities in order to secure scarce Depression jobs. In addition, labor-union organizers often needed to use an assumed name (and would need a matching Social Security card) when working in communities actively hostile to unions.

The Administration's attention to confidentiality matters is reflected in the detailed fashion in which exceptions permitting data sharing are specified and regulated. Confidentiality rules were outlined by the first (and still existing) regulation issued by the agency. Entitled "Disclosures of Official Records and Information," it spells out the situations in which SSA will engage in data sharing. The Internal Revenue Service has access to some of the information in SSA files, since it collects the Social Security "tax." The Administration also exchanges data with "closely related" federal and state public-assistance programs, where, to avoid duplication, each wants to know if the other agency is supplying an individual with financial support. In a few cases each year, the Administration supplies location information to the FBI or the Secret Service when the requesting agent stipulates that this cooperation is necessary "to protect against sabotage or espionage."

As a result of statutes passed by Congress, SSA must also provide location information on request to the Immigration and Naturalization Service on individuals suspected of being illegally in the country; in fiscal 1971, SSA supplied INS with such information in 15,000 instances. As a result of another congressional action, SSA will help the courts to locate deserting parents "when all other resources have been exhausted."

All these instances of legally permissible sharing operate on a case-by-case basis, requiring the outside agency to have a need for information about specific individuals. Administration officials and employees are also given the authority to "respectfully decline" attempts to subpoena information which is not included in specified sharing arrangements. A law passed in 1939 provides that no disclosures can be made except in accordance with SSA regulations; this legislation reinforces the Administration's rules but does not provide the kind of specific legislative definitions of confidentiality under which Census Bureau files are maintained.

The courts have steadily upheld administration rulings covering the confidentiality of SSA records. All but one minor ruling out of ten cases since 1966 supported the Administration's arguments against producing data.

The Administration receives many requests for information on individuals from police departments and local sheriffs: "They bother to ask," says an SSA official, "largely because they don't know of the confidentiality rules." In marked contrast to its cooperation with federal agencies, SSA refuses such requests. However, the Administration is subjected to considerable cross-pressure from Congress on this issue. For example, the House Ways and Means Committee and the Senate Finance Committee frequently call on SSA to make more productive use of its data, including greater sharing with law-enforcement agencies. In this regard, one congressman, irked at the adamant stance of the Administration, asked, "Are you defending the rights of murderers?" and on one occasion, an amendment to provide Social Security data to law-enforcement agencies whenever capital crimes are involved was barely defeated in Congress. On the other hand, civil-liberties-oriented committees, such as Sen. Sam Ervin's Constitutional Rights Subcommittee, have demanded that SSA tighten even further its privacy and confidentiality rules.

The Social Security Administration also receives and rejects requests for information from private individuals and organizations. SSA officials mention detective agencies, bill collectors, and wives searching for their husbands as among the most frequent sources of inquiries. Similarly, SSA refuses to sell lists of beneficiaries for commercial or other mailing purposes. The Administration is not specifically prohibited from doing so by law, but this service has never been a part of SSA or HEW policy, and would be contrary to the general nondisclosure spirit of the law.

In a limited number of special cases, where it seems of direct benefit to the individual, SSA will take a letter from a private inquirer and forward it to the person being sought, in care of his latest employer. However, it always remains up to the individual being sought to decide whether he wants to reply to the inquirer. One man, when contacted about an $8,000 inheritance, told SSA that it was worth losing the money to avoid being reunited with his relatives.

The Commissioner of SSA has the power to suspend any of the Administration's confidentiality rules, and he has used this in rare cases. For instance, where a defense attorney has felt that the location of a key witness might save his client's life, and the witness was in no legal jeopardy, an exemption has been made.

In administering the Medicare program, SSA does exchange medical and financial insurance claim information with physicians, hospitals, and the fiscal intermediaries which handle billing and document preparation. A recent amendment to the Social Security Act specifies that such exchanges of information should only go as far as is necessary for effective administration of the Medicare program. To some critics, however, SSA uses its power to define confidentiality rules far too broadly—protecting itself from newsmen and public-interest groups who might want to investigate Medicare abuses or failures of the program to provide adequate services. According to one critic, SSA has expanded rules designed to protect the privacy of individual taxpayers and beneficiaries in order to protect "Medicare's corporate servants," concealing important information on the quality of nursing homes and hospitals in the process.[4] SSA officials argue that they carefully monitor the quality of nursing homes and other facilities used in the Medicare program, refusing to certify those which do not meet important standards. To publicize "lesser deficiencies" in these institutions, they say, would create unnecessary concern on the part of program participants.

---

[4] As reported in the *Freedom of Information Digest*, Vol. 13, No. 5, Freedom of Information Center, University of Missouri, September-October 1971.

Over the years, there have been several convictions of private detectives for trying to bribe SSA employees to give them information. Administration officials could recall only two cases, however, where employees had made unauthorized disclosure of confidential information. In both cases, in 1947 and again in 1967, the employees involved were prosecuted, convicted, and fined or jailed.

SSA also takes great care in protecting its public reputation for confidentiality. Some years ago, Sam Ketchum, Dick Tracy's associate in the nationally syndicated comic strip, was shown using a Social Security number to reveal the identity of a "dognapper." Numbers were hard to get, he told his police colleagues, but he added, "Don't worry. I know the Bureau Director." The real-life director of SSA's Bureau of Data Processing, William Hanna, published the following pained rejoinder:

Dear Mr. Tracy:

Despite his claim, I have never met your flatfoot friend, Sam Ketchum, and he did not obtain from me the name of the person assigned the social security number tattooed on that stolen Manchester terrier. I call this to your attention because information in Social Security records is confidential and if I had done what Sam says I did, I could get a year in jail or a $1,000 fine or both.

SSA officials believe computerization of files has contributed to their security. In the manual era, the applicant's record was an individual ledger sheet. Thus if a person could get to the file drawer and then the ledger, he could check any record. Although entry to the files area was restricted by guards who checked workers' identification, it was impossible for the guards to keep track of everyone. Under SSA's computerized system, however, the individual first has to secure the tape from locked storage. Then, because SSA runs a batch-processing operation, the entire tape must be run to gain access to any single record.

Access Rights

Each individual has full access to his Social Security record, a policy that has remained unchanged since 1935. Name, address, Social Security account number, and date of birth are available, as well as the amount of credits accumulated and the applicant's insurance status. SSA officials emphasize that computerization has made individual access a great deal easier. Requests for information (SSA receives 2½ to 3 million annually) can now be processed overnight at a cost of a few cents each. In the event that there are inaccuracies in his record, the individual can have corrections made, or, if the Administration itself discovers an error which it thinks the individual should know about, he will be informed.

There are some medical or psychological reports which the Social Security claimants or beneficiaries cannot see. For instance, a diagnosis that the person has cancer or is a psychotic will be withheld from him when he has not been told of this by his own doctor. However, officials note that SSA will release this information to an applicant's medical or legal representative. Medical information is not disclosable at all for purposes of a workmen's compensation suit, even where the patient himself might authorize this. Criminal penalties are provided for any physician engaged by SSA who discloses such information. This policy stems from SSA's sense that if such disclosures were made, "physicians might submit less comprehensive and candid reports or even refuse to perform consultative examinations, to the detriment of the disability insurance program."

Since individuals can look at their SSA records, some employers, landlords, retail merchants, and other interested parties have managed to gain access to those records by applying pressure on the individual. For instance, a public housing authority seeking to examine the earnings records of tenants, provided each with a "release form." If the tenant wanted to stay in the housing project, he had to sign the form authorizing SSA to release the information. According to Commissioner Ball, the Administration had to provide the information in response to the individual's "request," even though they knew this was a means of circumventing SSA rules against disclosure.

Still another aspect of the individual's control over his own Social Security record is in cases in which the Administration permits individuals to alter the name or number under which their records are stored. SSA cooperates wherever the individual has a valid reason for the change, such as an attempt to escape a labor blacklist, or a notorious past. While the Administration maintains a record of the change, it allows a new number or a pseudonym to be used on the Social Security card. Commissioner Ball emphasized that "It is very important to allow people to establish a different identity and start over somewhere else. We need to know both the old and new identities, but we keep it confidential.''

The character of SSA's basic relationship with people covered under its programs has had considerable impact on its record-keeping policies. Unlike most government agencies, SSA does not have to make evaluative decisions about the individual's rights to benefits. In issuing numbers, keeping earnings records, and getting out the checks to retired beneficiaries or their survivors, SSA can operate without treating its record subjects with the kind of investigative inquiries typical of most social-service agencies. While it has to exercise some control over internal and external fraud, the Administration is more like an insurance than a welfare system: if the individual has paid his "premiums" and meets the explicitly stated requirements of the law and Social Security administrative rules, he is entitled to receive the specified benefits. Much of the Administration's philosophy of confidentiality and access rights stems from this fact. While recent changes in minimum benefits have given SSA program activities somewhat more of a "welfare" character than previously, the basic social-insurance outlook persists.[5]

In its disability program, on the other hand, SSA acts very much like a welfare agency might in giving out general assistance—making a close determination of eligibility, requiring documentation, and operating through a complex hearings structure. This aspect of its work generates the most extensive and sensitive individual records in the Administration—most of which are manual in character.

The Debate over Use of the Social Security Account Number

SSA officials in 1971-72 were deeply involved in the growing controversy over use of the Social Security number by outside agencies. Though it is often assumed that such use runs counter to law, no statute or administrative rule prohibits use of the account number in other record systems. In fact, an executive order by President Roosevelt in 1943 required that, as a means of avoiding

---

[5] Many beneficiaries receiving the minimum retirement benefits today are getting considerably more from the program than would be the case were the only determinant of benefit levels their contributions to the trust fund; revenue increases which make increases in benefits possible come out of the taxes of current wage earners.

costly duplication, any Federal agency establishing a new system for personal identification *must* use the Social Security number.

That order is still in effect. Ten years ago, when the Internal Revenue Service proposed to develop its own numbering system, the Bureau of the Budget and Congress rejected the proposal on cost grounds. Use of the Social Security number for all income-tax returns was approved instead, and almost every employed person in the United States must now have a Social Security number, whether or not his earnings are covered by Social Security. The Department of Defense also uses the Social Security number as identification in lieu of the previous military-service serial number. Its use by other federal agencies, such as the Veterans Administration, Civil Service Commission, and FAA, has been approved as well.

A very large number of nonfederal government agencies and private organizations are also using the Social Security number as an identifier in their record systems. On the state and local level, agencies such as motor-vehicle departments, hospitals, and libraries have adopted this system. In the private sphere, business firms, colleges, and banks are among those organizations requiring the number of employees, customers, and students. SSA does not encourage such use, but it has neither the funds nor the authority to police outside uses of its numbering system.

Criticism of this expanding use of the account numbering system has come from several quarters. We note in the profiles below, for instance, that after much debate in the state legislature, the Department of Motor Vehicles in New York was forbidden to require Social Security numbers on license applications. On several university campuses, a move to adopt the Social Security number for student records met with considerable resistance as well. At the federal level, use of the number was debated (and rejected) in the course of planning for the 1970 decennial census, and the number's use outside SSA was discussed in the course of Senator Ervin's 1971 databank hearings.

Dealing with the Issue

SSA has responded both to the complaints and to the prospect of becoming a "national numbering agency." In 1967, Social Security officials planned to set up a public advisory council, in collaboration with the Bureau of the Budget, with top-level representation from business, labor, and civic groups. This body was to examine the important policy issues involved in the use of the account number as a universal identifier. However, this action was delayed as a result of the change of presidential administrations in 1968.

In 1971, a high-level task force was created within Social Security to advise the commissioner as to what Administration policy ought to be. In their report, task force members suggest that use of the number will continue to spread outside the federal government, especially as more organizations computerize their record systems.[6] Since this continuing spread raises serious civil-liberties issues, the authors argue, SSA should be cautious in its support of nonprogram uses of the number—at least until some clear national policy evolves. Following these task-force recommendations, SSA would openly assist health, welfare, and educational organizations where proposed use of the number "involves clear advantage to society, and little or no risk to individuals." Assistance to organizations in such cases would consist of checking the numbers given by individuals to see that they are correct and issuing numbers to those who do not already have one. The task force suggests that a release form be obtained from each record subject authorizing such procedures, but it is recognized that this could be a meaningless provision in settings where the individual is in no position to refuse the organization's request for cooperation.

SSA officials point out that for many purposes, the account number is not a particularly good identifier, since the Administration has been flexible both in requiring little positive proof of identity upon issuing a card, and in its willingness to change an individual's file name or number. As a result, SSA is under continual pressure to "tighten up" its account-number issuing procedures. While the Administration has resisted doing so where this might lead to undue costs or inconvenience for applicants, its task force recommended expansion of the early (ninth-grade) enumeration program, and legislation which would provide criminal penalties against those "willingly furnishing false information on a Social Security number application with intent to deceive the Secretary as to [their] true identity."

Some Administration officials pointed out to us that, intended or not, such increased controls over the issuing process will have the effect of making the account-numbering system more

---

[6] Social Security Number Task Force, *Report to the Commissioner*, Social Security Administration, May 1971, 124 pp.

readily usable for record identification purposes outside SSA. Early enumeration in the schools, for instance, will make it difficult in future years for adults intent on fraud to secure multiple cards under different names—claiming on each application that they have never been issued one. The challenge to them will be, "How is it that you didn't receive a card when the rest of your ninth-grade class did?" The new penalties for supplying false information represent a concern for "proper" identification that has not characterized the card-issuing process in the past.[7]

The task force further notes, however, that any formal move to establish the Social Security number as a "universal identifier" might represent a burden on the Administration. To maintain sufficiently tight control over such an identification function, SSA officials suggest, considerable additional funding would be required if they were to keep this activity from cutting into their primary mission. The Administration also raises the issue of damage to its public image. The feeling of many is that whether or not it actually administers a national identification program, the concept of a universal identifier is so distasteful to many segments of the population that public confidence in Social Security programs would be undermined.

Testifying before Senator Ervin's hearings on federal databanks in the spring of 1971, HEW Secretary Elliot Richardson took a position somewhat different from that expressed in the SSA task-force report, emphasizing that he saw no civil-liberties problems inherent in the use of the Social Security number itself. Answering critics who have said that use of the common numbering system greatly facilitates the exchange of personal information among organizations, he argued that computerization really makes it unnecessary to have identical account-numbering systems. However convenient record linkage on the basis of Social Security number might be, the computer makes it possible to link records quickly and cheaply on some other basis. Stopping the spreading use of the number, he said, would not do much to keep organizations from exchanging personal data. Richardson went on to say that the "potential for invasion of privacy or breach of confidentiality of information lies not in the use of the number itself, but

---

[7]Considering such provisions in its attempt to fashion measures for a new welfare reform plan, the Senate Finance Committee voted in March 1972 to require that every child be issued a Social Security number upon entering the first grade, that legal immigrants to the country be issued a number when they arrive, and that the Administration assist in issuing numbers to welfare recipients who do not already have one.

rather in how the organization uses computerized collections of data which are indexed by the number."

There is today no formal HEW policy on the use of the number. This will be forthcoming, Richardson said, after he has studied the recommendations of the SSA task force, and after a special commission of outside experts—created by the department in February 1972—makes its report to HEW.

The Future

Assistant Commissioner Jack Futterman suggests that the growth of large databanks is inevitable. "Society will use computers and nothing will stop it. The question is how to put the proper standards of privacy and due process into the system." In the case of SSA, the future development of its programs and systems applications is dependent, in the first instance, on what additional programs Congress may ask it to assume.

SSA officials at middle-management levels have expressed concern about the impact that President Nixon's proposed welfare reform program would have on their operations if any substantial part of the record-keeping or administration of that program were to be assigned to SSA. Some of their concern lies in the expectation that acquiring responsibility for a welfare program might adversely affect administration of SSA insurance programs: the Administration would have to police fraud violations on a much larger scale and would be involved in applying far more stringent eligibility criteria, scrutinizing applicants in a fashion incongruous with social-insurance administration. If the Social Security number were used for individual identification under welfare reform, new controls would have to be instituted. Under current proposals, a federalized welfare program would also entail greater data sharing, as SSA, IRS, the Department of Labor, and state agencies would have to communicate in order to monitor the tight "workfare" eligibility process which the President has promised will be a part of the new program.

Federal Law Enforcement

More than 30,000 agents or officers perform law-enforcement functions in federal agencies; of these, 8,500 serve in the FBI. The remainder are in investigative and protective units scattered throughout the federal civilian and military establishment. Among the more well known of these are the Secret Service, the Bureau of Customs, the Criminal Investigation Division of the army, the navy's Office of Naval Intelligence, the Postal Inspector's Office, the Bureau of Narcotics and Dangerous Drugs, the Immigration and Naturalization Service, the Intelligence Division of the Internal Revenue Service, and the Bureau of Personnel Investigations of the Civil Service Commission. Some less well known but important federal investigative units are found in the Food and Drug Administration, the Alcohol, Tobacco, and Firearms Division of the Internal Revenue Service, the Coast Guard, the Securities and Exchange Commission, and the Civil Aeronautics Board.

These agencies, with their different overall goals and areas of jurisdiction, operate for the most part independently of one another. But many of them share information on an informal basis, and take part in some coordinated actions (as in the case of "task forces" established to deal with organized-crime problems on a regional basis). Within the law-enforcement field as a whole, informal "communities" exchange information about suspects, events, and trends of common interest. The best known of these is the "domestic intelligence community," made up of representatives from agencies such as the FBI, the military intelligence agencies, the CIA, and the Internal Security Division of the Justice Department.

While Congress makes laws defining what conduct is criminal and reviews the operations of federal law-enforcement agencies, considerable discretion still lies in the executive agencies as to how law-enforcement resources will be applied—who will be investigated, what techniques will be employed, what information will be collected, and how it will be interpreted and used. The widespread public debates in 1970-71 over U.S. Army surveillance of civilian political protests and FBI surveillance of black militant groups and campus activists illustrate the concern of many Americans when federal investigations touch on areas of constitutionally protected expression and dissent.

As a general matter, the investigative and intelligence files of federal law-enforcement agencies are considered "privileged" executive records and are not subject to public access under the federal Freedom of Information Act of 1966. However, when information about individuals is drawn from these files for use in civil or criminal proceedings, the content and sources of the information must be disclosed to satisfy constitutional rules as to due process of law. If the federal investigative agency does not want to reveal its sources, the executive has to forgo prosecution.

By 1971, computerized information systems had been adopted for some record-keeping functions within most of the leading federal investigative agencies named earlier. Some of their applications are highly sophisticated, such as the Secret Service's capacity to enter a set of personal characteristics (without name) into its computer and search for a match against a data base (in 1971) of some 50,000 persons whose identities and characteristics are kept in the file because they are believed to pose a potential threat to the President's safety.

Among these computerizing federal law-enforcement agencies, the Federal Bureau of Investigation has been the object of considerable commentary and protest recently; it is the subject of our next profile.

THE FEDERAL BUREAU OF INVESTIGATION'S NATIONAL CRIME INFORMATION CENTER

The FBI is described in official government publications as "the principal investigative arm of the United States Department of Justice." Created in 1908, during Theodore Roosevelt's administration, the bureau's first two decades were spotted with inefficiency and political corruption. In 1924, Attorney General Harlan Stone named the late J. Edgar Hoover as director, beginning a tenure of office (until Hoover's death in 1972) in which the bureau became a national symbol of "professional" law enforcement.

Over these years, the bureau has also been criticized by spokesmen representing a wide variety of positions on the national political spectrum. Sometimes the criticism has involved the increased power of the FBI in relation to local and state law enforcement, sometimes what the FBI failed to do (as with civil-rights enforcement in the South during the 1950s and early 60s), and sometimes the role of the FBI in controversial programs (such as loyalty-security investigations). Particular investigative methods used by FBI agents (such as telephone tapping) have also been the object of criticism, as have such matters as the uses sometimes made of FBI reports, and the public statements about political movements and social philosophies made by Mr. Hoover. Public support for the FBI has generally been very high, however. In 1971, the FBI came under broad criticism in the press and from some well-known congressmen for its surveillance of black militant and antiwar protest groups. At the height of the criticism, though, a national Gallup Poll showed that 80 percent of the public rated the FBI's role as either "highly" or "moderately" favorable. Only 4 percent answered "unfavorable," with 11 percent "neutral" and 5 percent with "no opinion."

The FBI "investigates violations of federal criminal statutes, collects evidence in cases in which the United States is or may be a party in interest, and performs other duties imposed by law or Presidential directive. FBI jurisdiction, which is strictly defined by law, covers 185 investigative matters."[8] These range from "classic" bureau activities involving bank robberies, kidnapping, interstate auto thefts, and internal security to more recent roles in the areas of civil rights, organized crime, and airplane hijacking.

In 1971, the FBI had a budget of $294 million. In round terms, its 19,500 full-time employees consisted of 8,500 special agents and 11,000 clerical, stenographic, and technical personnel. The agents conducted over 880,000 field investigations in 1970. The bureau is organized with a director, associate director, two assistants to the director, ten divisions, and a legal counsel. From its national offices in the Department of Justice building, the FBI coordinates the operations of 59 field offices and 400 suboffices throughout the country. (The bureau is scheduled to move in 1974 into its own 11-story, $100-million building at Tenth and Pennsylvania Avenues in Washington, D.C.)

Manual Files and Bureau Functions

As an exclusively investigative agency, the FBI is and has always been built on files. From the 1920s to the present, the bureau has maintained three major files containing information about individuals: fingerprint and identification records; a narrative or "central" file; and a name-index file.

Fingerprint and Identification Records. Since its creation in 1924, the Identification Division of the FBI has been the national depository and clearinghouse for fingerprint cards and arrest records collected throughout the United States. (Formal congressional approval for this function was given in a 1930 statute.) Though the total number of fingerprint sets on file was over 201 million in

---

[8] Federal Bureau of Investigation, *1970 Annual Report.*

1971, the bureau estimates that it has nonduplicated prints on about 86 million different persons. Approximately 19 million of these are in the FBI's "criminal section," representing fingerprint and arrest records submitted by local, state, and federal law-enforcement agencies for crimes serious enough to require taking prints. The cumulative record of an individual's arrests, dispositions, and sentences makes up what the FBI calls a criminal identification record or summary criminal history, popularly called a "rap sheet." Sixty million fingerprint cards are stored for 19 million individuals in the criminal section.

The criminal identification records are available to law-enforcement agencies throughout the country, which submit fingerprints of arrested persons by mail and receive back by mail any record of prior "criminal involvement." Fingerprint cards are also submitted by state and federal government agencies checking out the criminal history record of persons applying for certain jobs, permits, and licenses. FBI identification records are not sent to private employers, though Department of Justice regulations make a few exceptions, such as federally insured banks and railroad police. However, in many states, local and state law-enforcement agencies can get prints from the FBI and supply them to private employers.

Traditionally, the FBI did not regard a person as entitled to examine his criminal identification record to verify its accuracy or completeness. Over the years, the FBI would review the record with a complainant who came to the bureau with a specific allegation of inaccuracy, and would correct the record if errors were found. An FBI spokesman estimated that such "off the street" reviews averaged about ten per year. Apart from such exceptions, the bureau's view was that the individual should go to the local or state law-enforcement agency where an arrest had been made and ask to inspect it there (even if this meant going to several different communities or states in the case of a multiple arrest record).

Fingerprints for the remaining 67 million persons in the file make up what is called the "civil division." These are prints from military servicemen, government employees, and aliens; from applicants for jobs, licenses, and permits requiring fingerprint checks; and from voluntary submissions for identification uses. Civil-division prints are used to identify fugitives, amnesia victims, missing persons, and unidentified bodies, and to verify identities where these may be in dispute.

The Narrative File. The most sensitive of the three main files in the bureau is known as the "narrative" or "central" file. These are records generated by the various criminal, civil, applicant, and special investigations conducted by the FBI. Over 6 million records are in the file, identified by name of individual or group and containing a wide range of material. This includes credit-check and criminal-record information, reports of agent interviews, documentary materials, informant reports, "technical informant" data (usually wiretapping or room-bugging information), and data from other sources. From this base file, the bureau creates special lists that may be desired, such as the names of 10,000 persons to be picked up in case of invasion or war or special files, such as those on organized crime, radical groups, and civil-disorder incidents. Similar narrative records on matters of local concern are maintained at the field offices and suboffices, with exchanges to and from the central file.

The central narrative file forms the basis for FBI reports that go to various federal agencies for which the bureau does employment suitability investigations, to prosecuting and civil attorneys in the Department of Justice, and for various intelligence reports that the FBI prepares for civilian and military agencies of the federal government. The FBI also shares selected information from its file with local and state law-enforcement agencies; in 1971, the FBI estimated that it disseminated "340,000 pieces of criminal intelligence data" to other law-enforcement offices.

FBI narrative records are confidential. They are not open to public scrutiny under the federal "freedom of information" law, and also enjoy privileged status under federal judicial doctrine. Individuals or groups are not told there is a record on them and cannot see their folders. In the past, some officials in federal executive agencies authorized to receive FBI reports have released or leaked their contents. In addition, controversies over whether FBI officials or recipient agencies leaked information from reports on notables such as Martin Luther King, Jr., Bobby Baker, Congressman Cornelius Gallagher, and others have been well-publicized (and unresolved) episodes of the 1960s.

The narrative file contains a mixture of verified and "raw" (or unconfirmed) information. When providing a report, the bureau will indicate levels of reliability and confidence that it places on particular items of information. However, the bureau regards "evaluation" of the information to be beyond its function as an investigative agency; that belongs to the executive agencies which determine whether to prosecute, sue, employ, license, etc.

The Name-index File. The FBI name-check file is essentially a card index to the narrative records. It contains approximately 56 million cards, arranged by name of individual or group, and indicating whether there is information on that person or organization in the central file. About 2.6 million "name checks" were made in the index file in 1970, principally in connection with employment, licensing, or permit applications.

The FBI also maintains important laboratory files (samples of animal hairs, typewriter standards, tire treads, etc.) and statistical files (such as those used to produce the Uniform Crime Reports). However, these do not contain identified personal information.

Early Computerization in the FBI

The FBI had adopted calculating machines in the 1930s to augment its manual procedures. In 1934, it installed a punch-card system for searching fingerprints but had to abandon this and return to manual searching because the volume of prints submitted grew too large for the punch-card systems that then existed.

The FBI's first computer, an IBM 650, was installed in 1947, with a more powerful 1401 added in 1955, and an IBM 7070 system in 1958. These were used primarily for administrative and statistical purposes, in a batch-processing mode.

The first use of computerization to process individual records rather than statistics or payrolls came in 1963. In that year, the bureau began a "Careers in Crime" study to investigate "recidivism, mobility, and profiles by type of crime" and to help evaluate the effectiveness of the overall federal criminal-justice system. The criminal identification records (rap sheets) of 194,000 offenders under federal law were computerized. As new arrests, convictions, and other transactions for these offenders were sent to the bureau, the record was updated and reports of various trends and patterns were produced by computer analysis.

The Careers in Crime research showed not only that criminal activity was increasingly spilling over local governmental boundaries but also that the existing system for exchanging wanted-person, stolen-vehicle, and prior-arrest records between local jurisdictions and throughout the nation was too slow and incomplete to help local law enforcement. Though the FBI had been collecting and circulating "wanteds-and-warrants" by mail or teletype since the 1920s, the mounting volume of these records and delays in getting them out (especially to the officer on patrol when he stopped a suspect) persuaded the FBI management that a faster national system was needed.

First, however, top FBI officials had to be convinced that the new third-generation computer systems could provide necessary random-access storage, and that a dependable terminal-telecommunication operation could be developed. When internal briefings and other FBI staff work within the bureau persuaded the director of these new capabilities, approval was given in 1965 to design a computerized national system.

The FBI defined its role as providing the national index to records primarily supplied by and to be used by local, state, and federal law-enforcement agencies. Wanteds-and-warrants were selected because this was the most vital information for the man on the beat and the "apprehension process." The decision was made to hold off development of a national computerized "rap sheet" system because there were problems of standardization to be worked out and technical matters that made it, according to FBI Inspector Jerome J. Daunt, "unwise to rush the technology."[9] Furthermore, local and state law-enforcement agencies were primarily interested in the basic wanteds-and-warrants system at that time.

In 1965, Director Hoover announced plans for the National Crime Information Center. Since the money for this system had to come from Congress, the plan was submitted first for review by the Bureau of the Budget, then to the Appropriations subcommittees that pass on FBI budgets. Each of these approved the project, as did Congress in voting funds for the FBI. No enabling legislation for the new center was sought from Congress because a ruling secured from the Attorney General declared that the 1930 federal statute authorizing the FBI to collect and disseminate "identification and other records" relating to crime to local, state, and federal law-enforcement agencies was sufficient legal foundation for NCIC.

During 1966, while the system was being tested, the FBI director wrote an article describing NCIC in *Popular Science Monthly*. For "the average, law-abiding citizen," Hoover stated, NCIC meant only "good things." "[I] t will mean no intrusion whatsoever upon the right to privacy," since only persons on whom warrants for serious crimes were outstanding would be listed. NCIC "will guarantee the security of information in its files

---

[9] Efforts were begun at this time on several other computer applications, such as a modus operandi file of bank-robbery offenders and an automated fingerprint recognition system. These underwent slow but continuous development throughout the 1960s.

against access or removal by unauthorized persons." Furthermore, "nobody can misuse the NCIC data banks to embarrass you with some ancient traffic violation or tidbit of personal [gossip]. . . . No such information will be stored there."

NCIC went "on the air" in January 1967, with approximately 23,000 records of wanted persons and stolen property on its two IBM 360/40 computers. Fifteen police jurisdictions were connected to the system in this pilot phase. The information on each wanted person stored in NCIC was designed to tell an inquiring officer the offense for which a current warrant has been issued, the agency that placed the warrant in the system, and to supply basic identifying data about the individual. The ID data include name, sex, height, weight, date of birth, Social Security number, and armed forces serial number. The full criminal-history record (rap sheet) was not in the file; for this, an officer would have to contact the agency that submitted the warrant, or the FBI's manual identification file.

Early Civil-liberties Discussions about NCIC

To the press that watched the opening-day demonstration, an FBI spokesman emphasized that the bureau was "not planning a monster set of dossiers on law-abiding citizens." At the same time, he noted that "additional criminal information might be fed in as the system takes shape." Following the opening exercises, the American Civil Liberties Union wrote Attorney General Ramsey Clark expressing concern that the "additional criminal information" spoken of in 1967 might encompass investigative files containing "information concerning the individual's political beliefs and associations." The ACLU also raised the question of just what kind of "criminal record" would be stored; they noted that the failure of some local law-enforcement agencies to report the disposition of arrests to the FBI (especially acquittals and dismissals) and the FBI's policy of circulating such "incomplete" arrest records created injuries to persons with such records when they applied for various jobs or licenses. ACLU also asked about rules for access and controls over misuse. A spokesman for the Attorney General replied that NCIC was not a "centralized dossier system" but "a computerized index providing leads to documented information maintained by state law-enforcement agencies and the Federal Bureau of Investigation." He specified the limits and controls in NCIC, and sent along Director Hoover's *Popular Science* article to show that the bureau "has been concerned from the start about possible intrusions upon the right to privacy, and has taken the steps indicated in the design of the system to protect that right."

Operations of the NCIC

In early 1972, the NCIC system was running 24 hours a day, seven days a week, with about 76,000 "network transactions" handled daily. The time of response to an inquiry averages less than 10 seconds. More than 100 remote control terminals were located throughout the 50 states and Canada. Forty state and metropolitan agencies had their own computers directly linked to NCIC, allowing inquiries from over 4,000 local law-enforcement agencies to go through their systems. NCIC had a staff of 87 (9 agents and 78 clerks), and an operating budget of $2.8 million. An Advisory Policy Board was created in 1969, made up of 23 law-enforcement executives from agencies throughout the U.S., and offering recommendations on standards, procedures, and operations for the system.

"Active records" in NCIC on December 1, 1971, totaled 3.3 million, and were divided as follows, in rounded figures:

Persons	114,000
Vehicles	756,000
License plates	253,000
Articles	715,000
Guns	442,000
Securities	1,046,000
Boats	4,000

This distribution of about 3 to 4 percent "person" records to 96 to 97 percent "property" records has been typical of the NCIC system thus far.

During 1970, the FBI reported a daily average of 500 "hits," or positive identifications, on the system. Issues of the NCIC *Newsletter* and FBI *Bulletin* recount examples showing how officers around the country learned that persons, vehicles, or goods that they were checking out were indeed wanted, and of instances in which the safety of officers was protected through the "danger warning" provided by an NCIC identification.

The *Newsletters* particularly report examples of "interesting hits" that arose by police checking the identities of persons or vehicles in situations beyond those that would have led to such checks before NCIC. The March 1971 *Newsletter* reported as follows:

> Recently a young man hitchhiking through Kentucky was jailed by troopers at Pikeville when he made the mistake of stopping off at the Kentucky State Police post there to use the restroom. Troopers ran a check on him with NCIC. Before the man could leave the post, he was arrested as a parole violator from Lansing, Michigan. Similarly, an individual contacted a local charity in Independence, Kansas, requesting assistance money to return to Texas. His car description and license number were furnished to Independence police who ran an NCIC check. An immediate response revealed the vehicle had been reported stolen in Dallas, Texas, a week earlier. The man's transportation problem was resolved by the Kansas authorities. . .

In the November 1971 *Newsletter* there was a report of a man in Englewood, Colorado, who failed to dim his automobile headlights and was stopped by a local police officer. On calling for an NCIC check of the identification the man furnished, he was found to be wanted on a two-year-old federal warrant for embezzling funds in a New York City bank.

According to Jerome Daunt, inspector in charge of the NCIC system, there has been a substantial increase in apprehensions of persons with stolen vehicles by state and local police; for example, he notes that interstate stolen vehicles recovered and thefts solved are now at 43 percent of those reported, compared to 20 percent before NCIC.

NCIC records have already been accepted as valid evidence in federal courts. Under U.S. Supreme Court decisions, police officers must have "probable cause" (knowledge of an outstanding warrant of arrest) to make a lawful search of an automobile while making a personal arrest. Several audit logs of NCIC "hits" have been used to prove that police officers had the constitutionally required "probable cause" when they conducted the searches.[1]

System Safeguards in NCIC

Physical security for the computer center is provided by its location in a guarded building, and a guarded installation. To minimize

---

[1] See, for example, *U.S.* v. *Golembiewski*, 437 F. 2d 1212 (1971).

threats from an unbalanced programmer doing damage from within, two persons are always stationed in the center. Backup tapes are stored separately, and the files could be reconstituted if they were ever destroyed. Additional physical security measures are planned for NCIC when it moves into the new FBI headquarters building.

Each request is logged into the system to identify the requesting agency, terminal used, time of inquiry, and information sent. These logs are preserved on tape and could be used to trace any leaks that might be discovered. However, individual officers using the terminals are not required by NCIC to give their names or other personal identification.

The NCIC manual stresses that its information is for law-enforcement use only. A 1969 meeting of the NCIC Advisory Group noted the possibility of a user agency divulging information improperly and recommended that a penalty system be established. Under federal law, the FBI could cancel service to any law-enforcement agency that violated confidentiality rules; however, since state computers control the inquiries from local departments into the system, the states would have to enforce such an expulsion policy to keep a local or state agency out. (In 1971, the FBI endorsed the desirability of a criminal penalty being enacted to punish breaches of confidentiality.) The NCIC Advisory Policy Board also recommended that all local and state computer systems interfacing with NCIC should be either exclusively law-enforcement computers or under the control of law-enforcement personnel for the NCIC interface, a matter that we will return to later in the profile.

Inspector Daunt believes a greater accuracy and completeness has been achieved in the NCIC system than existed during the manual-record era. For example, existing federal warrants were checked back against court records before data conversion to see whether they were still outstanding. For the 1960-66 period, 38 percent of the warrants proved to be outdated or invalid and were thus not entered. In addition NCIC *Newsletters* and operating bulletins continually stress the importance of entering complete records, obtaining identifying information later that may not have been available at the time of initial placement of a warrant in the system, and similar "quality controls" in the operation. The NCIC staff makes periodic reviews of entries to identify "inaccuracies or improper procedures," not only notifying the contributor involved but also publishing instructions in the *Newsletter* to help correct such practices more generally. Despite the confidence NCIC management has in the accuracy of its records, users are expressly cautioned that an NCIC "hit" is not to be considered infallible proof of identity (since fingerprints are not used in the NCIC wanted system) and that regular identification measures should be applied later to establish identity conclusively. Each "hit" message instructs the inquirer to contact the agency originating the record for confirmation.

NCIC also faces a problem in getting agencies that have apprehended a wanted person or stolen article to notify NCIC immediately, so that a wanted status can be erased. Failure to cancel could lead, for example, to the owner of a stolen-but-returned car being picked up while driving his own vehicle. To reduce this risk, NCIC also requires periodic off-line validation of active records every 90 days by the contributor.

Because NCIC began as a "wanted" rather than a rap sheet system, the question of an individual getting access to his own record did not arise in this operation between 1967 and 1971. Presumably, the FBI would be happy to have anyone check in to see if he was wanted; a "hit" could then lead to instant arrest.

Computerizing National Criminal-history Records

While the NCIC system began as a file limited in scope to wanted and warrants, and with relatively little civil liberties opposition to that operation, the moves to bring summary criminal histories into NCIC have drawn far more criticism. The current debate had its origin in 1969. The Law Enforcement Assistance Administration (LEAA), the agency within the Department of Justice which funds innovations in the criminal justice field, initiated a project called SEARCH (*S*ystem for *E*lectronic *A*nalysis and *R*etrieval of *C*riminal *H*istories). First six, then ten states were given grants as a cooperative pilot project to develop a standard format for offender records. Top LEAA officials in 1968-69 spoke of the project's goal as an independent record-sharing system joining state and federal agencies.

The FBI served on the original policy committee of SEARCH but withdrew late in 1969, stating that its "workload commitments at that time did not allow FBI participation." Several persons active in SEARCH felt it was because the FBI intended to develop its own national criminal-history file and did not want to support the idea that it might be done by a state consortium.

However, an FBI representative rejoined the SEARCH project in April 1970.

By the summer of 1970, the sample state records had been computerized and the feasibility of a central index switching system in one state had been demonstrated. At this point, three alternatives for managing the central system were open to the Nixon administration: a multistate consortium, with one state serving as the message-switching center; LEAA itself, perhaps through a clearinghouse administered by the International Association of Chiefs of Police; and the Federal Bureau of Investigation. Those favoring the first or second solutions believed that lodging the national computerized system in the FBI would strengthen the FBI's already powerful influence over local and state law-enforcement agencies, leading to greater centralization of the police power in the U.S. "This system ought to remain in state hands," one prominent SEARCH official commented. "If we put all these records in the hands of a federal agency, we are working to diminish the role and responsibility of the states in law enforcement." If the system were to be federally administered, these spokesmen felt it ought to be in the hands of an independent federal "information-handling" agency created by Congress, rather than under the control of a "line" investigative agency such as the FBI.

These spokesmen also stressed the opposition of the FBI to proposals for installing civil-liberties protections in computerized information systems. In July 1970, a Security and Privacy Subcommittee of Project SEARCH had recommended the adoption of detailed standards for limiting data collection, assuring information confidentiality, setting controls on system users, and providing for system security. The report also recommended a right for individuals to have access to their own record to check its accuracy or completeness. The FBI had never recognized such a legal right of access and had never routinely permitted such access in the manual rap sheet file. Furthermore, it had sharply questioned the propriety of SEARCH spelling out a code of privacy and confidentiality rules when this was proposed by the Security and Privacy Subcommittee, though the FBI has said that it did not question the need for safeguards to be set.

The case for FBI control of the new national system was that it already had the national fingerprint file, which would be needed for basic identification, and had run the manual criminal record exchange for almost 50 years. The bureau had practical experience in computerizing rap sheets, going back to its "Careers in Crime" work that started in 1963. The FBI's position is that it always intended the criminal history record to be the basic file of its national computer system, but had started with wanted-and-warrants. Also, it was the NCIC's standardized classifications for general crime categories that were the ones adopted by SEARCH. Most important, the FBI had the national telecommunication system up and running already in NCIC; at a time of severe economic constraints, setting up a parallel system would have been a costly choice. Critics of this view, such as Joseph Hanlon, a columnist for *Computerworld*, replied that this was advocating "grafting an elephant onto a flea," and that the presence of the relatively small NCIC system was not a basis for placing the criminal-history function with the FBI.

In December 1970, after intense lobbying behind the scenes by all involved, Attorney General Mitchell transferred primary responsibility for managing the national computerized criminal-history system from LEAA to the FBI. The NCIC would not store the full summary criminal histories now in state and local files, but would serve as a national index, informing an inquiring agency of the presence and major aspects of a record; for more detail, an inquiry would have to be made to the state holding the primary record. A budget of $1.3 million for the first year of operations was approved by Congress in the FBI's fiscal 1972 appropriation, and the system began operations in November 1971.

The Civil-liberties Debate Moves into the Courts

While these developments were taking place, lawsuits in the federal and state courts began to challenge several key aspects of the way law-enforcement agencies were handling offender records under existing manual procedures. In a series of cases during the 1960s, lower federal courts ruled in favor of individuals who sued to have their fingerprints returned and their arrest records expunged when charges against them had been voluntarily withdrawn or were dismissed by the court, or when the individual was acquitted at a trial.[2]

These decisions stressed that arrest records were circulated widely by many local law-enforcement agencies to private and

---

[2] *U.S.* v. *Kalish*, 217 F. Supp. 968 (D. P. Rico, 1967); *U.S.* v *McLeod*, 385 F. 2d 734 (1967); *Morrow* v. *District of Columbia*, 417 F. 2d 728 (1969); and *Wheeler* v. *Goodman*, 306 F. Supp. 58 (W. D. N. C. 1969).

government employers, and were used in license and permit checks; official circulation of the "criminal record" in such cases operated as a form of punishment for persons who had never been found guilty of crime. Judicial notice was also taken of the greater tendency of black Americans living in ghettos to be the subject of round-up arrests, and arrests without later conviction were noted to take place frequently when police dealt with civil-rights groups in the South or antiwar demonstrations throughout the country.[3] However, these decisions affected only the individuals who sued to have their records expunged, or to get other specific relief, and the courts did not issue rulings setting general required practices for law-enforcement agencies.

In June 1971, the FBI's criminal-record procedures received a major blow. A federal district court in Washington, D.C., in the *Menard* case, ordered the FBI to cease disseminating criminal-history records for purposes of determining employment, licensing, or other benefits, even when the inquiring agency was a local or state law enforcement agency.[4] After taking extensive testimony from the FBI on how its criminal-history file was maintained, and while accepting the value of such records for direct law-enforcement purposes, Judge Gerhard Gesell ruled that the FBI's criminal record system "is out of effective control." "Arrest record material is incomplete and hence often inaccurate," Judge Gesell ruled. "No procedure exists to enable individuals to obtain, to correct, or to supplant the criminal record information used against them," or even to know that checks were being made for employment purposes. "The Bureau cannot prevent improper dissemination and use of the material it supplies to hundreds of local agencies," and "there are no criminal or civil sanctions" against misuse. There is no clear set of standards among the states as to which jobs ought to require criminal record checks and which need not. Finally, Judge Gesell declared, "Control of the data will be made more difficult and opportunities for improper use will increase with the development of centralized state information centers to be linked by computer to the Bureau."

In this situation, the court held, where government's circulation of arrest records reveals "episodes in a person's life of doubtful and certainly not determined import," this "clearly invades

---

[3] See *Gregory* v. *Litton Systems, Inc.*, 316 F. Supp. 401 (C. D. Cal. 1970).

[4] *Menard* v. *Mitchell*, 328 F. Supp. 718 (1971). The decision was on appeal in 1972 before the U.S. Court of Appeals for the District of Columbia.

personal privacy." To be permitted, there must be a clear showing by Congress that it authorizes dissemination of criminal records for employment and licensing checks, with a "national policy" specifying "adequate sanctions and administrative safeguards." Until Congress so acts, the court held, the bureau cannot continue disseminating records for uses other than direct law enforcement.

The FBI complied with the *Menard* ruling immediately, suspending national dissemination of records to local and state agencies for employment and licensing checks but calling for legislation to "correct" the situation. In September 1971, Sen. Alan Bible of Nevada introduced a bill to authorize such exchanges. The senator stressed the importance of criminal-record checks to prevent infiltration of organized-crime figures into the gambling and liquor industries in Nevada, and the need for screening of applicants for "sensitive" posts such as "the employment of schoolteachers, the licensing of lawyers, private investigators, real estate agents," and other positions. He also stated that legislation could be written that would provide the "adequate sanctions and administrative safeguards" for constitutional rights that the courts had discussed. While this bill was awaiting committee hearing and review, Senator Bible introduced a provision in a supplementary appropriation bill to authorize the FBI to continue circulating records as they had before the *Menard* case until June 30, 1972. This rider was passed by voice vote, was accepted by the House, and signed by President Nixon. Later, there were protests by liberals in Congress that the authorization had been "sneaked through," and they promised a full debate when appropriations were considered to cover operations beginning in July 1972.

FBI Policies for the Computerized Criminal History File

Meanwhile, a set of recommendations for the projected computerized criminal history system were developed by a Security and Confidentiality Committee created by the NCIC's Advisory Policy Group.[5] Drawing heavily on the SEARCH recommendations, the NCIC committee proposed that information in the new system include personal identification and public record data on the major steps of an individual's progression through the criminal-justice process—arrest, prosecution, trial, imprisonment, and pa-

---

[5] The committee consists of two members from each of the NCIC's four regions, plus one FBI member. The chairman is the Director of the Michigan State Police.

role. Only serious violations would be included. There would be no juvenile offenders, minor offenses such as drunkenness or vagrancy, disturbing the peace, or nonspecific charges such as "suspicion." No "social history" information, such as civil commitment for narcotics or mental illness would be included. All users of the system would be criminal-justice agencies: police, prosecutors, courts, correction, parole, and special criminal-justice units. Computers and terminals linked to the system would have to be either owned by criminal-justice agencies or, if using a partitioned segment of a multiagency computer center, the partitioned segment using the criminal-record system would have to be under the "management control" of law-enforcement officials. Criminal-history records would not be stored in databanks also containing noncriminal information, such as welfare, hospital, education, or voting-registration records. "The person's right to see and challenge the contents of his record should form an integral part of the system with reasonable administrative procedures." Rules for removing information would be based on state or federal laws and controlled by the agency that submitted the original record. A purge of a record would wipe out all personal-identification data in the file, as well as the criminal records. It was recommended that criminal and civil penalties for misuse of information be adopted, as well as model state statutes to cover privacy and security matters in computerized information systems of participating cities and states. The recommendations went on to specify a series of "minimum" practices for assuring accuracy of data and transactions, auditing and monitoring the system, and providing physical, personnel, and technical security measures.

In June 1971 Director Hoover "endorsed" these recommendations in testimony before the Senate Appropriations Committee and offered some observations about "legal aspects" of the impending system. "Computerization," he said, "does not enlarge or restrict the persons and agencies to whom the identification records are presently available." There *would* be arrests without disposition in the system when it began, he stated, but "the computer will be programmed to erase such arrest notations when and if the law so requires." True to his long-standing position, the director declared that "a person having a record should have no absolute right to see it." However, he added, "The FBI has no objections to a declared right of a person, by statute or judicial decision, to learn the content of his identification record and to protest alleged error therein on any occasion when it appears that the record is to be used against him in any manner."

The Summary Criminal-history File Goes On-line

In November of 1971, the FBI began operating its national criminal-history system, with 130,000 individual records in the file. An IBM 360/65 was installed at FBI headquarters for NCIC system expansion, in addition to the 360/50. One state with computerized criminal-history records had joined the full operation at its start; other states were expected to join the system by the end of 1972. Over 6,000 local, state and federal law enforcement agencies would be able to inquire into the system, as well as courts and correctional institutions. The individual record stored in the file includes personal identification data and numbers, arrest charges, the disposition of each case, sentencing details, custody history, and "supervision status." All of the policies recommended by the Advisory Policy Board were adopted as regulations for the system. These include a procedure to give a person who requests it a copy of his own computerized record; a procedure in which the computer periodically demands update from a police agency for any arrest record entered without disposition information; and the signing of written agreements with each participating agency forbidding dissemination of criminal-history information to unauthorized persons.

Future Plans

The FBI will be heavily engaged in developing its criminal-history and automated fingerprint applications in the near future. Over $1.6 million were spent between 1967 and 1971 on the fingerprint work, with a prototype announced ready for building in 1972.[6] According to Jerome Daunt, there are no present plans to put individual intelligence information into on-line computerized systems; Daunt observed that this area "should be left alone until we know how to use and protect it effectively."[7]

Debates over the FBI's expanding NCIC promise to be intense during the next few years, not only by itself but as part of the reconsideration of the FBI's role following the death of Mr.

---

[6] The FBI worked also on Procheck, a computer file and software program for identifying professional check forgers. Other computer applications included support of field investigative work relating to organized crime and "investigations relating to security."

[7] It should be noted, however, that the FBI regularly contributes information which goes into intelligence databanks maintained by the Organized Crime Intelligence Unit and the Inter-Departmental Intelligence Unit (IDIU) (for internal-security matters), both within the U.S. Department of Justice.

Hoover. On specific issues, there are bills pending in Congress to limit the dissemination of arrest records or to expunge conviction records for those who have demonstrated successful rehabilitation after serving prison sentences. A decision will have to be made whether only computers owned or operated by criminal-justice agencies will be allowed into the criminal-history network, or whether multidepartment computer centers operated by civilian employees at the local and state levels will be able to maintain the criminal-history file, under appropriate security measures.

There will also be broader debates, such as whether Congress should spell out safeguards for confidentiality, security, and individual access in the NCIC or leave the FBI's new administrative rules in effect. Beyond this lie proposals to reopen in Congress the issue decided in favor of the FBI by the Nixon administration in 1970: who should run the national criminal-history exchange—the states, the FBI, or an independent federal agency? And in 1972 LEAA moved to create a computerized network of state data centers, to provide a system of collecting crime statistics independent of the FBI's Uniform Crime Reports; whether this project would remain independent or would also be "annexed" by the FBI promises to be a lively issue in both the criminal-justice community and in the Congress.

What this agenda suggests is that the development of NCIC will go forward in the 1970s in a setting of serious debates as to federal-state relations, federal executive branch reorganization of functions, and civil-liberties claims.

State Regulatory and Licensing Agencies

Exclusive of those being used in education, there were 582 computers in use in state agencies in 1970, an increase of almost 50 percent over 1966.[8] Total EDP costs for these activities were estimated at $240 million, but there are wide variations in both

---

[8] In 1970, 733 computers were being used in state institutions of higher education. Data used here are from *Information Systems Technology in State Government*, 1970 Report of the National Association for State Information Systems.

expenditures and the distribution of computing equipment. The heaviest users were California and New York (with 49 computers each); the least use was in North and South Dakota and New Mexico, each with two computers. According to the National Association of State Information Systems, highway, finance and revenue, and motor-vehicle agencies are the three highest-volume users of computers in state government. More specifically, we learned from our own survey of organizations that more than 85 percent of the state tax and motor-vehicle agencies have computer applications to their files on taxpayers and licensed drivers. We have selected the New York State Department of Motor Vehicles to illustrate some of the uses of EDP for record-keeping at the state government level.

New York State in 1970 had 49 computers, 2,400 EDP employees, and spent $28 million on these activities. The state government exercises unusually firm budgetary review and systems-development control over agency computer usage. It also has a Statewide Information Systems committee that serves as an interagency body to consider matters of data standards, data sharing, and privacy and confidentiality.

New York State has *computerized* "people databanks" in at least 11 state agencies. These include the Civil Service Department, with personnel information on state employees; the State Labor Department, with a "job bank" file of unemployed persons run in collaboration with the U.S. Department of Labor; the New York State Identification and Intelligence System, which has files of fingerprints, wanted-person information, and summary criminal histories; the Department of Health, with files on vital statistics and communicable diseases (such as VD), a cancer register, and a physicians and nurses register; the State Tax and Finance Department, with a file of the names and addresses of state taxpayers; the Social Services Department, with files on children in institutions and recipients of Medicaid and welfare; the Department of Mental Hygiene, with a file of patients in state-operated facilities and some patients in state-aided private facilities; and the Department of Corrections, which has begun an "inmate information system" for the state's prison population. The State Department of Motor Vehicles is one of the largest computerized "people databanks" in New York State government, with information on 11½ million persons in its files in 1971.

NEW YORK STATE DEPARTMENT OF MOTOR VEHICLES

As America's romance with the auto has intensified, vehicle-registration and driver-licensing operations in every state have grown proportionately. Since 1924, when the New York Bureau of Motor Vehicles was created, the number of registered motor vehicles in the state has increased from 1.6 to 7.2 million, and the number of licensed drivers from 1.9 to 8.3 million.

To maintain records on this number of vehicles and drivers, the New York State Department of Motor Vehicles spent over $36.3 million in 1970 and employed 3,200 individuals in 12 district offices and 2 branch offices. Eighty-two county clerk's offices throughout the state supplement this work by acting as the department's agents. The department has responsibility for drivers' licenses, motor-vehicle registration, inspection, insurance, automobile safety, and, most recently, plays a role in the adjudication of moving violations occurring in New York City.

Manual Records in State Motor-vehicle Department

Prior to 1961, the bureau was a division within the State Department of Taxation. It maintained two complete and independent manual records systems, one in New York City and one in Albany. Under this system, as Basil Scott, Administrative Director of the Department, explained, "If you got two traffic tickets in Albany and two tickets in New York City, a strong possibility existed that no one would ever know that you had four. You might be able to get away with the violation, even though we had a special ticket control section operating to reconcile the N.Y.C. and Albany files."

The department maintained three distinct files in each location: (1) a licensed-driver file, (2) a registration file (which also contained insurance information), and (3) a convictions file (which included traffic accident reports and suspensions). Supplementing these all-paper files was a register of license-plate numbers on microfilm, which enabled police to identify the owner of a vehicle from the number on the car's license plate. In addition to its own use, the files were regularly consulted by government agencies, principally in the law-enforcement area. And because the files were considered "public records" by law, any private individual or organization could (for a small fee) obtain a copy of any record from these files.

By the late '50s, it became apparent within the department that the manual system would soon be overwhelmed. The annual registration and licensed-driver growth rate was then nearly 5 percent. From "one filing cabinet in the corner of the office," the bureau had grown to 50 million pieces of paper covering an area equal to two city blocks. George Syrett, Jr., Assistant Director of Data Processing, emphasized that by the late '50s the issuing and renewing operations for both licenses and registrations were suffering badly from massive backlogs. "Because all registration renewals were due in January, it took the first six months of the year to get these five million pieces of paper filed. If you came in to a department office any time before May, as often as not we didn't even know if you had a current registration."

The inability to provide current motor-vehicle information often delayed license suspensions for months, and this was considered a serious matter from a traffic safety standpoint. In addition, a driver whose license was under revocation might renew illegally and go undetected for weeks until his record caught up with him.

Computer Applications in Licensing and Registration

In 1957, the New York State Temporary Commission on the Coordination of State Activities conducted a thorough study of the state's Motor Vehicle Bureau operation. Its first recommendation was that the bureau be made an independent department. Thirteen of its other 68 recommendations dealt with the need for the bureau to computerize. In 1958, a feasibility study by the bureau reached the same conclusion.

In 1960, the bureau acquired an IBM 650; when it became an independent department in 1961, it added an IBM 1401. The first computer application pursued was the consolidation on one master tape of the separate driver's-license and conviction files from New York City and Albany. Over a three-year period, information on licenses, traffic convictions, accidents, and suspensions was converted to computer storage.

Plans for computerizing the vehicle-registration operations were worked out in a second feasibility study conducted in 1963. By the mid-60s, through the addition of more computers and peripheral equipment, information on licenses, convictions, and registrations was consolidated on magnetic tape files in Albany. At this point, the principal Motor Vehicle Department record-keeping operations were computerized.

Until 1969, however, a completely parallel manual system was maintained to service law-enforcement agencies. This was because the department's batch-processing computer system was not responsive to the "on demand" retrieval of records that police needed.

A third feasibility study in 1965 recommended that the Motor Vehicle Department adopt new third-generation computer hardware, and create an on-line system. By December 1967, the Data Processing Division was having its "fourth annual Christmas installation party"—this time an IBM 360/40. Christmas 1968 marked the arrival of an IBM 360/65.

Today the department uses two 360/65's. One computer is devoted to on-line operations and the second computer performs batch-processing applications, as well as providing a backup capability. Since 1969, 60 IBM visual-display units located in the central office have provided the department with immediate retrieval of all information in the license and registration files.

Approximately 95 local offices are connected on-line with the Motor Vehicle computer system by 300 typewriter terminals. These allow local offices to replace lost licenses and registrations in a matter of minutes, as compared with three weeks under the manual system and nine days under the batch-processing arrangement. Batch-processing remains an important part of the department's overall operations, however. The weekly update of all files continues in this mode, as does a great deal of statistical work.

New York State government exercises unusually close review and coordination of state agency computerization. At every stage in the growth of the Motor Vehicle Department's system, the office of Computer Systems Development in the Division of the Budget approved the plans. Over the 10 years of the system's life, its reputation within the state has steadily improved. One official at the Division of the Budget asserted, "The system at Motor Vehicles was designed ahead of its time. It's been magnificently successful."

The department regards computers as absolutely essential to its operations. The Director of Data Processing, Sam Mills, remarks, "With a continuing 4 percent to 5 percent increase in work per year, it's unbelievable where we'd be without computers. In a manual system we'd have at least 6,000 employes instead of

3,000." Staff cuts and other economies made possible through computerization, the department says, enable it to operate at reduced costs (as much as $3.5 million less than with manual procedures, according to one department estimate for 1967-68), while providing speedier and more effective service. For instance, while they have not integrated their license and registration files, either computerized file can be searched quickly by name or number, making cross-referencing between the two files quite simple.

Mills also believes that computerization has made possible better administration and control with the department. "Because each district and local office is connected by terminal to Albany, the computer system performs an accounting and regulation function. Now we're instantly aware of who's doing what and who's receiving how much money."

As a result of their computer capabilities the department implemented at least one new program that officials believe would have been impossible with a manual system. The Administrative Adjudication program, designed to relieve some of the pressure on city courts, began in New York City in July 1970 and provides for computerized scheduling of traffic-violation hearings. A traffic ticket is entered on the computer's complaint file (a subsystem of the license file) and is compared with the driver's past record. If the record indicates that this new violation, if proven, will result in disciplinary action, the driver is notified that he cannot plead guilty by mail. A hearing is then automatically scheduled and the computer prints instructions to notify all parties. At the hearing, the referee's computer display console will produce the motorist's past driving record only after an entry has been made that the dependent was found guilty. Even though this is public-record information, the referee is supposed to consider it only in the passing of sentence (suspension, revocation, etc.). The computer programming is aimed at discouraging him from using a driver's record to "decide" the motorist's guilt.

Through another recent development, the department assists the City of New York in controlling parking-law violators. The city's Parking Violations Bureau submits the license-plate numbers of vehicles involved in parking violations. On magnetic tape, the department returns information identifying the vehicle owner. If an individual accumulates three unanswered parking summonses over an 18-month period, the city notifies the Department of Motor Vehicles that the individual has been identified as a "parking scofflaw." The department will then refuse to renew that person's registration until it receives notification that the summonses have been satisfied. The newly computerized city system has been the center of a flurry of public protests recently. Handwritten summonses, it seems, are often hard to read; as a result, many mistaken plate numbers were forwarded to Albany for identification. Many individuals then received notices from the city's bureau for violations they had not committed.

Security and Privacy Concerns

The Department of Motor.Vehicles' computerized files include personal identification information on license holders, data about registered vehicles, conviction records for many types of traffic and criminal offenses, license suspensions and revocations, and mandatory accident reports submitted by those involved.

In addition to these computerized files, the department still maintains manual files of particularly sensitive information. One of these relates to mental and physical disabilities of licensed drivers. When an "impaired individual" (such as a paraplegic) is licensed to drive only under certain conditions (e.g., the presence of special controls in the car), a short notation to this effect is placed on his computer-generated license form; but the particulars relating to his case are kept in the manual medical-history file.

In describing the variety of information in this disability file, Joseph Donovan, the department's first Assistant Counsel said, "We accept lots of reports even anonymous tips concerning someone's health and driving ability. We often get calls from people explaining that their aged parents really shouldn't be driving anymore, or from people who want us to know that someone is an epileptic unfit to drive. When this happens, we immediately confront the accused and take appropriate action. The results of these hearings, include medical reports, also go into the file."

Sensitive or not, virtually all of the information in Department of Motor Vehicles files is legally defined as public-record data, and this status underlies the department's approach to data security.[9] Data Processing Division officials could not recall any

---

[9] In 1971, a clerk in the New York City Department of Motor Vehicles office was indicted for taking money to supply information to commercial firms. This was part of an indictment of eight private detective agencies, two airlines, four present or former policemen, and one court clerk for supplying confidential offender records to private employers. In the case of the Motor Vehicles employee, confidential records were not involved, since he provided

instance of outside penetration of the system, but note that various kinds of unauthorized access *have* taken place from within. Officials at the department recalled an incident a few years ago in which playful computer operators changed the address on the licenses of some of their friends to read "c/o Wilfred's Tavern." In building their on-line system, planners in the department made sure that the clerks using remote terminals would have access only to the information they actually needed. A district office terminal, for instance, will indicate that an applicant is or is not eligible for a license replacement but will not allow the operator to see the applicant's driving record. More fear is expressed about deliberate sabotage, as state police experts and others have raised questions about how data-processing personnel might handle various attempts to damage the system.

Through the American Association of Motor Vehicle Administrators (AAMVA), many jurisdictions exchange information on out-of-state violations. When a driver from another state is involved in an accident or incurs a moving violation, this fact is communicated to the department of motor vehicles in his home state. This is a manual operation, in which a special AAMVA codebook is used to interpret reported infractions—offsetting the differences in state laws.

The New York State Department of Motor Vehicles also participates in the National Driver Registration Service (NDRS), a computerized clearinghouse with names of drivers whose licenses are under suspension or revocation. Maintained by the U.S. Department of Transportation, the NDRS contains the driver's name, descriptive identifiers, state and license number, and the reason and length of the revocation or suspension. The file had between 1.3 and 1.5 million records on file during 1970-71. During 1970, state and federal agencies requested 15 million "name record searches," resulting in 121,000 "hits."

According to Duncan MacPherson, EDP Programming Supervisor, the department makes use of the NDRS in the same way that other states do, through manual inquiries to the system. When a New York State license is suspended or revoked, NDRS is notified. When someone with an out-of-state driver's license ap-

---

public-record data that could have been obtained directly for 50¢ an abstract. However, this employee had an arrangement by which he furnished the information to private detective firms for money payments. The clerk pleaded guilty to a charge of unlawfully receiving gratuities (totaling $250) from the Pinkerton Detective Agency. See New York *Times*, January 27, 1971.

plies for a New York license, his name is checked through the
Register. This prevents drivers from getting around state revocation laws by simply applying for a license elsewhere.

State and local police make frequent use of New York Motor
Vehicle records. Approximately 1,000 telephone checks are made
by police each day, with about 35,000 requests for written print-
outs per month. Most police requests are aimed at identifying
stolen cars, and therefore require information from the registration file. In some cases, a computer-generated microfilm copy of
the entire registration file is made available to large police departments, so that they can perform their own record checks. Ten to
fifteen percent of police requests are for driver's-license and driv-
ing-record information.

Sales to Commercial Firms

In both the manual and computerized systems, the Department of
Motor Vehicles has operated under legislative authorization to sell
information from its license and registration files. The New York
Vehicle and Traffic Law specifies that the Commissioner of Motor
Vehicles may, *in his discretion*, arrange by contract with the
highest bidder to furnish copies of all vehicle registrations. With
the exception of 1965, when Circulation Associates received the
contract, R. L. Polk and Company, a firm which handles direct
mail services, has regularly been the highest or sole bidder.[1]

Polk pays a fixed price per hundred registration records,
which are supplied on computer tape. By law, "any such sale of
registration information shall be limited to only that part of the
vehicle registration records describing the name and address of the
owner of the vehicle, and the make, model, year, weight, body
style, number of passengers and cylinders, fuel, license plate number, type of registration and transaction, validation and expiration
data and vehicle identification number. . ."[2] The vehicle-registration information that Polk obtains through contracts with the 50
states is not sold directly in that form. Normally, Polk extracts
information items from the motor-vehicle files and uses it to
prepare lists of names and statistical summaries which it sells to
advertisers. It also will take advertising prepared by a company
and mail it directly to a specified population, retaining control of
the lists.

---

[1] A profile of R. L. Polk appears below, pp. 156-167.

[2] McKinney's Consol. Laws C. 691 202 (3).

Such use of motor-vehicle information has raised public debate in the past five or six years. The department's Administrative Director, Dr. Basil Scott, suggested that even though "public record" information is involved, "We're getting our backs broken on this privacy thing—letters, articles, bills in the legislature every year. We have to be concerned about privacy." The department now receives a stream of complaints from state residents who have received mail solicitations that they do not want. These run about 100 a year. "Most of them," Scott said, "spring from the individual's annoyance and not out of any commitment to privacy. Because everyone knows that we sell our lists, we're a natural target. We check each complaint out carefully through Polk, but almost always it's not Polk that is involved. . ."

The department's Assistant Counsel, Joseph Donovan, suggested that "Of all the mailing list complaints we've had, only one was traceable to Polk. Some guy got a letter saying 'Mr. Jones, why don't you trade in your 1958 Merc and get a new Cadillac. . . .' " He also noted, "We get letters from parents screaming about pornography coming to their homes. I doubt that this is from our lists. After all, we have a huge list, and we're all on it; why wouldn't we all get that stuff if the company sending it out was getting its names from Polk?"

In 1967, a licensed driver and car owner in New York challenged the constitutionality of the New York statute authorizing the sale of registration information.[3] Corliss Lamont, chairman of a group called the Emergency Civil Liberties Committee, claimed that providing such information for "solicitation through the mails, by telephone and in person for the selling of merchandise resulted in considerable annoyance, inconvenience and damage to the plaintiff and others similarly situated." Further, Lamont alleged that the actions of New York State and R. L. Polk and Company "are in violation of the plaintiff's right of privacy and constitute a deprivation of liberty and property under the 1st, 4th, 9th, and 14th Amendments."[4] The federal district court disagreed:

The information sold by the Commissioner is not vital or intimate. It is, moreover, in the category of public records available to anyone upon demand. What the State has done in

---

[3] *Lamont* v. *Commissioner of Motor Vehicles*, 269 F. Supp. 880.
[4] *Ibid.*, p. 882.

practical effect is to tap a small source of much needed revenue by offering a convenient packaging service.

In his contrary thesis the plaintiff proposes to stretch the constitutional dimensions of privacy far beyond any reasonable foreseeable limits that the courts ought to enforce.[5]

Aside from this "packaging service," any individual or organization for a 50-cent charge can purchase the print-out of a specific license or registration record. Information such as motorist accident reports (which in many states are confidential) can also be purchased in New York for $3.50. The Motor Vehicle Department receives nearly $2 million per year in reimbursement for this service. For example, the Retail Credit Company, a leading investigative service for the insurance industry, buys approximately 1 million print-outs a year, primarily for use in its automobile and life-insurance reports. The insurance industry itself buys upwards of 100,000 print-outs per month. Sam Mills has noted: "With a manual system we could produce only 10,000 abstracts monthly; now, we do 20 times better, and the state gets $70,000 or $80,000 per month."

In recognition of the volume of this trade, the department is currently considering the request by the Retail Credit Company and some insurance companies to have on-line terminals installed connecting their offices with the department. MacPherson emphasized, "Their terminals will be programmed to access only certain information, so it won't pose any confidentiality problems." By contrast with institutional buyers, purchases of motor vehicle records by individuals are very low, totaling no more than 500 per week.

Donovan pointed out that even "the medical history information is public information, and we're powerless to prevent people from seeing it. We never question anyone with a legitimate need for the medical history records: attorneys, insurance representatives, Retail Credit, etc. We can't stop them. If a busybody or just someone off the street came in and wanted the records, I don't think we'd give it to them. But if they went to court, there's no question they could compel us to give it to them."

The department's data-sharing activities have prompted some legislative attention in the last few years. Hearings conducted by the State Senate Subcommittee on Right of Privacy in 1969 looked into the department's sale of lists and recommended that

_____

[5] Ibid., p. 883.

state law be altered to prevent the department "from taking part in this purely commercial venture." As of 1972, no action had been taken on this recommendation.

The Subcommittee also examined the question of soliciting Social Security numbers on driver's-license applications. At its hearings, the Subcommittee received numerous complaints from motorists who felt that being asked for their Social Security number on the license application was an invasion of privacy. The State Senate Subcommittee concluded that the state should forbid use of the Social Security number in motor-vehicle affairs, but no such law has been enacted.

The department has been asking for each applicant's Social Security number for several years. But the applicant supplies it voluntarily, and instructions on the application form state this condition. As a result, Scott estimates that as many as a third of their records do not contain the number at all. The department would like to make submission of the number mandatory, since having it on each file would make the identification function in its own operations easier. It would also make record-matching easier when it shares information from the files. Scott suggested that "we look at it as a way of protecting the motorist. We need a means of positive identification especially in our dealings with insurance companies. On many occasions we've revoked the wrong license because we get the wrong 'ident' from the insurance company and we have the man listed as not insured." Currently, therefore, they collect the number but do not use it. It is an item of information which does not go to Polk, for instance.

Future Prospect for Computerization

Officials at the department's Division of Data Processing expect the '70s to produce some important developments in their data processing operations. "There will be much greater use of our system by law-enforcement agencies," Mills predicted. For example, the department expected to open a computer-to-computer link with the state police sometime in 1972, to supplement the on-line terminal connections already present at the Nassau County and New York City police departments.

The department plans no significant changes in its basic computer system. Visual displays for on-line data entry and update is a major improvement in peripherals they hope to turn to in the near future. However, the department sees itself as basically "all automated, on-line," and that is what its basic operations require.

Municipal Law Enforcement

Having looked at examples of computerization at the federal and state levels, we turn next to local government. More than 1,700 computers were being used by municipal, county, and specialized-district governments in mid-1971. The first of our three profiles at this level of government will examine computerization within city police departments.

"The United States is primarily a nation of small police forces," a recent study of law enforcement observed, "each of which operates in its own independent sphere, and attempts independently to sustain its operations."[6] The 3,700 municipalities with populations of more than 2,500 employ about 200,000 uniformed police officers, providing a national average of about one policeman for every 1,000 citizens. New York City has the nation's largest police force, with about 31,500 full-time officers. Chicago, Philadelphia, Los Angeles, Detroit, and Cleveland have the next five largest forces.

City police departments in the United States have the dual responsibility of peace keeping and criminal investigations. Information plays a major role in both spheres, and record-keeping has traditionally been a critical and time-consuming activity. From the standpoint of confidentiality and access, police records on individuals, groups, and events fall into three categories: "public record information," such as "booking" records, traffic and accident reports, etc.; "investigative" or "case" reports, which usually are confidential until action is taken (such as indictment), after which they can usually be obtained by the individual himself (through his lawyer), and can be seen by the press; and "intelligence" or "raw" files, which are maintained within many departments by special police squads or bureaus that deal with areas such as vice, organized crime, and subversive activities. Police intelligence files are secret, and are generally exempted under laws which permit public or individual access to other law-enforcement files.

Adoption of computers by police departments took place steadily during the early and mid-1960s. A survey in 1969 which examined police departments in cities over 25,000 population found that 110 of the 251 departments responding were using

---

[6]D. L. Norrgard, *Regional Law Enforcement*, Pub. Admin. Serv. (1969).

ADP.[7] Sixty percent of these noted that they had not adopted computers before 1964. The major applications being pursued were to records on traffic-accident reports, parking citations, traffic citations, arrested persons, criminal offenses, and police personnel.

Since 1968-69, however, there has been an enormous spurt in police department use of computers. Though part of the response to the rising crime rates and civil disorders of the past decade, the turn to computer technology has been directly stimulated by the availability of federal grants to state and local law-enforcement agencies under the Crime Control Act of 1968. Approximately $30 million was given to such agencies for computerized information systems by the federal Law Enforcement Assistance Administration in 1970. Estimates are that the number of police departments using computers has probably doubled since 1969, and that many departments which already had computers have moved to more advanced applications and on-line inquiry systems. From our own survey of organizations we learned that approximately 20 percent of the police departments in cities of over 50,000 population had developed computer applications to their "rap sheet" (arrest and criminal history) files as of 1970.

For our profile, we will be examining the Kansas City, Missouri, police department, the twenty-first largest police force in the nation.

KANSAS CITY, MISSOURI, POLICE DEPARTMENT

Kansas City, Missouri, is the twenty-sixth largest city in the United States in population, with half a million residents. Founded in 1821, it grew up as a stop on the overland wagon route to the West, and then became a major railroad point after the Civil War. Today, Kansas City is a leading agricultural and industrial center in the Midwest. Racially, the city is approximately 75 percent white, 24 percent black, and 1 percent Puerto Rican.

Like other urban centers, Kansas City faces serious crime problems. In 1969, the city ranked eighteenth among the 102 standard metropolitan districts in the number of crimes commit-

---

[7]Paul M. Whisenand and John D. Hodges, Jr., "Automated Police Information Systems: A Survey," *Datamation* (May 1969), pp. 91-96.

ted per 100,000 people. City police investigated over 43,000 crimes that year, including 105 cases of murder and manslaughter. Serious offenses rose 23.8 percent over 1968.

The City Police Department

The Kansas City Police Department has an unusual legal status. The chief of police is selected by and is responsible to a board of civilian police commissioners appointed by the governor. However, the municipal government must set aside 20 percent of the city's operating budget for the police department, with special elections that pass on bond issues for any unusual police needs. The department's current chief, Clarence M. Kelley, is a native of Kansas City who spent 21 years in the FBI before retiring in 1961 to take his present job. In 1971, he had 1,000 police officers and 350 civilians under his command, with an annual department budget of $18.7 million.

The police department has a reputation nationally as a highly innovative law-enforcement agency. Its 60 sections, bureaus, and units include (in addition to its computer systems) a six-vehicle helicopter patrol, K-9 squad, crime laboratory, community relations unit (under a black captain), four neighborhood storefront centers, and an Office of Citizen Complaints. The latter is staffed by four civilian employees of the State Board of Police Commissioners and conducts independent investigations of charges filed against police officers. National racial tensions are felt in Kansas City, and charges of police brutality have been made by the Black Panthers; antiwar and youth groups have also complained of "police hassling" from time to time. In April 1970, one of the police storefront centers was bombed and two officers injured.

Manual Record-keeping and Initial Computerization

Prior to 1966, the department had the kind of manual record systems typical of local enforcement agencies. These included files of fingerprints, wanted persons, stolen articles, complaint reports, offense reports, investigative files, and management reports. Records were kept on standard forms and stored in filing cabinets. Electric accounting machines had been used to help prepare statistical reports, and the department had a standard radio-communication system for contacts between officers in the field and central headquarters. In the late 1950s, the department acquired an IBM 402 tabulating machine, which it used for payroll work and other

The Move to Databanks and Teleprocessing

Between World War II and the early 1960s, a program of annexation joined surrounding towns to Kansas City, forming a larger central municipality and doubling the physical area for which the city police were responsible. Under this program the city had become the fifth largest in geographic area in the country, covering 316 square miles. Since police manpower levels are normally based on population rather than area, this left the police with an unfavorable man-to-territory situation. In addition, radio calls from officers in the field requiring searches of the central files and radio-back had increased so heavily in volume that it was taking an average of 30 minutes to reply to a patrol officer seeking information about a person or vehicle. The department points out that, since the officer needed to know the "danger status" of persons he was investigating ("armed," "mental case," "known to resist arrest"), delays in response endangered officer safety and weakened police effectiveness.

Because of the high costs and recruiting difficulties associated with expanding the force, Chief Kelley decided to explore the use of computer technology to make the existing force more efficient. A civilian expert in data processing, Melvin Bockelman, was hired in 1966 to direct a study of field information needs for the department. Bockelman, who had 25 years of experience in the data-processing field, came to the job from computer work at the Air Defense Command in Colorado. The study was begun by asking officers in the field what information they needed most to operate more effectively. From the responses to such questions a system was designed within the department, under a guideline "to fit the computer system into existing police structure and operations and not fit the department into a computerized environment." Taking advantage of the new on-line capabilities of third-generation computers, a teleprocessing-oriented system was specified and put out for bids by manufacturers.

In 1967, an order was placed for an IBM 360/40 computer, with the purchase financed out of funds from a bond issue approved earlier by city voters for general police equipment needs. No federal or state money was obtained. The decision was made to obtain a computer for the police department, rather than to use computer facilities at the city data-processing center because the city's computer was a second-generation machine and did not have on-line capacity.

In July 1968, what was described in several national maga-

zines as the most "advanced" computer-based police information
system in the United States went into operation in Kansas City.
The computer was installed on the fourth floor of central police
headquarters. Video-tube display units were located in the various
zone headquarters of the department, all linked into the communication center on the first floor of headquarters. Hard copy from
the computer was provided by various keyboard inquiry units
installed in the computer center, the communications center, the
warrant control unit, and in municipal court. Today, the department's data-systems division has 64 employees. These are organized into units for computer operations, on-line telecommunication, management information systems, operating systems and
research, data control, data processing, and criminal-justice systems.

The heart of the police computer system is its databank of
information on persons, vehicles, and licenses, available for on-line
inquiry by officers in the field and for generating transaction data
for trend reporting, manpower deployment, and management decisions. Basically, the databank stores records on outstanding arrest
warrants, stop-and-pick-up orders on vehicles, and intelligence or
"status" information on certain classes of persons. The latter
include "nationally known organized criminals," "local organized
criminals," "local parolees," persons known to resist or assault
police, and a category called "mentals, militants, and activists."

For effective on-line use, these information categories are
organized into files by personal identification, license, address,
wanted and warrant, detailed charges, and status. The "person ID
file" contains name, alias, address, sex, race, birthdate, state of
birth, height, weight, eye and hair colors, driver's license number,
and criminal status. There is also a file on police personnel,
containing standard data collected on employees. By the end of
1968, there were almost 90,000 individual records and statistical
reports on-line; as of November 1971, this had grown to over
224,000.

The ALERT System

The primary application in the on-line databank is called ALERT
(*A*utomated *L*aw *E*nforcement *R*esponse *T*eam). An officer in the
field radios in to the communications center the license-plate
number of a car he is following or has stopped, or the name and
other identifying information of a person he is investigating. The
center then queries both the Kansas City computer and the FBI's

National Crime Information Center in Washington, D.C., to which Kansas City has had a computer-to-computer link since 1969. From these inquiries, the communication-center operator learns whether that license has been reported stolen in Kansas City or nationally or whether the individual is a "wanted person" or "law-enforcement intelligence subject"[8] locally or nationally. Any "danger" status attached to the identification is also furnished. An officer investigating a disturbance can also inquire by address for the names of persons on file who live at that location or within half a block on the same street. The report is then radioed back to the officer. The department says that the response comes back on the average, in 3-4 seconds, compared to 30 minutes before ALERT.

Though originally designed as a system for the Kansas City police department, ALERT has now grown into a regional criminal justice information system covering 10,000 square miles of western Missouri and eastern Kansas and a population of 1.5 million persons. Its 105 on-line terminals (of which 13 are printer-receivers only) service 6 county sheriff's offices, 22 police departments, the Kansas City (Missouri) FBI office, the Kansas and Missouri State Highway Patrols, the U.S. Postal Inspector's Office, 1 county prosecutor's office, 1 municipal court, and 1 juvenile court. ALERT terminals can now obtain information on drivers licenses and vehicle registrations directly from the motor-vehicle department's files, which are on-line from the State Department of Revenue.

The department added a "modus operandi" file to its system in 1971. When a crime is reported, details of the circumstances of the crime, physical descriptions of any suspects, and aspects of the criminal's mode of operations are coded and entered into the computer. Where a person is later identified and convicted, his name is then entered with this information. The file can then be searched to see if the details of a crime currently under investigation are similar to those of any past crimes. The computer produces a list of crimes committed in similar ways and, in some cases, a list of possible suspects.

During 1970, the ALERT system had almost 8,000 inquiries a day, adding up to 2 million transactions for the year. In 1969,

---

[8]This refers to someone who is regarded by a law-enforcement agency as a proper subject for various kinds of continuing surveillance, such as a leader in organized crime activities or an organizer of militant protest activities.

this produced 21,700 "hits," or positive identifications. The three largest categories of "hits" were city traffic warrants, stolen autos, and parole violators. The department also noted 88 hits on "law-enforcement intelligence subjects."

Computer-assisted Manpower Deployment

A second major application is called LEMRAS, the *L*aw *E*nforce-ment *M*anpower *R*esources *A*llocation *S*ystem, a software program sold by IBM. Geographic data on the city's 9,000 blocks, 16,000 intersections, and 69 patrol beats were fed into the computer, in an effort that took 3 man-years of work. Information on calls for services (440,000 for 1970) was then recorded into 627 reporting areas, producing a data base that has date, time of day, unit assigned, type of event, and service time used. From averages adjusted for seasonal and short-term fluctuations, LEMRAS pro-duces predictions of the number of calls for police service that will occur at a particular location at a given time. These are used by unit commanders for assigning men and services.

Additional Applications

The ALERT system was also designed to produce a wide variety of reports for the police department. Presently, the department gets computer print-outs of daily workloads for detectives and crime lab technicians, with monthly productivity reports for command-ers. The system also produces each morning a record of all serious crimes reported in the previous 24 hours, giving the location and status of the crime. The crime index for Kansas City and various other statistical reports are now done by computer.

Another major use of the system is to provide an automated court docket for the Municipal Court in Kansas City. This applica-tion also generates warrants when an individual fails to appear in court.

As a result of shifting administrative data processing to its computer, the department retired its 402 tabulating machine in 1970. It also replaced 95 percent of its keypunching machines with devices for direct entry of data onto tape.

Management Evaluation of the Computer System

Kansas City police officials have nothing but high praise for the computer. ALERT has "saved time for the cop on the beat," Assistant Chief James Newman noted. "If he doesn't have to stop a car that's not wanted, it frees him to do productive things."

Chief Kelley adds that ALERT "helps the individual citizen" as well as the department. Fast and accurate information "frees a great many people much more quickly from an investigation. It clears a person in seconds if he has no record or is not wanted. In the past, a person might be tied up for some time."

As for the LEMRAS application, the department says that its studies show its deployment predictions to be "95 percent accurate" in "projected results to actual activity."

Department officials feel that work analyses and management reports produced from the computer databank are leading to valuable changes in law enforcement operations. In addition, Melvin Bockelman, now Director of the Data Systems Division, notes that data produced by ALERT have "shown us where many theories and philosophies about police information systems were out of date before they were ever implemented." Department spokesmen felt that ALERT had made possible the unification of criminal-justice agencies "separated physically by geography, jurisdictional limits, and political entities" into "one common databank" containing "all facets of information for an entire region." Department officials also cite ALERT as playing a major role in helping reduce the crime rate for serious offenses in Kansas City during 1970 and the first half of 1971. Reported crimes in Kansas City dropped about 11 percent for the total period, while nationally, reported crimes *increased* by 11 percent.

System Safeguards and Civil-liberties Issues

Throughout its development, the department has paid attention to the protection of privacy and security in its computer system. All data stored in the computer are designated "privileged law-enforcement information." Physical security is provided by guarded premises and elevators, a locked facility for the computer and communication centers, and identification procedures for entry. Special precautions have been taken to detect wiretapping of the computer lines. Persons using the terminals must put in an identification number and know the special procedure for asking questions before they can obtain information. Every transaction is permanently recorded in an audit log; while used primarily to assure the proper functioning of the computer equipment and software, this procedure generates a record showing not only which terminal queried the computer but also identifies the person making the inquiry, the time, and the information provided to him.

To provide security on the "hard copy" produced within the Kansas City Department when one terminal requests a print-out, it is produced at another terminal; this "two-person" procedure helps discourage unauthorized uses, since collusion between at least two persons would be required for illegal access to be obtained. Print-outs are to be held under physical security safeguards or destroyed under specified procedures.

Under department rules, only authorized personnel from law-enforcement offices or other criminal-justice agencies (prosecutors, courts, etc.) may have access to databank information, with special restrictions on some data such as juvenile records. The computer system is not to be used for making criminal-record checks for private firms or agencies of government which are outside the criminal-justice field. The department's manual file of conviction information is open to employers, credit bureaus, or the press, but not its records of arrests that have not led to convictions.

An individual may review his own summary criminal history by applying in person or having his attorney apply. If a person claims there is an error or omission in his record, the department regards it as an obligation to change the record if it cannot substantiate the correctness of the record as it stands. An estimated ten such requests are made each month. Very few errors have been discovered, the department says, essentially because so much time and money is spent in ensuring accuracy. As a whole, the department believes that computerization has greatly increased the accuracy of its manual and computerized files, as a result of the correction and updating of all records, and the purging of old and incomplete data that began in 1967 and has continued under supervision of the data-control unit. One local attorney who has handled important civil-liberties cases involving the police said that the department's rule under which a person and his attorney have full access to all police records pertaining to the case (including such items as tape recordings of police dispatcher conversations), earns the department "a big plus on that basis alone. In other cities, a person would have to get a court order to obtain such access."

Behind these policies lies a philosophy about privacy and security expressed frequently by Chief Kelley and Data Processing Director Bockelman in speeches, magazine articles, and department training publications. Government should not surrender its right to collect and use data necessary for performing its functions, Bockelman asserts, but government agencies can design and manage computerized databanks that "will afford a greater guarantee of privacy and security than a manually based filing system could ever possibly afford." In a 10-point program of basic safeguards, Bockelman stressed the development of measures such as limiting what goes into the system in the first place, verification from source documents, employee education programs, audit logs in on-line systems, passwords and other inquiry codes, and disciplinary action in the event of improper use. The challenge, he said, is to see that systems are "rigidly controlled according to ethical procedures of our times."

Challenges to the ALERT System

Whether the department has the proper ethics and is providing sufficiently rigid controls has become a matter of some debate during the past two years. One issue that has arisen involves the databank's "intelligence" and "status" files. In 1970, the "intelligence" files contained about 2,500 "organized-crime subjects." The great bulk of these were persons from all over the country, on a list compiled by "national law-enforcement agencies" and made available to local police departments. Kansas City says it has "added about 25 underworld subjects from our local group, based on our own intelligence."

The "militants, activists, and mentals" list in the "status" file contained the names of about 600 individuals in 1971; this was also a list provided by national sources, and covers "people engaged in violent confrontation with the police." Bockelman explained that "these are mostly militants traveling around a lot, like the Black Panther party." The "activist" category had about 40 names and is a file of local persons "who advocate the overthrow of the government by force or engage in conspiracies along those lines." "Mentals" covers persons with a history of emotional disturbance associated with violence.

Only police officers are supposed to have access to the intelligence and militants-activists-mentals file. The department regards this as essentially a "flagging system" to warn the field officer of possible danger involving those he is investigating; the department's Intelligence Unit maintains far more extensive manual files on individuals, groups, and incidents than anything stored in the computer databanks.

Protests about the activist file began in 1970. A police officer visited a professor at the University of Missouri at Kansas City to "get the names of those people the professor thought were activists engaged in violence on the campus." When asked what he meant by activist, the officer said "those people who demonstrate." The professor reported to various university and civil-liberties groups that the police were collecting information about "demonstrators" to put in the computer. When local civil-liberties groups arranged a meeting with Chief Kelley to protest such a practice, the chief stated that only those advocating violent overthrow were in the file, not just demonstrators, and he defended the purpose of the file. But he agreed to take out of the files the names of anyone "not actively considered a potential danger." The chief says this was done, since he was persuaded that if only "potentials" were included, some "unfairness could result," such as their "receiving a ticket from an officer when someone else might only have received a warning."

The maintenance of such intelligence and status lists was also questioned by Sen. Charles Mathias, Jr., of Maryland, in testimony before Senator Ervin's Subcommittee on Constitutional Rights, which held hearings on databanks and civil liberties in the spring of 1971. Senator Mathias singled out Kansas City as an example of a department which had computerized information from "criminal intelligence and raw investigatory files." "Computers are bringing the ammunition for persecution, harassment, and idle gossip within the reach of every prosecutor and part-time deputy sheriff in the land," the senator alleged. "I do not know that the Kansas City system has been abused," he stated, and he added that he did not advocate eliminating the categories used in the databank. But he called for Congress to require rules for the systems it was funding without waiting "until abuses surface."[9]

In July 1971, a suit in federal district court was filed against the police department and Board of Police Commissioners by the Kansas City Vietnam Veterans against the War, with support from the local American Civil Liberties Union. The suit, among other things, challenges the collection of intelligence data about persons engaged in peaceful meetings and demonstrations and the creation of police dossiers that are alleged to exert a "chilling effect" on the exercise of free speech, association, dissent, and privacy. The attorney for the complainants hopes to bring out misuse of computer records in the case if and when it comes to trial. "Members of the Vietnam Veterans are often spotted by the police," he said,

---

[9] The Kansas City Police Department received a $150,000 grant from LEAA in 1970 to expand its computer data center and regional telecommunication system.

"sometimes for selling underground newspapers. When they are stopped, the police ask them for their name and Social Security number—they always ask for the Social Security number. The police then radio this information to headquarters and very often they will return, acting entirely differently. They'll line the guys against the car and frisk them or find other ways of harassing them." He concluded, "We believe this change in behavior is caused because the officer is told by the computer that these people are activists."

Another area of public discussion over the Kansas City computer system involved not the scope of its data but its system safeguards against unauthorized use. In November 1970, a local TV station, KMBC, revealed that the police department in Lenaxa, Kansas, one of the nearby towns which had recently received a terminal into the ALERT system, went to major businessmen and landlords in the town and offered to check out persons applying for jobs and apartments. The purpose was "to keep an eye on who is coming into town." (Lenaxa is a white middle-class suburb of about 5,000 persons.) The employers and landlords liked the idea, and the police chief began to run record checks for them. Thirty-two persons with past criminal records were discovered. The Lenaxa police chief defended his practice to the Lenaxa City Council by noting that "without the use of this computer, these 32 people would now be residents of our community."

The TV station that revealed the practice broadcast an editorial stating that "for the computer data to be available to private interests suggests the 'Big Brother' of Orwell's book, making judgments on the basis of incomplete and perhaps misleading information. An individual could find his present and future gravely affected—without knowing why." However, a newspaper article following up the story reported that the Kansas Attorney General's office had issued an opinion ruling that police departments had a legal right to release the criminal records to landlords or employers because such matters were public records.

When the Kansas City police learned of this action, it ordered the practice stopped immediately and said they would take the Lenaxa department off the ALERT system. "This information is to be used only by police personnel for official police business," Assistant Chief Newman told the press. "Strong notices" to this effect were issued to all users of the system.

One other instance of unauthorized use has been uncovered, in which an officer in another department used a remote terminal to obtain an arrest record and made it available to an employer.

Again, a reprimand was given. To date, no agency has been dropped from the system or suspended temporarily as a result of violating rules.

Future Plans for Police Computerization

The Kansas City Police Department expected to link up in 1972 to MULES (*M*issouri *U*niform *L*aw *E*nforcement *S*ystem), a computerized databank of the Missouri Highway Patrol containing statewide wanted-and-warrant information, and to the national summary criminal-history system being added to the FBI's NCIC. The department received an IBM 370 system in 1972 to handle the saturation of their present system by program demands. As for new applications, the department was working on COPPS, a *C*omputer *O*perated *P*lanning *S*ystem being developed in conjunction with the Midwest Research Institute, and had also begun work on a court-information system for the local circuit courts.

Municipal Government

The Kansas City Police Department illustrates a local-government computer system wholly dedicated to use by one city agency. In the next profile, we look at the data-processing activities of a municipal government as a whole—New Haven, Connecticut.

Sixty-five percent of the American population lives today in metropolitan areas (cities and suburbs), with over one-quarter of all Americans living in the nation's 150 largest cities. These contain in their departmental files some of the most important information about a citizen's public and personal affairs. Scattered through such files are data on birth, marriage, divorce, and licensing; tax affairs and property ownership; police, health, welfare, and education records; voter registration; and city personnel matters.

Efforts to use computer technology in municipal government have increased steadily during the past decade. An excellent overview of such usage can be drawn from a survey conducted by the International City Managers Association (ICMA) in mid-1970.[1]

---

[1] *ADP in Municipal Government* (Washington, D.C., International City Management Association, October 1970). Urban Data Service, Vol. 2, No. 10.

About half of 3,303 cities surveyed responded to a questionnaire by providing detailed descriptions of their use of computers and unit record (tabulating) equipment, which the survey combined in calling "ADP." Fifty-four percent of the respondents said they utilized ADP in some aspect of their municipal operations, about twice the proportion of cities that reported such use in a previous ICMA survey two years earlier.

Greater detail on municipal data-processing patterns was obtained by ICMA in a follow-up survey of cities with populations over 25,000. Among these, ADP use was greatest in the western part of the United States, among central cities, and in cities with populations over 500,000. Median ADP expenditures for cities over 500,000 was $1.75 million annually: $210,000 for cities between 100,000 and 500,000, and $43,000 for cities between 25,000 and 50,000.

Looking at the types of ADP applications in 332 cities, the survey found that 255 listed "housekeeping operations"; 137 "functional applications"; 22 "databanks"[2] and 39 said that they had "management information systems." On-line terminals in computer systems were found almost exclusively in the large cities. All the cities over 250,000 reported that they either leased or owned computers. The largest single user of computers among American municipalities was New York City, which spent over $22 million for computer operations in 1970.

Our project made site visits to four municipalities: one in the Northeast, one in the Middle Atlantic region, and two in the West. These ranged in population from 110,000 to 2.7 million. In the following profile we present an account of the efforts of New Haven, Connecticut, to develop a comprehensive central databank for municipal government.

NEW HAVEN, CONNECTICUT

In March 1967, the *New York Times* announced that IBM and the city of New Haven had begun what the *Times* called "the first attempt to program an entire city," coordinating "all the city's facts in a single pool." Within the next few months, articles on the

---

[2] A databank was defined in the survey as "a pool of data, usually organized on a municipalwide basis and intended to serve both planning and operating needs."

"IBM-New Haven project" had appeared in *Look*, *U.S. News and World Report*, the British press, the *Congressional Record*, and leading computer journals.

"What is involved in the databank," *U.S. News* wrote,

> . . . is an unprecedented coordination of facts about individuals. Lives of New Haven residents to a large extent are to become available to city officials at the push of a button—all in the interests of efficient government. Into the computer will go people's tax statements and their property holdings. Any brushes with the law, however minor, will be fed in. So will reports on welfare applicants, school and health records, and court decrees. All of this information, and much more, will be electronically cross-indexed and be available in a split second. . . [I] f all goes as planned, UMIS [the Urban Management Information System] and its central databank could be in full operation by mid-1968.[3]

Mayor Richard C. Lee of New Haven commented, "It's going to be fantastic. We've got all this information scattered all over the place now so we can't use it. But after it's all together, we'll get at it and make New Haven a national model."

Most of the stories noted that there were serious questions of privacy raised by what the *Hartford Times* called the "centralization and availability of information" in the New Haven databank plan. Mayor Lee said that the system had careful safeguards for confidentiality, adding, "I would fight invasion of anyone's privacy with all my conviction." Robert K. Lyons, the IBM project manager, said that "the computer system will allow only authorized officials access to stored data."

In 1972 New Haven has no UMIS. One city official said that, compared to the system envisaged in the IBM-City project, "our computer operations today are far more modest." And, he added, "it's probably a good thing for everybody that it worked out that way."

New Haven—"The Model City"

New Haven is an industrial city of 150,000 on Long Island Sound, about 75 miles east of New York City. Heavily Democratic in voter preferences, its population in 1970 was 69 percent white and

---

[3] "A City Where Computers Will Know about Everybody," *U.S. News and World Report* (May 15, 1967), p. 70.

31 percent black, Puerto Rican, or Oriental. Fred Powledge, a former *New York Times* reporter, called New Haven "a square city," despite the presence of Yale University in its downtown area. It has a seedy railroad station, he noted, a "Toonerville airport," an unpleasant climate, no exciting restaurants or night life, uninspired local political parties, and a dull daily newspaper. Yet, he observed, between 1953 and 1968 it became known throughout the nation as "Model City," the one municipality that had put together money, talent, leadership and energy in support of creative and successful urban redevelopment.[4]

At the center of Model City was Richard C. Lee, elected in 1953 at age 37 for his first two-year term as mayor and reelected steadily for the next 14 years. A regular Democrat from a poor Irish family in the city, Lee started his career as a reporter on the local newspaper, then spent a decade as director of the Yale University News Service. When he took office in 1953, he saw major parts of the city business district decaying into slums, an increasing flight to the suburbs, and city government performing as a sluggish mechanism, concerned with trivial affairs.

To mount a campaign of "physical and human renewal," Lee perfected what came to be known as "the New Haven method" in urban reform. The mayor brought together a collection of talented professional "urbanologists," organized a Citizens' Action Committee representing the "best people in New Haven," and developed a series of plans for replacing slum sectors of the city with new business, residential, and civic establishments. Money for these vast enterprises came from a mutually reinforcing combination of private foundations, government funds, and business investment. (By 1966, the city had attracted $250 million in redevelopment grants and investments, $75 million of it from the U.S. Department of Housing and Urban Development.)

Because he found the municipal government a set of departmental baronies, Lee developed a "parallel government," primarily by creating two powerful new agencies under his direct control to obtain grants and run the innovative programs. These were the Re-Development Agency and a body called Community Progress, Inc. (CPI). The latter, funded by more than $5 million from the

---

[4] Fred Powledge, *Model City: A Test of American Liberalism* (New York, 1970). Other accounts relied on for discussion of New Haven politics are Robert Dahl, *Who Governs? Democracy and Power in an American City* (New Haven, 1961); William Lee Miller, *The Fifteenth Ward and the Great Society: An Encounter with a Modern City* (Boston, 1966); and Allan R. Talbot, *The Mayor's Game: Richard Lee of New Haven and the Politics of Change* (New York, 1967).

Ford Foundation, made New Haven a pioneer in urban social action. Between 1962 and 1965, CPI developed the forerunners of later federal domestic program concepts such as the war on poverty, job retraining, Project Headstart, "neighborhood participation," legal services for the poor, and many others. From the perspective of the middle 1960s, New Haven seemed the epitome of reform-within-the-system or, as Secretary Robert Weaver of HUD put it, "New Haven is coming closest to our dream of a slumless city." It was in this context of activist reform government that the IBM-New Haven project was developed.

New Haven Government and Data Processing

Municipal government in New Haven operates under a mayor and a board of aldermen elected directly every two years, with each alderman representing one of the city's 30 wards. Since Connecticut abolished county units, the city performs some functions that would be conducted as county matters in other states. The major areas of city activity cover health and welfare, public safety, education, parks and recreation, public works, public records and city administration, and planning and development, organized into 45 separate departments and agencies. Municipal organizations and powers are governed by a city charter dating from 1897 (with minor revision in 1952), which Mayor Lee made several unsuccessful attempts to modernize in charter-revision referenda. The city budget for 1971-72 was $66 million; approximately 5,000 persons are employed full time on the municipal payroll, one out of every 30 city residents.

New Haven installed EAM equipment in its welfare department in 1935, and a similar operation was developed in the Department of Education in the late 1940s, to make simple lists for payroll. "Modern data processing in the city began in 1954," according to Assistant Controller Walter Turning, "about the time that the redevelopment program began under Mayor Lee." To economize on the separate payroll and check operations that were scattered in the various departments, and to control against check thefts, a centralized system using a 405 tabulating machine was set up in the Controller's Office. Improved tab machines were used until 1958, when the city obtained its first computer, an IBM 305 RAMAC. This was used for payroll and administrative housekeeping, with one additional application being a computerized index of individual criminal records maintained by the city police department, which could be searched according to modus operandi and personal appearance criteria.

In 1961, New Haven installed an IBM 1401 computer and converted its operations to magnetic tape. In addition to payroll work, this system took over assessment and tax-billing operations that the city had been running by renting time on the computer of an insurance company in Hartford. The 1401 was operated by the Controller's Office but it also did work for other departments. These included "number-crunching operations" for traffic and engineering department studies, critical-path scheduling for construction projects, welfare accounts payable, student scheduling for the schools, and police modus operandi records. Each of these operations was done as a separate run, through batch processing, with each department bringing in and taking away its own data. No central data base or integrated files were created. Financial and program monitoring through the 1401 helped Mayor Lee and the Re-Development Agency in preparing proposals and reports for funding sources. "The high-powered management people Lee brought in couldn't have functioned as well as they did without the kinds of data that the computer gave them," Turning stated.

By 1965-66, the city's data-processing work was bursting its available core storage. "We were burning the midnight oil trying to operate with the 1401," Turning recalled, "so we got an IBM 360/30 in October of 1966. We didn't place the order to perform new functions as much as to get our existing work done on time."

The Move to a Databank Approach

At this point, Mayor Lee began to see some new possibilities for the city's computer operations. In his "State of the City Message" in February 1966, Lee announced plans to establish a task force on modernization of the city's government, with its membership drawn from local business, labor, academic, and governmental talent. The first area assigned for task-force consideration was "The Application of Computer Technology." Noting that the 360 computer to be delivered later that year would "substantially expand our data-processing capacity," the mayor said that the task force should see whether this capacity could be used to build a "so-called databank," linking records from various city files into "a complete information system."

At approximately the same time, the Advanced Systems Development Division of IBM, a unit created to explore applications along the frontiers of data processing, decided to see whether it was feasible to assemble files from the major departments of a city into one unified data base for urban management.[5] If a system could be developed for one municipality, the hope was that it could be sold to other "progressive" cities, producing a significant market for IBM computers. Members of other divisions within IBM doubted whether it was either technically or political-ly feasible to develop such a total information system within one city, or whether anything done in one municipality with great expenditures of time and money could be applied to cities with different legal, administrative, or personnel patterns without mounting a similarly expensive effort. They also felt that IBM would do better to keep selling computers on a department-by-department basis, or to central service bureaus in cities. "We still have trouble getting the payroll to work properly," one such IBM executive commented, "so what are we doing with these far-out ventures that will only disappoint city managers and give data processors a bad name?"

However, the Advanced Systems Division was given approval to try the experiment; in early 1966, it selected New Haven from a group of candidate cities as its first choice for a pilot project. The Division noted that New Haven was a "model city" in both urban renewal and human renewal, that it had Mayor Lee's "national reputation" for urban accomplishments, it was a workable middle-sized municipality, was near the division's Mohansic Laboratory, and "has been a good IBM customer for a long time." The division arranged a presentation of the idea to city officials in April 1966, and a delighted Richard Lee signed an agreement shortly there-after to create the "IBM-City of New Haven Joint Information System Study."

The IBM-New Haven Project

The project began with IBM supplying systems and design special-ists and the city contributing office space and the time of various city personnel. A three-phase plan was adopted in 1966 which called for (1) a "relatively brief" feasibility study to "develop concepts"; (2) a "systems design" phase, of approximately two years; and (3) implementation, along phasing patterns to be deter-mined by phase two.

---

[5] This would parallel the work that another division of IBM was doing at the same time with Santa Clara County, California, in attempting a unified county information system. This is discussed in the next profile.

It was while phase one was getting under way, early in 1967, that the initial *New York Times* story appeared. "Before we were even halfway into the feasibility study," Walter Turning recalled, "overly optimistic blue-sky literature got into the trade press and popular magazines. This type of publicity created such enthusiasm within New Haven government that the city people began to believe there was something here already. They were expecting terminals on their desks any minute. They didn't know how difficult it would be to develop and manage the integrated system. But the publicity got out and they were being held up throughout the country as great innovators."

The feasibility study was completed in December 1967. Not surprisingly, it called for full-scale work to develop UMIS. What is needed, the report said, is to move New Haven "from a fragmented, departmentalized filing system to a massive, machine-readable, centralized file," enabling New Haven officials to deal more effectively with "the complex and dynamic urban environment." The city's information today lacked "comprehensiveness, accessibility, relatability, timeliness, and utilization," all of which could be provided by UMIS. This would be done by developing "transaction" files unifying data in five areas—"population, land, buildings, roads, and environments"—along with "functional" files on budget and other areas. The central files would be automatically updated by the transactions from each department. In this way, "information would be shared and duplication would be avoided." Nothing in the 27-page report on "System Concepts" mentioned privacy, data-access controls, or individual access to records, even though examples were given of increasing the use of personal records from police, health, educational, and tax files.

Phase two of the project began in 1968 when teams went to each department to study its assigned functions and organization, the records it maintained, the information it needed to make effective decisions, and "interdepartmental information flows." From these studies, the project staff (nine employees from IBM and six from the city) worked on the "functional specifications for a prototype system."

In April 1969, the project issued 27 booklets, each covering one city department, as well as two summary booklets, one on *System Design Concepts* and the other a *Summary Report and Guide*. The summary recommended that work on UMIS go forward in a five-year, two-stage design beginning with applications in the areas of police, land records, and financial controls; that the city should seek funds from federal, state, and private sources for the effort; that UMIS "should be organizationally responsible to the Mayor" through an "Office of Management Systems"; and that a "Citizens' Task Force" should be created to provide "community participation" in assuring protection of privacy.

In its specification of hardware and software for the "prototype system," the summary noted that there would be a "Central Persons File" with name, address, Social Security number, and date of birth, which would serve as the "identifier" file for persons known to the city. An "indicator" in that file would note which departments might have detailed information about that person, with access tables to ensure that a city official was authorized to see such data before he could obtain it from the "functional file." This was only one of the "technical, administrative and legal innovations" that the summary stressed would be necessary to "reduce the protection-of-privacy issue to a manageable level."

To the outside world, the IBM-New Haven project seemed to be a thriving and promising enterprise at this point in 1969. In fact, it was dead. Earlier in 1969, concerned about the growing debate over computers and privacy in the FCC, Congress, and the national press, and somewhat nervous about the "putting-it-all-together" publicity the New Haven project had been receiving, IBM management took a closer look at what was happening. Their judgment was that there was inadequate assurance that the unified data base could be achieved, either in technical terms or with respect to the organizational reforms that would be needed to carry out the ambitious project objectives. Further, the issues of privacy and security promised to generate serious public controversy. In this situation IBM decided to withdraw, closing out its participation in the project in 1969.[6]

---

[6] Ironically, some of the best writings up to that time on providing for privacy, confidentiality, and citizen access rights in a local-government computer system had appeared in the Joint Study documents or papers arising from it. For example, Charles P. Kindleberger, Jr., of the city team gave a thoughtful paper on "A Positive Approach Toward Urban Information System Security" at the 1969 meeting of the Urban and Regional Information Systems Association. Stating that "resolving the privacy threat may well be the difference between an information system that constitutes a successful government tool and one that is a fiasco," Kindleberger advocated that "Procedures [should] be established whereby the kinds of data recorded in a system, security clearance to that data, and a purge schedule for the data are explicitly set forth. The rights of individuals to review and challenge information will have to be stated, and the means of processing grievances developed. Many of the proposed operating procedures should be legally encoded in both municipal ordinances and a revised municipal charter." The safeguards outlined in project documents included exposure codes to limit a user's access

While IBM was taking a second look the sense of direction within the project had also become blurred. "There were meetings at the end," one participant reported, "at which everybody laid their cards on the table and said, 'We don't know what we're going to collect and how to handle it. Where do we go from here?' " City Controller Frank Kelly felt the central problem of the UMIS Project was the fact that city personnel practices and department structures would require major changes and a new city charter would have to be enacted before the proper base could have existed for the new central information system envisaged by the project.

The formal end of UMIS in New Haven came in 1970. The federal government had announced the formation of an Integrated Municipal Information Systems project, a multiagency venture chaired by the Department of Housing and Urban Development. This called for medium-sized cities to submit plans either for a total computerized city information system or one of four computerized subsystems (public safety, public finance, physical and economic development, and human resources development). The city's plan had to be developed and the project carried out in cooperation with a software firm and a university.

New Haven applied for one of the two citywide information system grants, viewing this as an ideal means of going forward with the UMIS blueprint. For its consortium, New Haven brought in the Joint Center for Urban Studies of Harvard and MIT, and the Travelers Research Corporation, of Hartford, Connecticut. IBM was asked to add its name to the submission and did so, since New Haven was still "a good IBM customer." However, HUD selected Charlotte, North Carolina, and Wichita Falls, Texas, to develop the "total systems." With this, New Haven's UMIS went on the shelf.

Current Computer Applications in New Haven

Late in 1971, New Haven acquired an IBM 360/40 computer, providing the city with its own on-line capabilities for the first time. Computer work for each city department is provided by a Data Processing Division in the Controller's Office, which operates under a general manager, two programmers, and a budget for 1971-72 of $321,000.

The Data Processing Division does service work for individual

---

to information, audit trails, terminals with unique codes, voiceprints for personal identification, and purge schedules for removing "stale" information.

departments in payroll and accounting as well as handling such
matters as general tax billing, vital statistics, municipal-bond accounting, budget composition and projections, incinerator billings,
and employee pensions. Based on suggestions from the joint study
for first-priority computer applications in particular departments,
the city has automated the processing of absentee ballots, payments to landlords and grocery stores under welfare programs, and
a few other high-volume operations. As Controller Kelly put it,
"These relieved us of a load that was choking us but didn't require
a big, sophisticated on-line system."

New Haven currently operates two computer programs that
go beyond routine matters in municipal ADP. The city has a DIME
file (*D*ual *I*ndependent *M*ap *E*ncoding), a computerized geocoding
technique used to retrieve aggregates of geographic information.
This program contains an entry for each street intersection in New
Haven, and allows the City Planning Department and an Ad Hoc
Data Users group to relate reports of police, fire, health and other
kinds of incidents to particular geographic locations.

The other advanced application is in the New Haven Police
Department, made possible by a grant from the federal Law
Enforcement Assistance Administration. This is an on-line Case
Incident Reporting System (CIRS), modeled after the Kansas City,
Missouri, Police Department's ALERT system.[7] In this application, information on police incidents is dictated by police officers
by radio to police headquarters, recorded, transcribed by secretaries, and then keypunched into the computer. The record includes date, time and type of incident, location, and persons
involved (by name, age, sex, race, relation to incident, and date of
birth). Four visual scanners in the police department allow retrieval and display of the name of each individual cited in case and
incident reports, and their relationship to the incident (arrestee,
complainant, victim, suspect, witness, etc.). Information can also
be retrieved according to type and location of incident, complaint
file number, and some other categories. Eventually, the system is
planned to include a warrant file, arrest records, summary criminal
histories, and a yet-to-be-defined "intelligence file." Detailed narrative information is presently still filed on hard-copy records,
though it is now indexed by computer incident-report number.
City personnel see CIRS as providing much faster and more
efficient circulation of information for field use, reducing manual

---

[7] See the profile of the Kansas City Police Department earlier in this
section.

file errors, and allowing greater access to stored data for studies of police deployment and similar management problems.

Mark Berger, counsel for the Police Department, said that "maximum thought for privacy and security went into the planning for the CIRS system." Special Police Order 70-71, "Disclosure of Police Records," provides that access to investigative and arrest records is limited to city police employees and a group of other specified law-enforcement agencies. The rules deny access to agents of the Internal Revenue Service, U.S. Immigration and Naturalization Service, "military recruiting investigators, welfare department investigators, and private detective agencies." A written and notarized approval by the arrested person is required before a record will be furnished to such other government agencies or private organizations.[8] In general, investigative reports are governed by the same regulations. Juvenile records are held strictly within the city police department and are not shared with other law-enforcement agencies.

While CIRS was based on the Kansas City system, it never adopted the "status codes" that the Kansas City system originally had. "In Kansas City," a New Haven police department spokesman commented, the program "put labels on people like 'mental' or 'homosexual' or 'militant.' We felt that this was an arbitrary and unfair practice." The New Haven system does allow a police officer to ask whether a person he is going to arrest may pose a danger of violence to the arresting officer; if the past arrest record or previous resistance to arrest justifies this a code signifying "arrestee dangerous" is displayed.

There have been few public comments locally about threats to individual liberties in either CIRS or any of New Haven's operating computer systems. Neither Dr. Ben Bursten, head of the local chapter of the American Civil Liberties Union, nor Tom Keyes, Corporation Counsel of New Haven, knew of any court actions challenging New Haven's computer operations. Keyes also emphasized that the city has never received any civil-liberties complaints about its present computer work, though there were earlier consultations with civil-liberties leaders about the UMIS project. The main reason for the absence of protests, Assistant Controller Walter Turning believes, is that the kinds of depart-

---

[8] A sample form to be used for such notarized authorization specifies the purpose for which the check is to be made, states that the individual understands he is *not* required by law to give such an authorization, and that unless such authorization is provided, the Police Department "would not provide this information."

mental records now computerized are, except for CIRS, almost entirely public-record information according to law.

Future Plans for Data Processing

New Haven in 1972 has no master computer plan that it is following. It expects to do more budget work, add a voter-registration file, and develop an on-line welfare case reporting system if outside funding can be obtained. As Controller Frank Kelly explained, "We'll seek federal or state funds on a program-by-program basis to computerize only those things that are doable."

New Haven's Development Administrator, Leroy Jones, feels that New Haven is "not disillusioned" about the potential of urban computer technology. "We're still interested in information banking, we want computers, we want management information systems. But you have to remember that today we're in a survival fight. When you're in that position you simply can't devote money or talent to frills."

County Government

Having seen a project for a unified municipal information system that never got to the implementation stage, we turn to a similar idea for a county central databank that is currently in the midst of development. Forty-seven states have county units in their governmental systems. Historically, the county has served as an important administrative unit in American governmental life, taking care of much road building and maintenance, courts and law enforcement, welfare, tax collection, land and debt records, and health facilities. Some counties also managed the school system. In recent decades, counties have grown in importance as problems in these basic fields have spilled over the lines of city, suburb, and unincorporated town. Especially in the western part of the nation, and in those places which have turned to professional county administrators or elected county executives to provide stronger central leadership, the county exercises a major influence on the lives of its citizens.

Counties maintain important pools of information about the people under their jurisdiction. As in municipalities, these records have traditionally been kept by and for each separate department, with the most sensitive files (such as welfare, health, and police records) usually governed by state or county regulations of confidentiality.

Though there has been no national survey of computer usage among counties, various sources indicate that the municipal pattern of adopting computing primarily for financial "housekeeping" and functional-area purposes (with a small number of databank and management information system applications), prevails in county governments as well. Some counties have become well-known nationally for their work in ADP, for example, Lane County, Oregon; Dade County, Florida; and many of the California counties.

In fact, California has more extensive computer usage at the county level than any other state, with 38 of its 39 counties having general purpose computers. The largest computer installation among the California counties is Los Angeles, and other large systems in the state include those in San Francisco (a combined county and city administration), Orange, San Diego, Santa Clara, and Alameda counties. The county chosen for our profile is Santa Clara.

SANTA CLARA COUNTY, CALIFORNIA

Santa Clara County, California, lies at the southern end of the San Francisco Bay metropolitan area. A rural, fruit-and-vegetable-producing community before World War II ("prune capital of the world"), its largest city, San Jose, had 60,000 residents. Today, Santa Clara County has mushroomed in growth into an urbanized area of 1.1 million residents. Half a million of these now live in San Jose.

Socially and politically, the county mirrors much of the diversity of American society. Some of its areas, like Palo Alto (with its avenues of aerospace-electronic plants and the Stanford University campus), are prosperous middle- and upper-class communities; politics here tends to be a contest between liberal Democrats and conservative Republicans. There are also sections of rural and urban poverty, with long-term heavy unemployment among blacks and Mexican-Americans, who make up about 15 percent of the county population. Welfare programs are a major concern, and recent cutbacks in aerospace operations have sent large numbers of engineering professionals onto the unemployed lists for the first time in their lives.

Like county governments throughout the western United States, Santa Clara provides a wide range of public services. These include welfare, law enforcement, public works, planning, tax assessment and collection, hospitals and health, courts, and voter registration. The county has more than 7,000 employees, and an annual budget for 1971-72 of approximately $235 million.

County Record-keeping and the Move into ADP

"In the early 1950s," a Santa Clara County document noted, the county "handled and processed information with few more refinements than in 1900." It had "faster typewriters, adding machines, and billing machines," but the "techniques of processing were based on one major criterion—manpower." Each county department gathered and stored its own information. In 1955, a punched-card system was installed, and repetitive work such as preparing payrolls, tax billing, assessments, budget, and maintaining the welfare rolls was done on this EAM equipment.

By the late 1950s, "demand from the departments . . . exceeded the capacity of punched-card equipment." When second-generation computers arrived, Santa Clara County moved to them promptly, installing an IBM 1401 in April 1961, "the first local governmental agency in the United States to receive such equipment." A second 1401 was leased in 1963. By mid-1964, both were on a three-shift, seven-day-a-week schedule, doing batch-processing work for the various individual departments.

By 1964, with third-generation computer systems arriving, the county's director of data processing, Karl Sheel, began to explore the possibilities of the new systems for county data processing with local representatives of IBM's GEM (*G*overnment, *E*ducation, and *M*edicine) marketing region. A county publication in 1964 expresses the mood of county officials at that point:

New total systems computers were being developed. These new computers made possible unique applications: They made it practical to cross organizational lines; they skipped over geographical barriers and boundaries; they could "draw a picture"; they could be fed intravenously by remote terminals. In addition, they had large "random access" storage, meaning that they could store a great deal of information and, at random and on call, seek out information and talk back to the person making the inquiry. The new total systems computers made possible a systems concept for data processing designed to provide centralized record-keeping with decentralized control.

The Birth of LOGIC

Spurred by this vision of new capabilities, County Executive Howard Campen called in department heads in November 1964 and announced plans for a comprehensive study of all department operations to explore the possibility of creating a "total information system" plan. The county arranged for the IBM office in San Jose to give a one-day course in computer fundamentals, county computer uses, and the IBM 360 system, a session to be attended by all department heads, the steering committee of the study project, and key personnel from the departments. Following this, IBM agreed to assign professional and technical experts to the county study and provided 18 hours of special training in documentation techniques for county personnel. For the next three months, teams of departmental specialists and IBM advisors made what the county has called "the most thorough analysis of data-processing applications ever attempted by an agency of local government." Duplications of information collection among the departments were recorded, a series of information subsystems were identified, and the design for LOGIC—*LO*cal *G*overnment *I*nformation *C*ontrol—was presented to the County Board of Supervisors in April 1965.

The basic idea of LOGIC was to build a "databank" containing ten "subsystems" with "information of common interest to many departments." The ten originally defined were: "People-General"; "People-Law Enforcement"; Property; Accounting; Personnel; Supply; Engineering; Hospital; Library; and Advanced Analysis. Storage would be on random-access equipment, so that a department could "reach in" and obtain "a specific item of stored information" rather than have to run through a whole file to extract the desired record. "Teleprocessing terminal units, tied directly with the central processing unit in Data Processing but located in the departments, would provide access to this pooled information." The advantages of this system, the 1965 report said, would be to share information on people and problems among the departments, eliminate duplication in collecting and maintaining information, and provide better and more timely reports to management. Significant savings on county operations were projected over the six years it would take to build LOGIC, from 1965 to 1971. The Board of Supervisors accepted the LOGIC proposal, placed an order for an IBM 360/30, and authorized the hiring of 14 additional programmers to start the work.

Looking back on the creation of LOGIC, top county officials cited two main explanations for the county's ability to mount such an innovative venture. The Santa Clara County charter (adopted in 1951) gave the county executive power to appoint all department heads other than the sheriff, district attorney, and assessor; this gave Campen the authority to bring department heads into cooperation where they might, in other California counties where they were directly elected, have resisted such an incursion on their independence. Secondly, the deep involvement that department specialists and department heads gave to the study (10,500 man-hours of work, with 125 county officials involved) made its recommendations more acceptable to county officials than the typical outside consultant's report might have been.

The local press had been briefed on the LOGIC proposal by the county executive before it was presented to the Board of Supervisors for approval, ensuring a considerable splash of publicity for what in one account was called the county's "giant step into the computer age." Among the generally favorable news accounts was one troubled editorial in the *San Jose Mercury News* of November 26, 1965, which asked "Must Computers List All Our Scars?" The editorial noted that government files contained not only welfare, probation, and hospital information on a person but also his "birthdate, income, property ownership, taxes, licenses, marital history, criminal record, IQ, educational attainment, draft status, incidence of venereal disease if any. . . ."

> When querying a computer will produce within a minute a print-out listing more facts about a citizen than he himself could find in six months of digging through his desk and dusty boxes in the garage, the individual's rights may need some attention.
>
> Has he any right to privacy? To live down his past? To guard against pressure and blackmail applied as a result of information manipulators knowing too much about him?

County officials must have been somewhat surprised at the fears expressed in this commentary, since they had not dealt with the privacy issue extensively in the 1965 LOGIC report. Only one sentence in that document had mentioned the question of confidentiality. Each department's information would be "instantly available" to any other department, they had noted, if such department "has a legitimate use for such information and . . . legally has access to the file."

Early Implementation of the LOGIC System: 1965-68

The first subsystem developed was "People-General." This was the largest application in the data-processing-bureau's batch operations. Since it already had a manual "people index," this application promised the greatest potential cost saving through conversion to on-line operation. By mid-1968, 250,000 names from the welfare files were put onto what was called the Alphabetic Persons Index (API). The information in the file included "Person identification Information," such as name, birthdate and state, sex, Social Security number, first four characters of address (for identification only), other names person is known by, and county departments which have information on the person. "Welfare Person Information" included such items as case name and serial number, family budget unit, discontinued and close dates, medical eligibility, and aid type. Finally, "Welfare Case Information" recorded items such as "all persons in a case"; case name, number, district and family budget unit; last contract date, and payee address.

Using API, county employees could secure, by terminal identification, data on any person listed in the welfare file, and a list of other county departments that had information on him. Welfare workers could obtain case data on someone coming into the office with a problem, and open a file immediately on a new recipient. The county medical center could also gain access to the welfare status file, for example, to determine eligibility for state or federal medical aid. Other departments with terminal access to API were Health, Juvenile Probation, and Adult Probation.

Other applications completed during this period included precincting work for the Registrar of Voters and refinement of the county payroll system. At the same time, programming was begun on a patient index for Valley Medical Center and a feasibility study was done for a "court automation" system.

Discussions of Civil-liberties Issues

In 1966, while congressional hearings were being held in Washington on the proposal for a National Data Center, the *New York Times* printed a long article about LOGIC under the headline "Coast Personal 'Dossier' Plan Stirs Fear of Privacy Invasion." The story stated that as a result of public speeches by County Executive Campen, a letter warning against dangers of invasion of privacy had been written to the *Palo Alto Times* by a local resident, and some county welfare workers had expressed "reservations about the availability of broad access to the names of clients."

The head of the General Services Agency, Robert A. Sorensen, under whose jurisdiction the Data Processing Center operated, explained to the press that all existing laws and rules about confidentiality would be carried over into the computerized system, and each department would only have access to data that it was entitled to have. He also stressed that data in the computer would be even more secure than in manual files because getting to them would now require technical knowledge.

However, civil libertarians were not wholly comforted when the then director of the data-processing center, Karl Sheel, was quoted as saying that those concerned about invasion of privacy were mainly the "higher educated . . . dreamers." "If you have no arrests, no outstanding warrants against you or if you're not on welfare or if you've stayed out of the clutches of adult probation," he remarked, you had no reason to fear anything from the system.

The *Times* story prompted local and national TV coverage of LOGIC's possible advantages and dangers. During this period, the county invited in a representative from the local American Civil Liberties Union chapter; he looked into the system and concluded that, as it then stood, it had adequate safeguards for privacy for its early operations.

Similar flurries of local publicity over "Big Brother" implications took place in 1967, when the welfare system went on-line ("LOGIC's Watching You, Folks," one newspaper headed its story), and again in early 1968, when a local paper went into the "ominous" possibilities of "a total information system" that can "mercilessly record our every indiscretion." Santa Clara County's provisions for privacy were also discussed in 1969, when a state legislative subcommittee held hearings on computers and privacy and obtained testimony from the county about safeguards in its system. (General Services Agency Director Sorensen testified in favor of stringent confidentiality rules and advocated passage of a state law giving individuals a right of access to their records.)

While these occasional public discussions were taking place in 1966-69 the county was moving internally to take up confidentiality issues as they arose in the course of data conversion. In 1966, while the welfare application was being put onto LOGIC, an opinion was obtained from the county attorney setting out which welfare records were confidential under state or federal law and which other county departments could have access to them. These rules, allowing access to the Health, Probation, and Hospitals Department but not to law-enforcement officials, were carried into the programming and terminal controls of the welfare API system when it went into operation. During 1968, studies of computer security policies were conducted and representatives of the county served on a subcommittee on privacy and confidentiality of a statewide Intergovernmental Board on Electronic Data Processing. (This board was composed of representatives from city, county, and state government computer systems in California and reported to the Lieutenant Governor.)

In 1969, another county attorney's opinion was written specifying which records from Health, Probation, Sheriff's Office, and Valley Medical Center might be put into the LOGIC system for sharing with other departments. Based on state law, the county attorney indicated that information considered confidential in terms of the general public might be shared with other county departments only when the purpose is "to serve the client" and when someone in the primary department makes a specific determination of that fact before granting access. In addition, the opinion listed three records that could *not* be shared through this process: information on venereal disease, on adoptions, and from the sheriff's investigative files. From these legal opinions, the county set up rules requiring permission in writing before data from one department could be shared with another department through the computer system. These were incorporated into the computer operation by "lockout" procedures on the terminals and authorization codes for individual identification.

Progress in the LOGIC System, 1968-71

By 1968, the six-year plan for achieving LOGIC had slipped by several years, with the county "hoping" for completion by something like 1973 or 1974. Problems of securing enough programmer-analysts, the need to continue existing application work for the departments, and the unexpectedly high costs of converting manual files into machine-readable language were, in the words of the data-processing director, George Vandermate, "not ignored in the original study" but "grossly underestimated."

However, work went forward on various subsystems. Another 250,000 names from medical records were put onto a patient index and added to API. The index had patient identification data (name, sex, birthdate, and Social Security number) as well as hospital information, such as diagnosis, eligibility for Medicare or MediCal, address and telephone number, and summary of account. This was used for admissions, eligibility, and patient accounting purposes.

The greatest surge forward for LOGIC in 1969-71 came in the field of law enforcement and criminal justice. While money from the county general fund became so short that LOGIC development had to be severely limited in other areas, large funds from the federal Crime Control Act of 1968 began to move out to local and state governments for projects such as computerized information systems. In 1970-71, Santa Clara received two grants totaling $650,000 for its Criminal Justice Information Control system (CJIC). Phase one, which became operational in 1971, is called "subject in process," and represents automation of a person's contacts with the criminal-justice agencies from time of booking by the police through arraignment, county jail, trial, and correction. Approximately 100,000 summary criminal histories from the manual police files have also been put onto the computer, providing access to the "known criminal population" of the county through terminals in city police departments, sheriff's offices, superior and municipal courts, district attorney's and public defender's offices, and juvenile and adult probation offices. Patrolmen in the field can radio in and get "the individual's present status in the criminal-justice process, his record of arrests, and his probationary status. . . ."

In January 1971, the CJIC Policy Committee adopted a Code of Ethics that specified civil-liberties guarantees for the system. "LOGIC subsystems do not form one huge databank, or 'people file,' " the code declares. "Access to various separate files is now, and will be, limited to those with the legal right of access and with permission of the departments responsible for the individual computer files." Participation in CJIC is limited to official criminal-justice agencies. No information may be placed in the system if "the data are not derived from official criminal justice proceedings." "An individual citizen has the right, after satisfactorily proving his identity, to view his own record in the CJIC files and to challenge the veracity of CJIC entries pertaining to him originated by participating agencies."

Several questions of civil-liberties import still remain to be decided by CJIC. For example, there has been discussion of whether to include a "violence potential" entry in an individual's CJIC file. Some CJIC participants have said this is too subjective and arbitrary a reference to include, while others have defended it as necessary for protection of the officer on patrol.

Effects of Computerization on Record-keeping Practices

Comparing record-keeping practices before and after computerization in Santa Clara County results in some interesting observations. In neither of the two main "people" files that were operational in 1968-71, the welfare and patient indexes, has the amount of information collected and recorded about each person been increased as a result of computerization. In welfare, far less personal information is collected on the initial application, essentially as a result of a shift in state eligibility criteria during the 1960s from a focus on detailed self-revelation to a requirement for a less probing proof of need: this change in program definition was faithfully reflected in the automated system.

Interviews with persons in the sheriff's office, probation department, and district attorney's office showed that an informal "reciprocity" system allowed county officials in these offices to get key personal information at times from colleagues or clerical help working in the welfare, health, or education departments, despite state law or county rules barring such access. Computerization did not eliminate such informal exchanges, but county officials say that it has, in some departments, limited the number of secretaries and clerks who have access to records, and thus might give out data improperly.

Future Plans and the LOGIC Timetable

In 1971-72, the Data Processing Center has a budget of $4,545,-000, and 225 full-time employees. The county expects to move ahead rapidly with its criminal-justice application, which is now "ten times bigger than the original LOGIC plan." Other subsystems will also be worked on, such as a Property Data Management Module to give all city departments access to the "current status of property and ownership in the county." The county has placed an order for an IBM 370 computer to handle its expanded processing and storage needs.

As of 1971, however, Santa Clara is still far from the integrated central databank outlined in the original LOGIC report of 1965. Technical and personnel problems, shortages of money, the pressure of providing service for regular department operations, and difficulties of linking information have all contributed to the "slippage."

In fact, some county officials doubt whether the "total information system" concept originally envisioned will be achieved in anything like the near future. Separate functional files will go forward, one county administrator explained, but the databank for decision-making support that LOGIC described presents difficulties that have not yet been solved. "Relations between people, and among people, property, and things are very complex; so little is known about them that the kind of 'data base' ideas discussed in the early days are still more wishes than anything else."

Commercial Organizations

Banking and Finance

In 1970, there were 13,700 commercial banks in the U.S., with assets of almost $536 billion. In addition, there were 5,700 savings and loan institutions, 500 mutual savings banks, 3,500 finance companies, and almost 24,000 federal and state-chartered credit unions (which handle loans for employees within businesses and for members of organizations such as labor unions). As is true of many American industries, there is a heavy concentration of business in the larger firms. In 1969, for example, the 50 largest commercial banks (out of 13,700) had almost 50 percent of the total assets. Legally, banks are chartered either by state or federal law, with various regulating agencies at each level supervising banking practices.

It is estimated that 60 percent of American adults maintain checking accounts in banks and that a large proportion also have personal savings accounts. Consumer credit, most of which is handled by banking and financial institutions, reached a figure of $127 billion of outstanding debt in 1970; $101 billion of this was in installment loans (automobile, other consumer goods, repairs and modernization, and personal). Today's commercial bank is a business-seeking institution, actively marketing personal loans and seeking credit-card customers.

The personal information built up in bank files is of various kinds. In addition to the dollar amounts individuals have in their accounts, the cancelled personal and business checks (which are kept on microfilm by banks, as required by law) contain on their face information as to who was paid, when, and sometimes include personal notes by the customer about the subject or purpose of the payment. There is also sensitive information in bank files on the credit and loan history of customers, the presence of safe-deposit-box accounts, trust and securities data, etc.

Protection of customer information from unauthorized or improper disclosure is also a critical aspect of maintaining good customer relations and has been reflected historically in a tradition of confidentiality applying to the banking transactions of individuals, companies, and organizations. Unlike Switzerland, however, where laws *require* secrecy in account and transaction information, and make disclosures without consent of the customer or legal direction a criminal offense, American legislation has not spelled out such guarantees of confidentiality. Furthermore, American rules for business regulation, tax investigation, and law enforcement have often worked to open financial transactions between individual customers and banking enterprises to scrutiny by executive, legislative, and judicial agencies.

Banks were prime candidates for computerization. While high-level banking decisions rest heavily on experience, informal knowledge, and intuition, the base of banking operations is heavily routine—repetitive arithmetic calculations, high-volume paper transactions, and large-scale communication of objective data. The sheer weight of these transactions began to strain bank clerical staffs sharply in the 1950s and 1960s. For example, more than 17 billion checks were being handled each year by banks in the mid-1960s. Further, the slogan that "time is money" applies with special pertinency to banking, where speed in the handling of transactions is not only part of the service expected by customers, both corporate and individual, but is critical in the major decisions about money exchange, investment, and loans made by top management.

Computerization entered the banking industry in the mid-1950s. The first large-scale, general-purpose computer was installed by the Bank of America in 1955. That early development was concentrated in the very largest institutions is shown in Table 2-2 for 1966.

EDP development is more widely spread in banking today, though the large institutions continue to lead in the extent to which their record-keeping operations are computerized. From our own national survey of organizations, we found that 64 percent of the commercial banks in our sample report some computer applications to records on current personal-checking-account customers. Further, many finance companies and credit unions have

Table 2-2*

Size of Bank Deposits	Number of Banks	Number of Computers
$250 million or more	174	955
$50-$250 million	599	398
$10-$50 million	2,305	399
Less than $10 million	10,567	none

*From a 1966 survey of 13,605 banks conducted by the American Bankers Association.

recently moved into heavy reliance on computerized record systems as well.

Our project visited three banks, all large institutions with major computerization efforts. One was a metropolitan "all services" bank in the East with several dozen branches, all located (as required by state law) within the city limits. A second was a midwestern, one-branch bank, with a strong commercial concentration in its business. The third, which will be the subject of our profile, was the Bank of America, located in California.

THE BANK OF AMERICA

The Bank of America is the world's largest privately owned financial institution. Founded by A. P. Giannini in 1904 as the Bank of Italy, it began operations in a remodeled tavern in the North Beach section of San Francisco. Giannini saw the advantages of statewide banking, which was (and is) permitted under California banking statutes. By 1930, when its name was changed to the Bank of America, "B of A" had established 353 branches throughout California.

In 1972 the Bank of America has 995 California and 95 overseas branches, over 200 administrative departments, and approximately 41,000 employees within the United States. International banking subsidiaries of the Bank of America are located in five major port cities of the United States. At the close of 1970, its total resources were $29.7 billion; net earnings that year were $163 million, up 6 percent from 1969.

As a "full-service financial institution," the Bank of America offers more than 100 types of customer services, producing $25.6 billion in deposits and $15.9 billion in loans in 1970. The Bank of America is also known for its commercial operations, with loans and lines of credit to large corporate enterprises in California, nationally, and throughout the world. Many people outside California use Bank of America Travelers Cheques, sold by banks and agents all over the world, and BankAmericard, an international credit-card system with more than 28 million cardholders. Recognized in every state and in 69 foreign areas, the card is accepted in more than 1 million merchant outlets, and processed $3 billion in sales in 1970.

Organizationally, the Bank of America administers its statewide banking complex through divisional headquarters located in two 52-story buildings in San Francisco and Los Angeles. State branch activities are organized into 12 semiautonomous regions, which operate under the general guidance of Statewide Regional Administration located in San Francisco.

Bank of America's Social Policies

Large financial institutions such as B of A have felt some pressure during the past decade from both governmental and private quarters to turn their funds and influence to dealing with social and racial problems. In its 1970 *Annual Report*, B of A discusses major social problems facing the nation, the bank's economic and social philosophy, and how the bank is discharging its "public policy responsibilities." The *Report* cites, for example, the bank's minority hiring programs (20 percent of its employees are nonwhite, largely concentrated in metropolitan centers like Los Angeles); the earmarking of some special loan funds for minority businesses, housing improvement, and housing projects; and special job-training programs for blacks and Mexican-Americans. The *Report* also mentions the bank's development of new "high-risk" branches in minority communities such as Watts and East Palo Alto, and the "local participation" provided in such projects for black architects and construction firms. "Profits are and must continue to be the central concern of any responsible corporate enterprise," the bank's 1970 *Report* noted, "but in the long pull, nobody can expect to make profits—or have any meaningful use for profits—if our society is wracked by tensions."

At the same time, the bank has found itself under sharp attack from the political left, black militant groups, and ecology spokesmen whose allegations included the charges that the bank was a major supporter of the Vietnam War, fostered racism in California, supported big farm corporations at the expense of oppressed farm workers, was "antilabor" in general, and exploited the resources of underdeveloped nations throughout the world, and the resources of California through its backing of large landowners.

In February 1970, unknown persons, allegedly students and others at the University of California at Santa Barbara, burned down the nearby Isla Vista branch of Bank of America, as a symbol of the "capitalist establishment." A few weeks later, a branch in Oakland was bombed, then a branch near the University of California at Irvine. From early 1970 until early 1972, more than 60 fires and bombings took place at B of A facilities, with losses estimated by executive vice-president Paul E. Sullivan at approximately $1 million.

Bank executives responded by deploring the violence of "a few students," but reaffirming their "great respect for the integrity, moral courage, and willingness to dissent" of young people. The bank urged continued financial support rather than any boycott of American universities. To demonstrate its own refusal to be "driven off by radical elements," the bank immediately rebuilt the two destroyed branches.

In newspaper ads, speeches, and other communications, top bank executives also answered the verbal attacks. President Clausen noted that as early as 1967 the bank had publicly deplored the effect of the Vietnam War on the economy, particularly withdrawal of funds needed for domestic programs; in 1970, then chairman of the board Louis B. Lundborg appeared before the Senate Foreign Relations Committee to term the war a "tragic mistake" and urge American withdrawal as a move vital for business as well as public interests. Other rebuttals by the bank included a recitation of its record in minority affairs, and its support of farm-labor legislation to help migrant workers. As for the charge of being a "capitalist" institution, the bank acknowledged "with pride" that it was part of the "market economy." Defending the American economic system for its record in spreading material prosperity and the capacity of its political system to provide needed social changes through democratic processes, the bank attacked those who take to violence "in an effort to force their views on the majority in American society."

From Manual Record-keeping to Initial Computerization

Bank of America's bookkeepers originally wrote account entries into three-foot bound "Boston ledgers," with daily account summaries and posting done by hand in pen and ink. The next step was the loose-leaf ledger posted by electrically driven bookkeeping machines. In the 1930s, the bank began utilizing punched-card equipment for operations such as trust and payroll accounting. Microfilm was introduced to provide improved audit and tracing facilities for checks and other transactions forwarded from the receiving bank to the payor bank.

After World War II, Bank of America found itself with what the principal architect of its data-processing systems, A. R. Zipf, called "cataclysmic 'paper problems'" created by the "booming postwar years" in California, particularly "the ever-increasing volume and cost of check handling." When business-machine manufacturers proved uninterested in developing machines to process paper checks automatically, the Bank of America commissioned the Stanford Research Institute in 1950 to help the bank design and develop its own system.

While this was under development (a period of almost six years), the Bank of America recognized, in Zipf's words, "not only the potential of general-purpose computers for banking applications but, more important, our need to develop a significant capability in the computer field." In 1955, the bank installed an IBM 702, "the first large-scale, general-purpose computer in any bank in the world." This acquisition, Zipf stated, satisfied the basic criterion followed in each of its hardware acquisitions and system changes: "cost-effectiveness." "In seven months," he noted, the cost of operation of the 702 "was less than the previous cost of performing the functions it had taken over . . ."

By this time, the Stanford Research Institute project had developed a prototype of an "automated bookkeeping system" for processing paper checks. Called ERMA, it utilized "Magnetic Ink Character Recognition" (MICR), consisting of the now familiar "funny little numbers printed in magnetic ink at the bottom of checks." These branch and account identification numbers were "read" electronically and the checks sorted accordingly. In 1956 the bank contracted with General Electric to produce and deliver 30 ERMA computer systems to automate all of its checking-account transactions, "the largest single nondefense order for computing equipment that had ever been placed" up to that time. By 1961, the 30 systems were installed and running in 13 regional centers, handling almost all of the bank's domestic-branch checking-account record-keeping. In 1958 the American Bankers Association adopted MICR as a national standard for handling checks, and the system has gradually become commonplace in American banking.

"By 1962," Zipf recounts, "we had computerized all of our volume record-keeping functions of consequence." The next step was to develop applications for providing computerized services to customers and businesses. This brought about data processing for BankAmericard (the general-purpose credit card the bank began marketing in 1959); payroll service for companies; a professional billing service for doctors and dentists; and various account, billing, and payment services for clients such as other banks, credit unions, mortgage companies, and charter travel services.

The Bank's "Second Decade" of Automation

As of 1964, the Bank of America had 47 computer systems, installed in 14 regional centers, representing a cost of $50 million, and devoted to a combination of in-house banking applications and service operations for outside customers. In mid-1964, with the announcement of third-generation computers and anticipating a need for greatly increased computer capacity by 1968, B of A faced a major choice: should they move to a single information system for their entire organization, along the lines of "total management information systems" that were then being widely discussed, or use an application-by-application (service-by-service) approach? Given the bank's over 900 branches, branch operations in 20 foreign countries, more than 100 banking services, and the very fast demand cycle of many of these, the bank concluded that the one-big-system approach was impractical, and an approach along functional, application-by-application lines was selected. In 1965 the bank did decide to consolidate its regional EDP operations into two large centers, one in San Francisco and one in Los Angeles, and to replace all of its general-purpose computers with third-generation IBM 360/65 systems. Many hundreds of programs had to be rewritten, at an investment of some 150 man-years. In early 1968, following delay of over a year because of difficulties with System 360 hardware and software, and the unanticipated need to redesign some applications, the conversion was completed and the two centers were running.

At this point, while B of A's system development efforts continued toward the automation of the remaining routine repetitive tasks, the focus of attention was shifted to information system planning and use of the data available through computerization for advanced operations research. Some operations research projects aided by computers had been going on ever since the mid-1950s; among these had been the development of a strategy for deciding how long to pursue overdue loans before charging them off as losses; a branch staffing model for manpower planning; and a loan credit-scoring technique to weigh those borrower characteristics that help to predict loan profitability. To accelerate developments in information systems and operations research, B of A created a Management Science Department in 1968.

Today, the Bank has four IBM 360/65's in its San Francisco Data Processing Center and three IBM 360/65's in its Los Angeles center. In addition to regularly scheduled processing for bank and business services, the computers are able to operate on-line, providing immediate response to terminal inquiries for credit authorizations requested from all California BankAmericard merchants. Prior to 1970, BankAmericard operated under a licensing arrangement with almost 4,000 local banks, which handled the processing of credit-card accounts for member banks on a local or regional basis. The Bank of America itself processed only the California BankAmericard accounts, which produced $610 million in sales during 1970. That year, over 31 million sales drafts were processed in California, based on 1.9 million California BankAmericard accounts.

Overall, according to Russell Fenwick, vice-president for systems and equipment research, the computer system represents one of the most advanced large-scale commercial installations in the United States. Operating costs of the bank's two data-processing centers were approximately $31.6 million in 1970. Except for on-line inquiries to obtain BankAmericard account status, data input is forwarded to the two computer centers for batch processing via a statewide air and auto messenger system. Branches prepare data-processing work (checks, time-payment coupons, BankAmericard charges, etc.) and put this into locked bags; these are picked up by messengers who deliver them to the data-processing center. A similar pickup system applies to business service work. When the bags reach the data center, they are opened, entries are sorted by class of information, prepared for input processing, and captured on magnetic tape or disk. Through this system, the postings for each individual account are done in the two data centers, not in the individual branches. The output of the centers is made up of the posted entries and output reports that are sent to the branches. Recurring reports to various levels of management are also prepared, as well as special "on call" reports. In 1970, this system was using over 180 tons of paper per month.

Personal Information Held in Computerized and Manual Files

"People records" at the Bank of America can be divided for ease of reference into three main categories, defined by the relationship between the individual and the bank. These are records on customers, employees, and "third parties."

Customer Records. The Bank of America has more than 14 million individual accounts in computerized storage. The major files include 7.2 million checking and savings accounts, 1.9 million California BankAmericard accounts, .9 million installment loans, .4 million mortgage loans, 1.1 million trust and shareholder accounts, and 2.1 million business service accounts of various kinds.

Information in these computerized files is drawn basically from two sources: the individual's application (when he opens an account, seeks a loan, applies for BankAmericard, etc.) and the transactions he then generates in using that service (such as writing checks and making deposits, paying his loan installments, etc.). However, only essential identifiers and ongoing transaction data are computerized from these sources. In the case of loans, for example, the bank does *not* computerize personal details from the application or information from the credit reports obtained from local credit bureaus or TRW-Credit Data Corporation (the national credit bureau which is the subject of our next profile); those are used by the bank officer for making the credit decision but, once that is made, the detailed information stays in manual files.[1]

Bank Employees. Until 1971, the only personal information computerized for employees was payroll information and a small quantity of current personnel data. The full employee record remained in file jackets in the personnel department.

In 1969, the bank retained the consulting firm of Information Sciences, Inc., to help them design a computerized Personnel Data System (PDS). Studies were done of information needs for personnel purposes, as well as tests of the "acceptability" to

---

[1] When applying its loan credit-scoring formula, the bank officer appraising the loan application takes the "indicator" items from the applicant's form and completes a scoring sheet to compute the applicant's credit score. There is no "computer scoring" of individual applications.

employees of various information items and their wording. The system, which became operational in 1971, reflected the results of this research.

Approximately 41,000 regular and part-time employees are currently covered by PDS, which operates through a coordinated input stream with the bank's payroll system. PDS contains approximately 75 classes of information about each employee, drawn initially from his employment application, and then updated by periodic inputs from units such as the bank's training department, benefits department, and the branch or department in which the employee works, which records basic changes in the employee's position and salary, gives performance ratings, etc. The stored information includes standard personnel matters such as identifying items, marital status, work history, education, benefits, vacations, absences, bank training courses completed, area of residence, and commuting time to work. About 10,000 executive-level employees supply a list of their skills, current memberships, and other activities.

From this employee data base, PDS automatically generates daily, weekly, monthly, quarterly, and annual outputs. Among these are statistical reviews for manpower planning, reports of unusual attendance and overtime records of specific employees for supervisor attention, and reports for supervisors to use in arranging training and education courses for the employee. When the system is in full operation, higher-level employees will be given an Employee Career Profile annually, for review and update (to include new skills, interests, etc.). The up-to-date information will then be available to higher levels of management for use in selecting candidates for open positions.

One interesting feature of PDS is its "general retrieval capability." In addition to allowing searches of the master file to prepare various reports and statistical profiles, this facility allows personnel officials to specify various criteria for a given post and then obtain a list of employees who fit these specifications. "For example," the bank notes, "a list may be needed that shows all employees above grade ten with three years experience in branch operations, knowledgeable in tax accounting, and having a performance rating of one or two." Combinations of most of the items stored in PDS can be retrieved in this fashion.

"Third-party" Files. The bank has computer files of information on prospective business customers with offices located in California. Data for these files originate from the DUNS California

Marketing File, with additional information supplied by bank officers. The bank also keeps computer files of payroll, billing, and other service information about persons who are clients or employees of the unions, professionals, and companies that subscribe to the bank's automated business services. This means, for example, that the bank receives from physicians the names of their patients, amounts owed, and similar data.

In addition to this kind of computerized third-party information, bank officers in each branch keep informal records on businesses in their territory which are not using Bank of America services but which are likely prospects for development as new customers. While no single system exists, branch officers are encouraged to be alert for marketing opportunities by developing information about local businesses and local officials which might be of use in personal contacts. This type of information is seen as useful in "personalizing" the business development process and may include business likes and dislikes, hobbies, special interests, names of members of the family, and other personal data. The information is accumulated in a variety of ways; it is not part of the formal records in the branch, and is not sent to central bank headquarters. There are no plans to computerize such information, not only because it is useful only at the local level but also because it is the kind of subjective and anecdotal information that bank management does not regard as appropriate for automation.

Privacy Aspects of Computerization at Bank of America

As a general matter, computerization has not led to the collection and storage of more information about each individual by the bank than it formerly put into its manual files. In fact, computerization has generally involved a skimming off from manual files of the most objective and frequently used data, with the traditional manual files retained for infrequent inquiries or legal documentation. Even in the case of PDS, with its 75 classes of items about each employee, and its capability for locating potential candidates for promotions, the information now collected does not differ in its character or sensitivity from what had been collected by the Personnel Department in the precomputer era.

Officials concerned with computerization at the bank believe that there is generally *less* information being obtained about employees, customers, and clients than was true in the precomputer era. According to Fenwick, "This is because of our reexamination of information needs; the need, on a cost basis, to squeeze data down to the minimum required for effective control, operation, and reporting; and our efforts to achieve better information rationality through the process of reducing unnecessary information flows within the organization."

At the same time, however, the expansion of bank services to include BankAmericard and the creation of its massive files—high volume transactions for 1.9 million accounts—is largely attributable to the availability of computer technology. Bank officials note that they cannot envision that operation being handled manually today.

Confidentiality Issues

Bank of America's *Standard Practice Manual*, the official statement of the bank's rules and policies, states that bank employees should maintain the confidential nature of customer relations unless authorized to do otherwise. This applies to virtually anything that the bank knows about a customer: what kind of accounts he has, the amount of money he has on deposit, his outstanding loans, money invested or held in trust, etc. Every person who joins the bank's employ signs an Agreement of Employment which has the following as its first condition:

> All accounts and transactions of customers with the Bank and operations of the Bank are to be held in the strictest confidence and not to be revealed to any persons within or without the bank without proper authority.

Actually, no federal or state statutes provide legal protection for the confidentiality of customer information, and there is no common law testimonial privilege for banker-customer relations. There have also been very few judicial decisions dealing with this question. The leading case is a 1961 Idaho Supreme Court ruling[2] which held that bank officials operated under an implied contract not to reveal customer information unless with the customer's consent, under authority of law, or in response to a constitutionally proper subpoena. "Inviolate secrecy is one of the inherent and fundamental precepts of the relationship of the bank and its customers or depositors," the court wrote.

In keeping with common practice within the banking world, the Bank of America does regularly disclose extensive information about its experience with customers (loans outstanding or de-

---

[2] *Peterson* v. *Idaho First National Bank*, 367 P. 2d 284 (1961).

clined, account balances, loan-payment performance, etc.) to other credit grantors, to local credit bureaus, and to the national computerized credit-reporting firm of TRW-Credit Data Corporation. As part of the credit-reporting system, this information is then available upon request to other "bona fide credit grantors," such as retail merchants, department stores, airlines, other credit-card services, and the like. Upon request, B of A also shares information about its former employees with the personnel officers of other companies and government agencies, following the usual informal practices for such interorganizational reference reporting.

Unlike many other banks, Bank of America has a formal written policy in its *Standard Practice Manual* specifying what information will be given out to government agencies and how this will be done. Inquiries as to patients' bank accounts will be answered for the state Department of Mental Hygiene and State Hospitals, for instance, and local and state welfare agencies are allowed to verify the deposit balances reported by welfare applicants. Agents of the FBI and Internal Revenue Service who have subpoena power and are able to demonstrate to the satisfaction of the bank that they are conducting a bona fide investigation and are not on a "fishing expedition" are given access to account information "upon presentation of official credentials." Except in criminal investigations, it is the bank's policy to notify the customer that such inquiry has been made and to disclose what information has been furnished to the governmental agency. It is the bank's policy to give the customer an opportunity wherever possible to seek a protective order from a court where information regarding a customer's business is sought.

Most such requests go or are directed to the local branches concerned and are handled by bank personnel there. Robert Fabian, senior vice-president and general counsel for the bank, states that, as far as he knows, the requests received from local, state, or federal officials to obtain account information are always honored if the inquirer has a "right to know" (by reason of law, court order, or other basis as outlined in the bank's *Standard Practice Manual*). Where the rules provided do not cover a given situation or there is some question about the "right to know," branch personnel are supposed to refer the matter to the B of A legal department.

Fabian further notes that "It is not at all uncommon for the bank to negotiate with law-enforcement officials for a more limited inquiry into account information than was originally requested, occasionally because the scope of the original inquiry may have been broader than appeared to be justified, but more commonly, because the inquiries are unduly burdensome or even impossible to comply with."[3]

The procedures for disclosing information in computerized files are the same as those used for information in manual systems; bank officials do not see computerization as having any significant effect on the rules and practices regarding confidentiality.

The bank's legal department, under Robert Fabian, has supervised each stage of automation to ensure that bank policies about confidentiality were followed in the computerized systems. For example, Fabian vetoed proposals from marketing officials in the bank who wanted to realize additional revenue by selling to direct-mail advertisers lists of names and account-derived information that could be generated through the computerized systems, including the list of BankAmericard holders. Fabian also saw to it, he said, that no "mail stuffers" are put into BankAmericard billing envelopes—things like "soliciting insurance or selling electric drills, hair curlers, and Teflon." Fabian regards such uses as an "improper intrusion into the privacy of our customers."

In the same vein, the bank has refused to sell lists of high-

---

[3] Bank officials indicated that they followed the same rules for access by law-enforcement officials to BankAmericard files as with other customer accounts. In 1970, they stated that they received 75 requests from all federal, state, and local law-enforcement agencies to examine accounts in the California BankAmericard system—the accounts processed directly by the Bank of America. These were related primarily to court actions for dissolution of marriages and bankruptcy cases. Law-enforcement officials are not allowed to make inquiries directly into the computer as to BankAmericard card-status or account files. Such inquiries go to the operations manager, who is supposed to examine each one to see whether it complies with Bank of America policies and then forward copies of the records to the requesting agency in a letter over his official signature. The total number of such requests for information from checking, savings, and all other accounts in the bank during 1970 was not available, since most of these requests are handled at the branch level, and no central record is kept of these.

Just what bank accounts government investigators should be allowed to inspect has emerged as a major privacy issue. During 1970-71, it was disclosed that bank records of various black militant, antiwar, and other protest groups had been subpoenaed by several congressional committees and were being inspected frequently by the FBI; in keeping with prevailing bank practices, in "criminal investigations," notice was not given of these inspections to the customer, a policy followed by B of A. In early 1972, while lawsuits testing the constitutionality of these practices were pending, the U.S. Treasury announced a set of regulations for record-keeping and reporting for all American banks. These regulations stemmed from the Bank Secrecy Act of 1970, a law aimed primarily at controlling illegal overseas transfer of funds by underworld figures and large-scale tax evaders.

However, the Treasury regulations were quite broad. They required banks to microfilm and keep for two years all checks in personal accounts; to credit customers to those seeking an "elite mailing list." When the Bank of America signed a contract to furnish account and "customer-performance" information to TRW-Credit Data Corporation, knowing that it would be circulated further for credit-granting purposes, it had a clause included to the effect that TRW-Credit Data customers were not to see or use the information furnished for noncredit purposes.

Information Security at the Bank of America

When asked why he robbed banks, Willie Sutton's famous reply was, "Well, that's where the money is." In this tradition, banks have a long record of taking measures to protect the security of their cash, negotiable instruments, and other valuables, and to guard against fraud in the keeping of accounts and records. As a consequence, computerization unfolded at Bank of America in a setting in which physical security and auditing controls were already major concerns. Adding to this the apprehension over deliberate destruction of bank property that began with protest demonstrations outside the bank in 1968 and culminated in the branch burnings and bombings of 1970, it is not altogether surprising that the Bank of America proved to have the most extensive and costly security measures for its computerized and manual

---

record for five years all nonreal estate loans over $5,000 and all transfers of more than $10,000; and to secure a social security number for all persons opening new checking accounts. Reports about the specified transactions were to be made to the Treasury. All records kept under the regulations would be open to IRS agents presenting subpoenas, without notification to customers. Information obtained from reports could be supplied to other federal agencies on their declaration that this was needed for "criminal, tax, or regulatory investigation."

Bankers across the country, joined by business, political, and civil liberties groups, expressed dismay at the Treasury rules. In June 1972, the ACLU of Northern California and the California Bankers Association filed lawsuits to enjoin the rules, alleging that they constituted a violation of customer privacy in bank records, an unbounded system of government searches, and a threat to the constitutionally-protected anonymity of members and contributors to political and religious associations.

B of A participated actively in the California Bankers Association lawsuit, and Robert Fabian publicly condemned the Bank Secrecy Act for creating "a whole bunch of records" that were at the disposal of "people in power, if they want to abuse it." Noting the complaints that B of A had been receiving from its customers, Fabian added that the Act was undermining confidence in "the banking system and the government."

On June 30th, a federal district court issued a temporary restraining order suspending the reporting and disclosure provisions of the Act while its constitutionality was being heard by a three-judge federal court. At the same time, Senator John Tunney of California announced that he was introducing legislation in Congress to forbid disclosure of account information except with a court order or, in the case of agency subpoena, notice tó the customer and an opportunity to contest the subpoena in court.

records of any private organization that we visited. Given the huge financial losses that would result if the bank's data-processing operations were to be halted or disrupted, B of A management notes, expenditures for security have a high cost-effectiveness justification.

Officials estimate that their EDP security measures currently cost something in excess of $1 million per year. Nevertheless, the bank's security committee orients itself to what it regards as "credible threats," and relies more on "reasonable" measures for physical protection and control over access than on specialized techniques or "excessive concern over remote contingencies."

The bank's Data Center Security Program includes alarm indicator panels, closed-circuit television systems, and, at central control points, bulletproof glass, uniformed security guards equipped with two-way radios, and guard stations with consoles controlling interlocked double-door entries and exits. To provide data security, magnetic tape containing critical data is transported to remote off-premises storage locations.[4] Presently, backup power for the data centers involves rerouting of public power facilities. Future plans include provisions for separate emergency standby power supplies in each center.

Bank officials see embezzlement of money rather than leakage of personal information as the primary threat from persons getting unauthorized access to data. To forestall alteration of figures for such purposes, the bank uses special auditing controls at each step in the data processing.

Individual Access to Records

When an individual maintains checking, savings, or other service accounts at the Bank of America, he receives (as he would in all American banks) periodic statements showing transactions made on the account. As a result of this system, B of A officials suggest, the accuracy of transactions in the computerized accounts is kept high; "the individual—the customer—is the best auditor we have."

As far as personnel files are concerned, most of each employee's record is open to him. In the new PDS, each employee will be given a yearly print-out of his Career Profile which will contain most of the objective information relating to him, including—for

---

[4] It was from backup tapes, which are updated to the last posting day, that the bank was able to reconstruct customer accounts at the Isla Vista branch the day after it was burned.

higher-level employees—a detailed skills inventory. Returning the forms with corrections and additions will be the employee's way of updating this part of his record.

Some parts of their respective records are not accessible to employees and individual customers. The employee does not generally have access to recommendations, detailed performance evaluations, or the results of employment or promotion investigations conducted by outside agencies, though it would be normal, bank officials say, for him to discuss some of this information with his supervisor. In the case of customers, they are not specifically informed when a credit report is drawn on them, though they may sign a general authorization for this type of record checking when applying for a mortgage or other loan. In addition, the customer may not be aware of the tradition among banks of the sharing of information about account status and credit performance through central credit bureaus. Credit reports are considered confidential by the bank and under most circumstances are not for the customer's eyes; information from a credit report, however, may be discussed with the customer in the course of the application process.

In 1968-70, the content, accuracy, and completeness of such reports, and the inability of individuals to know about and contest their use in credit, employment, and insurance decisions, were the subject of a series of congressional hearings.[5] Hearings on credit bureaus were also held by the California state legislature. The result of the hearings was the enactment in California and nationally of laws that have had major impact on Bank of America access practices.

The California Consumer Credit Reporting Act of 1970 applies whenever a loan application for personal, family, or household purposes is declined or a finance charge is increased because of a derogatory report from a credit-reporting agency. The individual must be notified that such a report was used, and, if he applies in writing within 60 days, he must be supplied with the name of the agency which prepared it. He can then apply to the credit-reporting firm to learn the contents of his record there and challenge its accuracy. In April 1971, the federal Fair Credit Reporting Act (FCRA) went into effect. Though similar in some respects to the California statute, the FCRA is a broader law

---

[5] Further discussion of the federal hearings will be found in the TRW-Credit Data profile that follows this one.

covering commercial reports for employment and insurance purposes as well as credit reports, and has been the subject of
explanatory guidelines by both the Federal Reserve Board and
Federal Trade Commission.

The Bank of America supported the idea that one should be
entitled by law to see his credit bureau file, if he has been denied
credit. Complying with that part of the state and federal laws has
been simple for the bank, officials note, but several other problems have been of greater concern. First, FCRA exempts from
regulation those organizations which are not commercial reporting
agencies but which give information to "third parties" on transactions with their own customers. Information about loan, checking,
and savings accounts can be shared with other financial institutions, but B of A cannot include "personal knowledge about the
consumer" such as "mode of living" and "personal habits," or
"subjective opinions" about rates of payments or credit rating. In
addition, B of A is not supposed to pass on to other financial
institutions or credit bureaus consumer information derived from
other organizations, such as another bank or the previous employer or bank personnel.

Another feature of the new law's impact on B of A is that
when the bank orders from a commercial agency an "investigative" report (based on personal interviews with neighbors, friends,
and former employers, to learn about "character, general reputation, mode of living, and personal characteristics") it must tell the
individual in advance that such a report is being drawn. The bank
uses such reports for deciding on FHA and VA real estate loans,
and for some of its own decisions about applicants for employment. If the loans are refused or employment is denied "wholly or
in part on the basis of information" from a commercial reporting
agency, the bank must notify the individual of this fact and, upon
request, supply him or her with the name and address of the
agency which prepared the report.

After the first six months of operation under the FCRA, at
the end of 1971, the bank reports that there has been "little
public reaction." B of A has not been involved in any lawsuits
contesting the procedures the bank has set up to comply with the
law, and B of A branches have not experienced large numbers of
consumer complaints. Bank officials believe that as a result of the
new federal regulations "there has been a reduction in the sources
of credit information and/or an unwillingness to speak candidly,

which is detrimental to the extension of credit." Also, delays in processing FHA and VA loans, because of the notification procedures required under the act, have caused complaints from builders.

Future Directions of Computerization

EDP activity at B of A is now shared among three coordinate departments: one for systems development and implementation; one for operational affairs; and one for operations research and management information purposes. Bank officials looking to the early 1970s expect to see increased use of new input devices (optical scanning and on-line data capture) as well as new output techniques (such as on-line status inquiry and direct, microimage printing of journals and registers). While on-line transaction processing will not be stressed, on-line status inquiries from branches to the data centers are expected to be added to improve service to customers on a statewide basis.

Greater use of currently available computerized information for the purposes of management control and improving operational decisions is a priority for the immediate future. Additional operations research projects are also planned for new credit-scoring areas, and development of market forecasting models for specific activities. Other work includes analyzing current management information subsystems. However, B of A does not believe, as vice-president Thomas Taggert put it, that the time has come "when a huge mathematical model residing in a computer" can provide management "with the optimum plan of the day."

On the whole, EDP specialists at B of A are (and have been for the past decade) dissenters from the visions that some bankers and computer experts have painted of a move into the "checkless and cashless" society. B of A spokesmen have been impressed with the fundamental difficulties of such a plan—developing a unique identifier; achieving cooperation among all the necessary banks and sales establishments; finding the enormous sums of money needed for systems-building; winning acceptance among the public, especially where "direct transfer" of funds from one account to another might mean that the customer loses control over when to pay due bills; and overcoming public fears about possible invasion of privacy through the creation of centralized personal transaction files. As a result, B of A looks forward in the 1970s to

more modest improvements with electronic transfer of funds[6] and
expanded electronic authorization of credit-card purchases as the
likely trends.[7]

Commercial Reporting Agencies

Each week, millions of decisions about individuals are made by
business enterprises as they grant someone retail credit, hire a new
employee or executive, accept a new insurance policyholder, or
approve a loan. Some uncertainty is involved in each of these
decisions, and the skill of the personnel director, loan officer, or
other evaluator lies in his ability to judge what qualities make an
individual a "good" or "bad" risk.

The degree of uncertainty differs from one type of decision
to another, but even though the actuarial studies of the life-
insurance underwriter may enable him to select new policyholders
with greater confidence than the personnel director has in selecting a new employee, the central ingredient sought after in each of
these situations is accurate and complete information about the
individual being evaluated.

The most frequently used source of information for such
decisions is the individual himself, who completes an application
containing relevant details of personal health, credit, or educational history and authorizes the business organization to verify the
truth of his statements. Verification of educational and employment records, current salary, etc., may be carried out by members
of the organization's own staff. They consult their own past
records on the individual, and contact sources of record information directly. Sometimes these sources of information will include
industry-run file systems, such as lists of persons who have already

---

[6] B of A vice-president Russell Fenwick is chairman of the Special
Committee on Paperless Entries (SCOPE) run by the San Francisco and Los
Angeles Clearing House Associations. This is an experiment in "preauthorized
'paperless' entries," to test the feasibility of a payments system through
computer and communications technology.

[7] National BankAmericard is currently participating in a pilot test of a
"less-cash" system arranged with IBM by City National Bank of Columbus,
Ohio; this uses on-line terminals in local retail outlets to authorize and
register purchases by participating BankAmericard customers. The charges are
made directly into their accounts, replacing the present "mail-in" system for
charge slips.

been turned down for life insurance, or who have filed false insurance claims. During the past 75 years, however, a large number of specialized firms have grown up to offer what has come to be called "commercial reporting" services. Banks, retail merchants, employers, and insurance companies purchase the information they need for business decisions from these private firms, instead of gathering it themselves.

The two main types of commercial reporting agencies are credit bureaus, which deal primarily in information for retail purchase and loan decisions, and companies doing preemployment and preinsurance investigations. Over the past century, credit bureaus have grown into a network of several thousand local agencies, each collecting and maintaining files of information about residents in its own area, and most exchanging reports through a trade association known as the Associated Credit Bureaus of America, Inc. The manager of one such agency, the Credit Bureau of Greater New York, has noted the range of information in his files: "information on age, marital status, dependencies, residential history, occupation, financial resources, bank references, manner of payment of accounts, loans and other credit extensions in the trade and lending institutions, and litigation history, if any." The sources of this information include "property records, landlords, employers, banks, credit references, court records, newspapers, trade periodicals, bulletins from protective agencies which handle frauds, and any other authentic source available."[8]

Though some credit bureaus also do preemployment and preinsurance investigations, the great bulk of such reports are done by a few major national firms. The largest of these, Retail Credit Company of Atlanta, Georgia, has over 300 branch offices, more than 7,000 employees, 45 million files on individuals and businesses, and produces more than 35 million reports annually. Other firms active in the field are Hooper-Holmes of New Jersey, Dun and Bradstreet's, and Fidelifacts (a national group of local investigation firms run by former FBI agents). Preemployment reports done by these firms are more detailed than credit reports in that they usually cover the character, reputation, and morals of prospective employees. A similarly "deeper" inquiry goes into reports done for insurance companies in the life, automobile, property, and health and accident fields.

---

[8] See *Report of the Subcommittee on Right of Privacy*, Senate Judiciary Committee, State of New York, May 2, 1969, pp. 9-17.

Most commercial reporting agencies make their profits entirely from selling information from their files; thus they have a marketing job of their own to do. Having compiled detailed records, they have to convince potential commercial customers that information from their files will be useful in resolving some of the uncertainty in business decisions.

Computerization did not move into the preinsurance and preemployment reporting firms in the 1960s. However, it did enter the credit bureau industry. Several local credit bureaus computerized their operations in the 1960s, and a newly formed firm, Credit Data Corporation, initiated first a regional and then a national computerized credit-reporting service in the mid-1960s. These developments took place alongside a growing concern from congressional spokesmen, consumer and civil-liberties groups, and the mass media over the way in which commercial reporting agencies were exercising their investigative power over the lives of 110 million consumers and some 50 million employees and executives.

Of the two credit bureaus and one preinsurance and preemployment reporting agency visited by our project, we have selected Credit Data Corporation for our next profile.

TRW-CREDIT DATA CORPORATION

Credit Data Corporation is a computer-based credit-reporting agency. It maintains more than 30 million records on individuals, has over 7,000 subscribers, and produced some 12 million credit reports in 1970. From centralized, on-line computer facilities in Anaheim, California, it services eight large metropolitan areas throughout the United States, with the files of one region accessible to all others. In contrast to the other organizations described in these profiles, Credit Data is an organization that was conceived, built, and operated wholly within a computerized environment, rather than moving into computerization after years of operation with manual files.

The Development of Credit Data

In a nation in which almost 2,000 relatively small credit bureaus serve local regions, Credit Data stands out as a firm which never was local in orientation. Its founder, Dr. Harry C. Jordan, a biophysicist, inherited a Detroit credit bureau from his family in the 1950s. Jordan was familiar with developments in the computer field and saw the possibility that computerized record systems might revolutionize the credit-reporting industry.

In 1960, he approached a number of major California credit grantors (mainly banks) with a plan for supplying reports specially suited to their credit-information needs. For some years, credit checking had been handled through a nonprofit, cooperative arrangement among the banks themselves. As the volume of loan transactions mounted and the banks found that they were becoming de facto credit bureaus, this system had become increasingly unsatisfactory.

Jordan proposed to create a computerized credit bureau which would supply up-to-date, reliable information of the type that credit grantors needed. When he convinced a number of the major banks in California to go along with his plan, and supply some of the financial backing,[9] Credit Data Corporation was born.

In 1965, Credit Data began operations on batch-processing computing equipment, serving 15 banks in the Greater Los Angeles area, with a satellite facility set up later to handle the San Francisco area. A similar computer facility was established in New York City, and arrangements were made so that the Buffalo, Syracuse, Chicago, and Detroit areas could be served from the two coastal centers.

As a first step in developing the company's computer files, selected records from each subscriber were microfilmed. Certain information was then taken from these microfilm records and entered into computer storage. The content of the developing computerized files was determined as Jordan exchanged ideas with a committee of subscribers which had been established for this purpose. Jordan's concept was that credit reporting should supply a credit *history* containing both positive and negative items of *objective* information on each individual. Evaluative notations such as "slow payer" should be eliminated. The credit grantor, he felt, should make the decision itself, by examining the individual's record of recent credit transactions. The principal sources of credit information in this new system were to be the files of fellow subscribers, with some additional data from the civil courts.

The banks and some of the retailers shared much of Jordan's thinking. They had traditionally required higher levels of accuracy

---

[9] Principal among these was the Bank of America.

and favored getting more objective reports than the retail firms and stores using local credit bureaus.

Credit Data files soon came to contain information on more than 30 different types of accounts, from bank auto loans to credit-card, department store, and mail-order charge accounts. Information on the status of these individual accounts included some positive items, such as "open account" or "closed account, paid satisfactorily"; historical descriptions, such as "account was delinquent 90 days, now current"; and more than 20 categories of negative reports, such as "credit not granted due to misstatement on application" and "account delinquent 30 days."

Credit Data and the Invasion-of-privacy Debate

Credit Data's development took place during a period of growing public concern about privacy and due-process issues in credit reporting. From 1965 through 1970, hearings were held on credit bureau practices before no less than three federal and five state legislative committees. The basic questions raised at these hearings were: What personnel information should credit reports contain? How accurate is the information reported by these commercial agencies? How complete are the derogatory entries in the files? What procedures are available for handling items of information which involve disputes between businesses and the consumer? And what precautions have been taken to prevent unauthorized access to credit bureau files?

As the issues surrounding credit reporting unfolded, journalists and congressmen took up Credit Data's promotional literature (which emphasized computer-to-computer links across the country and "instant response" to inquiries), and portrayed Credit Data as a prime example of the computerized databank of personal information growing up unchecked across the land. Whatever the critics' expectations when confronted with a firm having computerized files on 20 million persons, they were soon surprised to find Credit Data itself critical of credit-reporting practices and claiming to have better privacy protections in its computer files than existed in the manual files of other firms.

In testimony before Congressman Cornelius Gallagher's Subcommittee on Invasion of Privacy, which held the first congressional hearing into commercial credit bureaus in 1968, Jordan pointed out that Credit Data's subscriber committee had issued a Code of Ethics in 1962. long before the privacy implications of credit bureau operations had received national attention. In the code, they set forth what they saw as "undesirable practices" on the part of credit-reporting agencies, such as that of supplying credit ratings rather than "objective" credit experience information; putting "hearsay" information into the files; storing "outdated" information; supplying mailing lists derived from the credit-reporting files; and cooperating without question with law-enforcement agencies. Many of the activities criticized by Credit Data executives were found by Congress to be standard practice in other credit and insurance-reporting firms.

Throughout his testimony, Jordan suggested that the computer was less important than the rules set up for its use. He stated his belief that the computer "introduces more opportunity for control than it does for hazard," and that Credit Data's computerized files were easier to correct and keep up to date. He also stated that his firm was committed to the principle that the individual should be allowed to know what is in his file, and to correct any inaccuracies. At the close of the hearings in 1968, Credit Data was the object of guarded compliments from committee members.

By 1969, when Credit Data officials testified in support of the Fair Credit Reporting Act,[1] congressional response to the Credit Data philosophy was decidedly positive. Thanking Jordan for his cooperation in Senate subcommittee hearings, Sen. William Proxmire remarked that "your firm is an excellent example to the rest of the industry." (The "rest of the industry" pointed out that Credit Data could afford to take its position because it did not service the merchants who wanted more detailed information, and who often preferred having evaluative reporting from the credit bureau.)

In 1968, Credit Data Corporation was bought by TRW, Inc., a corporate conglomerate based in Cleveland, with strong aerospace and high-technology interests. TRW supplied funds for expansion of Credit Data operations, and the firm became known as TRW-Credit Data.

Current Credit Files

Credit Data's files contain more than 30 million records in 1972. It is difficult to know how many individuals are represented here, however, since the updating process results in some duplication. Making a "rough guess," a Credit Data executive said that records

---

[1] Some of the provisions of this new law were discussed in the Bank of America profile, pp. 127-129 above.

are maintained on about 25 million individuals. Disk units in the Anaheim computer facility store these records, and the processing is accomplished with two IBM 360/50 computers.

The financial histories which are Credit Data's stock in trade are compiled from information submitted by subscribers, and from some public record sources. From the courts come information on suits, judgments, bankruptcies, and other actions.

The accuracy of data in Credit Data's files hinges on four factors: how current the information is; the extent to which the source records from their subscribers are accurate; the amount of error which occurs in the process of transferring data from subscribers' files to TRW-Credit Data's files; and the success with which they are able to match an individual's identifiers with information about that individual.

As a matter of operating philosophy and under constant pressure from its subscribers, Credit Data attempts to keep its files up to date and accurate. Subscribers are required to update the information in Credit Data files as soon as they can (normally every 30 days at the minimum). Credit Data management maintains that subscribers would rather have no information at all from a given subscriber than to have old account information on file. Thus, there was general support for the expulsion of a few subscribers who could not make timely update reports. "Though we have many smaller subscribers," a Credit Data executive said, "we're really geared to the mass operator, not the local dress shop. If a subscriber can't keep up from manual records, for instance, we don't want anything from him." Seventy-five percent of their update comes in on magnetic tapes supplied by subscribers, and the update process for this data takes between five and ten days. Up to a month is required for extraction and coding of data which is received in manual form.

Current Services Provided

The process of credit reporting begins with an inquiry from a subscriber. One-third of these come in via teletype; others are received by phone and mail. The subscriber provides identifying information, on the basis of which a search of the computer files is made. This is by no means a simple process. Lack of low-cost storage had forced Credit Data to be highly selective in what information it gathers, and to abbreviate what it does store. Under the Credit Data retrieval system (as in many others) it is often difficult to make a match that is certain, even though Social

Security number and zip code have recently been added as identifiers.

In an attempt to prevent misuse of the credit report (as when an individual might be hurt by negative information mismatched with his name), all reports are issued with a warning: "It is possible that all of the above information may not pertain to the individual inquired upon." Each item of information on the report is assigned a "hit level," a code which indicates the nature and size of any discrepancies which exist between the identifiers supplied by the inquiring subscriber and those attached to that item in the computer file. For instance, if the name and address submitted on the inquiry form or over the phone matched a name and address in the file, but a different Social Security number were listed for that person, a number code would indicate this discrepancy. The extent to which such warnings are heeded varies considerably from subscriber to subscriber.

Credit information is reported over the telephone as a set of numerical codes. Via teletype and the mails, forms go out containing abbreviated statements which describe the status of each account which has been reported to Credit Data by participating institutions. Each form has a column for "negative" codes, another for "positive" codes, and a third for "nonevaluative" codes. This preliminary classification, a Credit Data official suggests, makes it easy for subscribers to "eyeball" the reports and separate out those which will require more attention.

For a smaller number of subscribers, Credit Data does several types of special reports. Accounts can be monitored continuously, for instance, so that a subscriber will be notified immediately if derogatory information is entered on an account they are concerned about.

The Fair Credit Reporting Act

The code of ethics which Credit Data and its subscribers set forth in 1968 included a provision permitting an individual access to his own record for challenge and correction. Consumer requests for such service amounted to approximately one-half of one percent of the total inquiries processed through April 1970 (about 350 such cases per month in its New York office, for instance).

In April of 1971 the federal Fair Credit Reporting Act went into effect. Credit Data executives were convinced that it would "create a landslide" of consumer requests for information when the act took effect nationally. In the New York City area, banks alone refuse almost 35,000 credit applications a month, and it was expected that the counseling load would mount as credit grantors told people that they were being turned down on the basis of a credit report.

To prepare for this increased demand, consumer counseling facilities in all Credit Data locations were significantly expanded, and new forms, instructions, and counseling literature were prepared. In the first month after the act took effect, consumer interviews quadrupled in number. The New York office, which had more than tripled its counseling staff since 1970, was swamped as phone lines and counseling offices were confronted with 200 consumer contacts a day. By December 1971, complaints had leveled off at seven-tenths of one percent of their total inquiries nationally, up only two-tenths of one percent from 1970. This amounted to approximately 8,000 inquiries per month.

A large proportion of the complaints they receive concern instances in which Credit Data reported a court action but no record of the disposition was available from the courts; this leaves the individual's record marred by the existence of a pending action. In the New York office a consumer counselor pointed out that "one of our greatest difficulties is in explaining to people that lawyers aren't always responsible, that the lawyer in a case often doesn't bother to file the court papers indicating that the case has been settled or dropped; and thus no conclusion is noted on the official record."

Disputed items are corrected, deleted, or where credit grantor and consumer disagree about the accuracy of the report, the consumer is allowed to place a short statement on file. When a report is drawn in such a case, the presence of an explanatory statement is automatically noted in reports. A code says "disputed account, contact local TRW office," but its text is not sent or read on the telephone unless the subscriber asks for it. The new Credit Data form also provides space for "disputed item" codes such as "merchandise not delivered" and "merchandise not usable." In keeping with its own long-standing policy as to when charges will be levied, consumers are not charged for counseling if the inquiry resulted from being denied credit or having had the terms of credit increased. Consumers whose inquiries are not connected with a specific credit application are charged $4.00.

To cover itself under provisions of the law that distinguish between credit reports and "*investigative* consumer reports," Credit Data instructs its subscribers that its reports are not to be used for preemployment or preinsurance screening. While Credit Data executives express confidence in the new law, they estimate that consumer counseling will cost the firm almost $500,000 annually, (about 5 percent of sales). They assume that the increased costs that will result from use of the act "will be passed on to the subscribers and, ultimately, to the consumer." Cost considerations may also lead "to removal of some perfectly valid information from the files." Where public record items are challenged, for instance, "the cost of checking them out may force us to just delete them without question instead."

Security and Confidentiality

Credit Data executives believe that the computer has improved the security of records in their files. Their operators and subscribers must "identify themselves to the computer by number" before they can get information from the files or make changes in a record. Credit Data executives have long said that this and other technological precautions make it much harder for persons to obtain unauthorized access in their system than in a manual credit-bureau operation.

Two cases of unauthorized access to the files were reported to us. One involved a former employee who was obtaining credit reports through using the identification number of a legitimate subscriber. When this was discovered, they changed the unique identification number which had been assigned, thus cutting him off from access.

In the other case, an employee tried to change his own record in the files. He was discovered when a keypunch operator noticed his name and wondered why an employee was submitting forms for changing his own record. He was fired.

Government Inquiries into Credit Data Files

In 1967, Credit Data refused a request by an agent from the Intelligence Unit of Internal Revenue Service to see the record of a New York couple. The district commissioner of IRS issued a summons to Credit Data demanding that it provide this information, but the president of Credit Data continued to refuse compliance at a conference on the summons before an IRS special agent. A hearing was then held before U.S. District Judge Sylvester Ryan, at which Credit Data argued that the "request for this information was part of a plan by the IRS to use Credit Data Corporation as a vast private databank for its own investigatory purposes . . . IRS does not dispute that it was preparing to serve 180 summonses on Credit Data Corporation requiring information on 180 different individuals." Credit Data called this an unreasonable search and seizure and raised the issue of privacy invasion as well.

The district court ruled against Credit Data, and this was affirmed on appeal by the federal circuit court.[2] In that case, Judge Lumbard declared that "The government has the right to require the production of relevant information wherever it may be lodged and regardless of the form in which it is kept and the manner in which it may be retrieved, so long as it pays its reasonable share of the costs of retrieval."

Passage of the FCRA partly covers this issue by providing that credit reporting agencies "may" allow government agents to obtain *identifying* information from their files. TRW-Credit Data considers the provision of credit information to government agencies a violation of the agreements under which the information is obtained. In a more practical vein, a Credit Data spokesman said that "requests from government agents are a nuisance. You have to take time to explain the reports to them; and, once you become a known source, they are on your back all the time."

The company's stated policy on this matter appears in a pamphlet entitled *You and the Fair Credit Reporting Act:*

> A governmental agency may obtain a report if it is considering you for a license or other benefit and is required by law to determine your financial responsibility or status. Any other information given to a governmental agency will be limited to name, address, and employment history, unless it is in accordance with the consumer's written instructions, or in response to an order of a court having jurisdiction to issue such an order.

Nationwide in 1971, the company estimates, not more than ten inquiries have been received from IRS and other law-enforcement agencies.

The Future

Aside from its efforts to further refine services as new needs are suggested by subscribers, no major changes in files or reports are contemplated for the near future.

However, Credit Data executives do not rule out important

[2] *U.S.* v. *Davey*, 426 F. 2d 842 (2d Cir. 1970).

changes over the long run, as the firm, its development phase over, operates as a profitable part of TRW's Data Systems and Services Divisions. Its parent division within TRW is heavily involved in innovative EDP developments, such as the development of point-of-sale credit-checking devices. While Credit Data executives fully expect to maintain their firm's identity, future expansion and uses of its huge credit files will depend heavily on TRW decisions as to marketing possibilities, cost considerations, and the social and legal "environment" for consumer reporting agencies of the future.

Insurance Companies

Five out of six American families are covered by life insurance. Liability insurance is written on more than 85 percent of the automobiles on the road. Over 90 percent of the homes in the nation are covered by fire insurance. And about 80 percent of the national population under 65 is covered under some form of private health insurance.

These policies represent billions of dollars in insurance coverage, supplied by over 3,000 insurance companies in the United States. Some handle only one "line"—life, health, accident, property, or personal liability; but many companies offer several lines or are part of a holding company which contains firms handling other lines. Most parts of the industry are characterized by great concentration, with a small number of firms holding a large percentage of the assets in any line. Of the 1,820 life-insurance companies, for example, the top 50 have more than 80 percent of the assets.

The basic principle of insurance is that a person pays a premium against the risk that some harm will actually take place, in which case he will be compensated in an amount or on a basis specified in the contract. The insurance company bases its premium charges on estimates of the likelihood that the insured risk will take place, when the event will take place, and the amount of the total payments likely. The process of accepting applicants for insurance involves disclosure of personal information from the individual and verification of that information by the company or someone hired to do this. In life insurance, for example, the individual often must supply personal history, medical history, personal habits, and employment information. For automobile insurance, companies require information on driving and accident history, personal and family information, and relevant habits, such as drinking. Several commercial reporting agencies are used by insurance companies in these lines to provide verification of the statements made on the individual's application form, and to supply information on matters of personal stability and morals that the companies consider critical to the application decision.

There are also intra-industry pools of information that are used for checking on applicants. These include the Medical Information Bureau (which contains medical information on persons already turned down for life insurance in previous applications to any of a large number of companies) and the Claims Index System (which has records of previous property and accident claims for individuals with any of the over 800 property and accident companies participating in the Index).

Generally, the information collected by life-insurance companies is used once, for the contract decision, but is not used again until a death benefit claim is filed. In the auto, health, accident, and property fields, however, policy coverage records and claims histories must be consulted whenever a claim is made by the policyholder.

Because of the enormous paperwork involved in the issuance of policies, collection of continuous premiums, and investigation and payment of claims and benefits, the insurance industry moved heavily into computerization in the 1950s, and has been one of the major users of computers ever since. More than 2,600 computers were in use in the insurance industry in 1970. Of the various insurance lines, the company we chose to profile is in the health field, though our project also visited a major life-insurance company and a conglomerate firm with all major insurance lines within its shelter.

Health expenses for the average American family have been rising dramatically in the past few decades, with the cost of an average hospital stay increasing two and a half times in the last ten years alone. To protect themselves against financial disaster, most American families pay for coverage from Blue Cross and Blue Shield plans, independent health-insurance plans, or private insurance companies.

One of the leaders in the health insurance field is the company treated in our next profile, Mutual of Omaha.

MUTUAL OF OMAHA

Among the largest and best known of the commercial health insurers in the United States is Mutual of Omaha, described in its advertising as "The people who pay. . . ." From its inception in 1909, Mutual has grown along with the health industry as a whole, and has become "the largest provider of individual and family health insurance in the world." It offers policies covering hospital and surgical payments; extra hospital expenses; the occurrence of specified diseases such as cancer; income protection for periods of illness or hospitalization; and a variety of supplemental plans designed to go into effect when others (such as Medicare or Blue Cross policies) stop paying.

Much of Mutual's growth has occurred over the past 20 years, during which its assets increased to over $568 million. The company is licensed in all 50 states, the District of Columbia, all provinces of Canada, Great Britain, Puerto Rico, Panama, the Canal Zone, and portions of the West Indies. Seven subsidiary companies also provide a wide range of other financial services such as life insurance and mutual funds.

Manual Insurance Records

As in other insurance firms, Mutual's underwriting and benefit-paying activities put it into the business of gathering information about policyowners from a variety of sources. Directly, or through its sales representatives, the company receives applications for insurance from individuals seeking a contract with the company; these represent one of the most important sources of information about the prospective customer. While applications differ from policy to policy, most require information about the physical, emotional, and occupational history of the individual. This may include the nature of an individual's work and duties, a history of injuries and medical treatments, and a listing of diseases ranging from high blood pressure and arthritis to cancer, syphilis, epilepsy and mental disorders. Some applications also include the question, "Are you and your dependents' morals and habits correct and temperate?" Mutual officials realize that it is unlikely that an individual would answer "no" to this question; it is put there essentially as a way of suggesting to the applicant that morals and habits will be considered. "Unless information from some other source should indicate some very gross departure from the accepted moral standards," a Mutual official notes, "the underwriting would not be affected by the written response to this question."

In processing the application, Mutual checks a number of sources of information, such as its own files on past applicants and current policyowners. Within the industry, a central file is maintained on individuals who have submitted false accident or health claims. "This reporting service operates more or less like an alarm system, periodically circulating special alert bulletins containing the names, addresses and other identifying information about those who have been reported by an insurance company as involved in fraud activity." Mutual suggests that this source is not used as a routine matter; only where conflicting or what appears to be false information on an application leads Mutual underwriters to be suspicious is a check of this source of information made.

As part of the application, the prospective customer lists doctors and hospitals from whom he has received treatment, and gives Mutual authorization to inquire into these sources; this is done by signing a statement such as "physician who has heretofore attended me or any listed dependent is authorized to give the Company such information thereby acquired as may be lawful." If important health history items are listed on the application, the salesman may check further with the physician or hospital, using the authorization which the applicant has provided. A Mutual official estimates that the company maintains health records on approximately 8.5 million individuals.

Finally, Mutual makes use of insurance "inspection" reports obtained either from its own inspection department or from commercial firms such as Retail Credit. "These are fairly minimum checks; we get something on general character—through reputation elicited from neighbors and references listed on the application—and we confirm things like employment, length of residence, and neighborhood environment." "Inspections are completed for only about 10 percent of our applications," Mutual official James Barrett says, "somewhere in the neighborhood of 60,000 inspections a year." About 35 percent of these are completed in-house by Mutual's own inspection department. "In almost all cases," Barrett says, "we call for an inspection because an application is incomplete or otherwise suspicious or because the policy applied for is a large one—for instance, to cover more than $300 per month in loss-of-time income." Hospital-insurance applications are rarely inspected, he said.

While there are rejections made, Mutual approves the great majority (at least 95 percent) of the over 600,000 insurance applications submitted annually to it by individuals. Mutual notes that policies are turned down for many reasons, but that by far the most common among these is health history. Working from actuarial studies which take into account age, sex, health history, geographical area, and other factors, decisions are made as to how great a risk the company is taking in approving the application of a given individual. Asked about the matter of homosexuality, a selection factor about which some protests have been raised *vis à vis* the life-insurance industry, a Mutual official said, "it doesn't come up and we don't look for it; and even if it did come up we wouldn't use it unless there were accompanying information with some real health implications. You have to realize that we want to sell insurance and that most of our policy applications go through without a hitch." A Mutual official further pointed out that race is not a factor in their underwriting. "Sometimes geographical factors come up," he said, "for instance, in parts of some cities where the health and hospital facilities and environment may be very bad. But race by itself just isn't a good criterion for accepting or rejecting an application." All applications are retained in Mutual files for approximately five years for future reference. Where an application has been rejected because it is incomplete, Mutual hopes that the individual will simply reapply. After a policy has been approved, a copy of the application is sent to the policyholder. He returns it indicating that he has looked it over once again and that the information in it is true.

The processing of benefits requests represents another occasion when information is gathered on policyowners. This involves communication of medical information to the firm—from simple diagnosis (where a policy pays as soon as a disease condition is discovered, for instance) to more detailed descriptions of medical procedures. Where investigations are made, Mutual officials say, they tend to be more detailed than the inspections completed in connection with underwriting since the control of fraud has to be among the company's concerns. When benefit claims are approved, payments go to policyowners or, if directed by the insured, directly to physicians and medical facilities for services rendered.

Computerization Comes to Mutual

Mutual's move to computers in the mid-1950s was by no means its first experience with business machines; the firm signed its first contract with IBM in 1927. This early step involved the use of a punched-card system to supplement the manual files then in use.

But even though the card system grew in extent and sophistication, Mutual's rapid growth after World War II severely taxed its home-office record-keeping facilities. For the years 1948-54, the company handled a yearly average of $5.1 million in new policy applications and $5.9 million in benefit claims.

In 1954, a committee from Mutual of Omaha and its life-insurance affiliate, United of Omaha, began to investigate the possibility of adapting computers to their record-keeping operations. At the time, there were very few insurance firms doing so, and it was not at all clear that the equipment available would be worth the investment. The following year, the committee made its decision that computerization would result in reduced operating costs for the company, laying the groundwork for expansion. A plan was then drawn up to automate some of the firm's most routine and costly high-volume tasks. At every step in the planning process, Mutual officials recall, cost-effectiveness was the key criterion. Mutual officials point to an industry study as evidence for the company's success in keeping costs down: its expenses of operation have been less than the combined average of the next 24 companies in its field.[3]

Mutual's first computer was delivered in 1957; "We just grew from that," James J. Kohanek, vice president for computer systems and programming, said. "Now we do everything but cut the lawn with those computers." Developing their computer applications steadily over the past 15 years, Mutual has become one of the largest computer users in the insurance industry.

At the heart of Mutual's record-keeping operations is its Consolidated Policy Accounting System (CPAS), covering its regular lines of individual policies and handling some $20 million in premium payments each month. This is a batch-processed file containing detailed records for each policy in force, including identifying information, premium payments, benefit information, etc.

In some of its advertising, Mutual prides itself on the speed with which policyowners get action on their benefits requests. The Mutual benefits file is maintained on-line and is linked with 35 of the firm's largest offices via a teleprocessing system. At the close of each business day, each of these offices "interacts" with the computer center automatically so that new benefits requests can be entered and adjustments can be made on those already on file.

---

[3] Standard Analytical Services, Inc., *1972 Independent Comparative Report.*

After a policyowner has contacted a local Mutual agent concerning a benefit claim, the agent can usually be supplied on an overnight basis with the account information he needs to begin processing the claim. The system handles 70,000 requests each month. Totally, the company issues nearly 9,000 benefit checks each weekday. On any given day, approximately 900,000 active benefit records are on tape, containing skeleton histories of the benefits granted under the policy, benefit details, and coded references to types of disability involved.

Early in its work, Mutual discovered that benefit histories were an important information resource for constructing new policies for health insurance and for considering new applications from individuals already covered under another Mutual policy. As a result the benefit histories of more than 5 million policyowners are stored on tape. Each contains a record of items such as diagnosis, benefits paid, and actions taken on the policy. Like the underwriting and current-benefits subsystems, benefits histories are available on an overnight basis to more than 30 remote terminals in the Mutual system.

In addition to active individual policies, the computer also handles the processing of benefits for its group-insurance programs, keeps some employee and agent records, and produces a variety of management reports.

Mutual also handles Medicare claims for several areas of the U.S., and does claims work for the government health-care program established for dependents of servicemen (CHAMPUS). For its Medicare work, it receives information on tape from the Social Security Administration computer system to determine the eligibility of claimants. By law and contract, this information cannot be used for any other purpose.

Mutual's computer system did not replace all other record-keeping, and manual files continue to play an important role in company decision making about people. Much of the sensitive information obtained in the course of underwriting and benefits investigations, for instance, is never entered into computer storage at all.

Those who helped develop the Mutual system do not think that computerization has increased the amount of information collected on each policyowner. Mr. Kohanek indicated further that the accuracy of record information in the files had been improved as a result of computerization. During the conversion process, he said, "we found mistakes, made corrections, and improved our overall accuracy as a result. In the precomputer system, many accuracy checks were not possible. With the computer system, some of these checks are now made automatically." "Even simple matters like illegible handwriting," are no longer as great a problem, since there is much less transfer of information from the files by hand to working forms."

Record Confidentiality

Within the health-insurance industry, there are some arrangements for information sharing. The protection of sensitive medical information which comes into Mutual's possession is solely its responsibility, since any legal protections which might pertain while the files are in the doctor's office or the hospital no longer apply once the information is passed on. Stating company policy, a Mutual official said, "We protect such information because of the highest regard for the privacy of the individual and the protection of the privileged information received from the physician or hospital." Emphasizing the confidentiality aspects of their operations, Kohanek said, "We have to protect our files; we'd lose our policyowners if we became lax on this."

Information on policyowners is shared within the industry, both when one firm makes ad hoc inquiries of another and through the industrywide pools, to which instances of insurance claim fraud are regularly reported. In cases where fraudulent claims for benefits have been detected, Mutual of Omaha forwards information on the policyowner and the general nature of the fraudulent activity to the industrywide file maintained specifically for this purpose. Company underwriters make the decision to forward an individual's name to this file when they feel that "they have sufficient reasonable grounds from inspecting company records."

Mutual's senior executive vice-president A. M. Hansen said that for other instances of sharing the company's rule is clear: "Information is released only upon authorization by the policyowner, upon court order, or where such is required by state or federal law." On occasion, law-enforcement officials (e.g., FBI agents with fugitive warrants) are given name and address information. "No medical or benefits information is released," according to Mutual officials, and rarely do law-enforcement officials ask for it. "FBI agents come around perhaps three or four times a month," said Mutual official James Barrett. "Usually what they want is location information or they are interested in the flight insurance area—for sabotage cases and for tracing the interstate movement of criminals."

Another reason for controlling disclosures, the company says, is to protect the company's sources of information. An internal memo to managers, first issued in 1965 and reissued most recently in 1970, stressed employee responsibility for "safeguarding confidential information":

> Each of us shares a responsibility to safeguard confidential information acquired during the course of the underwriting process. The seriousness of this responsibility cannot be overstated and a reminder from time to time is helpful, especially to our newer associates.
>
> If confidential information were to become available to an unauthorized person, however inadvertently, the consequences are obvious. Of course we would be embarrassed. . . . but any instance would have the potential of developing into more than embarrassment.
>
> It is extremely important to you, your agency force, your clients, and the Company, that we continue to merit the respect, confidence, and continued cooperation of our sources of information. Won't you please remind your office and sales staffs that. . .
>
> 1. The four-digit reason codes used on rejected applications and in correspondence are not to be discussed *with anyone.*
> 2. Confidential information which comes into your possession is *never to be released in written form outside your office.*
> 3. Confidential information is *never to be released in any form or discussed with anyone except authorized Company personnel*—authorized Company personnel being those persons to whom the information is essential in arriving at a decision which is properly their responsibility.
>
> Particularly such information is never to be discussed with the applicant/insured or the physician. Inquiries should be directed to the Home Office underwriters.

Mutual executives believe that customer records are indirectly protected by the accounting controls and physical security measures which have been taken—the former because of the huge sums of money involved in incoming premium payments and outgoing benefit checks. Kohanek suggested that the computer has resulted in greater management concern with physical security. A false bomb threat on Halloween night in 1969 prompted a reevaluation of security provisions, the placing of a former Treasury agent in charge of general security, and the design of new physical security arrangements for the computer facility. Protection of files from unauthorized access was part of the Mutual approach from the earliest computerization. Still another indirect protection is the fact that, to avoid having the data-processing center overloaded with ad hoc jobs, requests for information not covered by existing rules must be in writing and approved personally by Kohanek. The move to computers reduced the number of people handling and duplicating files as information flowed through the systems, and Mutual officials also see in this a general decrease in opportunities for unauthorized access.

Federal Demands

While the computer has made information from the files available more quickly to field offices (turnaround time on the payment of benefits was reduced from seven to ten days to 24 hours), Mutual officials indicate that this has not affected the confidentiality of the file. The increased processing speed serves the customer, they say, rather than endangering him in any way.

Both Kohanek and Hansen agreed that computerization had led to some greater demand for both identified and statistical data. Referring to new requirements on reporting payments to physicians of over $600, and recent federal demands for statistical information, Kohanek said that "the only reason we're asked to do it is because it *can* be done now by computers." Before computerization it would not have been practical to retrieve the requested data without incurring prohibitive costs; today the government knows that the data are more readily available at less cost than under a manual system.

To date, Mutual has used its own identifying number system for individual accounts in its files; this, they feel, is an additional security precaution against unauthorized penetration of the records. However, with increasing requirements for reporting by Social Security numbers (e.g., as in the case of reporting payments to physicians), the firm feels compelled to give "very serious consideration to using Social Security numbers as the identifiers." Kohanek said that the firm definitely does not want to adopt this system because it would "greatly increase the problem of confidentiality." But, he added, if they are required to use it more and more often, it just might make sense to switch to it.

Federal Constraints

The Fair Credit Reporting Act (which went into effect in April 1971) set extensive new regulations for certain operations by banks, insurance companies, and a wide variety of commercial information suppliers. Insurance companies must now notify applicants that they may investigate or verify items of personal information relating to the insurance decision. If insurance is denied on the basis of a commercial report, the individual must also be told of this and given the name of the company making the report, so that he may be told about and challenge its content.

Gene Retz, second vice-president for underwriting and renewal services, has been keeping track of customer inquiries and complaints under the new law; he said that the firm's offices have received very few inquiries, perhaps averaging five or six a week. "When we receive a call from a person whose application was rejected based on information received from a 'Consumer Reporting Agency,' we give them the name and address of the CRA. This gives the individual the opportunity to review the information and correct any inaccuracies. We haven't needed to correct any action yet on the basis of anything turned up in a customer inquiry, though we'd be glad to, if we found out that there had been some mistake." Retz said "that most people are pretty reasonable; they are willing to admit it when we explain how some information we have reflects badly on them."

"Many of the calls we've gotten," another Mutual official noted, "are the result of the notice people receive informing them that an inspection investigation will be completed. They want to know who we will ask, what the topics will be, and so forth. We certainly don't have any difficulty replying to any of these calls," he said.

Under the new law, if Mutual shared information from hospitals and physicians with other insurance companies without the policyholder's permission, it would be acting as a "Consumer Reporting Agency" and would be subject to several new requirements. Many insurance companies have changed their application forms as a result, so that blanket permission for such sharing is obtained. According to Don Langdon, an attorney in the Mutual general counsel's office, "We added a preinvestigation notice to our underwriting application and altered our authorization so as to include the policyowner's consent to obtain information from other insurers as well as doctors and hospitals."

The impact of the Fair Credit Reporting Act is also reflected in company policy on sharing even limited information from its files. For a number of years, Mutual, in common with many insurance firms, shared some information on its policyowners with Hooper-Holmes, one of the largest information suppliers to the insurance industry. By checking its files, companies can discover when and where a new applicant has been insured. Mutual supplied name, address, whether the policy was accident or health, and the birth year of the policyowner. But even with this limited sharing, Mutual officials were led by passage of the FCRA to reconsider their contract with Hooper-Holmes. While they saw little danger to policyowners in contributing to and using this source of information, they were concerned about what policyowners might think about this exchange. Mutual's contract with Hooper-Holmes was not renewed this year, and the company no longer shares information with them.

Under the law, inspections that are done "in-house" by the insurance company's own staff are not covered. As a result, the work that Mutual inspectors do for Mutual of Omaha does not come under the act. The firm also does some work for its subsidiaries, however, and the act is not clear as to whether this activity is exempt or not. "It is our position," said a Mutual official, "that what we do should satisfy the Federal Trade Commission requirements."

Mutual also believes that the public does not regard investigation of health, medical, and personal morals to be an invasion of privacy, when this is done for the purposes of deciding whether or not an insurance company will issue a policy or honor an insurance claim. This is a view widely held in the insurance industry, and members cite as support a national survey that the Retail Credit Company, the largest commercial reporting firm in the insurance inspection field, commissioned from Opinion Research Corporation, an independent commercial survey firm in Princeton, New Jersey.

Several questions about issues of privacy and commercial reporting inquiries were included in a larger list of questions that Opinion Research Corporation asked in interviews of a sample of 2,034 men and women over 18 years of age. On life-insurance investigations, they were asked, "If a person applies for a life-insurance policy, do you agree or disagree that the life-insurance company has a right to investigate this person?" Three areas of investigation were then listed: "Personal habits and character"; "Health and medical history," and "Financial integrity, which includes such things as credit rating and the ability to pay premiums on time." The survey found the following:

On health and medical history, 92 percent supported the inquiries and 6 percent opposed them (2 percent had no opinion).

On financial integrity, 66 percent agreed that the company has a right to inquire and 31 percent were opposed (3 percent had no opinion).

On personal habits and character, 58 percent supported inquiries and 35 percent were opposed (4 percent had no opinion).

The director of Opinion Research Corporation concluded from these responses; "The 'need to know' appears to be a principle that people apply to the invasion of individual privacy. Where there is a clear-cut need for the information, most people will support the gathering of confidential data."[4]

A Mutual attorney pointed out about the FCRA that "Like any new law, there is a period of adjustment by the company and the governmental regulating agency. Many things are often unclear to both parties. Also, a new act is expensive. We have to communicate its provisions to several thousand associates in the field, revise forms and procedures, and devote a lot of staff time to it." However, Mutual officials still believe the FCRA is worthwhile where it actually protects the consumer against error or inaccuracy in commercial reports.

More worrisome to Mutual officials, however, is the increasing federal regulation which the FCRA represents. They are concerned that the FTC (which is charged with administrative enforcement of the act) will take advantage of its broad or vague language "to increase its own power." This outlook reflects Mutual's position on matters of "government interference" in business activities versus a "voluntary approach under our free enterprise system."

Future Plans for Mutual

Mutual's data-processing future includes plans to use optical scanning equipment for application and claims processing. They also expect to pursue greater integration of files. Traditionally, Mutual

---

[4] John S. Schafer, "Privacy and the Public," *Inspection News*, Retail Credit Company, Atlanta, Georgia (September-October 1971), p. 17. We look more closely at this poll in Appendix B.

has kept the files on its health, accident, and life-insurance lines of its subsidiary separate, and computerization has not changed this so far. Each policy line operates independently and management cannot take profits from one line and apply these to make up for losses in another. However, integration of its data bases would provide better management reporting and Kohanek sees the firm moving in that direction in the next few years. Plans for a central information file—containing name, address, and policy information abstracted from several other files—are currently under study.

Such a system might permit them, for instance, to merge information from their flight-insurance and health-insurance files (which are and would remain separate) for marketing purposes. At present, such a system appears to be economically unfeasible, said Kohanek, "but maybe new technology might do it."

The Mailing-List Industry

In 1970, American business firms spent almost $19 billion on advertising for goods and services. About $3 billion of this amount went into mailings sent directly to potential customers in their homes and offices. Facilitating this process are the more than 1,500 firms which make up what is known as the "direct-mail industry." Growing up over the past century "behind the scenes" of advertising and marketing, these companies compile, exchange, sell, or rent names on mailing lists, and handle various aspects of the mailing operation itself, from the design of brochures to the addressing and mailing of the final advertising product. Aided by the relatively low costs made possible through third-class mail privileges, and the availability of "zip code" addressing, business, civic, educational, and political organizations sent out over 2 billion pieces of advertising in 1969. The volume of direct-mail advertising is such that, even with "success rates" averaging 3-4 percent, the industry estimates that this form of advertising produced some $30 billion in sales in 1970.

From the standpoint of those selling goods or soliciting contributions, the key problem is how to direct their mail appeals so as to reach the greatest number of potentially favorable recipients and avoid wasting material on unlikely prospects. To gather the names, addresses, and other "advertising-relevant" information that represent their stock in trade, direct-mail firms go to a wide range of public and private sources. These include official records, telephone books, city directories, membership lists, news clippings, customer lists, lists of contest participants, door-to-door canvassing, and convention rosters. From government sources come lists of pilots (FAA), boat owners (Coast Guard), ham-radio operators (FCC), and veterans (VA). Lists have also blossomed as the names of prospects are purchased outright, as in the case of information from motor-vehicle registration files, American Express customer accounts, and the files of major book publishers. Other organizations "rent" names from their files, often using an intermediary who addresses the mail but does not give the advertiser a copy of the list.

While no survey has been published of computer use within the direct-mail industry, the major firms are heavily computerized. An industry commentator noted in 1967 that "almost every firm processing a large volume of direct-mail business operates his own computer hardware, uses outside service bureaus, or is frantically figuring out how to physically and financially accomplish the transition."[5] Computerized files are updated and lists are generated at considerably less cost than in the precomputer era. Much of the information transferred in the direct-mail business is now handled on magnetic tape, and firms are better able to merge information from one file with that from another.

Hoping to win customers through "personalized mail, advertisers have also used the computer to marshal a number of facts about each individual on a list, and insert them at appropriate points in a standard form letter. One software house[6] even markets a computer program with which organizations can identify the ethnic group to which each individual in their files belongs. The company advertises that "more than 95 percent of individuals with 'Spanish' surnames can be expected to be of Spanish or Mexican descent, 85 percent of the Jewish and Polish surnames will be valid, and 90 percent of the Oriental name list will be Japanese, Chinese, or some other Oriental descent."

Still another example of computer-facilitated list production is the "Quality Index" marketed by the R. H. Donnelley Company. The index represents, in the company's words, "the most complete name-address saturation mailing list in existence. In structure, it is an electronic coding of tens of millions of consumer names together with a number of socioeconomic characteristics of the census tracts in which these families live."

---

[5] *The Reporter of Direct Mail Advertising* (February 1967), p. 106.

[6] Rise, Inc., of Los Angeles, California.

For our profile in this area we have selected one of the largest and oldest business service firms in the country, R. L. Polk and Company, of Detroit, Michigan.

R. L. POLK AND COMPANY

R. L. Polk and Company, a national firm with headquarters in Detroit and revenues of more than $70 million in 1970, is a diversified business engaged in publishing, research, and direct-mail advertising activities. The company began operations in 1870 as a publisher of city directories and statewide gazeteers (business directories). In this pretelephone era, salesmen had neither white nor yellow pages through which to locate potential customers. Polk's founder began by compiling a business directory for Michigan, listing the names and addresses of shopkeepers within walking distance of railroad depots. City-resident directories followed, as a service primarily for door-to-door salesmen, and Polk continued to expand along with the information needs of companies selling directly to consumers.

Today, Polk has more than 8,000 employees in 55 office and production locations in the United States, Canada, England, and West Germany. Its major divisions publish annual city directories; compile statistics on auto, truck, and other vehicle sales from state registrations; maintain a census of currently registered cars and trucks with ownership information; publish a twice-yearly directory of information about banks, bank officials, and selected securities dealers; provide marketing research and promotional services for banks and the auto industry; offer a wide range of direct-mail advertising services for businesses or other organizations wanting to reach the consumer directly with written messages; and supply statistical information on urban area characteristics for use by business and government.

While some of these activities involve working with statistical or property data, the collection, compiling, and use of individual names and selected characteristics represent the largest part of the Polk operation. In its promotional brochures, Polk describes itself as a supplier of information to American commerce with "a little information on each of millions and millions and millions of people." For its city directories, Polk notes that it has "recorded more than 263 million names in the last seven years." For its motor list and statistical work, it has "processed upwards of 1.2

billion individual yearly motor registrations, representing more names than the Bureau of the Census has recorded since it began counting Americans in 1790." And, in its direct-mail advertising work, for which Polk maintains what it calls the "world's largest selective circulation list," the company says that it sometimes has "as many as 200 million names and addresses on file." Allowing for considerable duplication on the various lists, Polk officials believe that the name and address of most of the 130 million adults in the United States today are included somewhere in the files of R. L. Polk and Company.[7]

In terms of the compiling and utilizing of name lists, three of Polk's divisions deserve more complete descriptions.

1. The City Directory Division publishes more than 1,400 "community encyclopedias" containing information on local residents, businesses, and organizations. The information is compiled by Polk "enumerators" who gather data through 25 million brief personal interviews annually. Information on almost 70 million individuals appears in these volumes. For every resident over 18 years of age, Polk lists name, address, marital status, occupation, place of employment, telephone number, and whether the residence is rented or owned. The directories are arranged in sections by name of the individual or organization (alphabetically), street number, and type of business. A new volume is produced yearly for 80 percent of the directories.

Polk advertising states that "the uses to which a City Directory can be put are virtually limitless. . . selling, buying, prospecting, credit reference, advertising, delivery, communications, mailing . . . even law enforcement." Police officials share this estimate of the city directory's value. A leading work on police intelligence states that using the current and previous city directories available at public libraries and other places "enables the investigator to check over an individual's personal history: his business connections, changes of address, marital status, movements within the city, and job changes."[8]

---

[7] In comparison, another major firm in the direct-mail industry, Reuben H. Donnelley, states that its Marketing Division's "Occupant List" reaches "over 56 million American families." Donnelley also offers clients "access to over 40 million passenger-car-owning families." *This Is Donnelley*, brochure distributed in 1971, p. 16.

[8] D. O. Schultz and L. A. Norton, *Police Operational Intelligence* (Springfield, Ill., 1968), p. 70. In addition, the Polk city directories were mentioned in New Left publications during 1970 as an excellent source for checking out personal histories of individuals suspected of being FBI plants. *Notes on Security*, by the Haymarket Collective, Cambridge, Mass., 1970.

2. Polk's Motor List Division compiles a list of every motor vehicle registered in the United States, drawn from official registration records in all 50 states and the District of Columbia. This file contains the names of almost 60 million individual vehicle owners, who own more than 75 percent of the cars and trucks on the nation's roads. Through its motor census, Polk states, the automotive industry is "the only industry that knows *who* buys its and its competitors' products . . . *when* and *what* they buy . . . and *where* the buyers can be reached. by name and address." Among the uses made of this file is for auto manufacturers to notify owners by certified mail to return their cars for remedying safety defects.

3. The Marketing Services Division (formerly the Direct Mail Division), located in Taylor, Michigan, is described by Polk officials as "the largest direct-mail facility in the world." Among other services, this division does market research for clients; designs and prepares mailings; administers coupon redemptions and contests; mails client materials to designated audiences; and rents or sells prospect lists.

An estimated 135 million names (with many duplications, of course) are maintained by the Marketing Services Division, making it Polk's largest file. To provide these names and addresses, Polk draws on its car and truck ownership files, its bank and business directories, its city directories, and on business prospect lists that it compiles from various sources or buys from other list suppliers. Polk's clients indicate economic, social, or other characteristics of the marketing population they are seeking and the size and location of the mailing they wish to do, and Polk provides either an existing list or a specially prepared list to meet that objective. A typical mailing that Polk would send out, for example, would be an advertisement for an expensive piece of luggage addressed to the registered owners of Cadillac automobiles in ten selected states.

Polk's *Catalogue of Mailing and Prospect Lists* offers about 1,500 lists that customers can draw on; these represent the "most popular" of the 10,000 lists of organizations and individuals that Polk obtains from its own files or through rental from other firms. Where the client wants to do his own mailing, the lists may be purchased in manuscript form, three-by-five cards, gummed labels, punched cards, or computer tapes. However, the more common situation is for customers to deliver their mail items to Polk, which will then address the items and place them in the mail.

The lists in Polk's 1971 catalogue offer names and addresses of a wide assortment of business establishments and individuals. Among the latter are individuals in various professions ("30,650 accountants—all kinds," "14,503 chiropractors"), in government posts ("10,190 city school superintendents," "2,000 city managers,"), in various business enterprises ("102 peanut butter manufacturers," "21,692 funeral directors," "30,193 retail hardware dealers"), and in civic organizations ("280,000 Junior Chamber of Commerce members").

The Move to Computerization

The kind of operations that it engaged in—collecting, sorting, printing, and updating names and numbers in very large quantities —made Polk a natural candidate for computerization. "Once, the human eye and hand were sufficient for Polk's keeping tabs on American commerce," a company publication about its computer activities noted. As the nation grew, however, the company moved to typewriters and electromechanical processing machines. By the 1950s, manual methods had become incapable of handling the increased volume of names and numbers effectively. Polk conducted feasibility studies over a two-and-a-half year period, looking at cost justification and possible increased speed of operations through computerization.

In 1958, the firm installed its first computer, an IBM 650 in the Cincinnati office, where the motor-vehicle registration list is compiled. Today, Polk has five computer installations. In Cincinnati, the Motor Vehicle and Motor Statistical Divisions share an IBM 370/155. The Marketing Services Division facility in Taylor, Michigan, has another IBM 370/155. The City Directory operation uses an IBM 370/145, located in Polk's Detroit headquarters, which also has three satellite systems (IBM 360/22's) which are used for input-output purposes. (These are located in Richmond, Virginia, Travers City, Michigan, and Cincinnati, Ohio.) Also in the Detroit building is an IBM 360/25, used for Polk's payroll, billing, and other administrative work. The fifth computer installation is a Honeywell system, used for all the work of Polk's Canadian operations.

There is no linkage between the five computers; each operates as a separate and independent system. However, there is considerable overlapping and exchange of data among the various systems. For example, the motor-vehicle registration data compiled in the Cincinnati office are sent on tapes to the Detroit office, where the information is used in preparing automotive merchandising campaigns, recall programs, etc. We already noted that information from the city-directory file or the motor list is drawn on to make up selective mailing lists for clients. In all, Polk maintains more than 50,000 reels of magnetic tape.

Polk officials in management and data processing speak in highly enthusiastic terms about what computerization has done for the firm's operations. Some of the advantages parallel those that other large data-handling organizations obtained from computers. For example, the enormous size of Polk's files meant huge storage-space requirements; even in punched-card form, these required some 20,000 square feet of space. With magnetic tape, this was reduced to 400 square feet of floor space.

However, advantages in updating several of their major files were particularly important to Polk. Prior to computerization, there had to be slow and expensive manual re-creation (retyping, resorting, etc.) of the directories issued annually or changed by periodic registration programs, and similar operations for many major lists. With the computer, it has been possible to update the tapes on which the directory or list are contained by addition, correction, or resorting programs. It is also easier to make corrections in a specific individual's record. "As new information becomes available on each individual on the circulation list," the company notes, "the computers prepare a new profile, keeping the circulation list current." Such new information includes changes in address, returns of coupons, subscription offers accepted, purchase clubs joined, and many other preferences.

As least as important has been the computer's impact on "selectivity," which Polk literature calls "the very heart" of its direct-mail services. Advertisers do not want to buy huge general lists; they want to pinpoint a particular group of potential buyers at the local, regional, or national level. Where selective lists had to be compiled previously by finding and typing entries from hundreds of thousands of large name sheets, these can now be produced from the master files through computer programming, and in a variety of formats (gummed labels, cards, print-out, etc.). A Polk publication noted that, after computerization, these were the services open to a direct-mail client: "He can specify individuals for their likelihood of buying certain products and in certain price ranges. He can specify geographical selection—by state, county, city, even postal zone or census tract. He can also specify by quality of neighborhood." According to Polk, a "truly selective list" not only costs the marketer less but also means that the customer receives less mail advertising in which he is not interested.

Computerization has not resulted in the merger of all of Polk's mail lists into one master file for the direct-mail work. Though this could be done technically, according to Donald R. Marine, the manager of data processing, it is not a business necessity and offers no business advantages. Either a customer finds what he wants in one of 10,000 lists that Polk offers, or a special list is prepared for him by mixing several lists or extracting a selection from a larger one.

Polk officials state that both speed and accuracy have also been improved by computerization. Removing old names and screening out duplications, which used to be very time-consuming operations, are now accomplished much more quickly and accurately. As to accuracy in general, Marine observed that "prior to computerization, lists were typed and little proofreading was done. Now, every entry is proofread."

Since the Polk files do not contain what is generally considered to be sensitive personal data, the company takes only what it terms "ordinary commercial security precautions" to protect its files from unauthorized penetration. "Security has never been a problem," Marine noted, and therefore "There are no physical or software security safeguards in the computer systems." However, Marine stressed that the magnitude of the files—50,000 computer tapes—is a deterrent to anyone who might consider trying to penetrate the system to browse around, since it would be extremely difficult and time-consuming for an outsider to locate the name and record of a particular person in this massive tape collection.

Officials of the firm stress that, basically, Polk "is continuing to process and publish information in much the same way that it has during the last 50 to 100 years." Computers "have greatly increased the speed and facility with which data can be tailored for both government and commercial use, but Polk's basic operations are unchanged."

Privacy Issues and Direct-mail Advertising

During the 1960s, complaints began to be raised that the placing of an individual's name on mailing lists and the sending of advertising and other unsolicited materials to his home represented an intrusion into his privacy. The issue was particularly sharp where the names on such mailing lists came from government files, such as motor-vehicle and driver's-license records, tax records, occupational license records, weapons registration forms, and similar files to which a citizen had to contribute his name if he was to obtain a government license or benefit or obey a compulsory registration requirement. Under public-record statutes and common-law doctrines at the state and federal levels, such government files were open to public inspection and copying by anyone, unless the records were among specific exceptions such as police, medical, and adoption files. Because the files were considered to be open to all, the practice had grown up of permitting commercial firms in the direct-mail industry to copy records from various large government files. This generated revenue for government departments and a service for various types of businesses and organizations.

The reasons for citizen complaints about mailing lists varied considerably. Some complaints involved the mailing of sexually oriented advertising that began in the late 1960s, under rulings of the federal courts that expanded the definitions of materials that could be viewed by adults without being legally punishable as obscene. Though a very small number of firms were involved in such sexually oriented advertisements, protests about families receiving such unwanted mail poured into Congress, giving rise to discussions about how the individual's name had gotten into the hands of those sending out sexually oriented mail in the first place. The fact that such firms were entitled to purchase government lists under public-record laws (and some did) was particularly resented by antipornography groups.

The result of this campaign was passage of a federal statute in 1970 allowing individuals to fill out a form at U.S. Post Offices indicating that they and others listed from their family did not want to receive sexually oriented mail. The names of those who so registered were compiled and all firms mailing sexually oriented mail were required by the law to obtain copies of this list and remove all such names from their files. Failure to do so would lead to criminal penalties. Furthermore, any commercial marketing use of this "don't send me sexually oriented mail" list was forbidden. By 1971, over 500,000 persons had placed their name on this list. The constitutionality of such legislation had been upheld by the U.S. Supreme Court earlier, in reference to a 1967 act dealing with "pandering advertisements," over claims that the law violated freedom of speech and the press.[9] The opinion of Chief Justice

---

[9] *Rowan* v. *Post Office*, 397 U.S. 728 (1970).

Burger stressed the right of the individual to judge what he considers obscene, and to protect the privacy of his home from such intrusions. "Main line" firms such as Polk and others in the direct-mail industry supported the campaigns to pass such laws and Polk had also maintained its own internal controls to make sure that no such mailings were done through rental or sale of its lists.

The part of the mailing-list-and-privacy debate that did involve firms such as Polk was the complaint that the sending of "junk mail" into the home represented an intrusion into personal privacy, as did unwanted telephone solicitations. During 1969 and 1970, various congressmen argued that the sale of government lists to commercial firms for direct-mail purposes was improper. Representative Jerome Waldie declared that when the citizen deals with government for some specific purpose, such as tax collection or licensing, he does not expect these dealings to lead to "other transactions" such as the receipt of mail solicitations. Several congressmen taking this position stated that it was the advent of computers that had fostered the great expansion of direct mail. Congressman Cornelius Gallagher, for example, deplored the fact that people's names were being "permanently and inescapably embedded in someone's money-making computer," and that this accumulation was now the empire of the direct-mail industry.

The industry position, shared by Polk officials, is that as long as the individual can throw away unwanted mail he is not being coerced in any way and his civil liberties are not being invaded. They argue that the great majority of people actually like to receive mail that presents offers, contests, or memberships or asks for contributions to worthy causes, and that it would be highly autocratic to deny this great majority the ability to receive such mail just because a very small number of individuals object. As for the sale of government lists, industry spokesmen (and Polk officials to whom we talked) stress that this is public record information open to anyone, not private or sensitive information. "We don't have anything in our files that is not available to everyone under the law," a Polk official said. "If anyone can get it, why not R. L. Polk?"

As for the computer being responsible for the growing lists, industry spokesmen stress that being able to make their records about individuals more detailed and current through computerization allows them to make mailings more selective, so that fewer people will receive mail in which they have no interest.

Judicial and Legislative Tests of the Privacy Issue

So far, challenges in court to the sale of government lists to direct-mail advertisers or other organizations have produced only decisions upholding those practices as lawful. In a 1967 case, a federal court rejected a suit by philosopher Corliss Lamont that sought to force the Commissioner of Motor Vehicles in New York to stop selling driver and vehicle lists to R. L. Polk.[1] "The mailbox, however noxious its advertising contents seem to judges as well as other people," the court ruled, "is hardly the kind of enclave that requires constitutional defense to protect 'the privacies of life.' "

A more recent case in Connecticut involved an invasion of privacy suit brought by a man named Chapin, with support from the Connecticut Civil Liberties Union, against both R. L. Polk and the state Motor Vehicle Department.[2] Chapin showed that he had received three pieces of mail advertising consumer goods as a result of the driver's license containing his name being sold to Polk. He alleged that this caused irreparable damage to his right to be left alone, and asked the court for an injunction banning further sale of such files. After reviewing the state public-record statutes and finding that the state legislature had not included motor-vehicle records among those government files that it had recently excluded from public viewing or copying, the court held that Chapin's petition must be dismissed. No injury had been made out that courts could recognize. "The pace at which our commercial world runs does not permit its inhabitants the seminarian solitude and serenity of the cloistered cleric without interference from the bustle of mundane life." Even if some limits needed to be placed on the sale and use of public-record information, the court concluded, this was a task for the legislature and not the courts, since no fundamental constitutional rights were involved.

This ruling is in line with recent federal court decisions under the 1967 federal Freedom of Information Act. The Federal Aviation Agency could not withhold lists of pilots from direct-mail advertisers seeking them, nor could the Veterans Administration refuse to give antiwar groups the names of former servicemen in Vietnam.

At the legislative level, more than 80 congressmen have joined Congressman Frank Horton, a New York Republican, in

---

[1] *Lamont* v. *Commissioner of Motor Vehicles*, 269 F. Supp. 880 (1967).

[2] *Chapin* v. *Tynan*, 158 Conn. 625, 264 A. 2d 566 (1969).

sponsoring legislation to amend the Freedom of Information Act to prohibit government agencies from selling lists for commercial purposes or other solicitations. "I do not believe," Congressman Horton explained, "that the Freedom of Information Act was passed as a license for commercial organizations to invade an individual's privacy. . . ."

A related bill proposed by Congressman Gallagher would require a firm to note on the mailing label the source from which it got the addressee's name; allow the individual to specify to the Post Office that he only wishes to receive soliciations from charitable organizations; and would make provision for the individual to get his name off any list, no matter what his particular objection to its being there. Commenting on the potential of the computer to protect privacy, Gallagher suggested that "Since the vast majority of these lists are computerized, we can use the ease of entering and altering data on a computer to protect the privacy of our citizens, rather than to invade it."[3]

The Direct-mail Industry Responds

By the early 1970s, criticisms by consumer and civil-liberties groups, in the press, and among legislators prompted the Direct Mail Advertising Association (DMAA) to develop a special program to deal with the issue of unwanted mail. The industry position had been that the great majority of persons either wanted or did not mind receiving mail advertising, but that some practical way should be found to meet the concerns of the few who did object. The solution they devised was a national Mail Preference Service, an industry-administered way for an individual to get his name taken off the lists of cooperating DMAA members, as well as for other individuals to have their names added to lists in areas of interest to them.

To use the service, someone seeking to remove his name

---

[3] In related areas, government regulatory agencies have recently begun to control deceptive practices used by some businesses to get prospects for direct mail lists. The Federal Trade Commission ordered Welcome Newcomer, of Washington, D.C., to stop making house calls on new residents that were presented as visits to inform newcomers of local services but in which the names and preferences of householders interviewed were marketed commercially. The FTC also ordered Metromedia, Inc., of New York City, to stop sending out a mail questionnaire that had offered 4 million householders "an opportunity to win fabulous gifts" in return for completing the questionnaire about habits and preferences. Metromedia did not disclose that the information obtained would be sold to direct-mail advertisers.

notifies DMAA. He receives a letter which explains that this service will remove his name from the lists of all cooperating DMAA members. It also notes that this will not mean an end to all mail advertising. ("Many direct mailers, such as your local merchants, religious and charitable organizations, alumni associations, political candidates and office holders, and so on . . . do not belong to DMAA . . . and can get your name from a telephone or city directory.")[4] Furthermore, the letter observes it will not stop sexually oriented mail, since "smut peddlers" do not belong to DMAA and, in fact, mail first class rather than third class to avoid postal inspection. The DMAA encloses a Post Office "antismut" form, just in case the individual is concerned with that aspect of mail.

As DMAA receives the completed name-removal forms, it compiles a list that is mailed every 30 days to subscribing DMAA members. DMAA makes the removal list available either in printout form, for small companies that sort their labels or envelopes by hand, and on computer tape, for large firms that can then use this as a filter on their computer output from basic files to prevent the production of lists for clients containing those names.

For those seeking to add their names to mailing lists, a separate form lists 22 major areas of consumer and civic activity that the person can check. This list is then circulated every 30 days to subscribing companies, who agree to use it to mail only for specific categories indicated by the consumer.

DMAA is frank in noting that it had mixed objectives in creating the mail preference system. On the positive side, it was a way to "demonstrate our responsiveness to the consumer and direct mail's unique ability to be selective" and "give consumers an opportunity to receive *specific*, desired types of mail advertising." However, it was also seen as a way to "give antagonistic consumers an opportunity to get off mailing lists" and "neutralize the small but vocal minority of critics and forestall restrictive regulations and legislation."

The Mail Preference Service was launched in March 1971. DMAA gave the plan wide publicity in some 13 test cities, receiving wide media coverage and reaching an audience they estimated as 20 million people. As of December 1971, they had received about 8,000 requests for forms, of which about 2,500 were completed and returned. Robert F. DeLay, president of DMAA, said that "this is positive proof that, contrary to what some would

---

[4] DMAA estimates that its members account for about 65 percent of all mailed advertising.

have you believe, the public *does* want to receive advertising mail."

By mid-1972, only half of DMAA's members had joined the Mail Preference Service. R. L. Polk had, for example, but Reuben H. Donnelley, another giant in the industry, had not. DeLay said he expected to have 85 percent of the members signed up by the end of 1972. "They better do it," a DMAA spokesman remarked, "otherwise government regulation is going to be enacted in the future."

In addition to receiving the monthly computer tape from DMAA, Polk has long maintained procedures for responding to an individual who contacts them directly and asks to have his name removed from various Polk publications and lists. For example, an official in Polk's Philadelphia office indicated that a man who had been contacted by Polk "enumerator" called and asked to have his name taken out of the city directory. He was asked to write a letter to the regional office that handled publication of that directory, and his name was taken out. Polk also makes what it calls "every effort to comply immediately" to remove names from its lists, if someone asks that this be done, though it is difficult to locate an individual name on a given list of any size because the files are not programmed for such removal procedures.

Future Plans and Prospects at Polk

Whether measures such as the DMAA Mail Preference Service or Polk's own procedures will forestall state and federal regulation in the future is an open question. Many persons within the industry believe that therer will probably be legislation regulating the sale of government name lists to commercial firms, and perhaps a system that allows the individual to indicate on a government form when he completes it whether he does or does not want to receive commercial mail. Others believe that measures being taken by the industry will allow "antagonistic consumers" to get off the main commercial lists and will make legislation unnecessary.

In terms of computerization, Polk is beginning an effort to develop teleprocessing to link its local offices to the main computer centers; presently, this is limited to the city directory computers in Detroit. For their motor list work, they are looking to put typewriters on line to the computer, and edit as the data come in instead of the optical scanning and sequential production they now do. "This will take several years," according to Al Francis, of the Data Processing Department.

Nonprofit Organizations

Colleges and Universities

Almost 7 million students were enrolled in American higher education in 1971, in 2,400 colleges and universities, over 5 million of these in four-year institutions. These include both public (city, state, and federal) and private (church-sponsored, independent, etc.) institutions, but broad similarities exist in the way they keep records on students, faculty, and staff.

Reflecting their history as institutions for training young men (and later, young women) in the principles of knowledge and culture and in preparation for "useful careers," colleges and universities have traditionally been paternal institutions in their relations with students. In law, university officials were long considered to stand *in loco parentis* (in the place of the parent), with authority to make rules for student behavior, administer discipline, and expel students for improper behavior. As far as faculty are concerned, American universities have had an uneven record of alternating between the provision of academic freedom for the pursuit and profession of truth, and the application of the prevailing community standards of social and political orthodoxy as controls over faculty independence.

In the late 1960s, much of the *in loco parentis* tradition was swept away in the wake of broad campus protests, leaving students with substantial autonomy in their personal and residential affairs. During the same period, high politicization of campuses also produced divisions within the faculties over the university's role in the larger society, and over curriculum and teaching priorities.

Colleges and universities maintain three principal types of personal records—on students; on faculty, administrators, and university employees; and on alumni. Student records include those of the central admission and registrar's offices; academic records in particular schools and departments; dean's office records of disciplinary matters; and records in special university service facilities, such as medical, counseling, and psychiatric offices.

Regular requests from outsiders for information from student files come from a wide variety of sources, such as prospective employers (private and governmental), professional and licensing authorities, and institutions of higher or continuing education. There are also inquiries from law-enforcement officials, legislative investigating committees, and judicial authorities in pending civil or criminal cases. Rules governing the provision or denial of such information have been the subject of strong debate at several points during the past two decades.

Though colleges and universities have been centers for research into computer theory and design, and installed computers early for faculty and student research, the use of computers for handling personal records and administering the institution's affairs has grown slowly. So far, the principal use has been in processing student records. Sixty-four percent of the colleges and universities responding to our own national survey reported some computer applications to registrar's office files on undergraduates.

From among the colleges and universities using computers, we selected one that would be expected to be highly advanced in systems design and EDP applications, the Massachusetts Institute of Technology.

THE MASSACHUSETTS INSTITUTE OF TECHNOLOGY

The Massachusetts Institute of Technology, an independent, co-educational institution with an endowment of some $216 million, is located on the banks of the Charles River in Cambridge, opposite Boston. The Institute was founded as a "school of practical science" in 1861, "where young men could learn exactly and thoroughly the fundamental principles of positive science with their leading applications to the industrial arts." MIT has been among the nation's elite educational institutions since the mid-'20s, and is particularly noted for the scientific, technological, and engineering achievements which have come out of its more than 70 specialized laboratories. Over the years, its curriculum has gradually expanded to include substantial programs in the pure sciences and in the humanities and social sciences.

MIT laboratories were important centers of theoretical and experimental work in electronic data processing, and computers are now used widely in research, teaching, and administration on the campus. As one faculty member put it, "This is the last place you'd expect to find anyone in awe of the computer; here it's a tool . . . like a pen."

In its five schools (Architecture and Planning; Engineering; Humanities and Social Sciences; Management; and Science), each with several departments, more than 7,000 graduate and undergraduate students work with a faculty and teaching staff of over 1,000. Through these departments, the Institute awards academic and professional degrees through the Ph.D. and offers a number of postdoctoral programs.

Faculty, students, and members of the Institute's research staff also work in a number of interdepartmental research laboratories, such as Project MAC,[1] widely known for the "interactive" computer systems which it has developed. Outside the Institute proper are laboratories in which both classified and unclassified research are conducted in such areas as missile and aircraft electronic guidance systems and communications technology. The Institute is administered under a president and a board of trustees (called the Corporation), and the academic side of the administration is divided into financial and nonfinancial lines.

Personal Records

Each member of the MIT community is the object of a number of record keeping efforts, with the largest collection of files relating to students. Although the Institute is a single administrative unit, its manual record keeping over the years has been characterized by high decentralization, each department and office having considerable autonomy in defining record content and use. Applications and other documents required for entrance are maintained in the Admissions Office. In the Student Aid Office are records on students (and their parents) who apply for financial assistance at some point in their Institute careers. (About 60 percent do so.) The Registrar keeps track of grades, class standing, and other "progress indicators." For some students there are records in the files of the student-run Undergraduate Judicial Committee, or in

---

[1] An acronym variously expanded to "Man and Computer," "Machine-Aided Cognition," and "Multi-Access Computers."

the files of the Faculty Committee on Discipline, which handles more serious infractions of university rules. Sensitive counseling records are maintained within the office of the Dean for Student Affairs and in files kept by the Freshman Advisory Committee and department counselors. The Campus Patrol also maintains some records on students—arising out of investigations into cases which range from drug offenses to theft, occasional suicides, and protest activity. If the student is employed on campus, records are kept in the Student Personnel Office. Finally, and more informal than most of the foregoing, are the records maintained by various student activities and fraternities.

The Office of the President maintains records on members of the faculty, as do the deans of the various schools and the department in which each member teaches. The Office of Personnel Relations maintains the principal files on nonacademic employees of the institute. For all MIT employees, payroll records are maintained separately from personnel records, and for faculty, staff, and students alike, the Medical Department maintains files. Employees must undergo preemployment physicals; and all members of the MIT community are eligible for ongoing medical care and psychiatric counseling through the Medical office. Psychiatric records are maintained entirely separate from the several medical records.

For those who are MIT graduates, records are maintained in the Registrar's files and in the Placement Office (if the individual has solicited its help in getting a job). In addition, records in the institute Alumni Office follow each graduate indefinitely.

Records on thousands of participants in social and psychological research are also to be found within the files of several of the Institute departments and individual faculty members. Faculty members and administrative officials from the various departments and divisions also have records about students in their personal files. These include grades, copies of letters of recommendation, inquiries from colleagues or outside sources, written materials such as student term papers, and many other types of information. Such individual files are usually kept with far fewer security precautions than the more central records of the Institute.

Computer Development at MIT

While several independent computer systems serve major laboratories, four on-line systems serve the Institute proper. They are operated by the Information Processing Center which falls within the MIT Information Processing Services Office directed by Robert H. Scott. These systems include two of the most sophisticated and flexible on-line systems in existence, which developed out of the interdepartmental Project MAC, an endeavor dedicated to creating on-line systems in which multiple users can work simultaneously in an "interactive" environment. While all of the facilities managed by the Information Processing Services Office probably have some administrative or social research records, they are primarily used for student and faculty research that involves little storage of information on identified individuals.

It was not until the 1960s that EDP was applied to record-keeping on individuals at MIT. Today, there are extensive computer applications in the personal records of the Admissions, Student Aid, Registrar and Alumni Offices, and for the Institute's Personnel and Payroll offices. More limited and specialized EDP applications have been developed for a large number of other departments including the Medical Department, the Psychiatric Service, and the Educational Council. The records of other departments, the Dean of Students' Office, and individual faculty members remain largely manual.

In the precomputer era, there was little in the way of centralized directon for the record-keeping operations of the Institute. As a member of the EDP staff remarked: "It's really a very ordinary university; there was heavy duplication and inefficiency, and the responsibility for record-keeping was very diffuse, to say the least." In the early '60s, the Registrar and Alumni offices began to work together on computer applications designed to relieve the pressures of increasing record volume. While the size of the Institute's student community had grown only modestly, the number of transactions had increased considerably, and keeping track of routine information on past and present students was becoming increasingly expensive. In addition, there were some tedious and complex chores—such as course scheduling—which were seen as ripe for computer handling.

What began as ad hoc cooperation between offices grew into an independent operation, known as the Office of Administrative Systems, set up to handle data-processing operations for about 30 nonfinancial administrative offices. Included among these were extensive record-keeping programs for the Registrar and Alumni offices, for Admissions, Student Aid and the Educational Council, and for many systems which are not directly related to record-keeping on students or alumni. In 1971, the Institute administrative data-processing and systems development activities were unified through creation of a new office of Administrative Information Systems.

Taken together, these computerized files contain a broad range of information on students and their families. Loans, scholarships, earnings from work, and the financial condition of the student's family are kept track of in the Student Aid Office system. Grades, class standing, and other academic performance indicators are a part of the registrar's computerized files. For the 7,000 students who apply to MIT for admission each year, high school grades, recommendations, test scores, and activities are recorded, along with some information on geographical, socioeconomic, and ethnic background. Where the student had applied for admission with financial assistance, his family's income and assets are covered. Computer applications for the Alumni Office enable it to follow and estimate the graduate's potential as a fund-raising resource.

More limited applications have been developed for the Medical Department. Over the past ten years, visits to the clinic jumped from 30,000 to 75,000 per year, and out of an attempt to understand this rise, the medical staff began to monitor the use of facilities and staff time. Patient visits are recorded, along with diagnoses, medical procedures, and the length of time spent on each case. The Psychiatric Service has developed its own computer programs, and these are maintained by and are only accessible to psychiatric personnel. These grow out of staff research interests in psychiatric epidemiology. Patients fill out special forms on which they provide 15 or 20 items of background data, which can then be merged with diagnostic information. At present, no diagnostic information is stored in computer-readable form, however.

On the financial side of the administration, EDP developments began around 1964. At that time, according to Mr. Paul Cusick, vice-president for business and fiscal relations, computer applications were developed "primarily to get people paid—very routine, very functional systems." Salary, payroll deductions, pension information, and medical plan eligibility are currently handled via computer as part of the general payroll operation out of which records are kept and checks generated.

In the electrical engineering department, Prof. James Bruce (now associate dean of the engineering school) developed a system designed to reduce the heavy load of routine, tedious work connected with managing the department. An on-line system, it helps at times of budget preparation and for arranging teaching assignments—tasks which "used to take an inordinate amount of time and were always done with a lot of wasted motion."

Computer developments in all three of these areas were marked by some internal resistance and political problems. In the electrical engineering department, for instance, very little of what might be considered sensitive information was put into the system. But by tradition at MIT, information on salaries is considered highly sensitive. "When we first proposed the system," Bruce said, "people said to me: 'you're not going to put salaries in the computer, are you?' I said, 'yes—and it will probably be as secure there as it is in my office right now.'" Use of the system developed in the electrical engineering department is now being extended to all departments within the School of Engineering.

Each of the universitywide administrative systems now run on two IBM 360/30's in batch-processing operations. The application in the electrical engineering department, however, is developed for the far more sophisticated "Multics" system operated by the Information Processing Services Center.

The Computer's Impact

On the broadest possible level, Scott suggested, little real reorganization of administrative functions has yet to occur as a result of computerization, although some "progress" has been made in this direction within individual offices. "For example," he said, "the Admissions office is still the Admissions Office, even though many of its data-handling operations have been computerized; and it always will be—even if it some day works off a much larger, centralized data base."

Those involved in computerization efforts within the Institute point to important increases in processing speed and efficiency, especially in the Registrar's Office, where student records are easier to keep up to date and "much better course schedules are prepared than when it was done by hand." Cusick said that the results are "pretty obvious" in the Business Office, which handles some four to five hundred million dollars a year in checks, "not ten of which are signed by hand."

Cusick further pointed out that some information on faculty members is more accessible now than it was in precomputer days. As part of an effort to control toll-call costs, the data-processing staff was asked if they could provide a list of calls and charges incurred by each faculty member. Much to Cusick's surprise, the telephone company had been supplying the Institute with a tape containing just that, and the information was available within a very short time. "If travel records were on tape," he assured us, "we would also be able to get a print-out of faculty itineraries— since one travel agency handles much of the travel by Institute faculty; and of medical claims submitted by faculty members— since most are covered under Blue Cross." However, there is currently no need for these data, he added.

General Civil-liberties Issues in Student Records

Like any university, the Institute has to face questions about the propriety and confidentiality of faculty and staff records, but the most extensive set of privacy concerns surround the records on its students. For most students, MIT is something of a "total environment"—providing not only education but also bed and board, counseling, medical care, recreation, financial support, and the social and interpersonal context for much of the student's life. But as in other educational institutions, the classic *in loco parentis* relation between student and administration which once dominated this environment has been fundamentally challenged in the past half decade, not only by radical students branding the Institute as an accomplice in war and racism, but also by many other students who demand freedom from administrative control over their personal lives while on campus. Accompanying these changes, some but by no means all members of the MIT community feel, has been a marked decline in the trust among students, faculty, and administration.

Each record-holding unit within MIT has a set of specific rules regarding access to records by members of the Institute community, but several civil-liberties dilemmas are evident in these. Faculty members are encouraged, for instance, to know as much as possible about their students. Yet medical, psychiatric, and some of the registrar's files are not open to them, and student records in the dean's office are closed as soon as any sensitive material has been entered.

The explicit or implicit permission of the student is required before a response to outside inquiries may be made. While Institute officers maintain that this rule is followed closely, an equally important problem concerns the content of communications to outsiders. Especially where background investigations for security clearances are concerned, the student may not know what a faculty member or other Institute personnel have communicated to investigators; sometimes, the student may not know that any

Institute personnel have even been contacted. Other classic issues in handling student records have arisen at MIT, including those surrounding the communication of even limited information from Psychiatric Service files and those connected with the propriety of contacts among campus and local police and the various administrative offices. Psychiatrist-in-chief Dr. Merton Kahne receives requests for information, and notes that "most of the students who come to see me are not by any stretch of the imagination 'sick'; but you have to be very careful how outsiders interpret anything close to being a 'psychiatric' record." For this reason, Kahne said, "release of information from our department in all instances requires the explicit approval of both the patient and the psychiatrist-in-chief. In some cases the Psychiatric Service supplies the student with a copy of what was communicated to an investigator, and, less frequently, advises a student *not* to communicate certain details of a problem to an investigating agency. "I'm not impartial in all this; there are times when it is simply better for a student to keep certain aspects of a problem to himself. . . ," Kahne commented.

The question of law-enforcement contacts has been a source of concern to other Institute officials. William Speer, associate dean for student counseling, remarked that "We've been frightfully informal about all this because there is a very high level of trust here; we trust the campus patrol, and I think a large fraction of the students trust us. Our campus police are the best, and they have only limited and informal access to information about students through us." Speer went on to say that "we are looking at this whole thing closely now, however; we want to make sure that we are not being a little naive. It occurred to us, for instance, that there could even be links among the police on different campuses, or contacts between them and industrial security people—with whom we have in the past only cooperated in the most careful way."[2]

Since "Dow Day" protests at MIT in 1967, there have been various student protests about campus recruitment, ROTC, and war-related research in MIT laboratories, such as the development in MIT's Draper Laboratory of a guidance system for the controversial MIRV missile system. A dean suggested that, during 1970—when there was considerable campus unrest at MIT and which we frequently heard referred to as "our year of trouble"—

---

[2] Recent disclosures from FBI files and in the course of court cases indicate that it is "standard practice" for campus police and other personnel to be used as informants by the bureau.

some disciplinary action had to be taken after a student protest. "To identify those involved," he said, "we used some photo work. This was the first time we'd had any real trouble on the campus, and this incident—this whole year, I think—engendered mistrust between some students and the administration."

The access which students have to their *own* records varies from file to file, but as a rule they cannot see records containing recommendations (such as may be found in admissions and dean's office files), or their files in the Psychiatric Service and the Student Aid Office. The clearest exception to this lack of access occurs in the case of medical records, which under Massachusetts law are open to the patient. Physicians in the Medical Department, however, feel that this conflicts with good medical practice, and patients are strongly discouraged from looking at their own medical records.

Commenting on student access to their own counseling files, Dean Speer said that, "During our year of trouble, more students came in to see what was in the Student Counseling files concerning their campus political activities." But even though more frequent, he said, the number was (and is) still very small; "I can't remember more than 15 or 20 students who came in to check that year; whenever this occurs now, we just sit and discuss what's in the folder. As best I can tell, no one leaves feeling dissatisfied."

The Computer and Confidentiality

Most of those with whom we spoke at MIT suggested that computerization of administrative files had neither altered fundamentally the records which are kept on students nor changed the way in which decisions get made about them as individuals. Nor has the computerization of student files affected the confidentiality of student records. Most important in this regard is the fact that the working files are still for the most part manual—even those which may be produced and updated by computer. In fact, almost all the files on computer have their manual counterparts. And, in many cases, the most sensitive information in a file is not in computer storage at all. While medical "encounter" forms are computerized, and include diagnosis information, the most detailed and sensitive personal data in these files remains in manual form. Psychiatric encounter forms do not include diagnostic information at all, and all psychiatric records—both computerized and manual—are stored under identification numbers "only the department can decipher."

Dean Speer suggested that he would never put any of his counseling records on computer. "First of all there isn't enough volume; second, much of it is too trivial; and sometimes there is very personal information in the file which doesn't belong out of this office." Data-processing personnel at MIT, however, believe that the computer files are at least as well protected as their manual counterparts. In each of the computer systems developed, some precautions were taken to protect the confidentiality of data in the files—from the scrambling of identification numbers in the psychiatric systems to the "password" protection system available to "Multics" users.

Administrative actions were taken as well. Memos to staff members in the Office of Administrative Information Systems have noted that the records processed there are the responsibility of the client offices, and that information from one office cannot be passed to another without the "specific approval of the file owner."

MIT's computer systems have been the subject of a number of news and magazine stories relating instances in which students or employees were alleged to have made unauthorized access into the system. A recent issue of *Modern Data* magazine, for instance, published a letter from a reader describing a student who managed to penetrate the software security on an MIT computer system. According to the writer of the letter, "The following day, when routine computer processing was done, the following sentence was found overlaid onto every record in computer memory: 'The Green Phantom Was Here.'" In a letter of reply to the magazine, Scott said that this was a wholly apocryphal and untrue story. The editor, in reply, agreed that they had failed to run their usual check for accuracy on this item, and apologized for printing it.

Data processing personnel do relate a few "war stories" about breaches or near-breaches of the computer system. Some of these were serious attempts to cheat the system and get free computing time, while others were more in the way of practical jokes, "created by students with high technical competence, time on their hands, and interesting senses of humor." These few instances, Scott said, sometimes give rise to fictitious elaborations which make the papers, but none of these involved unauthorized access to personal data.

Civil-liberties Concerns within the Institute

Several leading faculty members at MIT have been vocal in discussing computer and privacy issues in American society as a whole, including Dr. Robert Fano, Dr. Jerome Wiesner (now president of the Institute), institute psychiatrist Dr. Merton Kahne, and Prof. Joseph Weizenbaum. Testifying before Senator Ervin's hearings in 1971, Wiesner suggested that "1984 . . . could come to pass unnoticed while we applauded our technical achievements. The great danger which must be recognized and counteracted is that such a depersonalizing state of affairs could occur without overt decisions, without high-level encouragement or support, and totally independent of malicious intent."[3]

A recent "test" of the security of student records has also sparked campus interest in civil-liberties protections. Freshmen in one class undertook to probe the security of confidential campus administrative files. Much to the chagrin of administrators (including the Psychiatric Service and the Office of Student Counseling), the students succeeded very well. "Using nothing more sophisticated than a screwdriver to jimmy a few doors and desks and a simple ruse or two to distract personnel who might otherwise have objected to their poking around," one administrator noted, they managed to show that one could quite easily gain access to a number of manual files containing information on students and faculty. Computer files were not among those to which the students secured access.

The Ad Hoc Committee on Privacy

Within the past three years, several universities[4] have established committees or study groups to look into privacy issues in the academic environment. An Ad Hoc Committee on Privacy of Information at MIT was formed in 1968, and included faculty, administration, and student members. Its report[5] was issued in 1971, and reflects a great deal of wrestling with complex social and technical issues.

The committee recommended that the Institute itself take responsibility for protecting the privacy rights of its members. As a general rule, it felt the obligation is on the record holder to justify his need for identified personal information and to state how long a given record will remain in the files. Further, the

---

[3] *Federal Databanks, Computers and the Bill of Rights*, Hearings before the Subcommittee on Constitutional Rights of the Senate Judiciary Committee, February and March 1971, Part I, p. 762.

[4] Stanford, Harvard, Wisconsin, and the University of California among them.

[5] Reprinted in *Tech Talk*, the MIT official weekly newspaper, May 19, 1971.

committee suggested that only the individual himself can define how "sensitive" a given item of personal information is, and that it is the responsibility of Institute offices to respond creatively to individual perceptions in this area.

The committee developed the idea that individuals have a prima facie right to see files which concern them—except where exercise of this right would conflict with protection of the privacy of others. With respect to the sharing of personal information outside the Institute's boundaries, the committee urged that it be standard practice to reveal as little as possible beyond information on an individual's academic performance and professional capabilities. This, the committee said, applies to security-clearance inquiries as well, which have to be handled with special care. Even when it is clear that an individual's extracurricular activities are relevant to the security investigation underway, the committee suggested,

> It is essential that the privacy of the faculty/student relationship, and the special responsibilities of the university for unfettered intellectual development and debate, not be forgotten. Casual reporting of, in particular, a student's activities and ideas during the most critical period of his intellectual experimentation could mar his career for life. Even when a person is asked, or feels compelled, to act in his role of citizen of the larger society, he can express his candid opinion about the suitability of some individual for work requiring security clearance without divulging the information on which his opinion is based.

The Committee noted that some of the files on campus were poorly protected and that, while they discovered relatively few violations of confidentiality resulting from unauthorized access to files, "the damage done by privacy violations cannot be directly repaired, and its consequences cannot be readily foreseen. For this reason, *preventive* measures are of special importance. This point must be stressed because the need for preventive measures is too often overlooked or dismissed in the absence of serious violations, particularly when the costs of such measures is appreciable."

A particular concern in the origin and throughout the operation of the committee was the rapid growth of on-line computer systems within the Institute. A report by a special subcommittee on "on-line data bases" concluded that these were, in fact, more easily protected than some of the manual files and batch-processing computer operations. Therefore, it recommended that two of the latter systems not be used at all for storing and processing sensitive personal information.

In closing, the committee suggested that the Institute must be sensitive to the relative powerlessness of individuals in large organizations, and the extent to which coercion is implicit in much of the administrative and research data gathering which goes on in a university setting. Recognizing that genuine conflicts can arise between the civil liberties of different individuals (as in the conflict between a physician's right to keep his working notes private and the patient's right to see his own medical record), they recommended that some third-party mechanism, such as an ombudsman, be established so that members of the Institute community could appeal disputed issues over privacy and records.

The Institute faculty has since voted to "accept the basic principles underlying [the] report," and to establish a standing faculty committee "to gather information and develop experience about privacy matters."

The Future

During the next few years, the Institute will be developing a number of new computer applications in record-keeping and converting many of its current functions to on-line operation. The two universitywide administrative systems will be combined into a single system late in 1972. It is also likely that some increased integration of files will occur and, according to Robert Scott, "one of our objectives is to combine some of the record-keeping functions now handled by separate offices to reduce duplication and minimize error. There is some resistance to this in some cases, so we'll do it in small stages and not try to implement a grand plan all at once. First we'll develop some sharing of data across jurisdictions; then we'll end up by merging the files along functional lines."

In addition, use of the Social Security number for both staff and student files has recently been decided upon, and this move is expected to generate campus debate, as it has at several other educational institutions.[6] But it is clear that the Institute moves into the future with the administrative and technical means to

---

[6] At Stanford University a committee on privacy has recommended against allowing the use of the Social Security number for purposes of identification in university record systems. At MIT, the psychiatric service has decided not to use the Social Security number for its record-keeping, even if most other university files on individuals have or will adopt it for identification purposes.

increase computerization; whether and how the guidelines of its Ad Hoc Committee will be used to balance conflicting policy interests will be of importance not only for MIT, but as an example for American universities as a whole in the 1970s.

Behavioral Research

During the past few decades, research into individual and group behavior has grown enormously in both quantity and importance in the United States. Such "behavioral research," as it is often called, involves many types of investigative efforts. These include social science projects in psychology, sociology, anthropology, and political science; medical research; market and public opinion research; and data collection by government agencies such as the Bureau of the Census and the Department of Health, Education, and Welfare. Behavioral research is carried on in a wide variety of institutional locations, including government agencies; industrial enterprises; in special projects, bureaus, and centers housed within colleges and universities; in nonprofit institutes and centers; and in commercial research enterprises.

Three qualitative developments in the conduct of social research have led to growing concern over matters such as the ethical or political boundaries for inquiries and the confidentiality of personal data once they have been obtained. First, more behavioral research is being done today on subject-areas that are socially and legally sensitive, such as investigations of alcohol and drug use, sexual behavior, and political and civic activity. Second, there has been increasing stress on what is called "panel" research, in which the same individuals are studied over long periods of time. Finally, much behavioral research deals with "dependent persons" in mental institutions, prisons, hospitals, and other involuntary settings. Research with children also falls within this category. These trends involve problems of consent and voluntariness that raise important ethical and civil liberties questions.

The advent of computers has stimulated some developments in behavioral research about which further civil-liberties issues have been raised. With computers, it has become practical to conduct studies on far larger populations than was feasible through manual methods (such as 500,000 schoolchildren in the national education assessment, Project Talent). In some cases, computers also make possible the collection and analysis of more elaborate and detailed data. The result is a growth in the number of large computerized files of identified and potentially sensitive data about individuals.

The establishment of data banks in the research area has also stirred some concern, whether they were designed as repositories for research data from completed projects (perhaps 20 of these central data collections already exist), or as collections of data from which new research might be conducted by several researchers simultaneously. While the use of such storehouses of data is not yet widespread, proposals in this direction continue, especially where federal funding is heavy. Most recently, a member of Congress introduced a bill proposing the establishment of a National Research Databank.[7]

The absence of legal privilege for these files makes questions of collection and maintenance particularly important. Even where professional and scholarly ethics of confidentiality are strong, no legal right of confidentiality for information exists for behavioral research. Data can be subpoenaed by legislative committees and courts, and penalties for contempt of court await those who do not comply.

For our profile in this area, we have chosen the research arm of a leading national education association, the American Council on Education.

THE AMERICAN COUNCIL ON EDUCATION

The American Council on Education (ACE), founded in 1918, is a nongovernmental council whose voluntary membership includes schools, universities, and educational associations. It had 1,700 institutional members, and a budget in 1970-71 of $2.5 million.

Separate commissions of the council deal with such matters as relations between the federal government and educational institutions, university academic affairs, and problems of higher education planning. ACE is run primarily by and for educational administrators, and the issues with which it has most frequently dealt are "those which are likely to cross a college president's desk." The council has also been involved in efforts to measure the performance of institutions of higher education, developing concepts of institutional accountability.

---

[7] Congressman H. R. Collier, in H. R. 8732 in June 1971.

The ACE Office of Research

ACE research activities began in 1956, with an award of $375,000 from the Carnegie Corporation to establish an Office of Statistical Information and Research (OSIR). Between 1956 and 1963, this office developed slowly, essentially offering fact books on higher education to colleges on a subscription basis. In 1965, the OSIR became the Office of Research, with Dr. Alexander W. Astin, an educational psychologist, as its director.

An ambitious research plan was developed by the first three members of the office staff, Astin, John A. Creager, and Robert Panos. It called for annual questionnaire surveys of entering freshmen in a large, representative sample of colleges and universities, with follow-up studies of some of the same students in subsequent years. Astin and the council's then president, Logan Wilson, were primarily interested in the assessment of higher educational institutions, and hoped that this project would make it possible to appraise the impact which different college environments have on students. Their other objectives included developing and publishing national profile data on a wide variety of student characteristics such as race, career choice, and attitudes on public issues; and the development of trend data useful in the evaluation of manpower needs, student and faculty mobility, and financing. This plan, called the Cooperative Institutional Research Program (CIRP), became the major ongoing project of the Office of Research.

The Office of Research, working through the established lines of communications and auspices of the council, obtained cooperation from nearly 300 institutions in the research plan. As a result, in the flurry of activity which characterizes the orientation and registration process for college freshmen, more than 200,000 such freshmen sit down each year to answer a battery of ACE's demographic, opinion, and attitude questions. The questionnaire is administered by local college personnel. In return for their cooperation, administrators receive summary data describing the national college population and a summary statistical description of their own freshmen. Occasionally they receive more specialized feedback, as we will discuss below.

A number of short-term studies conducted by the Office of Research depend heavily on contact made, and the institutional and student samples established, for CIRP. The studies have focused upon such things as minority groups in higher education, campus unrest and change, and the development of research methodology. The latter involves appraising the veracity and consistency of student reports of their own experiences and attitudes, so that researchers can have a better sense for the validity of the data they gather. Most recently, ACE researchers have been involved in evaluation research on the open-enrollment program of the City University of New York.

The Content of CIRP Inquiries

In both the CIRP surveys and studies of smaller scale, the data are typically collected through self-administered questionnaires, although some personal interviews are used for more intensive research. The identity of respondents is obtained (name and home address); this is needed because, even though the research results are presented only in statistical form, CIRP is designed to track individual student development over time. Defending this research practice in a paper, Astin suggests strongly that there has been far too little such longitudinal research in the social sciences. As a result, there is much that we are unable to know about the effect of institutional and other environments on individuals. The object in the case of CIRP is to predict and describe the impact of early college experiences on later achievements and activities. This kind of research is virtually impossible without the ability to link an individual's records gathered at different points of time.

The CIRP questionnaires are four pages in length, and ACE researchers pride themselves on the amount of "interesting" information they can elicit through fewer than 30 multifaceted questions. Freshmen were asked to supply information on their education and family background; to answer "self-image" items in which they rate themselves along dimensions as diverse as "academic ability," "stubbornness," and "political conservatism"; and to complete career preference questions. In questions on past school activities, one class of freshman students was asked whether, during the past year in school, they had "Demonstrated for a change in some racial or ethnic policy? . . . Demonstrated for a change in some military policy? . . . Demonstrated for a change in some administrative policy of my high school?" In the same multiple-response question, students were asked about work habits, whether they used tranquilizers or sleeping pills, and religion. Public-opinion questions were also a part of the survey, and students responded to items on women's rights, the death penalty, legalization of marijuana, college "open-admissions" policies, and the way in which college administrators have handled student protests. Many of the questions are changed from year to year. Most of the questions, however, are considered by the Office of Research staff to be "relatively innocuous," and they believe that students themselves do not usually regard the questions as sensitive.

Participation in the CIRP survey (as in all ACE research) is voluntary. However, institutions are not required explicitly to point this out to students unless the students ask; the voluntary aspect is implied in the cover letter accompanying the questionnaire ("we ask that you cooperate in the research . . ."). In addition, ACE promises (on the questionnaire itself) to maintain the confidentiality of responses. Within ACE, some questions have been raised about the way in which freshmen interpret the voluntary character of the research. Caught up as they are in what is for some a bewildering adjustment process during registration, they may feel more pressure to participate than ACE intends—especially if the local administrators consider that they need the results of the research. Whatever the reasons, very few freshmen refuse to take part.

Computerization at ACE

In a very real sense, large-scale research at ACE was made possible through computerization. This proceeded in three rather distinct phases. Prior to 1965, the office had no real need for computers. None of its programs involved the processing of large data files. Statistical information in tabular (rather than raw) form was acquired from sources external to the council, put together in appropriate form, and passed on to subscribers.

The second phase began with the development of CIRP in 1965. With the annual acquisition of extensive data on over 200,000 individuals, computerization became essential. The early computer applications in this second phase were conducted by an outside service bureau, after programming by the Office of Research staff. The locally administered questionnaires were sent to a commercial firm where identified documents were scanned by a sensing device and all marks indicating responses were transferred to magnetic tape. These tapes were sent to the Office of Research, checked for errors and internal consistency, and finally processed to produce *statistical* condensation of data. Follow-up surveys involving questionnaires mailed to and returned by students who had previously participated in CIRP were processed in a similar manner.

After processing CIRP data, national reports were (and are) prepared on student characteristics. Six such statistical reports have been issued annually since 1966, each covering over 200,000 freshmen and some 80 items of data. Institutional reports based on the particular college's freshmen are also prepared. These too, are statistical reports, devoid of student identification. They are returned to the respective college for use by college staff, and no institution is permitted to see the data pertaining to any other institution.

Also a part of routine processing is the generation of magnetic tapes with *identified* data, at the request of the institution. By ACE rules, institutions may obtain such tapes on their own students, provided that the students are informed at the time they participate that responses will be returned to college personnel. Before such tapes can be prepared and sent, the chief executive of the institution must certify to ACE in writing that students were so informed at the time they completed the form, and that the questionnaire information will be used only for research purposes. No further checks on fulfillment of this requirement are made by the Office of Research, since ACE researchers believe that college administrators recognize the ethical and practical reasons for adhering to this requirement. Furthermore, they suggest, if a local administrator really wanted to violate the requirement of confidentiality he could Xerox copies of the questionnaires as they were completed or "simply design and administer his own questionnaire locally."

Special analyses of CIRP data are also prepared. In the case of longitudinal data, computer applications are used to study such things as the "prediction" of student behavior (e.g., dropping out in the sophomore year) from attributes obtained at some earlier point in time (e.g., freshman religious attitudes, parental educational level, sources of college finances, and race).

The third phase in computerization at ACE involved the development of a databank for use by both the ACE staff and outside educational researchers. The system installed at ACE is essentially an elaborate computer program which permits the outside researcher to specify the kinds of data analyses he requires, and have ACE do the analysis at nominal cost. The total system makes statistical analyses possible on over a million freshmen, though analyses on this scale have rarely been done. Longitudinal data on subsamples from the total file are also accessible through the same system and most requests for data have been of this nature. Institutions themselves can also be studied, as descriptive data (such as affiliation, endowment, and student-teacher ratio) on each or some of 300 colleges and universities is combined with data from the student surveys.

Since the databank facilities became available in 1969, fewer than 50 outside researchers have made use of the data in it. This low level of use reflects, in part, the fact that the system is both young and that service is only a secondary objective of the office. As the system becomes more widely known, and the data in it more attractive to outside researchers, the level of use is expected to rise.

Until 1970, the office used a commercial service bureau in Maryland to process all data. A shift to in-house computing was initiated in order to consolidate the staff, to enhance collaboration between computing staff (who were in Maryland) and the ACE staff (in Washington), and also to minimize expenses of computing. ACE took over complete operation of a large (XDS SIGMA 5) computer in 1971, installing an office staff member as chief of operations.

Confidentiality of Research Records

In 1966, several members of the ACE staff and board of directors initiated efforts to have the council issue a formal public statement on the release by college officials of data on students to government agencies. The House Un-American Activities Committee (HUAC) was holding hearings on student activism at that time and had threatened to subpoena the membership records from student groups on some campuses. After some internal debates over the propriety of ACE entering this area, and some fears that a statement might jeopardize "good relations" between government and universities, the council issued a formal statement which recognized the need for colleges to act in accord with the law (e.g., supply the data if subpoenaed), but suggested that colleges ought not to be "pressed into the dubious role of informant." Colleges were urged to stop keeping lists of student organization members if they could, and to challenge the scope of HUAC subpoenas if and when they were served. Concerned about another aspect of the privacy problem, a member of the research staff, Robert Panos, began to work on the problem of confidentiality in research records; in 1968, he organized a professional symposium to sound out other researchers on this topic.

Around the same time, objection to some aspects of the CIRP survey developed. The National Student Association challenged ACE for its CIRP research effort. "We are dealing," said NSA president Robert Powell, "with a national study, financed by government, housed by an institution of college administrators, which deals not with institutions but with individual behavior at a time when all forces of power in the nation are attempting to control that behavior." Replying to the charges, ACE researchers noted that it was far more likely that their research would help students than hurt them. Responding to requests from the NSA and the American Civil Liberties Union, the ACE research staff agreed in 1968 to two changes in the CIRP questionnaire: modification of the instructions to students and an end to the use of the Social Security number as identifier.

In 1968, the research office began a study of Campus Unrest and Change, a three-year project supported by the National Institutes of Mental Health (NIMH). A sample of students who had participated in earlier CIRP surveys were now to be interviewed in order to study the way in which students became involved in campus protests and the impact of such actions on them.

Though the campus unrest study involved no more than 40 students on each campus, the interviews conducted were very detailed and the topic was highly charged. As a result, ACE experienced its first widespread resistance and protest. An article in the SDS newsletter *New Left Notes* was entitled "There's a Man Going 'Round Doing Surveys," and urged all SDS members and sympathizers not to take part. The campus unrest study, SDS spokesmen said, was in reality a "form of counterinsurgency research," designed to produce profiles of the student protester—profiles which could then be used by admissions departments to systematically exclude "protest-prone" students from the campus. Further, it was argued, there was no reason to believe that social scientists would refuse congressional committee requests for data, when so many college administrators had honored them in the past.

Ad hoc protests, challenging both the purpose of the research and confidentiality provisions occurred at several campuses, and numerous critical articles and editorials appeared in student newspapers, such as that in the Columbia University *Spectator* entitled "Fold, Spindle, and Mutilate!"

Members of the Office of Research staff believe that the student protests alone have not been responsible for altering research procedures. Protests have generally been short-lived and the number of students who refuse to take part or who use the tactic of supplying bogus answers is, they concluded, "so small as to be utterly insignificant as far as the validity of our research was concerned." The council itself, according to Logan Wilson, was virtually unaffected by the protests over the campus unrest study. "We simply knew that the protests were misdirected. Right from the beginning of our program in 1965, for example, great care was taken to separate physically all data from all identifying information and to keep identifying information locked in high security vaults." "Our staff," he said, "has probably thought and done more about this problem than any other group of researchers in the field."

The protests by students indirectly set into motion forces which were difficult to ignore, however. Realizing that the campus unrest study might raise some eyebrows, NIMH assistant director for extramural research Eli Rubenstein had set up an ad hoc advisory group before the work even began. As this group met throughout 1969, it became increasingly concerned about the security of the data being gathered, especially as the Justice Department adopted a "hard line" on campus protest, and Senator McClellan (heading a special investigatory committee) began to threaten to subpoena student witnesses to campus unrest. The advisory committee was composed of well-known social scientists,[8] and its views could not easily be ignored.

During this period, the U.S. Office of Education approached ACE with a request that the Office of Research submit a proposal for supplementary funds for its studies of campus unrest. A proposal was drawn up and was being evaluated at the same time that radical and student criticisms were being leveled at ACE. With the cooperation of Dr. Rubenstein from NIMH, a large colloquium was set up, with representatives from the ACE Office of Research, the Office of Education, and student groups such as the National Student Association. While this colloquium played no formal or official role in the USOE's evaluation of the ACE proposal, some of the participants from the Office of Education had expressed concern about the criticism which ACE was receiving. According to some who were present, the meeting was "a stormy session at points," but ended with the Office of Education participants somewhat more satisfied with the arrangements ACE had made to protect the confidentiality of data in its files. While the funds were eventually granted, the Office of Education's expressed concern

---

[8] Kenneth Keniston, David Riesman, Christian Bay, Amitai Etzioni, Joseph Kaufman, M. Brewster Smith, Andrew Greeley, and Seymour Halleck.

represented one more source of pressure on the ACE research staff.

At the same time, though considered less important by ACE Office of Research personnel, four or five institutions said that they would refuse to take part in the following year's CIRP survey. While the loss of a few participants was not crucial, there was some fear that a bandwagon effect might develop—resulting in the loss of a significant number of institutional participants. No such move occurred, however (possibly because the withdrawals received less publicity than ACE had anticipated), and some of the universities that dropped out returned the next year. For a time, though, the apprehension at ACE had been real.

Meetings of the ad hoc advisory committee produced some "heated exchanges" during this period, and at least one member threatened to resign publicly unless the committee put itself on record with respect to protecting the identified data in ACE files. The committee finally issued a statement covering both the CIRP and the Campus Unrest research programs. This included the promise that *identified* personal interview information would no longer be gathered at all in the Campus Unrest study, and that special precautions would be taken to protect CIRP data from inappropriate use. All of the researchers involved were to agree specifically not to divulge identified research data, even in response to subpoena, and the committee said that it would "support with all legal means any such refusal." In short, researchers explicitly said they "would go to jail" rather than cooperate in a breach of confidentiality.

The Council Research Office Responds

Under pressure from research subjects, guardian groups, political organizations, participating colleges, and funding sources, and pushed from inside by some staff members and the advisory group, the ACE research staff began the development of alternative strategies for coping with problems of confidentiality. Thinking back on the controversy, Astin said, "We soon realized that we were naive in thinking that people would believe us when we said we'd go to jail rather than give up data in response to a subpoena— even though we really would have done so." Indeed, some critics said that this promise was not a real protection, since all it would take was a policy reversal on ACE's part to make the data vulnerable once again.

Within ACE, the first substantial research on protective strategies was conducted by the Office of Research staff members, and out of this developed the elaborate LINK file system for the CIRP survey data. The system was designed (1) to eliminate possible use of research records for applications other than professional social science research (such as law enforcement or congressional use under legal subpoena, or through illegal appropriation of data by some other party); and (2) to eliminate the possibility of the researcher himself "snooping" into research files.

The principal feature of the LINK system is that the computer tape which makes identification of CIRP respondents possible is stored out of the country. The tape used for research in this country contains identification numbers that can only be matched to names through use of a special LINK file tape—which is stored abroad. "Actually," Astin recalled, "this was suggested to me by a former attorney for the Justice Department. He said, 'Why don't you do what the Mafia does: store your sensitive records out of the country where they cannot be obtained by subpoena?' "

Under contract with a foreign research institution, the LINK tape (which allows one wave of responses to be linked for comparison on a person-to-person basis with responses from subsequent waves) will not be returned to the U.S.—even if ACE requests it. Some of the processing must therefore always be done out of the country. This makes the identified CIRP responses free from subpoena, since ACE no longer controls the process of matching names with responses.[9] The potential (and drawbacks) of the LINK approach to protecting confidentiality have been commented on in print by ACE staff members such as Astin and Robert F. Boruch.[1]

While the LINK system does, for all practical purposes, prevent subpoena of the computerized files, the identified CIRP data remains technically vulnerable at several points. As Boruch and others on the Office of Research staff have noted, any of the staff could have copied all of the tapes prior to full operation of the LINK system, and local college administrators and workers in the document processing firm also have access to the *manual* survey returns files before they are destroyed. But the research

---

[9] For a detailed discussion of how the LINK file works, see A. W. Astin and R. F. Boruch, "A 'Link' System for Assuring Confidentiality of Research Data in Longitudinal Studies," *American Educational Research Journal*, Vol. 7, No. 4, 1970, pp. 616-24.

[1] Boruch joined the staff of our project in November 1970, on a partial leave of absence from ACE. During the final analysis of data and revision of this manuscript, he had left ACE to join the staff of the Social Science Research Council and the faculty of Northwestern University.

staff at ACE feels that the risk of such violations is minimal, since the administration of the survey and early processing of the data take place over a relatively short period of time. More important, says Research Director Astin, is that there is currently little real threat of unauthorized access. "LINK was a specific defense measure. Most people didn't understand how it worked, but it satisfied some. But really, I don't think anybody wants our data—or wanted it then. There's no real legal use for it, for instance; students don't sign the questionnaire—so it's not a legal document —and there is some probability that, if we did match names with responses, we wouldn't even have the right person; questionnaires do get mixed up at times. Certainly no court is going to accept information like that. A congressional committee is a possible interested party, I suppose, but there are easier ways for them to get the kind of information we've got on file."

Future ACE Research Activities

The CIRP questionnaires were administered according to schedule in the fall of 1971; when the data have been LINK-processed, a sixth wave of responses will have been added to the ACE databank. No protest was heard at the more than 300 participating colleges and universities. Whether the LINK system actually protected ACE files from real external threats or only safeguarded its public image, the technique has sparked interest among social scientists. For some, it is a protective measure they might employ in their own research files, though the cost of setting it up and operating under its restrictions might be prohibitive, and in some research situations it would provide a false sense of security. For others, it defined the kind of timely protective and political response to be expected of social science research institutions when they handle sensitive data that might be subject to violations of the confidentiality promise under which they were gathered.

Religious Organizations

Approximately 128 million Americans were reported to be members of organized religious bodies in 1971. Included are 69 million Protestants, 48 million Roman Catholics, and 6 million Jews. Five million persons are scattered among religious groups such as Jehovah's Witnesses, Christian Scientists, the Church of Latter-day Saints, and the Seventh Day Adventists.

Since there are federal and state constitutional provisions guaranteeing freedom of religion and non-religion in the United States, Americans of legal age are free to belong or not to belong to a religious group as they wish. They are also legally free to leave a religious body whenever they please, though to do so they may have to bear a disruption of social and family ties.

Religious groups vary in the degree to which members will tolerate inquiry into or interference with their personal lives, exercise control over some part of their children's education, and in the proportion of time and financial resources members are expected to contribute. But whether the required self-disclosure is occasional and shallow, or approaches the confessional depth which more totally involving religions can demand, the members of many religious groups accept scrutiny which, on the part of government, would clearly by regarded as unacceptably intrusive.

Most religious groups are busy record keepers. Into the local registers will go entries for baptism or blessing, confirmation and bar mitzvah, marriage, and specialized religious ceremonies. Local records are usually kept of financial contributions and assessments, attendance of children at religious schools, and activities of the many clubs and societies attached to the local church or temple. Many religious groups keep records on a national basis on ministers, priests, and rabbis, to facilitate the search of congregations for new pastors and to aid in the administration of national religious affairs.

Catholic, Protestant, and Jewish organizations in the United States have not made extensive use of computers as yet for their administrative affairs, though several Protestant denominations are presently working on a computerized system for their professional personnel. However, one religious body is well known for its early adoption of computer technology, the Church of Jesus Christ of Latter-day Saints (the Mormons). It is the subject of our next profile.

THE CHURCH OF LATTER-DAY SAINTS

The Church of Jesus Christ of Latter-day Saints was officially organized in 1830 in New York. Because of heavy persecution in various eastern and midwestern states, to which the church moved in search of religious freedom, the Mormons trekked west in 1846. They reached Salt Lake City, Utah, in 1847 and settled there permanently, creating their own self-sufficient community in the desert. Non-Mormons emigrated to Utah during the decades that followed, and the territory became a state in 1896, after the Mormons officially rejected the practice of plural marriage (polygamy) in 1890.

Today the church has more than 3 million members, primarily in the United States but with communities in more than a score of other nations as well. Mormons believe in the Bible, the Book of Mormon, a Trinity, baptism, repentance, and the laying on of hands; they do not regard themselves as Protestants, and are not part of the National Council of Churches of Christ.

The church has always been an authority-centered religion, believing in an all-male priesthood, strong parental authority, industrious work and thrift, and strict morality in sexual and personal lives. Members may not smoke, drink liquor, or use "stimulating" beverages such as tea or coffee. Geographically, the church is organized into units called missions, branches, wards, and stakes, with various church societies performing work in special areas such as teaching, youth life, and genealogical research.

The church depends on a voluntary lay ministry rather than a career priesthood, with males called to fill the posts of local bishop, stake president, and higher offices in the central church administration. Church doctrines hold that Negroes cannot serve as priests, and there are only a small number of blacks in the church. Members support the church with a voluntary tithe of one-tenth of their income, and are expected to undertake unpaid missionary work for the church.

Growing out of its history as a total community in Utah, the church maintains not only religious institutions such as churches, schools, and mission homes but also owns and manages a wide range of commercial enterprises. These include the Hotel Utah, TV station KTVA, and the *Deseret News* in Salt Lake City. They also manage their own extensive welfare program for church members, believing that this should not be left to the state. To support these relief efforts, they produce and store food, clothing, and other materials in a chain of farms, storehouses, and granaries. They also run a placement service to help out-of-work members get jobs. Where a member is not disabled, he is expected to work for the relief he receives.

Traditional Record-keeping in the Church

Personal lives of members are kept under close watch in the church, and detailed records for the central administration are compiled by local bishops on the individual's attendance and participation at meetings, offices held, tasks given, services and missions performed, tithes paid, and family performances in the home-fellowship program. Over the years, four sets of personal records have grown up within the church.

1. A cumulative record sheet for each member is prepared and kept by the local bishop, in the ward or branch in which the church member currently resides. A copy is also kept up to date in the Presiding Bishop's Office in Salt Lake City. In a standardized format, these sheets contain the member's life progress in the church: date of birth, current address, parents' names, date of marriage, names of spouse and children; the dates of the performance of various religious ceremonies and duties (blessing, baptism, confirmation, etc.); and voluntary posts held within the church (deacon, teacher, priest, elder, etc.). The date and places of missions served for the church are also recorded. On the back of the form are notations of a member's transfers to different local church bodies as he might change his residence. Date, place, and cause of death closes the membership record.

Information dealing with the moral life or personal behavior of a member is not entered. When the local bishop learns about personal or family matters germane to the church, this is kept in his memory or his informal notes, but not in official records. The basis for this policy lies in the church's fundamental belief that individuals must be forgiven their trespasses not only by their fellow men but also by their church. To compile a permanent record of improper behavior that would follow a member throughout his life in the church might lead some officials to prejudge that person when considering him for church duties, and would inhibit reformation and personal growth. In addition, as one local bishop commented, "it would be like double jeopardy," making a person pay twice for the same transgression. Members guilty of a "serious transgression" are dealt with by a church court.

When a member transfers to another ward of the church or when a local bishop finishes his term, the membership records passed on to the new bishop do not generally contain narrative or evaluative information. In special cases, however, a slip may be attached to the record saying that before the new bishop calls the member to a church post or approves his doing certain work in the temples, he should communicate with the former bishop. Several local bishops interviewed said that they had used this procedure, giving as illustrations members who were sexually promiscuous or held some improper doctrine ("someone who believed we should have polygamy again") and had not made honest efforts to reform or follow approved doctrines. Informal communication might also be used, such as a telephone call by a bishop to whose ward a member had moved asking the former bishop what kind of church work the member or his family might be especially fitted for, or asking about the history of a serious problem that had come to the attention of the new bishop, such as "a youngster who seemed to be in real trouble."

A church member is able to see his local record and have any item corrected if it is inaccurately recorded. This is usually handled as part of the regular conferences bishops have with members about their yearly activity. Except for a parent seeing entries for his minor children, no one other than the member or church officials dealing with membership records can see an individual's sheet or the central membership file in Salt Lake City. No list of members is given to outside private, governmental, or commercial bodies.

If a member decides to leave the church, he can have his membership records destroyed, leaving no trace either locally or in the central file that he had ever been a church member. If he returned to the church later, a new record would be opened and his data recorded again. The church may "disfellow" a member if he is engaging in improper conduct; when in such status, he cannot hold the priesthood but can attend meetings and partake of the sacraments. The church can also excommunicate someone, as when he is living in open adultery or has become an active member of another church, and will remove him from the membership records. Both these actions require hearings before special church bodies, with extensive procedural safeguards for the member.

2. Records of a member's tithe payments contain a note of the amount that the member stipulated as a tenth of his income for that year; the receipts for weekly installments; and a cumulative total of the amount actually paid in at the end of the year. Generally, a member's statement as to what his tithe would amount to is accepted by the local bishop and the central church, and no investigations or credit checks are done to verify a member's income.

3. Because the Mormon church does not have a professional ministry, there is no central personnel file for ministers such as is kept in many other major religious denominations. Personnel and salary data are kept for those serving as paid employees in the church's central administration, persons employed in various com-

mercial enterprises run by church bodies, and full-time school-teachers.

4. Finally, the Mormon church believes that every person who has lived on earth will have an opportunity to live again at a future moment of resurrection, and with the same family that he was part of on earth. To do this, the person must accept Jesus Christ and his scriptures, as defined by Mormon doctrine. For members of the Mormon church, qualification entails performing in a church temple the basic ordinances of baptism, confirmation, marriage, etc.

Because billions of persons lived and died without accepting Christ, Mormons believe that they should, by serving as "proxy for the dead," afford such deceased persons the opportunity to choose Christ at the time of resurrection. Church members, therefore, do research as to the birth, marriage, family, and death of nonchurch members, as drawn from historical or genealogical sources, and place these records in the master geneealogical file maintained by the church for the time of resurrection. This is done at the initiative of the Mormon church members, with no approval or permission sought from the heirs of the person so nominated.

Mormon officials note that "The church does not accept names of persons for this purpose within 110 years from the birth of the person whose record has been submitted. Any record which has information which might be of an embarrassing nature (such as illegitimate birth) is not available to the public, but is retained in a confidential file by a Special Service Section."

The duty of research has made the church's Genealogical Society (founded in 1894) the largest genealogical organization in the world. By the late 1950s, the Temple Records Index Bureau at the society's headquarters in Salt Lake City had over 25 million three-by-five cards, each containing vital statistics and notes of the performance of ordinances for a living or deceased person. The cards were stored in over 800 filing cabinets. The society also maintained an enormous library of printed and microfilm records of genealogical information—histories of families, churches, and communities, and registries of names and historical events from all over the world. The church states that it has 5 billion names in its genealogical records.

Although the church runs an extensive internal welfare program, distributing food, clothing, and goods, no central records are maintained about who is receiving welfare in a ward; details of a particular case are known to the bishop, the financial clerk, the

Relief Society president, and one or two other local officials. Only statistical summaries are sent outside the local ward.

The Initial Decision to Computerize

Until the early 1960s, the personal-record systems just described were kept in traditional manual forms, with some EAM equipment used for payroll and related activities. By the mid-1950s, church officials became alarmed about the size and annual increase of the genealogical records. The 25 million cards in its Temple Records Index Bureau were increasing by more than 1 million cards a year. The floor in the bureau's main library had buckled so badly that special girders had to be installed to support it.

When this condition became known throughout the church, several members who were professionals working in data processing suggested that the society consider computer storage and processing. The committee of high-ranking church officials created to consider this idea was rather skeptical at first. They doubted whether investing in expensive computer equipment would lead to savings in costs over the manual operation. More important, they feared a loss of control over the records in going from traditional paper documents that anyone could read and care for to a mysterious form of electronic storage and retrieval understood and controlled by computer specialists.

The members proposing computerization convinced church leaders that, even if no money were saved, computerization would lead to better utilization of the genealogical records than had been possible through manual techniques. They also convinced the review committee that the computerized file could be developed in full conformity to church doctrines covering the form and use of these records. When it was shown that church members who were data-processing professionals would design and run the computer system, this met the officials' concern that persons insensitive to Mormon religious tenets would control the files.

Though the decision to computerize the genealogical file was made in 1957-58, it took almost ten years before problems of system design, data conversion, and operating procedures could be worked out and automation begun. (Meanwhile, the church installed an IBM 1401 in 1962, using it primarily for the church's own financial accounting.) Attempts were made to convert the existing genealogical cards into computerized storage by means of optical scanning. Because the cards were of different-colored stock and contained frequent erasures and strikeovers, this did not prove

feasible. Other problems included identification and documentation for accepting entries to a record from the church member
submitting it, and devising the proper sorting keys to use for file
organization.

The Current Computer System and Its Applications

To work out these procedures and run its administrative and
commercial ADP, the church created a new organization, called
the Management Systems Corporation (MSC). This became the
church's data-processing center, and also accepted commercial jobs
to fill up its unused computer time. The director of MSC, Bruce
Smith, had been one of the computer professionals in the church
who suggested computerization originally. The MSC steadily enlarged its computer capacity during the 1960s, so that by 1970 it
was using an IBM 360/65, with assorted printers, disk drives,
magnetic tape units, video display terminals, and other peripheral
equipment.

As of 1971, computerization had been applied to four personal-record files in the church. All new genealogical records and
updating submissions to them are now computerized, with conversion of the 35 million existing records scheduled for gradual work
in the future. Payroll data for church employees were put on the
computer, but information on preemployment history, job evaluation, current skills, and similar matters remains in the manual
personnel file jackets. Tithing records were computerized and local
bishops receive a computerized print-out of weekly and annual
payments that one bishop said "has lightened the bookkeeping
load enormously."

In 1970, a program was begun to put membership records on
the computer. Local bishops have been notified to acquire special
typewriters and use new forms for the optical scanning device that
will be in operation.

There are no plans to create and computerize individual
welfare records. Bruce Smith explained that one of the prime
objectives of the welfare program—to provide dignified work for
recipients and train people for jobs elsewhere—would be undercut
if the local, informal record system were replaced by computerization. This decision was sustained even though the lack of central
records has allowed some instances of fraud, in which a church
member joined more than one local church ward and drew welfare
benefits in each. In one case in California, a member enrolled in 14
wards before he was discovered. A few cases such as this may seem
alarming, Smith noted, but "the number of abuses is not sufficient
to justify creating a record system that follows people around."

Comparisons between the Manual and Computerized Files

As already noted, existing church rules about information collection and record-keeping were rigorously followed in the computerized systems. The same information is collected for membership and genealogical records as was collected before computerization was adopted; no additional questions or commentary were added to the individual forms. The church's policy on not recording derogatory data on members was carried over fully into computerization. As Smith put it, "Our philosophy doesn't make the church data-omnivorous."

The church prepared carefully for the forthcoming conversion of its membership records to computerized storage several years ago by having local bishops call in each head of family or individual member, show him the existing manual record, and ask him to verify the correctness of all items. Anything the individual considered inaccurate or incomplete was corrected on a showing of the proper information. As for the genealogical files, the church's Data Processing Committees believes that the new procedures of requiring identification from the members who submit information and production of original source documents to prove the facts submitted have greatly increased accuracy over procedures in the manual era.

MSC officials do not see why outsiders would try to obtain personal information from their "people records" through theft or stealth. As a result of this judgment, the physical and technical safeguards for the computer system have been aimed primarily at providing security against wanton or mischievous destruction of equipment, ensuring confidentiality for "sensitive" pay records, and guarding against such dangers as accidental programmer or operator errors or monetary fraud. These safeguards are not talked about in public, on the theory that describing them might make it easier for skilled intruders to overcome them.[2]

There is no greater sharing of individual data within the church than before computerization. The MSC sees itself as the trustee of information for the "owning" departments of the

---

[2]To protect its genealogical records against deliberate or accidental harm in what the church calls "an uncertain world," and to have them available whenever the resurrection comes, the church invested millions of dollars to hollow out a solid granite mountain near Salt Lake City and create a top-security records vault. A completely self-sufficient facility, with provision for automatic sealing of the site in case of nuclear blast, the vault has six huge rooms, each capable of holding 880,000 rolls of microfilm. At present, only one room is used, and this is not yet full. A separate room is used to store the computerized genealogical records and other computer backup tapes.

church (the Genealogical Society for that file, Controller's Office for employee payroll, and Presiding Bishop's Office for membership records). The basic rule, Bruce Smith observed, is that "we don't release anything unless to the owner of the information, or on authorized signature from someone who has both a need and authority to justify release."

As for outside release of information, the church is still one of the least "data-sharing" organizations in the nation. Despite its increased technical capacity to generate lists of names or search its records, it still gives out no credit information, sells no lists to advertisers or fund-raising groups, does not share information with other religious groups, and will supply only minimal information to government or press inquiries. For example, it would verify the fact of membership or of the use of a member's car on church affairs if the Internal Revenue Service wanted this to support a tax deduction. But it will not confirm or release the fact of membership where individuals do not want to be known publicly as Mormons, or where present or former membership might be used to embarrass someone in his social or political life. Both before and after computerization, a person who leaves the Mormon church out of religious or personal disillusionment, or for any other reason, can have all his records destroyed, leaving no trace of his former membership.

Unlike most other religious groups in the United States in recent years, the Mormon church has not faced serious protest movements among its membership or lay ministry. One of its publications, *Dialogue* magazine, contains occasional articles by church members criticizing various church doctrines or practices, such as its policy on barring Negroes from the priesthood, but these expressions have a strong "reform within the family" character. As a result of this climate of strong trust by members in the doctrines and leadership of their church, and the sense of a "loving community," the personal information sought for counseling, home-fellowship programs, and church records is given freely or considered legitimate for the church to be concerned about, even where it deals with very sensitive aspects of personal, family, or ideological life. The ultimate safety valve, of course, is that anyone can leave the church if he becomes disenchanted or feels oppressed. None of the church members, local bishops, or central administrators interviewed could recall any protests by members about civil-liberties aspects of the church's record-keeping policies.

Future Plans for Computerization within the Church

In the next three to five years, those in charge of the church's data-processing activities foresee their work with personal records involving computerization of the membership file, gradual conversion of the accumulated genealogical records, and greater use of the computerized data base to give church management better reports on trends in church operations. MSC officials do not see anything like integrated files or a "total management information system" for church affairs emerging in the near future. Because of the substantial autonomy American law gives to religious bodies to conduct their internal affairs without regulatory supervision, the church anticipates few government interventions in its record-keeping or data-sharing policies. The church marches to its own drum, and its computerization effects have carried over with precision the church's rules and philosophy as to collection and use of personal information for church life.

Hospitals and Health Centers

The 340,000 physicians and 26,000 hospitals in the United States are all deeply involved in the problems of medical record-keeping—long cited within medicine as a source of both inefficiency and extraordinary expense. There were more than 30 million hospital admissions in the United States in 1970, and some 850 million individual visits to physicians. As individual records have grown in volume and complexity, problems of accuracy and timely retrieval have mounted as well, affecting the work of health personnel who depend heavily on the information contained within them. Records, or parts of them, circulate among physicians, hospitals, and insurers; within hospitals they move between central record rooms and the points of use.

Where the physician knows his patient very well and is in direct contact with him, the medical record is not always necessary for his immediate care. But the patient's medical care is increasingly provided by a complex network of specialized professionals and institutions. More and more families are involved with group medical services, using different physicians at different times and receiving treatment in several locations. Here, the patient's medical record serves as a principal means of communication among doctors and health facilities. Almost 7 million Americans moved across state lines in 1970 alone, creating the need for transfer of medical records to new locations. The reporting required for insurance underwriting and claims processing, hospital accreditation and other regulatory and law-enforcement activities, and for health department monitoring of communicable diseases, also involve the transfer of substantial amounts of information from medical records.

For the most part, the medical community has not yet turned heavily to computerization to solve its medical record-keeping problems. A 1970 survey of hospitals in the U.S. reports that "55 percent of all hospital information processing applications are still performed by hand,"[3] and in our own national survey only 24 percent of the hospitals in the sample reported computer applications to their patient medical records.

As in many other fields, computerization has progressed furthest in hospital accounting and billing operations, with some other applications to laboratory reporting, patient admissions, and scheduling. Because the patient's individual medical record is a basically narrative document, it is difficult to reduce it to the kinds of codes and abbreviations which might make computer storage relatively inexpensive; instead, massive storage would be required for any system that was designed to accept the record in narrative form.

Early attempts at computerization in medical institutions have to some extent increased the amount of attention focused upon confidentiality issues. Questions are being raised by professionals within the health field about what kinds of protections exist or should exist in medical data systems. Central to these discussions are two themes: the low level of protection existing in current manual medical files (said one physician, "Newspaper reporters have 'plants' in my hospital. A twenty-dollar bill will buy any information"), and the problems which may arise when medical information is passed into the hands of nonmedical institutions which handle insurance, claims record-keeping, etc.

Legal complications accompany these technical ones. Where reports and orders must be *signed* by a physician, no method for duplicating this function on the computer has yet been devised. Where medical records move outside medical institutions and outside the care of medical personnel, in many cases they are no

---

[3]Hospital Financial Management Association, 1970.

longer protected by laws which privilege the relationship between health personnel and patient. A further factor in the development of computerized medical records is that medical institutions have had relatively little money to put into the development of computer systems, and have had difficulty pulling medical personnel away from health-care tasks for system development.

These and other barriers, and the fact that many developed clinical-record computer applications are not yet "paying their way," explain why there is no health institution operating today with anything near a fully computerized medical-records system.

Two additional factors need be mentioned as background here. First is a philosophical shift in several quarters—Congress, the labor movement, and among some civic groups—to the position that, even though almost two-thirds of the health care in the U.S. is currently paid for out of private funds, high-quality medical care is a right to which every American is entitled, rather than a privilege of birth or wealth. This developing public opinion finds its expression currently in national health-insurance plans being debated in Congress.

Second, in contrast to the picture of limited development we presented above, a few institutions have developed far more comprehensive or sophisticated computer systems. Examples are an on-line psychiatric record system developed for a small hospital and the "interactive" computer system developed to take a medical history from a patient through a question-and-answer process. Among the more advanced users of computers for clinical medicine is the Kaiser-Permanente Health Care Program, the subject of our final profile.

THE KAISER-PERMANENTE MEDICAL CARE PROGRAM

The Kaiser-Permanente system had its origins in the "paternal capitalism" of one of America's largest industries—the Kaiser industrial empire which grew up on the West Coast prior to World War II. In order to reduce the cost of providing health care for its employees, Kaiser established its own system of hospitals, clinics, and participating physicians. In the Kaiser shipyards of World War II, the medical needs of 100,000 employees were met through the successful operation of this system.

At war's end, however, layoffs threatened the continued existence of what Henry J. Kaiser was later to call "the new economics of health care." As membership in the plan dropped below 14,000, Kaiser was forced to open the program to the public. Today, the Kaiser-Permanente program has become the largest, and one of the most successful, group medical plans in the nation—providing "total" medical care for over 2 million persons in California, Oregon, Hawaii, Colorado, and Ohio. The program operates on a nonprofit basis under the Kaiser Foundation, and members are treated in more than 30 clinics and in 21 Kaiser hospitals and laboratories, with medical services for the program supplied through 2,000 full- and part-time physicians who participate in the various Permanente Medical Groups.

For a set fee, the program—which is both insurer and medical provider—agrees to meet all of the members' health needs, from examinations and inoculations to long-term hospital care. When this arrangement was first established, it was considered a radical answer to some widespread and pressing problems in medical economics. Hospitals and other health institutions had been criticized for their poor fiscal management, and physicians for encouraging unnecessary (but often profitable) hospitalization and surgical procedures. Under the Kaiser program, physicians are salaried or are partners receiving per capita payments; since the program operates on a tight budget, there is pressure to avoid unnecessary medical expenditures. The emphasis at Kaiser is on *preventive* medicine—keeping its members healthy and catching health problems before they become costly in human or economic terms.

The prepaid structure has had the effect of keeping Kaiser premiums low (averaging $450 a year for a family of three or more) compared to those of other plans. In addition, Kaiser-Permanente members "spend less than half as many days in the hospitals as other Americans."[4] Still another result of this combination of health insurance and care is that a comprehensive set of medical and administrative records on each member exists for use within the system, rather than being scattered among several unrelated institutions. Limited administrative records on program members are stored centrally, and files on some patients—principally medical examination reports—are in central computer storage. Most patient records, however, are stored manually in the offices of participating physicians and within Kaiser health facilities.

---

[4]*New York Times*, September 13, 1971, p. 1.

Computer Development at Kaiser

Kaiser-Permanente's professional and economic commitment to the notion of "preventive medicine" led it, in 1950, to be among the first U.S. medical-care institutions to undertake a "multiphasic health screening" program in which record-keeping was supported by card-punching and sorting equipment. Yearly intensive examinations were offered to members along with a battery of tests designed to identify health problems early. Though approval of this new program was not unanimous among Kaiser-Permanente physicians, [5] most facilities adopted the system.

As in many other medical institutions in the U.S., computerization efforts at Kaiser-Permanente began with accounting and billing, in 1954. By 1971, in Kaiser-Permanente's northern California region, there were "more than 400 programs utilizing EDP in administrative and financial areas. This includes generating group direct billings, mapping address and coverage changes, and providing statistical profiles."

In 1960, the multiphasic screening program led Kaiser-Permanente into its first experience with computer applications in medical record keeping. The multiphasic checkup program had come under attack for its failure to organize the collected data properly and make them convenient for use. The Kaiser Medical Methods Research Department—which had developed the program—decided that computerization might improve utilization of the data, and developed a pilot study along those lines.

Kaiser's move to computers was prompted also by increasingly costly and inefficient manual procedures. The patient medical records were stuffed with documents such as lab test results, surgical summaries, notes by physicians and nurses, identification information, and sometimes even basic accounting data. In most cases, the physician lacked time to review an entire file, and had to try to extract hurriedly those items critical to the patient's current problem.

Coupled with the problem of effective record use was that of record-keeping cost. Kaiser Medical Methods Research investigators discovered that "information commerce" (record keeping and other patient care communication) accounted for 29 percent of

---

[5]The staff at one of the northern California hospitals voted not to switch to the multiphasic approach, preferring instead to handle diagnostic screening "in the traditional way."

this hospitals' operating cost, with manpower representing most of this expense.

In 1968, the National Center for Health Services Research, an agency under HEW, awarded Kaiser funds to begin the development of "a computer-based system that will support the medical data requirements of one million health plan members, one thousand physicians, and a large corps of professional and paramedical contributors to patient care." The pilot project is being conducted in the San Francisco Bay area Kaiser facilities. The foundation hospital there, and its associated clinics, provide services for 125,000 Plan members.

For this pilot project, the Medical Methods Research (MMR) group selected applications which seemed achievable within the state of the technological art and given the problems common to medical record-keeping. First, they would "acquire and store in the computer record of each patient, on a continuous basis, all hospital and clinic diagnoses, results of all laboratory tests, X ray, pathology, and electrocardiographic examinations, and data concerning all drugs dispensed or administered." Second, they would "provide initially limited, but progressively expanding, services to the professional and technical staff such as printed reports of test results and, in the hospital, visually displayed and printed sets of data" (doctors' orders, medication schedules, laboratory specimen labels, etc.). Finally, the project would seek "to provide a broad and flexible data base for clinical, epidemiological, and health services research."

Initially the pilot-study applications were run on an IBM 360/50, but have been changed to an IBM 370/155. The operations are organized so that Kaiser payroll, accounting, and billing information is processed independently on a Honeywell computer and is kept separate from medical data and information on patient use of the facilities. Eventually the medical and administrative files will share a common data base.

In the computer files at present, the Patient Computer Medical Records are "in the process of being built." Beginning with the results of multiphasic screening exams, MMR researchers have developed one by one the ability to handle data from other clinical sources. Since 1969, data from out-patient pharmacies and medical offices in the San Francisco area have been entered. More recently, clinical lab test information on both in- and out-patients has been collected and in-patient data stored.

Since June 1969, on-line typewriter terminals in five out-patient pharmacies have allowed pharmacists to enter more than

1,000 prescriptions daily directly onto each patient's record stored in the central computer in San Francisco. In addition, the system handles each year 1 million clinical laboratory tests and 60,000 multiphasic screening examinations (from the San Francisco, Oakland, and Walnut Creek multiphasic laboratories).

The medical record established for each patient and updated on each visit is like its manual counterpart in form and content.[6] Identification data in the file include medical record number, Social Security number, name, address, birthdate, sex, and blood type. In addition this section contains enough identifying information on family members and relatives to permit cross-referencing among these records. The medical data section of the record includes historical information on past illnesses and complaints, observations by Kaiser-Permanente physicians, test results, preliminary and firm diagnoses, and reports on medical procedures which have been ordered or performed. Every patient contact with the San Francisco Kaiser-Permanente facility generates a "visit" entry into the computerized record.

At present, only part of these data are made available on-line. In the San Francisco Bay area facilities, physicians are provided on-line retrieval of multiphasic reports. During 1972, more laboratory test information, patient drug orders, and drug-use information have been added to the records which are available on-line.

The Computer Impact

Assessing the impact of their new system, MMR researchers believe that "the computer medical record system has probably had a small impact so far on the general record keeping practices in Kaiser-Permanente medical centers. Essentially the same quality and quantity of data is being kept as before." Some new data are kept only in the computer system, however, such as those used for special research phases of the multiphasic program "which have not as yet proven to be of clinical value."

A member of the MMR staff, Dr. Edmund Van Brunt, project chief of the computer data acquisition system, pointed out that the system is really "a long-range research and development program." Whether large-scale computerized medical files can provide the kind of reliable and sophisticated service required, or whether the costs of adopting computer systems for medical record-keeping will be too high, are questions still to be answered.

---

[6]The general contents of a hospital medical record are specified under California law (California Administrative Code, title 17, group 2, section 280).

A survey of physician reaction to the computerized system is currently underway. Dr. Morris Collen, director of the MMR Department, believes that the more experience doctors have with the system, the more they will like it. Originally, there was a feeling among some Kaiser physicians that computerization would somehow "dehumanize" the practice of medicine. However, Dr. Collen feels that "just the opposite is true. Because of the computer the physician will have more individualized information about his patient—more complete and more accurate than he could possibly have gathered before."

Kaiser-Permanente has more concrete information about *patient* reaction to the use of computers in medical record-keeping. Since 1964, studies have been conducted of patient opinions about the multiphasic program, in which the use of computers is immediately apparent to the patient. "With computer cards and questionnaire in hand," the patient starts through the battery of more than three dozen tests. Data-processing cards are used to enter the test results, which include body measurements, medical history, chest X ray, EKG, spirometry, eye examination, hearing tests, and laboratory analysis of blood and urine. Data from the tests are fed directly into the computer for immediate analysis. The computer then summarizes the findings and indicates where additional tests seem advisable. Within a three-hour period, almost all of the examination results have become a part of the patient's permanent computerized medical record. Kaiser researchers note that "patient satisfaction" with this system of examination has consistently been very high among test groups surveyed each year.

The new computer system may also have had some impact on the accuracy and completeness of patient records. Dr. Collen notes that "errors have become so common in traditional medical records that physicians are accustomed to handling them, from finding a woman's lab test in her husband's file, to prescription errors in the hospital." But Collen feels that the problems needn't be as great in a computerized system. Under our operating definitions, he said, "some 10 percent of our computer records contained 'errors.' We don't know what the error level in manual files is, but it certainly couldn't be less! Gradually we hope to get the computer file error level down to around 3 percent. To go to 0 percent error would be prohibitively costly, and probably isn't possible, anyway."

Mr. Lou Davis, manager of the MMR computer center, noted that some medical records at the San Francisco Hospital were once accidentally erased (by overwriting) due to an error in the computer system. To ensure recovery after this, backup tapes are maintained from which a record can be reconstructed; the manual files could also be used for this purpose if necessary. To handle the problem of "input error," periodic checks are made by comparing the computerized medical record against paper files.

Medical Records and Confidentiality Issues

Both the revelations made by patients to their doctors and records arising out of medical care have been treated as confidential for centuries. The tradition reflected in the Hippocratic Oath is also recognized in law; many states have established the "doctor-patient privilege" and extended this to medical records in hospitals, clinics, and other health facilities. Unauthorized disclosures from medical records have not played a prominent role in the drama of increasing concern about privacy. There are occasional instances of reporters writing about the illness of a celebrity or of "political" leaks of medical records from VA or army files. But for the most part, the medical community has received relatively little criticism connected with unauthorized disclosure.

Patient charts in the offices of Permanente Group physicians are kept in central record rooms. In Kaiser Foundation hospitals, medical records on past patients are also stored in the medical record room under the general supervision of a medical record librarian. These are filed by the patient's medical record number, and must be signed out under the responsibility of a physician. In keeping with a well-established medical tradition, psychiatric files are stored separately and special permission is required for their use. When the patient is in the hospital, his record is moved to the appropriate ward, where it is in most cases stored in restricted files at the nursing station.

No medical information is stored in the central administrative files of Kaiser. Since Kaiser is both insurer and medical provider, members need supply no claims information. This aspect of Kaiser-Permanente insurance operations sets it apart from other plans (such as Blue Cross-Blue Shield or those offered by Mutual of Omaha) in which the insurer—a nonmedical institution—must process and retain claims forms containing medical information.

Under California state law, adult medical records and communications between physicians and patients are privileged, and medical records in Kaiser Foundation hospitals and clinics—whether in chart rooms, on the ward or elsewhere—are similarly covered. While the law protects health records to some degree, the medical record is also a legal one. With or without permission of the individual, the court can subpoena the entire medical record. Most frequently, however, records go to court at the request of patients involved in actions such as disability and malpractice suits.

Information on births and deaths is reported to the California Department of Public Health. The same department also requires that infectious diseases (e.g., VD) be reported, and maintains the state's Tumor Registry. Reports on Kaiser patients who are also covered under Medicare or MediCal[7] are sent to appropriate agencies or to intermediaries which handle billing. Cases of gunshot or knife wounds, reported rapes, and the physical abuse of minors have to be reported to local police. In addition, the names, addresses, and injuries of accident victims must be supplied to police on request.

Under California law, and by tradition within medicine, individuals do not have access to their own medical records; Kaiser officials suggest, however, that "the patient has considerable control over his record since he must sign releases permitting its use." While he is often not in a position to refuse (as when he is seeking life insurance, for instance), the patient must sign a release form before his records or "abstracts" from them move outside the Kaiser-Permanente system. A Kaiser-Permanente policy information sheet reads, "If the patient is conscious and can communicate with the doctor or nurse in charge, or relatives, he should be asked whether he will permit any information to be given and his decision is final."

In developing computer applications at Kaiser, MMR investigators paid considerable attention to privacy and security protections. Physical security at the San Francisco Bay area computer facility consists of locked premises and a guard service that operates after regular duty hours. Mr. Lou Davis noted that an "audit trail" is kept on all transactions, and while this will not prevent unauthorized inquiries from within the system, he feels "it makes such penetration more difficult to achieve without detection."

As they moved from manual to computer applications, MMR retained the same basic rules of data sharing as obtained for manual records. These stated:

---

[7]California's supplementary medical insurance plan.

All data within the patient computer record are subject to the same regulations governing their privacy and confidentiality as are data within our hospital record room. This requires controls for protection of the computer records to specified degrees of user-imposed privacy. . .

Davis was quick to point out that there had been no instances of unauthorized access to the computer files. Kaiser-Permanente has suffered a few incidents involving leaks, but in each case the unauthorized release of data was traced to a clerk working in the manual files. Even when the computer files become more central to Kaiser operations, Davis said, he thinks the tendency will still be for individuals to go to the hospital record room for information, rather than the computer center.

The Future

Researchers in the MMR Department hope to expand the pilot-project operations. In the Kaiser Foundation San Francisco hospital, 21 video display terminals will be located in the patient care centers, and through these, hospital personnel will have on-line access to parts of the patient's medical record. Diagnoses, signs and symptoms, drug and nursing orders, medication schedules, and the results of clinical and other tests will be entered through the terminals. The record will be continuously updated as physicians, nurses, and technicians use it. Protections against misuse of the files will "develop over time," but will principally depend on identification of both terminals and the individuals using them. As currently envisioned, control over individual access will be accomplished by means of a machine-readable special identification card. From this card a device will electronically read the identification data coded on it, including perhaps some notation as to what files the individual is allowed to access through that terminal.

Officials in MMR assert that even with the new IBM 370 they will move cautiously in computerizing some parts of the manual files. "At the present time we have no intention of replacing hard-copy records," Davis said. Looking further ahead, Kaiser-Permanente officials say that the system will be expanded to the other hospitals in northern California, if it "proves out" in San Francisco.

Compared to Scandinavian countries, the United States has moved slowly both in the development of comprehensive preventive health-care systems and in the computerization of medical records, laboratory testing, and patient monitoring. But within the United States, the Kaiser-Permanente program is on the "leading edge" in both areas. Very few other medical institutions have moved as far as (or beyond) Kaiser's pilot project in the development of a computerized medical-record system.

Part III

Site-Visit Findings from 55 Advanced Systems

Trends in Computerization
of Personal Records

Drawing on the 55 governmental, commercial, and nonprofit organizations to which we made site visits, we have looked in detail at 14 organizations that are actively computerizing their "people records." With the exception of U.S. government classified files, which we did not include in our study, the profiles offer a panorama of the kind of large organizations whose collection and use of personal information has given rise to current public debates over the effects of computerization on civil liberties. At the same time, the profiles indicate those issues of record-keeping and civil liberties that are special to each field.

Now, we move from descriptive case studies to an analysis of the 55 site visits as a whole. A few words about our approach and assumptions in this analysis should be helpful as a guide to these chapters.

First, our focus is deliberately empirical. Rather than discussing hypothetical uses of the computer and its "potential" capabilities—an approach which has led to great confusion in the public's understanding of the computer's impact on record-keeping—we report what we found to be happening today in the 55 computerizing organizations we studied. Readers will recall from the general methodological discussion in part one that our judgments as to the computer's real impact on record-keeping within the site-visit organizations are based on a wide-ranging examination of materials, including interviews with executives, heads of user departments, and data-processing personnel; internal documents, forms, and procedure manuals; interviews with organizational specialists, civil-liberties groups, and individuals familiar with the organization's operations; transcripts of relevant legislative hearings and court cases; and a variety of public media sources.

Second, it is useful to recall the scope of record-keeping activities represented in these organizations and some of the distinctive characteristics of the sample we selected. Twenty-nine of these organizations were governmental and 26 were private. The government agencies covered the fields of law enforcement, motor-vehicle registration, welfare and social security, education, health and hospitals, taxation, personnel and civil service, military service, courts and criminal justice, management services, and statistics and planning. The twenty-six private organizations we visited included manufacturers, banks, insurance companies, private universities, religious bodies, airlines, hospitals, health services, newspapers, information suppliers, and computer service bureaus.

As a group, these 55 do *not* represent a cross-section of organizations. We deliberately chose organizations that are highly advanced in applying computerization to their personal record systems, especially those that have received the most publicity in the trade and general press for their pioneering work with automation, and whose computerizing activities had drawn the most attention—in terms of civil-liberties issues—from the mass media, legislative investigators, regulatory bodies, and civil-liberties groups.

Many of the managements we chose to study are generally regarded as leaders in their respective fields. They have been able to devote considerable in-house financial resources to experimentation with computers or have been exceptionally skillful in obtaining outside funding to carry on such work. These are the kind of organizations chosen by computer manufacturers (or who themselves approached the manufacturers) to cooperate in experimenting with the latest computer hardware or with advanced concepts in system design and software. Furthermore, most of these 55 organizations are still ahead of the mainstream in their fields, and their decisions about new computer applications in the 1970s are likely to produce many of this decade's leading-edge applications. If one can visualize a frontier of organizational activity along which American society should be setting up its scanning equipment to discern the early effects of computer technology on civil liberties, these organizations represent the proper terrain for such an outpost.[1]

Third, we use terms such as "all," "the majority," "a minority," or "a few" in describing the distribution of computer applications and record-keeping practices across the site-visit organizations. This strikes us as the appropriate level of precision for the kind of qualitative case studies we have conducted; reporting our

---

[1]To explore how far our conclusions about these "high technology" organizations could be generalized to the mainstream of organizations in each field, a survey questionnaire was developed and mailed during the winter of 1970 and the spring of 1971 to managers of 2,121 organizations across the nation. Treating respondents as competent observers of record-keeping in their own organizations, we asked questions about the computer's impact on specifically designated files within each organization (e.g., personal-checking-account files in banks). In all, anonymous responses were received from managers of 1,541 organizations, representing random samples from organizations in 14 different areas, including banks, health and accident insurance companies, life-insurance companies, colleges and universities, hospitals, city, county and state law-enforcement agencies, regional and state welfare departments, state education departments, regional school districts, and state departments of motor vehicles and taxation.

As we had expected, the survey instrument proved extraordinarily difficult to construct. The results we received reflect this fact; several of our questions were misinterpreted by respondents and the rate of nonresponse or of "don't know" responses to some items was quite high. On the whole, however, it is clear that many of our site-visit findings (for instance, regarding the computerization of sensitive and subjective information, the general impact of computerization on record-keeping operations, and the accuracy of data in computerized files) also hold for mainstream organizations in the same fields. In other cases, we found either that we could not draw an unambiguous conclusion from the survey data or that the responses from this wide range of managers in 14 fields conflicted to some extent with the picture we derived from site visits to advanced organizations (for instance, with respect to the question of the computer's impact on the "amount" of data collected on each individual).

Two sections of our survey produced data which have no direct counterpart in the presentation of site-visit findings which follows. We asked respondents to tell us about the level of civil-liberties complaints their organizations receive from record subjects and to comment on whether or not they see a need in the future for new administrative, legislative, or technological safeguards for civil-liberties interests. This material is discussed, together with the rest of the survey findings, in Appendix A. The survey report is detailed and quite long. Since much of the discussion of specific findings is either similar to the discussions which will follow in this part or represents necessary methodological digressions, and since the full range of findings is difficult to summarize succinctly, we have placed the entire report in the Appendix. However, we make reference to specific sections of the survey report throughout the chapters which follow.

findings in percentages might create a false image of the precision necessary or attainable through the case-study approach. Wherever possible, we refer back to the profiles for illustrations in the hope that this will give readers the fullest possible context within which to judge the points we make. Throughout part three, we also refer to site-visit materials from about a dozen additional systems we visited. Before using these identified accounts, a draft of the description to be used was sent for review and comment to the organization named. Other examples drawn from the remaining organizational sources are used without identification, generally because they involve off-the-record statements. Site-visit organizations were not asked to review our general findings; these represent the judgments of the project.

Finally, we approached the site-visit analysis with the premise that whether or not computerization of record-keeping leads to a lessening of civil-liberties protections for the individual is an empirical question. Computerization *may* have that effect in particular situations; or it may not change existing rights of individuals in any significant way; or it may actually be employed to increase the civil-liberties protections afforded to individuals. To assess such questions, we note changes in record-keeping practices that we saw taking place, then apply as a standard of civil-liberties "measurement" the legal rules and social norms as to privacy, confidentiality, and due process in record-keeping that prevailed in each field during the period in which these organizations undertook computerization activities.

With these explanatory notes, we turn to the presentation of our site-visit findings, analyzing first general trends in computerization, with particular attention to the current state of "databank" developments.

Trends in Advanced Organizations

INITIAL COMPUTERIZATION
FOR HOUSEKEEPING FUNCTIONS

The first stage of computer utilization for our site-visit organizations was automation of their financial record-keeping operations. This generally took place in the mid-1950s, as the organizations adopted first-generation or early second-generation computers to improve the processing of payrolls, billing, and other financial affairs. Such efforts had no significant effect on civil liberties. From the standpoint of civil-liberties concerns, the organization's right to collect information for employee payroll or client accounting was not disputed, and personal data that were transferred from manual records or EAM punched cards into computer-readable records was not generally of a type regarded as sensitive (except, for instance, where the leakage of someone's salary to his associates might be a problem). This "housekeeping" automation also did not alter the basic patterns of record-keeping. It did not lead to increases in the scope of data collection; identified data were not shared more widely than had previously been done; and organizations did not change the way they determined rights or opportunities for those on whom they kept records. Nor were any such changes intended; managers had distinctly modest intentions when they installed computers for internal housekeeping. They saw themselves adopting machines as "faster clerks" to process their routine financial affairs more efficiently. There was no expectation that the organization's structure, its decision-making outlook, or its relations with those on whom it collected information would be altered by this step. Civil-liberties spokesmen raised few alarms in response to computerization of this kind.

High-volume File Automation

The second phase of computer utilization by most of our site-visit organizations involved the automation of high-volume service transactions and in most cases took place in the late 1950s and early 1960s. For some of our organizations, this represented an expansion of their initial computerization. The Bank of America, for example, installed its first computer for housekeeping in 1955, then automated its personal-checking-account operations between 1957 and 1961. In other organizations, the automation of high-activity files represented a first move to computers, as with the Social Security Administration's computerization in 1956 to handle earnings records.

Most of the 55 organizations we studied are presently in this phase, which we call *file automation*, and most have automated only *some* of their high-activity files. They intend to automate others when time and funds permit. Perhaps a quarter of the sites we visited (represented by organizations such as Bank of America, Social Security Administration, and TRW-Credit Data Corporation) have automated *all* of their high-volume files involving records on clients, customers, or citizens. These "highly computerized" organizations still have in manual form a variety of less active, though important, files whose content, frequency of use, and special purposes have not made them suitable or cost-effective to automate.

Thus every one of the 55 organizations that we studied is conducting its record-keeping today with some manual files operating alongside the EDP systems. In some cases, important files are not computerized in any respect, and for many other organizations, principal manual "working files" are updated periodically from computerized master files. We saw no wholly computerized enterprise, either in the form of an older organization which had computerized all of its manual files or a new organization established after computers became generally available.

We saw in the profiles that file automation has taken place under a wide variety of administrative arrangements. In some multidepartment organizations, each department or bureau that had a high-activity file and could provide a cost justification for automation got its own computer. In other organizations, initially or at a later stage of computerization, a central data-processing bureau was set up within one department (such as finance) or under the organization's central administration. This service bureau then provided computing facilities for automating and processing the files of various users within the organization.

Still another pattern was for a computer in one organization to be used as a data processing center for departments or agencies in other government jurisdictions or for one firm to service other business and nonprofit organizations. An example is Alameda County California, whose Data Processing Center operates a computerized Police Information Network exchanging "wanted-and-warrant" information among several dozen municipal police departments in the San Francisco Bay Area. We also saw in our visits to two computer service bureaus that many organizations with computers continue to have computer processing done by these outside commercial organizations, when, for instance, they could not cope with peak demands or needed special data-processing services that were not economical to provide internally.

Throughout our 55 organizations, managers saw such file automation as an absolute necessity to cope with the tremendous increase in transactions with took place in the organizational world during the 1950s and 1960s. Readers will recall managers throughout the profiles saying that they were "drowning in a sea of paper," that "intolerable delays" were taking place in many of their basic file operations, and that it was impossible to hire and retain enough competent help to get the jobs done.

These rising transaction rates are illustrated in the table 3-1, which covers some of the service demands made on the types of organizations we studied. In looking at these large percentage increases in transactions, readers should keep in mind that both the American population and the number of persons in the work force increased by only about 50 percent over the three decades between 1940 and 1970, and by only some 25 percent in the "base point" years before computers arrived (1940-55).

The first point to observe in this table is how heavily transactions mounted between 1940 and 1955, the 15 years *before* computers became generally available. The timing of these increases contradicts the notion that the rise in transactions can be explained by the availability of computer processing itself.

The primary cause for these mounting rates of paper transactions varied among the different fields or activities involved. Some represented drastic increases in the number of people covered by a government program, leaving public agencies with no alternative but to cope with the greater paperwork in any way possible. Such expansion of programs occurred, for instance, in county and state welfare departments, the Social Security Administration, and the Internal Revenue Service. In other fields, the increases reflected forces such as rising affluence in American society, as in the volume of airline travel and hotel stays, the number of students in higher education, and passports issued for travel abroad.

Absolute increases in the number of clients, customers, and citizens covered under a program did not account for all of the transactional crush. The volume of transactions *per person* also increased in some activities for which files were kept, as in the number of personal checks written monthly by each account holder. In the welfare field the number of services (each involving different transactions) provided for a given client also increased, as for instance when new medical assistance programs such as Medicare were added to the government's welfare support for the elderly poor.

We found some instances in the business world where the computer did contribute to the increasing volume of service "demands." Commercial organizations under pressure to expand of course deliberately stimulate the purchase of goods, credit, and services, willingly accepting some "paper problems" in return for the increased business brought in through expansion. For such

Table 3-1

INCREASES IN THE VOLUME OF ANNUAL TRANSACTIONS
AFFECTING ORGANIZATIONAL DATA PROCESSING

TYPE OF TRANSACTION	PRECOMPUTER ERA			COMPUTER ERA		OVERALL INCREASE
	1940	1955	Increase 1940-55, Percent	1970	Increase 1955-70, Percent	1940-70, Percent
Checks written[a]	1.2 billion	2.1 billion	75	7.2 billion	243	600
Telephones in use[b]	19.3 million	56.2 million	191	120.2 million	114	522
Individual social security payments[c]	222,000	8 million	3,504	26.2 million	228	11,702
Individual federal tax returns[d]	14.6 million	58.3 million	299	77 million	32	427
Public welfare recipients[e]	4.6 million	5.6 million	22	13.3 million	137	189

Airline passengers[f]	Originating 3 million	Originating 42 million	1,300	Enplaning 171 million	307	5,600
Persons entering hospitals for treatment[g]	10.1 million	21.1 million	109	31.7 million	50	213

[a] *Checks Written*: These figures are the result of an estimate prepared for the project by the American Bankers Association. They represent a very rough estimate based on Federal Reserve Board statistics. Both personal and commercial checking transactions are included.

[b] *Telephones in Use*: These figures include both personal and business phones in the U.S. They are taken from *Statistics of Communications Common Carriers*, a publication of the Federal Communications Commission.

[c] *Individual Social Security Payments*: This estimate was prepared for the project from the records of the Social Security Administration.

[d] *Individual Federal Tax Returns*: These figures represent nonbusiness returns filed by individuals (including joint returns) for the years indicated. They are taken from *Statistics of Income, Individual Income Tax Returns*, an annual publication of the Internal Revenue Service.

[e] *Public Welfare Recipients*: Recipients under five different kinds of programs are included: Old Age Assistance, Aid to Families with Dependent Children, Aid to the Blind, Aid to the Permanently and Totally Disabled, and General Assistance. The figure for 1940 does not include APTD recipients, as that program had not yet been established. Sources include *Historical Statistics of the United States: Colonial Times to 1957* and *Statistical Abstract of the United States, 1971*. Both are U.S. Department of Commerce, Bureau of the Census publications.

[f] *Airline Passengers*: These figures represent an estimate prepared for the project by the U.S. Air Transport Association on the basis of Civil Aeronautics Board statistics. The percentage increases between 1955 and 1970 and 1940 and 1970 are exaggerated to some extent by the following change in recording definitions: for 1940 and 1955, the figures refer to *originating* passengers; if, in the course of a trip, a passenger took more than one plane, he would only be counted once. The figures for 1970, however, refer to *enplaning* passengers; if a passenger took three different planes to reach his destination, he would be counted three times. This difference in recording definitions has the effect of *exaggerating* the percentage differences from 1940 and 1955 to 1970.

[g] *Persons Entering Hospitals for Treatment*: Figures for 1955 and 1970 are from *Hospitals, Guide Issue*, an annual publication of the American Hospital Association. The 1940 figure was taken from *Historical Statistics of the United States: Colonial Times to 1957, op. cit.* All three figures include multiple admissions of the same individual in a given year.

TYPE OF TRANSACTION	PRECOMPUTER ERA			COMPUTER ERA		OVERALL INCREASE
	1940	1955	Increase 1940-55, Percent	1970	Increase 1955-70, Percent	1940-70, Percent
Persons covered by private hospitalization insurance[h]	12 million	107.7 million	797	181.5 million	69	1,513
Motor-vehicle registrations[i]	32.5 million	62.7 million	93	108.4 million	73	230
Passports issued[j]	26,000 (new and renewals)	528,000 (new and renewals)	1,931	(New only) 2.2 million	317	8,362
Students enrolled in colleges and universities[k]	1.5 million	2.6 million	73	(1969) 6.9 million	165	360
Applications received for federal employment[l]	1 million	1.7 million	70	2.9 million	71	190

| New York Stock Exchange Transactions[m] | 282.7 million | 820.5 million | 190 | 3.2 billion | 290 | 1,032 |
| Pieces of mail handled, U.S. Post Office (all classes)[n] | 27.8 billion | 55.3 billion | 99 | 84.9 billion | 52 | 205 |

[h] *Persons Covered by Private Hospital Insurance*: All data for this entry are from *Source Book of Health Insurance Data*, an annual publication of the Health Insurance Institute, New York City.

[i] *Motor-vehicle Registrations*: All data for this entry are from *Historical Statistics of the United States: Colonial Times to 1957*, *op. cit.*

[j] *Passports Issued*: Figures for this entry are from *Summary of Passport Statistics*, an annual report of the U.S. Bureau of Customs.

[k] *Students Enrolled in Colleges and Universities*: Data for this entry are from *Statistical Abstract*, *op. cit.* and *Historical Statistics of the United States: Colonial Times to 1957*, *op. cit.*

[l] *Applications Received for Federal Employment*: Figures for this entry are the result of an estimate prepared for the project by the U.S. Civil Service Commission.

[m] *New York Stock Exchange Transactions*: This entry is the result of an estimate prepared for the project by the Research Department of the New York Stock Exchange.

[n] *Pieces of Mail Handled, U.S. Post Office*: Figures for this entry were taken from *Statistical Abstract of the United States, 1971*, *op. cit.* and *Historical Statistics of the United States: Colonial Times to 1957*, *op. cit.*

firms, the arrival of the computer made it possible to handle such expansion at lower cost or to begin expansion into new areas with the computer's capacities specifically in mind. BankAmericard services, for instance, began to be marketed in 1959 with computer applications a part of the initial operations, and the number of charges per account in California BankAmericard rose from 5.7 receipts per month in 1959 to 16.3 monthly in 1970.

Some of these increases in the volume of personal record transactions were spread out over many organizations, such as all hotels or colleges. But in some cases, a single large organization (for instance, IRS or Social Security Administration) or a very few large institutions (such as the largest banks or welfare departments) had to accommodate most of the pressure of mounting transactions in their field of activity.

Whatever the particular reason in each case, the transactional surge of the 1950s and 1960s confronted our 55 organizations with a critical problem. It is difficult to say what might have happened if computers had not been available at this moment. One can speculate that some transactional growth would have been slowed, that more extensive use might have been made of EAM equipment, and that the organizational services provided would have been less elaborate in many spheres of activity. But the fact of history is that computers *were* available at just this moment in the evolution of American commercial and governmental affairs. Second- and third-generation computer systems offered far greater storage capacities and processing speeds than anything feasible in the manual era. These computers were vigorously marketed by computer salesmen who knew the transactional pressures facing managers and who could operate secure in the knowledge that managers and officials understood little about the systems that were being sold. Moreover, decisions to computerize were being made at a time when the nation at large saw advanced technology as one of the great blessings of our age.

In this setting, it was natural for managements to turn to computers as an ideal means for solving the problems of transactional growth, especially in the kinds of organizations represented by those we studied. There was undoubtedly a "bandwagon effect" as well in some of this computerization; having a shiny computer installation on display behind glass walls was an organizational status symbol of the time. There was also an early overconfidence in the technology. In many organizations, the prospects and opportunities of technology were admired while its limitations and the problems of its effective integration into the organization were minimized or ignored. But these were secondary elements compared to the computer's promise for dealing with the increases in transactions.

It was during this file automation phase that the civil liberties issue began to emerge. Computerization had now reached files with sensitive personal information about every American—files in education, health, welfare, social services, law enforcement, taxation, motor-vehicle registration, credit, insurance, and a host of similar fields. Social commentators in the period 1962-66 began to ask how automation was going to affect the patterns of privacy and confidentiality that had prevailed in the precomputer era, and whether or not automated processing would change the way organizations made important judgments about citizens, clients, employees, or customers.[2]

FROM AUTOMATED FILES TO CENTRAL DATABANK PROJECTS

While civic concern over file automation was emerging, a third phase of computerization appeared on the organizational scene. At about a third of our sites, plans were announced in the middle or late 1960s for the creation of "computer databanks." To analyze what the databank development meant, we have to define some terms and set out for purposes of comparison some baselines from the manual file era.

No standard definition exists of *databank*. It has been used by organizational and civil-liberties spokesmen to describe just about any large or small assemblage of data about people or things, sometimes in wholly manual form and sometimes computerized. At many points the term has been used in a pejorative fashion; just as records thought to be improper are often called "dossiers," so media commentators and the public often (disapprovingly) label as "databanks" various files about people that organizations use themselves or share with one another.

We have used *file automation* to refer to the computerization of single file systems within organizations. These single files are distinguished from computerized collections of data shared by separate departments or organizations, which we will call *shared central databanks*.

---

[2] In the project survey, respondents were asked to note the year at which they first developed computer applications to the files we designated. Their responses are analyzed in Appendix A, pages 417-419 below.

File automation—whether for financial housekeeping or for basic high-volume operations—typically does not involve merging data on the same individual from several different departments, and it is not ordinarily pursued to increase the sharing of data among departments or organizations. Even where some centralization accompanied file-automation efforts, as in the case of a bank pulling together its checking-account files from each branch, this generally resulted in a central file which covered more people but did not enlarge the pool of information on each person.

In contrast, shared central data banks are intended to have the following traits: (1) data about each individual are drawn from files hitherto in separate departments or bureaus within the same organization or from separate organizations; (2) these data are either organized into one centrally located file, or the several files (wherever located) are interconnected in a system capable of assembling a composite record on an individual when needed; and (3) the pooled data on each individual are set up to be shared by users in participating departments, bureaus or organizations according to some plan of anticipated and authorized inputs and inquiries.

This characterization of shared central databanks incorporates the elements we found frequently attributed to "databanks" in the computers-and-privacy literature of the 1960s. It is clear from the characterization that there were in the precomputer era and there are today *manual* shared central databanks with some of the same traits as automated ones. We saw several during our site visits. For example, there are centralized interorganizational networks, in which one agency manually collects, maintains, and disseminates records of the same type for a group of users or customers. The FBI's fingerprint identification system operated as a service for local, state and national law-enforcement agencies for four decades through manual procedures. An example from the life-insurance field is the Medical Information Bureau, which has for years collected records on persons turned down for life insurance on medical grounds, and has made data from these records available to participating life insurance companies wishing to check out new policy applicants. Only very recently has this organization computerized its files.

We also saw manual databank networks serving organizations of different types that had some kind of common interest, as with the credit bureau reports made available to banks, retail merchants, auto dealers, and other credit grantors, and the lists of names furnished by commercial mailing list suppliers to business firms, charities, religious organizations, and political groups wishing to reach specified populations through the mails. Common to all of these centralized manual-record networks is the fact that the participants in any one provide data of roughly the same nature—be it credit information, criminal histories, or medical reports.

The Databank Proposals

There were three significant differences between manual central databanks and the computerized versions proposed in the 1960s. First, computer software and hardware were intended to provide more regular, more rapid, and, if desired, more complex compilations of data about persons or groups than when employees had to consult separate records on an ad hoc basis and search laboriously through manual files. Dramatic increase in speed of access for update or administrative action was emphasized by managers as being a critical feature of many central databank proposals. Particularly where specialized interorganizational networks (such as the New York State Identification and Intelligence System) were involved, observers envisioned that this increased speed and ease of access would increase the use of central files and the extent to which information on individuals was shared.

Second, some proposals for shared central databanks called for a degree of centralization which did not exist in the manual era for the particular files involved. TRW-Credit Data pulled together credit information from a larger number of sources than had been available through any single manual source previously; the FBI did the same with wanted-person data.

Third, and most important, is the fact that some organizations proposed central databanks which were not only faster and easier to use, but were qualitatively different from anything which existed in the manual era in that they would merge different kinds of data about a given individual into a single record. Many single organizations and jurisdictions such as counties developed computerized data-processing centers; in their conventional form such facilities store and process—independently of each other—the many different files of information belonging to separate departments of the organization. Having different types of files in the same *location* was a matter of operating efficiency and did not mean that data from one department file were merged with data from another. But some of the proposals of the 1960s went beyond this to propose shared central databank facilities which would organize information from such different files into a single data base, to be shared by the whole community of users. The range of information about a given individual available to each user was to be broadened.

We can recall from the profiles examples of both kinds of central databank proposals outlined above.

1. Some organizations managing manual information networks for a user group set out to computerize this operation. We saw such file centralization in the FBI's creation of the National Crime Information Center to automate wanted-and-warrant information and in the automation of the manual credit bureau operation in one large commercial reporting agency that we visited. There were also some new organizations formed to apply computer technology to such network functions, such as TRW-Credit Data Corporation (for credit inquiries) and the New York State Identification and Intelligence System (for statewide fingerprint identifications and the provision of summary criminal-history records to criminal-justice agencies). But whether converted from existing manual systems or first conceived as computerized systems, these interorganizational databanks have as their main feature the fact that the *same* kind of data from each user is centralized for faster update and use.

2. The executives of some local government jurisdictions—cities, counties, and special districts—announced in the 1960s that they were going to bring information from their different departments and agencies into a common computerized file. Their purposes were to avoid the duplicate collection and recording of information about the citizen; to automatically update the central record as any department had a transaction with that person or took an action affecting him; to make the central record available for use (usually by on-line terminal) by an (authorized) department that needed to make a decision regarding that person; and to allow the jurisdiction's central management timelier and richer statistical trend data than had been previously available. We saw plans for such a jurisdictionwide central databank at New Haven, Connecticut, and Santa Clara County, California, and the main feature of these efforts was that each user would be merging a different kind of data into the central file.[3]

---

[3] Another concept of information reorganization through computers was also widespread in the 1960s. This was the concept of a "management information system" (MIS), sometimes called a "total management information system" (TMIS) to suggest the integration of all information sources and uses under the control of central executives. These conceptions almost always included a shared central databank as one element of a larger, more dynamic,

In contrast to the proposals for specialized interorganization networks such as the FBI's NCIC, the jurisdictionwide databank proposals obviously represented an effort to utilize computer technology not merely to do the old things faster, but to do new things with information. Here, managers were going beyond "transactional necessity." They were seeking to transform the information function in their enterprises, to achieve both richer files of information for making decisions about individuals and a richer data base for management planning and evaluation purposes.

It was the launching of such jurisdictionwide databank projects in the mid-1960s that stirred the deepest civil-liberties concerns. Managers of organizations creating computer databanks announced proudly that they would bring different files of personal information into "common storage," that more effective use of data would be made by the various departments of their organizations, and that central managements would have the capacity to reach bodies of personal information that were once too costly to reach as a regular resource because they were scattered and did not have common identifiers. These proposals led civil-liberties spokesmen to suggest that it would now be even more important for an individual to have knowledge of what is collected about him, access to his file for verification and challenge, and public review of the way in which precomputer rules of privacy and confidentiality would be altered by the central databank efforts. On the whole, civil libertarians feared that information on too many aspects of the individual's life would be united in one comprehensive record portrait at the local level.

The Realities

One of our prime objectives in the site studies was to learn how far advanced organizations had progressed in their computerization efforts at the time of our visits. Having followed up on most of the systems after the site visits, we can draw the following map of EDP developments in personal record-keeping as of mid-1972. Our focus here is on the existing state of computerization; in the next

and more top-management-oriented reorganization of the information function. We discussed such MIS and TMIS projects on our site visits, and the New Haven UMIS plan—Unified Management Information System—is one example of such.

two sections we will be treating in detail the effect of these computer operations on record-keeping practices and civil liberties.

FILE AUTOMATION: HERE AND "IRREVERSIBLE"

For the great majority of our organizations, file automation was the goal being reached for by their managements, and this is the phase of computerization at which these organizations stand today. What is significant for public policy understanding is that these managers conceive of computerization as neither an experiment nor a matter of much choice. They see it instead as a necessity for conducting large-scale programs in a complex, industrialized society in which demands for government services and pressures to develop new consumer markets in the business world produce a tremendous crush of record-keeping transactions. No organization that we visited has turned away from its computer and gone back to clerical help or EAM processing for its high-volume operations, regardless of how much delay, confusion, extra cost, and managerial frustration may have been experienced in the course of computerization.[4]

This is not merely a matter of being unable to hire enough competent clerks to handle the paperwork. During the past decade, the structures and procedures for record-keeping in the organizations we visited and the managerial outlook on information processing as a task have been fundamentally altered by reliance upon the computer systems. The organizations' employees and executives have come to depend on the speed of computerized information handling in their daily work. For all the occasional "foul-ups" that take place, managers say, the citizens, clients, customers, and members who are their record subjects have grown accustomed to a given level of diversity and quality in organizational services—whether they have been conscious of the computer's role in maintaining this level or not. Furthermore, interorganizational relationships throughout the country in many cases have come to depend heavily on exchanges of computerized data. In this setting, the managers we spoke to regard as essentially ignorant or Luddite anyone who believes that large-scale organizations have a meaningful choice in the matter of computer usage.

---

[4] See the discussion of our survey respondents' perceptions of the need for computers, Appendix A, pages 444-446 below.

At the same time, managers in most of the organizations we visited have recently developed a more realistic approach to computer technology. There is considerable skepticism about the far-fetched claims made for computer capabilities by technological enthusiasts, and increasing concern over the heavy financial costs to the organization for hardware and software. There is also a desire by these managers to exert greater control over the development of computer applications—to recapture some of the remarkably large zone of discretion that was given up to data-processing specialists in the days when computer systems were treated by many managers as mysterious black boxes.

As the computer magazines put it, this is now the era of "Users Lib." The key questions of computer usage that we found most of these managers asking today are how to improve the productivity and cost-effectiveness of existing operations, how to use the data generated by existing programs for more effective reporting to middle and top management, and how to achieve better integration of computerized processes with management's decision-making functions. Within this context, the trend toward file automation is regarded by these organizations as utterly irreversible.

COMPUTER DATABANKS—FEW AND FAR BETWEEN

The majority of the organizations we visited did not attempt to create and are not presently working on shared central databank systems. Only a minority (about a third) of these managements have committed financial and staff resources to computer databank projects. Of these, operational systems have been achieved in only one of the two types of central databank projects that we outlined earlier, the centralized interorganizational network. Computer systems linking groups of users or customers to a central file (either by on-line terminals, teletypes, or by telephone-operator procedures) have been achieved in several areas. The FBI's NCIC system and its new Criminal History File, the Kansas City Police Department's ALERT System, the New York State Identification and Intelligence System, and a wanted-and-warrant network serving a metropolitan region through one county data-processing center we visited all illustrate such uses in the law-enforcement field. The computerized credit bureau operation of one commercial reporting agency we visited shows successes in that field. The

Medical Information Bureau has become an on-line computer system linking insurance companies and their offices to the central file in Boston.

We see in these successes a common thread: each builds upon an existing system or on a well-established model. One large central file, typically following the basic format as to content set in the manual era, was converted to machine-readable form. In the on-line systems, such as that of the FBI, users are linked into the system by remote terminals. In other systems, such as the credit bureau, users phone names and identifiers into operators and get credit report responses back by phone or mail. In each of these systems, what was already a working databank using paper records and a teletype or telephone communications system in the manual era was converted by computerization and telecommunications into a system faster in its input and retrieval of records from the central file and faster in its transmission of information to and from central and field units.

Turning to the other type of central databank—that operating on a jurisdictionwide basis in local government—we did not find any of the proposed systems in actual operation at the sites we visited. Our profile of New Haven described how the Urban Management Information System (UMIS) conception never got past the feasibility-study phase. No other municipalities we visited have operational central databanks, and the demonstration projects in total municipal information systems being funded by the Department of Housing and Urban Development are still in early stages. Similarly, our profile of Santa Clara County showed that the ambitious LOGIC system—initiated in 1964-65 and projected for full operational status in 1971—is still a series of independent subsystems functioning primarily in only two spheres, social services and criminal justice. We visited six other counties—four in California, one in the Southeast, and one in the Northeast—and confirmed that there were no central databanks in these counties either. There were central data-processing facilities in most, but the files of user departments had not been merged and were not accessible through programs which could link records located in separate files. These organizations indeed had automated files in operation, but their central databank projects had either been discarded or had been converted into what was usually called "subsystem development leading to the prospect of a unified databank in the future," an embarrassed way of saying that things were going to take a lot longer than they had expected and there was no central databanking there yet.

Once we had established to our satisfaction that there were no central computer databanks of the kind which had raised civil-liberties alarms among our advanced organizations, we had little trouble reconstructing why we had been surprised to learn this fact, and in anticipating why a great many readers may also be surprised by it. First, many organizations announced their central databank plans in the mid-1960s, with timetables showing that their systems would go gradually into operation over the next three or five or seven years. The system plans and feasibility studies, as is the nature of this literary form, would spell out what would be done at each stage as though the plan would unfold with the inevitability of death and taxes. Press releases from these organizations or from computer manufacturers and software houses involved in the project would have been sent out to the media. The stories written from them would usually make the implications seem immediate to increase news value, as journalism is professionally wont to do. From there, the stories would radiate out to magazines in the particular field of activity (county government, law enforcement, welfare, etc.). At this point, the accounts were picked up by congressional spokesmen concerned about privacy and civil liberties, writers for law reviews and liberal magazines, and the television networks, in all of which the announced plans would be further treated as though they were moving inexorably to fruition. And because the technology was new and unfamiliar to so many people, few distinctions were made and applied between file automation, central interorganizational networks, jurisdictionwide databanks, and data-processing centers; it was all "Computers!"

As a result, by the time we did our site visits in 1970 and 1971, spokesmen from a remarkably wide range of fields and interests simply took it as a truth that central databanks were humming in New Haven and Santa Clara County, and at banks, insurance firms, credit-card companies, universities, and dozens of other major holders of personal records. There were neither follow-up stories in the press nor empirical studies as yet which might document what was and what was not there. As for organizations involved and their hardware and software suppliers, their managers were not eager to volunteer a public account of their present status, except occasionally to answer the attacks made on them for supposedly riding roughshod over civil liberties through their computerized operations.

It is beyond the scope of this report to analyze in detail the technical, organizational, and political problems involved that have impeded the building of central databanks. However, it will help to understand, in a basic way, the kinds of problems that kept the organizations we visited from realizing the organizationwide or jurisdictionwide plans they had announced. We observed four characteristic problems.

1. Many of the original databank plans were remarkably global in their requirements for restructuring organizations along the lines of what computer professionals have come to call "blue sky" conceptions. In order to create the central database required, and to have line employees, middle managers, and top executives use the information system in what systems experts regard as the most effective way, system designers were in effect calling for massive alterations in the structures, functions, and personal power relationships of organizations. Where this kind of thinking characterized databank plans, we found that resistance developed up and down the lines of the organization, leading top management to modify or ignore the central databank plan in favor of a set of more gradual and incremental steps.

This seemed to be particularly true in local government, when the financial costs and organizational disruptions were weighed against the need to keep vital public services flowing. In one county we visited, for example, a very "blue sky" central databank plan had been formulated in the early 1960s. By the time we visited the county in 1970-71, a new data-center director had been installed who explicitly rejected the grand design of his predecessor. "We would have had to reorganize the county departments entirely to carry out that plan," he noted, "and even if we did that, and spent twice our budget, there is no guarantee whatever that the databank would work." As a result, the new data-center director was pursuing department-by-department automation of files. "By the end of the 1970s," he said, "we *may* have the elements of a unified information system through our efforts. And we will have spent a lot less, made fewer mistakes, and fulfilled our mandated duties far better than the 'one big system' ideas that were being considered here before."

2. The conceptual problems of relating data to organizational goals, programs, and decision-making patterns are far from simple. In welfare departments, police departments, and many other government agencies, it is by no means clear what factors about individuals or events are the critical ones for predicting future needs or helping determine what organizational policies ought to be. Precisely because computers require the most explicit instructions as to what should be stored, how they should be

processed, and how to use the information, designing a central databank in which different types of files will be integrated brings to the surface many of the unknown factors and much of the ignorance with which complex social and economic affairs are actually conducted. People can muddle through but computers cannot. As a result of these problems in selecting and weighing the critical data, we saw organizations that decided it was simply too early in the development of unified information systems to attempt the central databanks they had been considering. The director of administration in one large city commented to us, "I'm just not bright enough to design a central databank for this city, and I don't think anyone else is today, except as a research project. We did our feasibility study but it's shelved until we know more about what affects what in the urban setting."

3. Even where the organizational and conceptual problems were overcome and we saw organizations committed to building central databanks, major technical problems soon developed. These arose not so much with the hardware equipment as with the design of software. At what might seem to be the simple end of the scale, organizations found that their existing manual and/or computerized files usually had different personal identifying numbers or labels attached to individual records; or that the records had such different formats that the process of data conversion would have been enormously complicated, or that substantial changes would have been necessary in the future operating procedures of some departments.

Even when such problems could be solved at costs the organization could accept, more fundamental software problems often emerged. Despite the power and flexibility of computer systems, they are still essentially master index and rapid communication systems in their handling of information. When data are assembled in a central data base, users can get answers to inquiries about individuals, things, events, or conditions only if the designers of the system have anticipated those questions and provided the programs capable of locating the necessary information for retrieval. Many who proposed central databanks visualized that data from the system would become available in an almost unlimited variety of types and combinations, each responsive to a management need of the moment. However, the software available in the organizational world in the past decade has not been able to provide a system working with the kind of browsing flexibility that a human researcher can invoke when using a book or a library. The importance of this limitation is that those seeking to build central databanks today have had to try to provide the software for all potential inquiries by users of the system. We saw that these attempts to anticipate future information needs proved so difficult at several municipal databank projects that the databanks never got off the ground, even though the system plans that had been drafted were widely publicized as administratively and politically impressive.

4. Several "lesser" factors contributed to the collapse of central databank projects at organizations that we studied. The shortage of federal funds for databank experiments and the drying up of tax revenues that accompanied the economic recession of the past few years were a part of the reason for cancellation or shelving of some databank projects that might otherwise have been continued as experiments during these years. The need for the data-processing unit to continue providing existing services and programs proved so great at some organizations that developing the new software and conducting the data conversions needed for moving into databank plans had to be postponed. Again, we heard at site after site that it always seemed to take longer than had been anticipated to automate the necessary files and to develop the software for the initial stages of databank development, a tendency toward underestimation of development time and costs that has been widespread in the history of computerization.

Lest our discussion be misunderstood, we must emphasize that we are *not* saying that central databanks within single organizations or as jurisdictionwide systems are technologically impossible, or that they will never be built. We are saying that we found nothing in actual operation among our 55 organizations today that fits the definition of these systems we have outlined, and that none is ready to appear in the immediate future. We are also *not* saying that there are no civil-liberties problems because we found "only" computerized interorganizational networks and file automation among these advanced organizations. We take up the civil-liberties issues in detail in the next two chapters. But our task in this chapter was to describe as precisely as possible what is actually in operation, as the first step toward separating fact from fancy in this area.

Effects on Privacy, Confidentiality, and Due Process

We examine in this chapter some widely held beliefs about the effects of computers on civil liberties that we did *not* find taking place among the advanced organizations we visited. These beliefs will be divided into two groups—those relating to privacy and confidentiality standards in record-keeping and those involving the provision of due process for individuals who are the subject of organizational decisions.

Before taking up these points, we should note that the organizations we visited were remarkably free between 1955 and 1970 to pursue automation without direct legislative or regulatory-agency measures dealing with civil-liberties aspects of computerization. The only exception before 1970 at our 55 sites was one municipal ordinance requiring that written permission of the "owning" department be given to the director of the city computer center before information from its files was released to another city agency or officer.

Between 1970 and 1972, we saw the development of a *few* legal interventions that affected computerizing organizations. For example, the state and federal fair credit reporting acts, though containing no language about computers as such, provided new rights of notice and challenge in commercial reporting, as we discussed in several profiles. More directly concerned with computerized systems were the federal court ruling limiting the FBI's dissemination of offender records to nonlaw-enforcement agencies through the NCIC; a state mental health records act authorizing institutions to participate in a multistate system for the computer processing of patient records, but requiring that personal identifiers be removed before facilities exchanged or forwarded patient data; and a municipal ordinance creating guidelines and a citizen's review board to cover privacy and security aspects of a microfilm criminal-history file which city police were developing under a federal grant.

These few exceptions only underscore the more basic finding; the organizations we studied have been able to proceed with their computerization for almost two decades on the basis of laws and administrative rules that prevailed in their fields in the late 1950s and 1960s. It is these existing concepts of civil liberties that we take as the basis for considering the effects of computerization.

Impact on Privacy and Confidentiality

When computers began to spread through the organizational world in the early 1960s, many commentators were convinced that they would overturn the traditions of limited data collection, compartmentalized storage, and controlled circulation that made up the American approach to government record-keeping and which had exerted a general influence over private record-keeping as well. A typical formulation of this concern appeared in *Privacy and Freedom*, published in 1967:

> [O]nce an organization purchases a giant computer, it inevitably begins to collect more information about its employees, clients, members, taxpayers, or other persons in the interest of the organization ... The inevitable result is that the [organization] acquires two or three times as much personal information from respondents as was ever collected before, because of the physical or cost limits of acquisition ... [In addition, there is more] sharing of data among those who use the machines ... information exchanges among units within the same large organization, such as police and health agencies in a state, or among independent organizations with common interests, such as life-insurance companies ... [There is also] the growth of central data pools in many important fields from education and health to banking, civil defense, and social science analysis ... [I]n return for putting its data into the central pool, an organization is able to draw on the total collection ...[1]

---

[1] Alan F. Westin, *Privacy and Freedom* (New York: Atheneum, 1967), pp. 161-62.

Summing up the effects of these "inevitable" results, the analysis concluded that "the impact of computers on organizational life is to destroy practical boundaries of privacy in record giving which were once as meaningful in this area as walls and doors were to conversational privacy before the advent of new physical surveillance technology."

Our finding is that this analysis does not fit the computerized record systems in existence in 1970-72. To see why this is so, we should begin by noting that there are two elements in the *Privacy and Freedom* statement. First is an empirical question: has the acquisition of computers led to increased collection, integration, and circulation of information about individuals? Second is a question of social judgment; if such increases do take place in a particular field or industry, or even in all organizations, does this automatically constitute an infringement on civil liberties, or will that outcome depend on additional factors, such as the need for the information, whether consent was given, whether safeguards are installed to prevent misuse, and similar matters? Keeping these two elements in mind, let us look at the privacy and confidentiality areas.

Privacy and the Collection of More Information about People

In assessing whether computers have led organizational managers to collect more personal information about people than was collected in the manual files, we use "more information" in the sense that civil-liberties spokesmen have used it, referring to widening the scope of substantive inquiry about the individuals on whom records are kept, either by asking questions about areas of personal life not included previously or probing in greater personal detail areas already covered.

To investigate this problem, we asked employees and executives about their desires or needs for more information; at selected organizations, we also looked at the content of data-collection forms and stored records used before and after computerization. At the three manufacturing firms whose personnel data systems we studied, for example, we compared the information about employees kept in all the manual records with what went into the computerized systems. At Santa Clara County, we compared welfare intake forms under the manual system with the new computerized ones. Similar inquiries were made in studying the FBI's NCIC system, the New York State Identification and Intelligence

System, the Census Bureau, the Social Security Administration, and others.

In a majority of the organizations we visited, our clear finding is that the content of computerized records about individuals has *not* been increased in scope compared to what was collected in their manual counterparts during the precomputer era. The explanation for this lies in a combination of two factors—managerial intentions and the state of the computer art during the past 15 years.[2]

In talking to employees and executives about whether they saw a need for more extensive information about those on whom they maintain records, we found that line employees and departmental managers in most organizations did not feel that they needed greater information about individuals in order to carry on their basic programs. As a result, they did not press for increases in the scope of information during the reviews of record content and data utilization that accompanied computerization of their active high-volume files. They wanted information about individuals made available more quickly, as in the credit-reporting, law-enforcement, and airline-reservation systems, and they wanted records to be more complete as to the information items already called for. "We have all the information we need to run our programs," one typical comment noted, in terms that were also expressed in the system plans of the city involved. "Our problems are to get the information on time, in usable form, at the place where it is needed, and in the hands of the persons who make the decisions."

In a similar vein, top executives in most of the organizations we visited do not feel a need to have a broader range of information gathered about individual clients, customers, and citizens in order to make managerial decisions. Timely and selective trend information about conditions and program operations are the key information needs seen by top managers. Because of this perspective, top managers did not produce "shopping lists" of information items to be collected when file automation took place.

We also looked at this question in terms of intelligence units within law-enforcement agencies as a whole that were included within our site-visit group, examining the issue of collecting broader information for computerized files at the Organized Crime Section of the Department of Justice, the Intelligence Division of the Internal Revenue Service, the New York State Identification

---

[2] We saw some instances in which the computer *indirectly* affected the scope of information collected. These are discussed on pages 223-229 above.

and Intelligence System, the Kansas City Police Department, and a county police department. Here, a comparison of information scope in manual and computerized files does not reveal an increase in the latter because intelligence units in the manual era already operated under a virtually unlimited concept of what personal information should and would be collected. Depending on the type of intelligence activity involved, information was regularly collected on such intensely private matters as the subject's finances, day-to-day movements, sex life, associates, and political beliefs. Such broad scope was justified by those in the intelligence community on the grounds that protection of public order and prevention of serious crimes or subversive activities were involved, that the information was kept secret, and that if formal government sanctions were imposed on any individuals investigated (criminal prosecution, denial of benefits, etc.), the methods used in the original information collection and the truth of the information reported could be tested in the ensuing judicial or administrative proceedings. Since there were no boundaries of privacy set by law or custom in the scope of intelligence data collected before computerization, we found that computerization was not leading to broader data collection. There wasn't any "more" to move up to.

The main exception we found to the general state of managerial intentions with regard to "more information" is an important one. Within some organizations, research or evaluation units are charged with analyzing how well the organization is performing. Similarly, planning units analyze what new policies and programs need to be undertaken and what future needs will be for current programs. While many evaluation and planning studies use data about people already collected by the organization in its program operations, we often found a desire to seek new information about reaction and impact directly from a sample of those in the programs being studied, or to bring together data necessary for evaluation from various files that are not normally merged or combined for any program purpose.

Where organizations had widened the scope of information collected, such evaluation and planning units were often responsible for the collection of more detailed information from individuals for computer storage and analysis. Among the examples we encountered were a mail survey of the income-use patterns and life styles of the elderly administered for the Social Security Administration by the U.S. Census Bureau, and a survey of attitudes toward family life, political participation, and education conducted in a poverty area by the planning unit in one Southeastern county. In a project studying utilization of city facilities, persons using welfare, health, and other social service agencies were issued plastic ID cards with personal identifiers embossed on them. When visiting a city agency, they were asked to insert their special ID cards into an imprinting machine which registered the time, date, and agency. From such records, researchers hoped to discover patterns in the use of city agencies and services that were not visible through examination of existing records.

In these and similar research situations, the wider data collection was intended not for making decisions about the specific individuals surveyed or monitored, but only for general evaluation or planning. However, the individuals participating in such research efforts were often dependent upon the government organizations sponsoring the research—for public assistance and other benefits or services. In some cases it was *not* clearly stated that participation was voluntary and that individuals could decline without any harmful consequences to themselves. Even where this is stated, it is often difficult to convince citizens or clients that they could afford to refuse participation. In terms of confidentiality, we found some individuals skeptical that identified data held in research files would be denied to the organizational managers if they should want identified information about individuals for investigative or administrative purposes. As a result, the Social Security Administration surveys drew protests from SSA recipients that were aired at Senator Ervin's hearings on federal databanks in 1971; local civil-liberties groups protested the county poverty-area survey we mentioned; and a local welfare rights organization protested the municipality's attempt to measure the use of city services.

The general orientation we found among user departments and top managers in most organizations—that they did not have unmet needs for broader information about individuals—was reinforced by the patterns of computerization and the state of the technological art during the past 15 years. Readers will recall from the profiles in part two and earlier in part three that automation of files has taken two main paths. In one pattern, the organization sets out to convert an entire existing record in a manual file into machine-readable form. Such full-record automation may be for batch-processing operations, as with the auto-owner's file at R. L. Polk, or it may be for on-line use, as with the driver's-license and vehicle-registration files at the New York State Motor Vehicle Department. In this process, the managers could decide to convert the record exactly as it was, to collect more items for the computerized record, or to reduce the items to be collected in the computerized record.

In the second type of computerization, the organization set out to select from its manual file a relatively small portion of information that it needed for fast retrieval or special analysis, retaining the full record in manual storage. Here too, the organization could decide to use only information already in the larger manual record or to seek new and more detailed personal data for the computerized record. Examples of this selective process are the ALERT file at the Kansas City Police Department, the FBI's NCIC system, and the summary earnings file of the Social Security Administration.

When managers considered how much information to put into each of these types of computerized files, the state of the art in computer technology during these two decades exerted pressures on them to *avoid* the expansion of their existing records or to skim off the least possible information for the special files. Some of the reasons for this have already been described in the profiles, but it is well to summarize these technological pressures here.

1. The cost of converting information from manual to machine-readable form has been quite high, especially with the keypunching techniques primarily relied upon during the period. Missing information had to be collected, data elements had to be standardized, and other costly procedures had to be followed. Highly skilled employees were required, the accuracy of keypunching had to be verified, and basic procedures for data collection usually had to be reorganized. These heavy costs led managers to approach automation with a desire to keep the information in each record at an absolute minimum.

2. For all the large storage capacities of third-generation computer systems, these still proved to be limited in relation to the huge manual files in many organizations, where maintenance of records on millions of persons was often the rule. Especially where on-line retrieval was necessary, as with Credit Data Corporation, limiting the amount of information to be stored on each record thus became an absolute necessity for cost-effective operations.

3. Though processing by computer is extremely fast, each processing operation still costs money. As the expenses of using automated systems began to mount, almost always beyond the original estimates of the data-processing plan, many organizations

began an active search for ways to eliminate the processing of unnecessary data.

4. At the output stage, organizations found that print-out operations were also costly, and created problems of paper storage as well. Furthermore, finding ways to avoid "drowning the decision maker in information not needed for his decisions" became a concern of computer managers in this period. Both of these factors enhanced efforts to reduce the information in computerized records wherever possible.

Put together, problems of cost and efficiency created a situation in computerizing organizations that bore little resemblance to the critic's picture of managers suddenly able to manipulate mountains of data at little additional cost in dollars or in organizational trauma.

To deal with these difficulties in data conversion and EDP operations, many organizations set up automation committees to review the data that were to go from larger manual files into the new computerized records. These committees were generally made up of representatives from top management, user departments, and experts in systems design and computers, with the latter drawn sometimes from within the organization and sometimes from outside consulting firms or computer manufacturers. Such automation teams generally looked at what data were presently collected, how necessary management considered each individual item to be, how frequently it was used, and who needed the data for decision making. These questions were not always answered in a definitive way, either in empirical or management-policy terms. But the effort often worked against an automatic transfer of the entire manual record. Organizations we visited started with the premise that users had to make a positive case for inclusion of each data item in the computerized file before it would go in.

As we examined the content of manual and computerized records in the 55 organizations, we did find some instances in which important additional personal information was added to the computerized files. On careful examination, however, these did not prove to be a direct result of computerization, but of other causes. One such factor was legislative changes in program coverage and administration that required collection of more information. For example, new laws required that banks and employers obtain the individual's Social Security number to facilitate linkage of interest and other income payments to the individual's income-tax files. Another factor is that private and local government organizations have had to collect additional items of information to satisfy the reporting requirements of federal or state grants-in-aid agencies.

Computers have often facilitated the setting of these new programs and rules. Mutual of Omaha officials suggest that reporting requirements were set by regulatory agencies precisely because they knew these could be accomplished without undue burden through computerized operations.

We also found a few computerizing organizations that are collecting *less* personal information in these files than in the manual era. Again, we found that this was a result of new legislative policies and changing social norms, not automation per se. Questions about race, religion, nationality, sex, and ethnic background have been steadily removed from the files of many organizations as a result of prohibitory statutes and public opinion. Similarly, changes during the 1960s in social conceptions of what entitles a person to welfare aid have led some county systems to reduce the scope of the personal information they collect on intake forms, as questions of identification and need were retained but historical reconstructions of the individual's personal life (common-law marriages, history of jobs held, etc.) were eliminated.

Thus, our basic finding is quite strong—*the organizations that we visited have not extended the scope of their information collection about individuals as a direct result of computerization.*[3]

The qualitative aspects of data being computerized are as important as the quantitative aspects. Stated most generally, we found that the information that is considered most sensitive and subjective in each type of organization has *not* yet been put into the computerized files, but is being maintained in manual records.

The definition of what is "sensitive" personal information varies considerably among different types of organizations, depending on the relation between the individual and the organization, the uses made of the data, and similar factors. Whatever information is defined as most sensitive within each organization, however, is not generally going into computer files. In the Social Security Administration, for instance, the medical records a claimant must submit for certain benefits are kept in manual form in the district office and are not computerized. In a computerized personnel system that is being created by several Protestant denominations, the automated information about ministers will *not* include either information concerning divorce or performance

---

[3]Discussion of our survey respondents' opinions on the question of "more" data collection is in Appendix A, pages 420-424 below.

evaluations in former posts, since church executives regard these items as too sensitive to offer in print-outs made available nationally to church committees seeking new ministers; such information will remain in the paper personnel jackets at national headquarters, or at the local church level. Even in almost totally computerized systems that we visited, such as one small metropolitan health plan, the files considered most sensitive (psychiatric summaries, lab reports on venereal disease, and employee medical records) are stored only in manual form.

The exceptions that we found to this trend were in organizations which collect only public record or objective transaction data about the individual and put all of this into their basic record. An example from our profiles is TRW-Credit Data, which differs from many local credit bureaus in not collecting information for preemployment or other "character" reports. Another example is R. L. Polk, which gets and stores a very small amount of information on each individual or household from public records or organization membership lists, none of which Polk regards as sensitive.

We are not suggesting that computerized records contain no sensitive or subjective data; we are pointing out that, compared with the manual files from which they were derived and which are still in use, computerized records in most organizations tend to be more objective and less sensitive in character.

The reasons for this treatment of sensitive and subjective information lie in basic factors accompanying computerization. Organizations moving into computerization have pursued the most cost-effective applications—usually their largest, most high-volume, routine operations. This makes computerization of infrequently used and smaller files—generally the more sensitive and subjective ones—a low priority. Moreover, subjective files are usually filled with lengthy narrative statements rather than the short, objective, and standardized items that are most easily and economically converted to machine-readable form and processed by computer. Thus we found that Retail Credit Corporation has computerized several of its regional or local credit bureau operations, but has *not* moved to automate its more sensitive preemployment and preinsurance records and reporting.

In addition, managers appreciate the fact that security problems attached to sensitive and subjective records often involve unauthorized inspection by their own employees as well as outside parties. Thus we found many managers preferring to keep their most sensitive and subjective files in manual form, either under lock and key in their own offices, in special parts of larger record rooms, or in the hands of the individual executive or employee who compiles such records. We also found many organizations concerned that they might incur possible legal liability or public-relations injury if they put the information they regard as most sensitive or subjective into their computer systems, thereby having to keep formal records of its presence there. In the health department of one university we visited, for example, physicians expressed great reservations about putting their rough notes into the computer. There was no technological or economic bar to including short narrative statements in the patient's record. But here, as in other computerized medical record systems, physicians were concerned that if these were in the computer system, there was a strong chance that their tentative "working hypotheses" and comments about patients might be seen by the patient himself (in states giving patients a right to inspect their medical records) or by lawyers handling malpractice suits. As a result, the decision was made to exclude such notes and comments from ongoing computerization.

The civil-liberties implication of this trend is that the more subjective information used by organizations to make judgments about people—in law-enforcement intelligence, personnel work, medical diagnoses, educational advancement, etc.—is not yet being put onto computers. Thus, any attempt to set rules of privacy, confidentiality, or due process that focuses exclusively on computerized records, on the theory that most of the critical decisions about people are being made out of these, would be inadequate and misleading. Most of the decisions about people are still being made with the aid of manual records today, and it is here the civil-liberties issues will remain heavily centered for several years to come.[4]

Confidentiality Issues: Information Consolidation and Data Sharing

Once personal information has been obtained by an organization, the important civil-liberties issue becomes one of confidentiality—who within or outside the organization is allowed access to a given record or file? In analyzing this question, it will help bring the issues into proper focus to draw together some features of precomputer organizational life described in the profiles.

---

[4] Our survey responses relating to computerization of sensitive and subjective data are discussed in Appendix A, pages 424-427 below.

In the precomputer era, files on persons were scattered in various locations throughout the typical large organization. Where an organization had a central headquarters and regional offices, files on a given individual might be maintained in both locations. Where organizations had various bureaus and departments in their main building, these would maintain some files on employees, clients, or subjects, while other files were likely to be kept in central record rooms, from which they could be checked out or where they could be consulted by employees. Some centrally stored personal records were considered open to all employees, others required that the employee be a member of a particular bureau, and still others were kept under strict security and were limited to a few designated persons in the organization, depending upon the type of file and the nature of the organization.

The point of noting this diversity of file-keeping practice is that such sharing of identified information from bureau to bureau, among regional offices, and from regional office to and from central headquarters occurred regularly during the manual era. The mails, teletype, telephone, phototransmission, and radio sets were used for the data transmission, and many organizations moved extremely high volumes of information about people through these media. In addition, the central record rooms often had different files of personal information stored together. Record clerks and archive directors would apply rules of confidentiality to determine access for persons within the organization, or for outsiders who asked to examine specific files. A person with access to files in a central record room, and collecting information from various bureaus and regional offices, could accumulate a lot of information about the subject of an inquiry. We documented such consolidative use of manual files in most of the organizations we visited.

We also saw that data-sharing rules differed in their formality and extent of enforcement in the precomputer period. Four types of general situations can be usefully distinguished:

1. Law or organizational norms sometimes defined personal information as strictly confidential and barred its disclosure beyond the primary organization. Examples from our site visits were the Census Bureau, the Mormon church, and adoption records in social agencies. Such situations were (and remain) highly exceptional in the organizational world.

2. Law or organizational norms sometimes designated information as confidential but specified a class of other agencies or organizations with whom this information would be shared, and

the procedures under which this was to be done. Examples from our profiles included the Social Security Administration, the social service agencies at Santa Clara County, Bank of America, and the Kansas City Police Department. This is frequently the case where sensitive personal information is collected but there is no desire to seal off the data entirely.

3. Under American law and practice, most personal data in government files (with the exceptions for investigative, security, medical, and similar records that we have already noted) are considered public record information, accessible to the press and to any person with a "legitimate interest." Examples discussed in our profiles were public-employee salary information, welfare rolls, criminal conviction records in the courts, tax records, motor-vehicle and driver-registration records, and personal vital statistics.

4. Finally, there were situations where no laws or clear administrative rules were specified. Here data-sharing decisions were left to line employees or were decided on an ad hoc basis as questions arose. In this setting, we saw formally sanctioned exchanges of information among organizations in the same industry or field, as among life insurance companies and universities. There was also cross-industry sharing, as among personnel departments in various kinds of organizations, and with the credit reports circulated among various types of retail or other financial enterprises. In addition, informal or officially unacknowledged sharing of data took place under the "information buddy system," which hinged upon personal relationships rather than formal organizational arrangements. Frequently this sharing was not generally known to the public, and was even in direct violation of formal confidentiality rules. Such sharing was occasionally exposed and sometimes punished, as in the case of unauthorized release of information from law-enforcement records or intelligence files, but it remained a continuing aspect of organizational life.

Comparing data sharing in computerizing organizations with these precomputer patterns, our clear finding is that precomputer rules have *not* been altered in computerizing organizations; rather, customary practices have been reproduced with almost mirrorlike fidelity. To use our fourfold classification for illustrative purposes:

1. In no organization that we visited with clear preexisting rules forbidding sharing outside the organization have practices changed as a result of computerization. Computerized census information remains entirely confidential, open only to sworn census employees. It is still not used to "administer, regulate, or prosecute" any person. In another organization we visited, infor-

mation from a computerized disease registry was maintained under the same confidentiality rules as had existed prior to automation.

2. Where there were specified data-sharing provisions, these have been continued in the organizations we studied. We saw in the Santa Clara County profile how the legal rules governing circulation of welfare, health, hospital, probation, and law-enforcement information were spelled out by the county counsel as guides for the computerized operations, and how these have been followed. In those instances where there *has* been sharing of data to new classes of users, this has been precipitated by new administrative rules or new legislation, rather than engendered by computerization itself. An example is the requirement that universities supply the federal government with names of students receiving aid under federal scholarship and assistance programs—a change that has occurred since, but not because, many universities have computerized their student aid files.

3. In the public records area, we found that greater volumes of information have been made available to users because of computerization, and often to a larger number of users. But the *class* of users has remained the same, in keeping with prevailing social and legal policies. For example, more name and address lists have been generated by direct-mail firms purchasing information on computer tapes from government agencies. The buyers are the same direct-mail companies, and the ultimate consumers are the same business, charitable, religious, and political organizations that were customers in the precomputer era.

4. Finally, where there were no preexisting legal or administrative definitions of confidentiality, this lack of clear definition remained in most cases. But in some organizations the most significant effect of computerization has been to *evoke* administrative rules providing new definitions about use of the computerized data; we saw this especially where a central computer facility handled such files from multiple departments in government and private organizations. When the files were in manual form, under the lock and key of each department, it had a sense of control over "its" records. But when the information was converted to computer storage, the departments had to be promised by the data-center director (or the head of the agency under which the center operated) that each department's data would be protected. General rules were set as to data sharing and a procedure was created ensuring that each agency would retain the power to

approve or disapprove requests from other departments for use of its data.

We saw this proprietary concept enunciated by formal documents at the time of computerization at municipal and county-wide data centers, at multiagency state computerized facilities, and in various types of private organizations. In many organizations we were able to examine the record of requests for such use, and verify approvals and denials according to the rules of confidentiality laid down.

We also found that computerization has not halted the informal or "buddy system" exchanges that existed in the manual era, and may even have increased their volume in some cases. We discuss this topic at length in the next section.

Thus we found that nothing in computerization itself has produced a sharing of identified information to a broader class of users within multibureau organizations or among organizations than before computers. Where changes in patterns of confidentiality have taken place among the organizations we studied, the cause was new legislation or administrative rule, prompted by basic program changes or new social policies.[5]

One important example of data consolidation at a site deserves mention. In one bank, the data-processing group had just completed (successfully) a project by which a customer who accepted the bank's offer of a "consolidated statement" was able to obtain a monthly print-out of the status of his major activities at that bank: checking and savings account, loans, cash reserve, and credit-card balance. To make this consolidation possible, the bank had to draw together the information on each customer from a variety of different computerized files that had previously been completely separate. This required verification of customer name in each account, and the monthly posting of the information for the consolidated statement from each separate file. In terms of confidentiality, this operation did not raise civil-liberties issues, since the creation of the comprehensive statement was done only if a customer asked for it and there was no disclosure of information to anyone beyond the rules that the bank had followed prior to its computerization. However, this example illustrates that no technological or organizational barrier exists to the consolidation of information about an individual from separate files; it is a

[5] Survey findings relating to the computer's impact on data sharing are presented in Appendix A, pages 427-429 and 437-442 below.

matter of whether the organization wants to do this and will spend the money and manpower to assemble such consolidated reports.

Impact on Due Process

Under this heading, we deal with the due-process tradition in organizational decision making. This tradition has two major elements. First is what the law calls "procedural due process," by which the individual is generally supposed to be informed of the information relied on by government to determine his obligations or benefits, and under which he is given some kind of review procedure for challenging information drawn from his record when government action is taken affecting him. The second aspect embodies what American law terms "substantive due process." This is the principle that executive and regulatory agencies of government should not make decisions in ways that are arbitrary or capricious, as this will be defined by legislative codes or judicial decisions. We will apply these two concepts of due process to the computerization of records by government agencies, and consider the relevance of these concepts of "fundamental fairness" to certain private sectors of record-keeping as well.

Procedural Due Process in Computerized Record Systems

One major concern of civil-liberties commentators has been that information put into computer storage will lead to more decisions being made about individuals without their knowledge, and without opportunities for inspection or challenge. "You don't know what the computer has on you" has been the popular way the fear has been expressed.

In part one, we noted that individuals in the precomputer period were often unaware that files existed about them in various governmental, commercial, and nonprofit organizations. People did not normally devote much thought or attention to the fact that their transactions generated a long trail of files—tax and land records, school records, medical records, government license and benefit records, etc. In a dim way the individual knew that papers or folders existed containing information that he had supplied, but this usually became noteworthy only when the individual himself had to furnish the record or when he discovered that some benefit or privilege had been denied on the basis of his record. Furthermore, there were various files in the manual era about which most people knew nothing, essentially because the operations in which these records were used were clandestine or of low visibility for some other reason. The work of commercial reporting agencies in the credit, preemployment, and preinsurance fields illustrates record-building activity in the private sector about which most Americans were largely ignorant. Police investigative or intelligence files dealing with persons suspected of involvement in criminal or subversive activities are a prime example from the public sector.

As for each *individual's* knowledge of records about himself, since computerization, we found that general public awareness of the existence of files and the types of people covered in them has increased rather than decreased during the past 15 years. The main reason for this is growing public sensitivity to the records-and-liberty issue in recent years, as part of the discussion of invasion of privacy. Popular books, media programs, congressional hearings, lawsuits, discussions within civic and professional groups, and other stimuli have made people far more aware than before of the general patterns of organizational record-keeping. For example, public awareness of files kept and used by commercial reporting agencies increased substantially after the publicity given to this area in legislative hearings of the late 1960s and passage of the Fair Credit Reporting Act of 1970. Far more people are aware of the existence and use of police and army intelligence files in 1972 than before the publicity and hearings devoted to these activities in 1968-71.

As we looked at *public* knowledge about record-keeping this follows the same lines of knowledge and ignorance today in the 55 organizations we studied as it did in the manual era: how much an individual knows depends on the type of organization and file involved, the degree to which the individual is judged by that record for rights and benefits, and the amount of visibility given to a particular record-keeping activity by the press, guardian groups, and the legislature.

We noted that a great many special files were created in the manual era about which the individuals recorded in them were unaware (and often intentionally kept that way). These included records on sales and business prospects; on potential appointees for judicial posts, executive offices, and faculty positions; on research subjects; and a host of others. There has been considerable publicity given recently to the discovery by congressional committees that computerized files have been set up for some low-visibility record-keeping activities of organizations, such as the file of "persons of law-enforcement interest" maintained by the U.S. Passport Office. Our research indicates, however, that most such special-purpose files have not yet been computerized. In our 55 organizations, a list of the *computerized* files of which the "record subjects" are unaware would be far smaller than a list of *manual* files which lie beyond the knowledge of those on whom records are stored. We saw no instances in which managers thought that computerization of a file would be a good way to decrease its visibility or make access by individuals to their own records more difficult.

Furthermore, where the public has become insistent that the individual know that a record has been used to affect his interests, as with passage of the Fair Credit Reporting Act of 1970, our site visits showed that the requirement of notification operates as effectively on record systems that are computerized as on those that are not. In other words, nothing in the computerized system necessarily impedes the execution of such public policies.

Turning to the individual's right to access and challenge, our site visits indicated that where there were rules allowing access and challenge before automation, as with bank customers to checking accounts, army veterans to their service records, or Social Security account holders to their earnings records, these rules have been carried over fully into the automated systems. Where computerization was introduced into fields in which considerable variations in policy existed (as in law enforcement, where some agencies allowed individuals access to their summary criminal histories and others did not), automation has not changed this picture of diversity: local police agencies continue to follow their precomputer rules. Where judicial or public pressures led some of these agencies to afford a right of access that they had *not* previously given, this was executed whether or not the organization had computerized the file in question.

The key point is that the presence of computers has not impeded such organizations from moving to afford rights of access and challenge. Rather, we saw in several of our visits that the computerized system allowed an access policy to be carried out with considerable efficiency. Systems at these sites could produce a print-out or display of an individual's credit history, summary criminal history, welfare status, etc., when the individual asked to see it, or to discuss its content, and have a counselor go over the record with the individual. If any errors were found, the official was able to correct the automated file as easily or more easily than he might a manual file. In some on-line systems, he could show the individual immediately by a new print-out or display that the correction had been made and that the corrected version would be the one subsequently provided to those using the system.

Our basic conclusions, then, are that the public debates over records and computerization have had the effect of increasing both public and individual awareness of files during the past decade; that computer record systems have followed, rather than altered, preexisting rules of notification and access; and that new legal rules of procedural due process have been followed equally well—or poorly—in computerized and manual file systems.[6]

"Substantive Due Process" Issues

The other aspect of civil-liberties interest in organizational decision-making is what we have called *substantive* due process. Here, we are drawing a broad analogy to the legal doctrine that regulatory and administrative agencies must not make their decisions in the determination of rights, benefits, and licenses on the basis of arbitrary and capricious criteria. Civil libertarians have expressed fears that computer systems will replace "human judgment" with dangerous "machine rigidities," and therefore introduce a new element of arbitrariness into decisions about individuals.

We paid attention during our site visits to three specific fears of this kind that have been voiced in the databanks literature: (1) that computers lead decision makers to treat "print-out" as "gospel"; (2) that computers lead to reliance on "rigid codes" to decide issues about individuals; and (3) that computers create "unforgetting and unforgiving" record systems.

Reliance on "Print-Out" in Judging People

It has been said that officials in computerized organizations are more likely to base their decisions about people on information contained in the "print-out," rather than judging the "whole person." The assumption is that the computer will somehow come to dominate the otherwise understanding clerk or official who will give great weight to what has come out of the "infallible" computer system, on printed sheets or the video display tube. Believing that the information must be accurate and complete because it has been produced by the computer, officials therefore will treat it as more trustworthy than written records, will be less inclined to doubt its reliability, and will be less willing to take into account

---

[6] The issue of individual access to records in the organizations surveyed by mail is discussed in Appendix A, pages 430-432 below.

what the individual himself says or provides in the way of written documentation.

An initial difficulty with this analysis is that it betrays considerable ignorance of organizational reality in the precomputer period. For example, it romanticizes the age of the clerk in a way that Franz Kafka and every person who has ever encountered a literal-minded bureaucrat would find laughable. All types of large organizations encourage their decision makers to rely on the records; indeed, this is usually considered as a step toward more fair and objective treatment of clients, customers, and citizens, since officials will be less able to introduce their own personal biases. Such reliance can also produce misjudgments about people because of incomplete data or biased reporting. Certain types of organizations that operate without much public visibility or scrutiny have been especially prone by their nature, mission, and procedures to rely on "the record" and are likely to produce a higher proportion of erroneous judgments than organizations operating in full public view. This tendency was documented during the 1960s by congressional inquiries into the way preemployment and preinsurance reporting agencies affected the rights of those reported on, when the reports tended to be accepted without doubts about their accuracy by the employers and insurance companies which bought them.

Apart from such special cases, however, the history of organizational life in the United States is replete with instances where the public became aware that bad judgments were made out of reliance "on the record," for instance, by evaluators for the army, the Foreign Service, corporations, churches, labor unions, and most other large institutions. As a result, our legal and social norms have stressed the desirability that organizations, particularly in government, should state the criteria on which decisions about specific individuals are based and provide procedural due process as the critical safeguard against misjudgment through the use of records; however, the degree to which these rules are imposed on particular government agencies or carried over into private organizational life has been a matter of continuing conflict and adjustment. Any analysis of the computer's impact on decision making must start with the fact that there have been long-standing problems over undue reliance on records by bureaucracies in the manual era.

In our 55 organizations, we observed that what primarily determined the role that a standardized record would play in an evaluator's decisions was his interpretation of the organization's instructions to him on this matter, expressed or implied; whether the record was delivered out of manual or computerized storage was of little consequence.

We can examine this issue by looking at three types of decision situations we found on our site visits. In the first type, information to be weighed is essentially objective and fast action is needed; here, we found computers being used to generate a "go" or "no-go" signal. Examples are the point-of-sale terminal from which a retailer checks an individual's up-to-the-minute status or "floor limit" under a credit card, or a police officer's use of NCIC to learn whether a car he is following is officially listed as a stolen vehicle. Because of the need for swift decision in these instances, and the computer's capacity to supply on-line response, the printout or video display indeed controls the immediate decision affecting the individual.

Note that this development follows the precomputer pattern in two ways. First, records also controlled some "fast-action" decisions in the manual era since what were then "rapid" methods of communication (radio or telephone) were used to call for a clerk to check a manual record and respond immediately. Secondly, in both the computerized and manual versions of fast decision making, the individual has an opportunity to challenge the decision later, by saying that he has not exceeded his floor limit on his charge card, or that his car is not the one reported stolen. We saw no indication that challenges to a computerized file's accuracy were less likely to be heeded by clerk or official than challenges to the accuracy of information lodged in manual files. Further, there were manual-era situations in which decisions were made *without* information from records (as where a police officer followed his hunch and stopped a car driven by someone who "didn't look right"). It is not at all clear that the individual was always better off in such cases.

A second kind of decision is where the organization has more applicants for a given program, service, or benefit than it can accommodate, and has developed certain "objective" minimum criteria for identifying which individuals it wants to select. We found banks, life-insurance companies, colleges, welfare agencies, and many other organizations using computerized data to help evaluators make such decisions. Examples of such criteria would be the use of a minimum salary level as the major criterion in issuing a charge card or making a loan; requiring a bachelor's degree for entry into a management training program; or using income below a certain level for a given family size as a criterion for welfare eligibility. Reliance on the computerized record was heavy in these situations because the decision was intended to rest on the presence or absence of what was regarded as objective information about a minimum status or attainment. The criteria the organization chose for making its selections may have been good or bad, from the standpoint of the individual and for society; but the use made of this kind of information was no greater in computerized than in manual settings.

Third, there are kinds of decisions in which organizations could not work on the basis of standardized, objective criteria alone. They expected their evaluators to weigh subjective characteristics, interpret necessarily incomplete factual summaries, conduct personal interviews, or invite self-descriptions by those being evaluated. That evaluators were expected to take various kinds of "organizational risks" with regard to clients and customers, and this was anticipated in the policies set by the organization. Among the most advanced of the computerizing organizations we visited, for example, "factor-rating" systems had been developed to help evaluators make such decisions. One example is the credit-scoring formula used to weigh personal credit histories to help bank officers make loan decisions. Another example is the Internal Revenue Service's computer-assisted sorting of personal income-tax returns; this selects for audit, on the basis of special parameters, those returns which are likely to result in tax liabilities different from those the individual himself determined. In both instances, organizations use the computer as a preliminary selection technique which supplements work done by officials—a personal conference with the individual, for instance—with the ultimate decision made by the bank or tax official.

In the 55 organizations that we visited, we found a strong awareness on the part of organizational personnel of the possible errors that hardware, software, and operator failures could create in computer-generated output.[7] In describing the progress and travails of computerization in their enterprises, top managers, user departments, data-processing directors and staffs, and line employees whom we talked to would almost invariably regale us with their favorite "computer screw-up" stories. Such persons displayed far from a "garbage-in-gospel-out" attitude in their use of computerized output. They knew the kinds of errors that could be made, and also knew where there were manual records to check should

---

[7] Our principal discussion of accuracy in computerized files appears in the next section; here, we are considering this as a factor in due-process issues.

questions arise about the accuracy of the computerized record. We did find an abundance of instances where people inside the organization used the computer as an excuse, saying that "the computer did it" when they knew—or should have known—that the problem was one of human error in data input, programming, or operations. Outside the organization, such explanations that the computer "screwed up" often would be presented uncritically by the press, since human error is all too common and nowhere as titillating and newsworthy as the idea that the machine erred.

In this regard, one must distinguish "treating the print-out as gospel" from the problem of automatic billing and dunning letters that have set off public anger about "dumbbell machines." The latter are situations in which an organization has set up its computer operations in a way so that several cycles of billing or dunning letters continue to go forward even though a person has tried—by letter or telephone call—to bring to the attention of the organization that an item is being contested as inaccurate. In the precomputer era, a clerk could check the item and set the matter right in a reasonably short time, such as before the next billing. But many organizations did not consider it worth the time and money to create a man-machine procedure which would stop the automatic billing and dunning output in their computer systems. There is some evidence to suggest that the public does not always accept use of the computer as an excuse. A recent national survey reports that while 24 percent say that they had had trouble getting a computerized bill corrected, only 3 percent attributed that trouble to the computer; 15 percent said instead that their trouble in correcting the bill was "the fault of the company's personnel."[8]

As a result of public anger at this situation, rules are now pending before the Federal Trade Commission and legislation has been proposed at the state and federal levels to force organizations to provide a personal response to customer complaints within a reasonable time, such as ten days after receipt of a protest.[9] The point to note is that this represents a case where organizations have set up an automatic procedure that is not capable of interruption and correction as rapidly as consumers want. It is not a question of relying on the print-out as absolutely right, but of how

---

[8] *A National Survey of the Public's Attitudes Toward Computers*, sponsored by the American Federation of Information Processing Societies and conducted by Time, Inc. See our detailed discussion of this survey below, pages 491-494.

[9] Connecticut passed such a law in 1971. See *New York Times*, June 4, 1972, for a review of such consumer legislation.

quickly an error can be corrected in the computer file or a conflict can be adjudicated through human evaluators.

Thus our basic finding is that we did not find "print-out" being used to sort and sift people in some automatic fashion in decision-making settings where more personalized and subjective decisions were typical in the manual era. We did not of course compare, over long periods of time, the behavior of decision makers using computerized files with that of evaluators working from similar manual files. Thus it is possible that there are some differences of a subtle nature between the way that clerks and officials regard computer output and the way in which information derived from manual files is regarded. But we saw nothing to suggest that such differences are yet affecting individual liberties in important ways. We did find that more of the fast, "go—no-go" type decisions are being made today with the aid of computers; but it is clear that similar decisions were made in the past without computers, and we do not see these as violating principles of substantive due process as long as the decision is known to the individual and timely appeal to primary records is available to correct any error.

Computer Coding and Organizational Decisions about People

There is no doubt that the need to reduce storage and processing costs has led organizations to seek abbreviations for the words and statements contained in the personal records that they computerize. This has prompted some civil-liberties analysts to conclude that reduction of written text to such "abbreviations and codes" has a harmful effect on the decision process, by causing organizational evaluators to "force-fit" people into categories that do not reflect the subtleties that a narrative record might convey. For example, during recent public debates over the U.S. Army's CONUS intelligence file on persons who might be involved in future civil disorders, it was disclosed that in the computer code, the number 134.295 designated a "non-communist," while 135.295 was the number assigned to alleged "Communist party membership" *or* "advocacy of communism." Commenting on this difference of one digit, Senator Ervin deplored the fact that CONUS intelligence analysts looked at the political utterances or activities of young people who did not have formal memberships and "sometimes chose a designation arbitrarily in doubtful cases."

To analyze this problem, we should again recognize that the use of abbreviations and codes in record-keeping did not arrive with computers as some commentators assume; they have been part of organizational practice for centuries. They were developed to deal with high-volume transactions by providing standardization and permitting "shorthand talk" among record handlers. In many computerized systems, preexisting codes and abbreviations from the manual record systems we carried over verbatim into the automated operations. In fact, the presence of such shorthand systems often made those records the prime candidates for computerization in the first place.

The civil liberties issue is therefore whether the adoption of coded entries or print-outs in computerized record systems affects the fairness of organizational judgments about people. It would seem clear in the army CONUS intelligence example that the vice in this practice (apart from whether the operation should have been conducted at all) was that classification of an individual as a Communist party member or advocate of communism was made despite the lack of adequate information, and that the shorthand employed was not fine enough to permit distinctions between actual members of the Communist party and those thought by the analyst to "advocate communism." Whether the label took six or sixty digits to record, whether it was spelled out in full text or not, and whether the record's format was handwriting, typing, or computer storage, this fundamental abuse of codes would remain.

At our site visits, we found that the use of codes in the computerized files was generally a carryover of abbreviations that had previously been used to save staff time and record space. For example, Credit Data Corporation employs a system of numbered codes (e.g., "01" means Open Account) which incorporate what used to be a check-the-box technique in manual credit reporting systems of other credit bureaus. Since most of the codes are based on relatively objective account status information from users (e.g., "account 60 days delinquent"), their meaning to users is for the most part unambiguous. We see no civil-liberties difference in the use of a computer-printed card with a set of fully defined abbreviations and having those items appear on the forms used in manual credit bureau reports.

Furthermore, we encountered some situations in which more detailed categories were used for the description of individuals after computerization than had been the case in the manual coding system. At a psychiatric hospital we visited, for instance, nurses on floor duty used to fill out nursing notes at the end of each shift, describing the general psychological and physical condition of each patient as this had been observed in the course of the shift.

Nursing personnel were required to write something about each patient; but having little time for this activity as they were going off duty and knowing that physicians on the staff made use of the notes infrequently, only the most cursory comments were made on the patient's chart. The nurses developed shorthand notations and informally agreed-upon summary phrases (such as "hostile and withdrawn" or "cheerful and cooperative") for describing the patient.

After the nursing-notes process was automated, personnel were required to choose from over two hundred short descriptive phrases in several categories. The code numbers they check for each patient are stored on computer, and each day a summary is printed out in narrative form so that physicians can review several aspects of the patient's recent behavior on the ward. The hospital staff reports that finer distinctions are recorded now for each patient than under the manual system; looking at the list of possible choices in several categories (e.g., "activities on unit," "patient reaction to medications") jogs the nurse's memory. The new summaries and analyses (such as predicting the outbreak of assaults on a given ward) which the computerized system has made feasible have also increased the overall importance of the nursing observations. As a result, nursing personnel report that they are more willing to devote time and attention to the reporting task.

Certainly the computerization of records has in no way discouraged the use of code numbers and abbreviations, and there is little doubt that careless use of labels such as "troublemaker," "unruly child," "heavy drinker," "subversive," "slow payer," "psychotic tendencies," and similar shorthand, in whatever form these are recorded, can have harmful effects on decision making about individual careers, privileges, and benefits. This possibility must be guarded against in any humanely oriented system. But in the organizations we visited, it does not appear that computerization of files led to any greater misuse of shorthand notations than was present in the manual era. Again, protection for civil liberties lies in making the criteria for decision known to those affected, giving persons rights to contest the basis for conclusions reached on their histories, and forbidding what society sees as improper or inappropriate use of codes in any kind of record medium. To ban computers but allow a handwritten note of "Communist" to be made improperly about someone, or through a pencil check on a printed form, would give no genuine protection to constitutional rights, and might generate a false sense of having "done something" about an important problem.

Computers Create Unforgiving and Unforgetting Record Systems

Throughout the "antidatabank" literature, it is said that the computer is an "unforgiving" machine whose "unforgetting memory banks" operate to confront individuals with their past mistakes and make it impossible for them to start afresh. Whether the file concerns criminal arrests, college disciplinary records, or employment histories, information is seen as lodged more permanently in a computerized file than in manual record-keeping. The civil-liberties danger of permanent record systems is that they violate the American "second-chance" tradition. Many citizens assume, out of a variety of religious, humanistic, and psychiatric orientations, that it is socially beneficial to encourage individuals to reform their lives, a process that is impeded when individuals know (or feel) that they will automatically be barred by their past "mistakes" at each of the later "gate-keeping" points of social and economic life. Because the computer is assumed not to lose records, to forward them efficiently to new places and organizations, and to create an appetite in organizations for historically complete records, the computer is seen as threatening this forgiveness principle.

In analyzing this assumption, we should recall that the "forgiveness" principle has always been a humanistic *exception* to a more basic feature of American cultural tradition—the strong belief in personal responsibility. Under traditional American definitions of religious and political ethics, individuals are morally accountable for what they *chose* to do with the opportunities and choices that confronted them in life. In this perspective, with its roots deep in the Puritan heritage, individuals should be judged by their acts and their achievements. If they had acted in violation of community or legal norms, but had *repented* and *reformed* themselves, or if standards had changed over the lifetime of the individual, forgiveness was a generous principle sometimes applied. But the *basic* principle was that the evaluator (the church, police, school, employer, credit grantor, etc.) should *know* what errors or "sins" an individual had made, and should then treat individuals properly according to the life histories that they had ("voluntarily") created.

Organizations had increasingly built up permanent record systems during the late nineteenth and twentieth centuries, as part of the tradition of obtaining detailed, longitudinal records in education, employment, law enforcement, credit, and other spheres of life. Furthermore, the tendency in formal organizations to keep rather than destroy records was well established. It is easier for organizations to file and forget records than to review them continuously and enforce retention rules. Thus the chance of escaping your record by moving from one place to another was already heavily diminished by the middle twentieth century, even with manual record-keeping practices.

Among our 55 organizations, we found that whatever the organization's practices had been about such matters as wiping out records after the passage of time, forwarding a record to new employers or schools, or contributing items of information on specific request, these same policies have been carried forward rather than changed in the computerized systems. Computerization as such has not led to either an expansion or a contraction of existing "forgive and forget" policies.

We also observed that computer technology was quite capable of having the system "remember" only what the human programmers and operators instructed it to preserve, and to have it "forget" on similar, humanly originated commands. For example, we noted at TRW-Credit Data the setting of programming instructions for removing from the central file those bankruptcy items older than seven years, in compliance with the Fair Credit Reporting Act. Similarly, as the FBI profile illustrated, if information about an arrest is put into the NCIC computerized Criminal History System, without a conviction noted, and the courts or Congress specify later that these items should not be preserved, it will be technically possible to wipe out all incomplete records without altering those records which do have convictions noted.

Thus the key question about subsequent erasure or noncirculation of derogatory information was *not* a technical matter in the organizations we visited. It was an issue of social policy, on which society has to choose between the "forgive and forget" and "preserve but evaluate" theories of record-keeping in each substantive area.

From the entire range of issues discussed in this section of "negative findings," several themes emerge with great clarity. First, the increased collection, consolidation, and circulation of personal information that civil-liberties spokesmen believed to be taking place as a direct and inexorable consequence of computerization are not happening as yet in the advanced computerizing organizations that we examined. Similarly, there has not been the ebbing away of procedural and substantive due process that civil-liberties commentators assumed to be an inevitable result of automated information handling. In each of the major fields of private and governmental activity that we studied in our site visits, preexisting norms and practices have been closely reproduced in the computerized systems; and where new laws or policies have been enunciated affecting civil-liberties interests, the computerized operations have embodied these just as fully as the manual ones. Whatever our children may see when they look at computerized record-keeping in the year 2000, the first 15 years of automation have simply not as yet altered relationships between people, data, and organizations in the ways projected by those who first looked with anxious eyes at the relation of computers to civil liberties.

Why the Misunderstanding?: A Case Study

The obvious question is why and how such a gap in understanding developed between what databanks are actually being used for in organizations and the statements about such use that have been presented by many serious journalists, lawyers, and social scientists. To understand this process, we have selected a key instance to treat as a case study in the origins and dissemination of mistaken information. Our example involves two very important areas of computer usage—on-line computer reservation systems and credit-card companies whose files probably contain information about the movements and expenditures of 50 to 75 million Americans.

In June 1968, an article appeared in *Look* magazine under the title "The Computer Data Bank: Will It Kill Your Freedom?" Describing the capacities of computers to produce a trail of records about the citizen and the way in which police and "other" investigators were already using these new resources, the article gave the following account of how the "innocent" American Airlines SABRE reservations system "invades [the traveler's] privacy":

> American's computer can be queried about any traveler's movements in the past two or three months. In a furious burst of speed, the electric typewriter spews out a dossier;

flights traveled, seat numbers, time of day, telephone contact, hotel reservations, etc.

[A] computer expert for the airline says that 10 to 15 investigators a day (Federal, state, local and other) are permitted to delve into the computer for such information. Some of them want (and get) a print-out of the entire passenger list of a certain flight to see who might be traveling with a particular person.

This account from *Look* was then adopted in many journalistic and legal articles about the new capacities of computers. It was used prominently in *The Assault on Privacy* (1971), a book by Prof. Arthur R. Miller of the University of Michigan Law School. In this study, the airline-reservations system example was used to warn against the "record prison" allegedly being built in America because "the computer can and is being used to analyze seemingly unrelated data on large numbers of people to determine whether a particular individual's activities bear any relation to the conduct of other investigation subjects or groups." The solitary example given of such use in the present was "American Airlines' deceptively innocuous flight reservations computer," with the *Look* magazine account being quoted as evidence. Professor Miller then mentioned the "recent expansion of computerized reservation services to include hotels, car-rental agencies, theatres, and sports arenas," concluding that investigative uses of these systems are "clearly the wave of the future in the surveillance field." Readers were cautioned not to forget "the trail being left by your Carte Blanche or American Express cards; it may be an interesting one, especially if you happen to shop or dine at the same places as some Mafia *capo* or suspected subsersive."

Professor Miller's acceptance and use of the *Look* account led to its repetition in reviews of his book by journalist Robert Sherrill in the *New York Times* and by former Attorney General Ramsey Clark in the *Saturday Review*. Ralph Nader described the same two- or three-month surveillance over past flights, fellow passengers, and telephone contact numbers as a capacity of the American Airlines computer in an article on privacy that he wrote in 1971 for the American Civil Liberties Union, part of which also appeared in the *Saturday Review* in 1971. Throughout 1971-72, references to large-scale investigative use of airline computer reservation systems were made by various spokesmen at congressional hearings on databanks, on national TV programs about computers and privacy, and in forums about privacy held before civic groups and other audiences. Usually it was implied that what was said to be true about American Airlines was also within the capacity of computer systems in other travel, entertainment, and credit-card companies.

Since we made a site visit to American Airlines, studied the operations of the SABRE system, and examined several credit-card systems, let us reconstruct what is right and wrong about these accounts.

Passenger information in the SABRE system was (and is) organized into two separate parts. The current file is an on-line reservation system that contains passenger travel data for the current date, one day back, and 320 days into the future. The past-date file is maintained on tape, off-line, and contains information from two days before current date to 60 days back, the period for which such records are required to be kept by Civil Aeronautics Board (CAB) regulations. After 60 days, the tapes are written over with new data and used again, with no permanent retention of the erased records made on microfilm or any other storage medium. Inquiries for passenger flight information further back than 60 days would have to go to manual records maintained by American Airlines, which consist solely of the ticket copies and accounting data.

The type of data maintained about passengers is the same in the current and past-date files. It consists of items such as name of the passenger, flight number, date, point of origin and destination, telephone contact, information about ticketing arrangements, offices from which reservations were made, notations of reservation requests and changes, any special requests (kosher food, wheelchair needed, etc.), and various land-travel arrangements if made by American Airlines services (car rental, reservations at American Flagship hotels, sightseeing tours, etc.).

We start, then, with information collected by the airline directly for service to its customers, set up in the computer system in a current on-line file and a past-date off-line file, with more limited manual records of tickets and payments kept as they always were. Now we can contrast this with the version presented by the commentators quoted earlier.

1. The *Look* article said that "10 to 15 investigators a day (Federal, state, local, and other) are permitted to delve into the computer for such information." If this were true, it would mean 3,650 to 5,470 such investigative inquiries a year, clearly a major use of the reservations systems by law-enforcement agents and "other" persons, the latter presumably being private detectives or

other private information gatherers. What the *Look* reporter was actually told in a brief telephone interview with a computer programmer, according to American Airlines officials, was that 10-15 past-date checks a day were made by American Airlines—almost all of which related to *customer complaints*. These involve problems of missing baggage, cancelled flight continuations, failure to get special food ordered, etc. These customer complaints require officials at the American Airlines Data Processing Center at Briarcliff, New York, to go into the past-date file and check the original record. However, a few of these three to five thousand yearly searches, less than 5 percent, do deal with law-enforcement inquiries, as we will describe shortly.

2. The *Look* account suggests that, given a traveler's name, his "movements in the past two or three months" can be obtained as print-out. This is wholly false; such a name check was never possible through the programming used in the SABRE system and cannot be accomplished in the system today. To enable the system to do this, the Director of Data Processing notes, would require not an easily inserted new instruction to the computer's routine program but a reprogramming of the entire operation. The present SABRE system (and its soon-to-be-installed replacement, SABRE II) require that name, *date*, and *flight number* be provided before a passenger record can be obtained from the tapes by an inquiry. There is no way to put in a name alone and get out a 60-day past itinerary for a passenger and the contents of those reservation records. Precisely the same is true of the current file. Name, date, and flight number are required. The need to specify date and flight number in addition to the name the person used when traveling substantially reduces the "browsing" capacity of the American Airlines System. Checking at another highly advanced airline reservations system, that of Trans-World Airlines, we learned that their system works exactly the same way.

It is possible, as stated in the *Look* story and accounts relying on it, to insert a current or past-date and flight number and find out whether a person was a passenger on that flight, as well as to obtain the names of the other passengers making the flight. Or a name can be checked for a particular future date and flight. This was exactly what could be and was done in the precomputer era, when such lists were kept manually and telephone inquiries were made into local and regional reservation centers. A slightly faster version of such flight-by-flight checks is what the SABRE system allows, not the total-itinerary version.[1]

The SABRE system is programmed in this way because it serves business needs and fits technological constraints to have it so. The airline is not running a surveillance system and has no customer-service or business-information need to retrieve travel profiles for each passenger. Programming to create such a "name only" search capacity would mean requiring the system to search each name against the 322 days that are loaded into the current file and the 5,000 flights or segments of flights the airline has each day. The past-date file would require a search of 60 days times 5,000 flight segments. This would be very expensive, especially if it included the programming necessary to minimize and cope with errors from false matches—a large number of which might be expected with only the name as identifier. It would also consume such substantial amounts of computer time as to interfere with the heavy use already made of the system by 2,500 field agents.

3. It was said in the *Look* article that the airline permitted "Federal, state, local, and other" investigators to "delve into the computer" for past travel information. As it was in precomputer days, American Airlines policy is to supply passenger information to law-enforcement agencies upon presentation of the proper subpoena. The number of law-enforcement requests compiled within both the manual and computer eras has averaged about

---

[1] To test the surveillance potential of the SABRE system, one member of the site-visit team (in July 1970) asked whether information about his past travel on American Airlines could be obtained from only his name and telephone numbers (office and home). Permission for making such an inquiry was obtained from the appropriate executive, and, a few hours later, our staff member was shown a print-out containing the *number* of trips he had made during the past six months from New York to his two most frequently traveled destinations, Washington and Boston. No flight numbers, dates of trip, telephone-contact numbers in Washington or Boston, persons traveled with, or other data maintained in the SABRE sytem were—or could be—provided by the airline. Provision of the number of trips and destination for our staff member stems from a special "frequent traveler" record kept by the American Airlines Marketing Department. A special program takes off the SABRE tapes the telephone numbers from which a specified large number of trips are booked, along with the name of the traveler and the place of destination. Salesmen from the Marketing Department are able to use these three items as leads to encourage continued or increased use by frequent travelers on American. No law-enforcement or other investigative requests are filled by the Marketing Department from these tapes. Any such requests would be forwarded to the general counsel or the Security Office.

10-12 *a month*, not "10 to 15 a day." This amounts to 120 to 144 a year, not the 3,600-5,400 claimed in the *Look* account; and this total should be considered in the context that more than 12 million passengers per year make trips on American Airlines.

Despite increases in air travel during the past two decades, law-enforcement requests have remained approximately the same for the past 20 years, according to the recollections of company security and legal officials. "It is now easier to comply, once we have determined that the request is proper," the general counsel of American Airlines notes, "but the volume has not increased." Half the requests come from federal inquiries, mostly the FBI, and half from state and metropolitan police departments. The airline's policy is that no private investigators are granted access to passenger information from the SABRE system. Inquiries from insurance companies (checking into accident or baggage-loss claims, for example) are dealt with from manual ticket records in the accounting department, not by use of the computerized record system.

The way in which law-enforcement requests for prior flight records were and are complied with also does not operate as the *Look* story implied. No outsider gets direct access into the computer, in the sense that "delve" suggests. SABRE reservations agents in the field cannot make inquiries directly into the past-date system, since this is not on-line; thus, they could not fulfill such requests from the airport terminals informally, even if they wanted to.

When law-enforcement agencies wish information from either the current or back computer files, they apply to the head of the airline's Audit and Security Department. Before 1971, he reviewed the requests and made the decision as to compliance. Since mid-1971, as a result of concern to tighten the procedures for such access, responses to such requests are coordinated with the airline's vice-president and general counsel.[2] Under his supervision, a subpoena is required in every case that does not involve "hot pursuit" of a criminal suspect. Even subpoenas have been

---

[2] The reason for requiring the general counsel's approval was the recognition of the problems the airline security manager would have in saying "no" to law-enforcement officers on whom he has to depend for cooperation in matters of airport theft, hijacking, and other crimes. "I cite public concern over privacy and let them blame me," the general counsel remarked. That the cooperative ethos is a real problem can be appreciated by noting that American Airlines was indicted and pleaded guilty in 1971 to paying a New York City police officer to supply the airline's personnel department with criminal record reports on prospective employees, drawn from the confidential files of the police department's Identification Section, in violation of law.

declined where these were thought to be improperly broad. For example, some time ago an agent of the Internal Revenue Service called on the general counsel and asked for passenger lists on special chartered flights between New York and Las Vegas that are sponsored by certain Las Vegas hotels to bring "heavy bettors" to their hotels free of charge. The counsel refused to supply these lists, citing the passengers' right to expect confidential treatment of this information. When the IRS agent wrote out a subpoena and presented it, the counsel then said that he would prefer to wait until the subpoena was enforced in court before complying, as it appeared to be a "fishing expedition." No attempt was made to have the subpoena enforced.

There are no remote terminals in the department of Audit and Security or the general counsel's office. When a law-enforcement request is granted, the inquiry is forwarded to the director of the Management Information and Data Processing unit in Briarcliff, New York. His staff goes into the on-line system or runs the back-record tapes, and the information is then furnished to the Audit and Security Department for transmittal to the law-enforcement agency. In cases of emergency, this can be done quite rapidly.

To check on the accounts of the SABRE system that we received at the airline, we interviewed an experienced law-enforcement investigator who works in the intelligence area; his specialty is the organized-crime field, in which tracking the movements of alleged leaders or couriers is a major surveillance activity. He confirmed that investigators do go to airline officials and employees when they have specific information about a suspect being on a particular flight or going to or from a particular place on a known date. Airline officials cooperate, he noted, some when the investigators show credentials and some requiring a subpoena. Responses are slightly faster since computerization, he noted, such as several minutes for a check of whether an intelligence subject was on the flights of one airline from New York to Chicago on a given day, compared to the half an hour it took before. But he was emphatic in stating that computerization had not fundamentally altered the way such investigations were conducted.

5. In *The Assault on Privacy*, we were also told not to forget about Carte Blanche and American Express cards, since the trail being left there "may be an interesting one, especially if you happen to shop or dine at the same places as some Mafia *capo* or suspected subversive." This adds two fundamental errors to the original *Look* mistakes. First, it suggests to the reader that the

computer systems of these credit card firms are the same kind of on-line individual operations as airline and hotel reservation files. They are not. American Express, for example, does not store on-line the individual charges made at each place of purchase by each cardholder; these records are kept either on tapes for batch-processing or on microfilm for permanent storage. The only relevant on-line application is a system containing summary information on the accounts' history of amounts over which a credit analyst must approve continued charge activity. (This aspect will be discussed below in greater detail.) The same absence of on-line billing records prevails in the two national bank credit-card systems whose operations we studied on site visits.

6. It was also stated that, as a result of computers, the individual's purchases could be correlated with those of "some Mafia *capo*" or "suspected subversive." Unlike an airline, which has clear business and safety needs to compile the names of all those who are on a particular flight, credit-card companies have no business need to compile lists of all those who eat at a particular restaurant on a particular day, or shop at a specific store, or fly on a particular airline. Thus, no programs to draw such information together are to be found in the American Express computers, or those of other credit-card companies. In view of the huge volume of transactions, American Express officials point out that the cost of compiling such information would be prohibitive. An investigator seeking to do the correlation that was described in *The Assault on Privacy* would have to know the names of the two or more credit-card holders whose activities he wanted to investigate and seek to get copies of their charges from American Express records. A microfilm copy is made of each charge slip as these come in from American Express establishments, from which one could obtain the date of charges, the establishment, and the amount of charge. An investigator could apply to American Express to get these records, trying to match up the places visited for a given period, but this is almost exactly what he would have had to do in the precomputer era. The computer has not brought about anything like the opportunities for efficient and speedy correlation or the capability of record surveillance that have been described.

Furthermore, the procedures by which American Express provides customer information to law-enforcement officials do not permit the kind of random searching by investigators that have been suggested. First of all, the basic records involved are not on-line and accessible by terminals; they are on computer tapes and microfilm. American Express policies require a subpoena or court order before any customer information is provided, and once approved, no direct access is given *any* investigators to the secured areas where the company's microfilm records and computer tapes are kept. When the subpoena is presented to the American Express Inspector's Office, an employee goes into the secured areas and prepares the microfilm copy or computer print-out; it is then furnished to the investigator. As far as the volume of such inspections, there were approximately 75 million charge transactions made by American Express' 3.8 million cardholders in 1971. The company's attorney who reviews investigative requests indicates that there were, for that year, about 25 law-enforcement subpoenas (15 of those from the FBI); about 100 from the Internal Revenue Service, primarily in tax fraud cases; and about 100 in compliance with court orders in civil litigation involving a cardholder, as where a wife files for divorce and seeks to prove that her husband had a higher standard of living than his statement of assets and income would permit.

There is one on-line application for American Express credit cards which should be mentioned. This is a system which provides a profile for video-tube display of each customer's spending level by month for the last year, and last two years, including subtotals by type of expense (airline, hotels, shops, restaurant, etc.) for charges authorized within recent periods. This is primarily a fraud-control device aimed at catching users of stolen credit cards before they can run up huge charges. When a business establishment calls American Express operators to obtain authorization for a cardholder's requested charge of a substantial purchase, the operator can see from the display whether this particular purchase is very different from the averages of the customer's previous monthly or yearly use.

A minor difference would not lead to any further inquiry, but where the charge sought is different in the extreme (a one-way first-class airline ticket to Hong Kong, or ten expensive dresses bought at one time in a Fifth Avenue boutique), the operator can request further verification of identity (by asking questions about home address or other matters in the microfilm copy of the customer's original application for the card). Or, in certain circumstances, he could refuse to approve a particular charge. However, this on-line application has no information dealing with the particular places at which the customer has shopped in the past or the kinds of goods he has purchased, and it would not make it possible for anyone who got to the terminals and broke the software protections employed there to learn whether "some Mafia *capo*" or "suspected subversive" also charged a ticket to Hong Kong on Pan American Airlines.

In looking over the errors involved in these accounts, one major point deserves noting. There are files considered secret by their owners or classified under government rules, or in organizations which would refuse most requests for information about their systems. Journalists and scholars are faced with difficult problems in checking the accuracy of accounts published about such organizations; when efforts to make checks prove fruitless, one can understand how the existing accounts continue to be used without verification. But the American Airlines example is a different case. Company officials there would have responded to any journalist or academic commentator who sought the truth about the original *Look* account. Company officials say they received no such inquiries, and the way in which the supposed computer capability and law-enforcement use are portrayed in these writings indicates clearly that the *Look* story was not checked further. American Airlines did send the *Saturday Review* a letter of correction after Ramsey Clark's review of the Miller book appeared, and it was published by the magazine. The same possibilities for verification were present for American Express and Carte Blanche, but the Miller book and other articles are still circulating an erroneous version of what computers are making possible at these organizations. As a result, countless readers still rely on these faulty accounts.

In leaving this episode, let us stress in the clearest possible fashion that we are not saying that computers *cannot* be used in the way attributed to the American Airlines reservation system. We noted that programming *could* make it possible to enter a name alone and get out a list of all past trips and the information associated with them. Tapes *could* be kept longer than 60 days. And airlines and other travel and entertainment companies with computers *could* let 10-15 investigators a day submit requests or even operate the terminals themselves. They could if there were important business or organizational reasons for them to organize their computerized record-keeping in that way, and if problems of cost, efficiency, legality, and safeguarding of customer goodwill by protecting confidentiality did not outweigh the possible business benefits. The critical fact for Americans to know is that these things are *not* being done today, nor have they ever been done before in these computer systems.

It is important to know this for three reasons that are crucial to public understanding of computers and civil liberties. First, people must understand that most of the information-analysis capabilities computers make possible are not present in the hardware when it is delivered. Such capabilities must be chosen deliberately by users of computers and put in as the files are designed, programming instructions are set, and other ad hoc system efforts go forward. As we saw, American Airlines had no operational reason to install the costly name-search capability in its reservation systems, and did not do so. What managements are doing with computers is therefore a question of empirical fact, not a general computer capability which one may assume without evidence that particular organizations have brought into being and are now using.

Second, if we assume that computer users are already doing things they are not, we risk surrendering without a fight the border between properly limited and surveillance-oriented computer applications. For example, as American society comes to grips with the problem of computers and civil liberties, we might seek mechanisms to ensure that name-search scanning capacities of the kind falsely attributed to the present American Airlines reservations system are not installed by managements in a computerized operation unless these are necessary for the organization's operations and proper safeguards against unauthorized or improper use are provided, perhaps with review of these issues by some kind of supervisory agency. The question whether such border-control measures should be adopted can hardly be understood and properly considered, however, if the public and opinion leaders assume that the borders have already been obliterated.

Finally, American society may want to reexamine the standards and procedures by which law-enforcement agencies obtain access to records of individuals kept by credit-card companies, travel and entertainment firms, etc., regardless of whether these records are in manual or computerized form. We noted this issue arising in the Bank of America profile, with test cases now pending which argue that notice to the customer and an opportunity to contest the legitimacy of subpoenas should be required in most cases before individual records are made available. Such issues need to be analyzed on their merits, as we shall do below in the next section and in our final discussion of public policies. The policy questions that the issues raise can only be blurred if society thinks that both elaborate surveillance data and widespread access to them by law-enforcement officials have suddenly become existing facts as a result of computerization within these organizations.

Effects on Record-Keeping

We turn here to significant changes in the collection and use of personal information which *were* introduced by computerization of records in the 55 advanced organizations we studied. We will treat these changes under five main headings:

1. The production of more up-to-date records, containing fewer omissions.

2. Greater utilization of information in the files.

3. Faster handling of inquiry-response transactions.

4. Creation of new or enlarged networks for interorganizational sharing of information.

5. Creation of larger data bases and information systems than would have been feasible through manual procedures.

We also take up in this section two topics which have played important parts in public debate over the computer's impact on individual rights. These are:

6. The accuracy of information in computerized systems.

7. Information security in computerized files.

We should note again that our focus here remains one of empirical analysis. In part five, we will take up both the sociopolitical setting of the databank debate and the implications for public policy that are raised by the findings of our study.

More Up-to-date and Complete Records

In the last section we observed that computerizing organizations are not generally collecting or storing more items of information about each individual in their computerized files than was the case in the manual era. We also noted that the most routine and objective information was being computerized, while more subjective and narrative information about individuals in each type of organization typically remained only in manual files. At the same time, we saw that, relative to the past, there are records on a greater number of people and more transactions per person in many computerized record systems that we studied, reflecting general trends in the growth of business services, government social programs, and government regulatory functions in the past two decades; computerization has assisted in this expansion, we noted, but was not the primary cause of it.

The move to EDP has affected some record-keeping more directly, however, and the first major computer impact we observed was that standardized records in computerized systems tend to have fewer omissions and the information in them is more likely to be current than when the same records were maintained only in manual systems.

For many important types of decisions about citizens, customers, or clients, organizations require information about the individual's current status, and some means of making this up-to-date information available to the person who actually makes the decision. Up-to-date credit histories are required for bank loan and retail credit decisions; law-enforcement agencies need to know the current "wanted" status and other particulars concerning suspected persons or stolen vehicles; the dollar amount of purchases outstanding often must be known before a credit-card holder can charge additional merchandise; social service agencies want to know about existing welfare aid being provided to clients who apply for immediate additional assistance; airlines depend upon immediate knowledge of existing reservations for customers who are requesting changes in their travel plans; and before issuing a refund check, the Internal Revenue Service needs to check whether the person has already received one for the year and whether or not he has an outstanding tax debt from a previous year.

Our clear finding from the site visits was that the process of data conversion for computerized systems has led to the creation of more up-to-date individual records than these organizations achieved in the precomputer era. In some cases this was the result of updating manual records in the course of conversion. In one state law-enforcement identification system we visited, though officials could give us no precise figure, they noted that a substantial proportion of the summary criminal histories being converted to machine-readable form were found to be out of date, with no dispositions entered for many arrests; where these could not be supplied by research into original court records, the notation of arrest was not carried over into the computerized record. For other organizations, however, computerization has resulted in a considerable increase in the extent to which individual records are up to date. Throughout our site visits, we found that organizations with on-line systems were able to obtain and circulate "status" information that was far more current and timely than in their precomputer record systems. A review of the profiles about the FBI, Kansas City police, TRW-Credit Data, Bank of America (for California BankAmericard), New York State Motor Vehicle Department, and Santa Clara County will show these on-line status reporting systems at work.

The capacity for keeping personal records more current in computerized files reflects the effect of three elements which characterize many EDP systems: terminal devices for supplying input to a central computer from the field and the supporting communications systems which make rapid two-way transactions possible; the increased processing speed of the central computer unit—particularly real-time, random-access processing capacity; and the fact that it is often in the interest of system users to comply with update rules. For some organizations, much of the updating of files is accomplished on-line from the field. A wanted-person notice can be entered on the FBI's NCIC computer within minutes of being issued by a local police department which has an NCIC terminal. As a replacement for a lost license is issued at a local Department of Motor Vehicles Office in New York State, the facts of this loss and reissue are entered on the person's record. For these organizations, the presence of terminals in the field and the random-access feature of their computer systems have a critical effect on the maintenance of current records. But even the batch-processing of update information has given some computer systems a time advantage over their manual predecessors. We saw that both Bank of America and TRW-Credit Data accomplish much of their file updating through batch-processing. Their computer systems allow for more frequent input of new information to massive files than would have been feasible in the manual era.

Once information becomes available for fast retrieval by field units, users themselves have a strong interest in keeping data up to date. Where these units did not update records as quickly as called for in the system, we noted that the central-system managers could monitor these delays and take measures to secure greater compliance. An example of this is the FBI's success in getting more timely reporting of the arrest of wanted persons and retrieval of stolen vehicles into the NCIC system. We also saw in the FBI profile that its new computerized criminal-history system, in response to judicial and civic-group pressures, has a feature by which organizations which have submitted records of arrest without disposition are to be automatically queried on a regular basis to enter the missing information as soon as court disposition is available. There are sometimes limits on the control which a central record keeper can exercise, of course, as we saw in the case of TRW-Credit Data; they could compel users to provide update from their own files more frequently, but they could not solve the problem of getting better update from the civil courts, whose reporting systems remain painfully slow.

Closely related to the problem of keeping records up to date is that of ensuring "completeness." For records of predetermined content, it is important that facts of identification or substance not be missing altogether if decisions are to be made in standardized fashion. In many of our site-visit organizations, it was clear that the review of record content occasioned by some of their computerization efforts served to focus attention on the problem of omissions from standardized records. This effect was particularly visible in law enforcement, county government, medical, and credit record-keeping systems. In the FBI's NCIC system, inquiries are not accepted unless all the important identifying information on the person is supplied. Similarly, the New York State Identification and Intelligence System makes persistent attempts to obtain complete rap sheet records from its user agencies.

In some systems, computer programs have been devised to "flag" incomplete records; we saw this, for example, at the Internal Revenue Service and in a medical records system. In developing an on-line records system in a small psychiatric hospital, programs were developed to reduce the number of some of the common record errors and omissions. Logical consistency checks were programmed so that if, for example, a staff member in 1972 entered a patient admission date as 5/12/74, an "error" message would flash on the screen. A similar measure was introduced to ensure completion of items on a "mental status" report which require either a narrative comment to be entered or else some indication of the severity of a symptom. If the physician moves to a new item without providing the required comment, a reminder flashes on the screen; this continues and does not allow the reporting of additional data until the item in question has been completed.

The computerization of three personnel record systems (one at Bank of America and two in very large manufacturing firms) illustrates other important effects of the computer on the completeness and timeliness of individual records. In these cases, computerization either led to the creation of a central personnel record file where such records had once been kept only in regional offices (and only a central *payroll* file had been maintained) or they increased the likelihood that the information about a person in a central personnel record would actually be used in placement and promotion decisions. It is reported that employees in the latter case have given more cooperation to updating their records in the newly computerized systems because they believe that doing so can mean increased opportunities for them.

Greater Use of Information in Files

Even though the scope of personal information collected has not been significantly increased in the computerized systems we studied, we did find many organizations making more effective use of the information already in their files. A good impression of this process at work can be drawn from a series of examples involving computerization at the Internal Revenue Service (IRS), one of our site visits.

1. Prior to computerization, most individual tax returns were examined only to record the fact that a return had been filed, to extract the tax payment (or note the amount of refund due), and to classify the return according to income. From each income level defined, a proportion of returns was randomly selected for audit. The total number of returns selected for audit depended then, as now, on the number of personnel available for audit operations. However, the process for identifying which returns are to be audited has changed dramatically since the introduction of computer processing. Every return is examined for possible audit after summary information has been extracted and entered into a computerized master file. A computer program examines a number of factors, weighs and scores each, and produces a score which indicates the likelihood that the individual's tax liability will

change if the return is audited. These scores serve as a guide for the selection of between two and three million returns for audit.

This example is significant in three ways. First is the fact that, even though it is IRS personnel who make the final determination of whether or not to audit a given return, computerization ensures that all returns receive more detailed attention, with more uniform application of selection criteria, than was feasible in the manual era. Second is the fact that application of the improved screening capabilities has reduced substantially the proportion of audits from which no change in tax liability results. Though the auditor does not know before he begins on a selected return whether the tax liability will increase or decrease, he can be more certain now than before computerization that some change is likely. Third is the fact that no more *items* of information are obtained from the taxpayer for the computerized system than were previously required, but far greater *use* is being made of the information that is there for purposes of tax enforcement.

2. In the manual era, IRS often wanted to compare the taxpayer's report of wages and interest income with that reported directly to IRS by employers and banks. However, this was feasible only when a specific individual audit was initiated; comparing these reports of income for all, or even a sizable proportion of taxpayers, was simply too cumbersome, costly, and time-consuming for the IRS to do through manual processing. Now, with computerization, a comparison program is being developed which may eventually do this automatically for all individual returns filed.

The idea has already been tried successfully on samples of returns. The IRS currently receives many of its information returns (from banks, employers, etc.) on magnetic tape, and data-processing officials there note that it is only through computer processing that the move to matching these with the taxpayers' returns will be feasible.

3. The IRS has traditionally tried to detect the filing of duplicate returns, in which the same individual, during a short period of time, files several returns in which he claims that a refund is due him. In the precomputer era, in keeping with its "speedy refund" policy, IRS sent out the refund checks and only later (if at all) discovered that duplicate refunds had been made. Now, before issuing a refund check, the computer examines Social Security number and/or address to see if the individual has already been paid a refund for that year.

4. Before automation, taxpayers owing money to the United

States for past tax liabilities would be paid nevertheless any tax refunds due them because of the difficulty of searching debt lists before honoring refund claims. Now, IRS computers check automatically to see whether the taxpayer claiming a refund has any federal tax obligations for previous years. If so, that amount is deducted before the refund is paid.

5. Still another instance of greater use of information is that the IRS computers compare returns in the current reporting year with those of the previous year, to identify quickly and to print out a list of individuals who filed one year but not the next. Previously, many nonfilers would be identfied only after a considerable time had passed.

6. Finally, the IRS uses statistical information drawn from selected returns to produce a tax model of the United States which is used for various predictive and analytic purposes. Through this mathematical model, for example, the IRS can provide estimates to Congress of the effect that a proposed change in the tax law would have on the production of revenues for a given class of taxpayer, for sectors of the economy, and for overall national tax revenues. Again, the data used for this model were in the files before computerization, but they were not available on a timely basis from the manual system, and could not be analyzed as easily.

As these varied examples show, the IRS is clearly making greater use of information from its files for both tax enforcement and for program evaluation and planning by management. These uses are a direct result of computerization.

We saw another type of increased use in one county we visited (not Santa Clara) whose data-processing center included computer applications in its welfare, probation, and law-enforcement files, and an on-line central index of individuals having contacts with various social service departments. The fact that a resident is receiving welfare is public information (by state law) and can be obtained from the central index not only by employees of the social agencies but also by police and probation departments. However, personal details of a welfare client's record are declared confidential by the state administrative code, and are not supposed to be revealed to other government agencies or private parties. Under the access controls of the data center, only authorized terminals in the welfare department can put in the individual's identification number and get out details of the case. On the other hand, police and probation officials frequently want to obtain from welfare records the latest address of an individual they are investigating or otherwise seeking to locate, even though this is not allowed under the agreements as to data access set by the various agencies using the central file. By using the central index, however, the police and probation officials can find out that John Smith is receiving welfare, and can also learn his case-file number. According to an official in the data-processing center,

> . . . once someone in an agency who is not authorized to get into the details of a welfare record finds out the ID number of a person on welfare—which he can get from the central index—he can then inquire by private telephone to a friendly welfare worker or supervisor about the status of that person with welfare. The friend enters the number, gets the address information, and passes it along. Of course, this kind of informal exchange took place before the computer as well. The difference is that such exchanges are now more probable and efficient. . . . Before the computer, it was too much effort for the police. . . . Now, it is easy, so it's done.

This practice is known to some officials at the computer center, but the problem has not been considered serious enough, or has not received sufficient public or legislative attention, for efforts to be taken to dissuade or bar officials from such practices.

It should also be recalled from the Kansas City Police Department profile that the "checking out" of prospective tenants and employees by the Lenaxa, Kansas, police department arose essentially because a terminal was installed linking this suburban department to a central on-line data base. As the system was then set up, the Lenaxa chief could enter a large number of names and get responses without arousing the attention of anyone in the Kansas City department. In the manual era, even if Kansas City replied to record queries by nearby police departments, a sudden deluge of requests by letter or telephone call, requiring manual searches of records by clerks, would have been more likely to produce questioning about the reason for the sudden upsurge of business from this small town.

Another aspect of greater use is the increased efficiency of computer systems in producing the names of persons in a large data base who fit combinations of characteristics that have been specified in the original organization of records and the computer programs. We saw this in the capacity of Bank of America's Personnel Data System to accept a list of career history elements and skills for which they were searching and get out the names of qualified employees. The same capacity of computer systems was used by the IRS to set parameters for selecting income-tax returns for audits. We also noted this capacity in a state health department we visited, in which the names and records of doctors being reimbursed under a state health program were printed out whenever the doctor reported that he treated more than a certain number of patients or performed more than a certain number of particular surgical procedures in a month. The objective here was to identify possible cases of fraud or improper practices for direct investigation. In a national credit-card company we studied, certain spending patterns that were outside the "regular experience" of each cardholder are monitored either to see whether the card might have been stolen or whether the individual using it was going beyond his capacity to pay. Perhaps half of the 55 systems we visited, including a large life-insurance company and the U.S. Secret Service, made similar use of the computer to identify individuals for further investigation.

In all of these instances, it should be noted that there were fundamental limits present: when setting up its data base and writing its instructions for the computer, the organization had to specify the items of information on the basis of which it might want to search each record in the future. If a need developed to identify full-time employees with more than three children, for instance, the computer system could not produce such information unless these items had been defined in advance as possible bases for searching the files. With the condition of predefinition met, the computer systems we saw were providing a much faster, larger-data-base version of traditional punched-card sorting, in which decks of cards are machine-searched to extract those with the specified punched items on them.

Looking over these aspects of greater updating, completion, and use of information in computerized records, it is clear that the basic effect of these changes is to allow some organizations to rely on more current and complete records than they had available in their manual records, and to manipulate information in the records more effectively for the application of the organization's criteria to those individuals about whom it makes decisions.

Faster Handling of Inquiries

Faster handling of transactions is such a well-known advantage of computer systems and was documented so fully in the profiles that a lengthy discussion of this development is hardly necessary here. In both batch-processing and on-line systems, computerizing organizations are able to speed up each individual transaction as well as reduce the time required for data-processing operations involving millions of records. Typically, in the precomputer era, even a "top-priority" information request from a field unit to search a large file maintained at central headquarters took half an hour or more to fulfill by radio or telephone communication and a search of manual or EAM files. Now, in computerized systems such as those used for airline reservations, law-enforcement "wanted" notices, and credit records, response times of under 30 seconds are not unusual for the entire transaction, from call-in to presentation of the reply. What is critical in these systems is both the flexibility of the communications system and the speed of on-line computer processing.

We noted on the site visits some instances in which the capacity of a central computer system to return an answer rapidly to a local unit led to major changes in the way field activities were conducted and decisions were made. Police officers in patrol cars throughout the nation are "checking out" more vehicle license numbers and querying the central system more frequently to see whether persons they stop or survey are in the wanted file than they did before state and national on-line "wanted" systems were initiated. Before, when it took half an hour to several hours to get a response, officers in the field would check only the most serious cases, essentially those persons they could hold for a while or vehicles that were parked. Now, as we saw in the FBI profile, a good deal of random checking is being done by officers in departments which have a direct link with NCIC's fast-response system. In the case of the Kentucky youth who stopped into a state police unit for information, it is unlikely that any check would have been made on him in the manual era.

An example from an entirely different area is the increased use of point-of-sale terminal devices for checking the validity of department store charge cards and for determining whether or not the customer has exceeded his allowable charges for the month.

Upon presentation of the card, a clerk can query the store's computer file (whether it is located in-house or stored in a service-bureau computer off the premises) and get a "go" or "no-go" response in seconds. In the precomputer era, such transactions often took 10 to 30 minutes and represented both an inconvenience to the customer and an expense to the store—in the form of the salesperson's time, and in the danger that a harried clerk would forgo the routine check because it was both time-consuming and embarrassing.

As these examples suggest, speedier response leads to greater use by the local participating units or officials in a central system. We found not only more requests made from the field by users, but also faster corrections of errors (as in credit reporting by TRW-Credit Data) and faster updating of current status (as in law-enforcement wanted-person systems or charge-card authorization). Previously, with long delays in response time and the decision-maker's awareness of lags in the circulation of correction or update sheets, local officials had to rely more on their own initiatives or on intuition than on the record. Now, with the awareness that records are more likely to be up to date and easily accessible, they expect to use the central information system more effectively to help with their decisions. In one hospital we visited, for example, doctors were found to be consulting the results of lab tests more frequently after computerization of lab reports than had been the case when it took longer to get them to the physician.

In asking managers about the effects of speedier transactions on their record-keeping, we heard two main comments. First, it was stressed that the increase in speed in these situations was not at the expense of accuracy; managers noted that the information being communicated was as accurate (or even more accurate) than when it was being transmitted more slowly in the precomputer era. Secondly, managers said that getting critical information about a client, customer, employee, or citizen more quickly enabled the organization to provide better services, and to reduce costs. One national finance company exploits this position in its radio advertising, stating, "Our computer gets your record faster so that we can spend more time in what really matters—helping with your money needs. . . ."

Creation of
New Interorganizational Networks

In the precomputer era there were organizations in the same field that regularly shared identified information (as among law-enforcement agencies, credit bureaus, personnel departments, colleges, life-insurance companies, etc.). There was, as well, some regular exchange of information among organizations in different but related fields (e.g., among banks, retail establishments, and employers for credit-reporting purposes). In the last section, analyzing changes in record-keeping practices that have not yet taken place as a result of computerization, we observed that computerizing organizations in these fields were sharing information in much the same way that prevailed in the manual era.

However, we did observe the emergence through computerization and rapid communication systems of regional and national data systems that are linking more closely organizations that had shared information in the manual era, and that these networks are giving rise to some new patterns of information handling and use. Perhaps the most striking examples from our site visits are in the field of law enforcement. In one Western county, several dozen local police departments created an information network for the exchange of wanted-and-warrant information—a system which parallels the regional network for 300 Kansas and Missouri law-enforcement agencies operated by the Kansas City Police Department's ALERT system. The FBI's National Crime Information Center and the new computerized Criminal History System together comprise a national computerized network, with more than 40 law-enforcement and criminal-justice agencies having computer-to-computer links into the system, and over 4,000 local agencies able to enquire through these state and local agencies.

Different in character but displaying some of the same consequences are the National Driver Registration Service (described in the New York State Motor Vehicle profile) and the regular exchanges of tax return information between the IRS and 48 of the 50 states. Neither of these is an on-line, high volume network of the NCIC type; but in each case, the computer has made it possible for a central body to become an important source of administrative information about individual citizens. Before the computerized file at NDRS was established, there was no central source which state motor vehicle departments might draw upon, and there was no practical way in which each license applicant could be checked through each of the other states. For state tax departments, the IRS had for some years represented an alternative source of information on their taxpayers, but one that was highly inconvenient to use before summary information from federal tax returns became available on computer tape. The new system dramatically increased the volume of federal returns that could be regularly compared with state returns.

Several other consequences flow from these increases in the speed of transactions. Because the data centrally available become more useful to each participant, the frequency and volume of the information flow tends to increase. In the case of the law-enforcement networks and the NDRS, the *number* of participating agencies also expands in response to the advantages the network represents. The more completely a network covers its assigned area, the more useful the central files become to each participant. And, as network participation becomes an integral part of the participants' normal operations, they become increasingly dependent upon the system; realistically, they are unable to withdraw. In law enforcement, for example, they may even abandon their own local wanted-and-warrant records, knowing that these are available from the central file. Even if they do not, how could a local or state law-enforcement agency operate if it were denied access to warrant-and-wanted information of summary criminal-history data in state, regional, or national databanks?

This feature of such networks increases the power of the central record-keeping unit. The system managers, usually with advisory committees of organizational participants, begin to standardize record content and reporting procedures, creating uniformities where traditionally there were significant diversities which impeded the flow of information. Furthermore, the network management can monitor compliance by the system users so that whatever rules are established will be followed more closely than would have been the case in a decentralized, manual system. The effectiveness of such monitoring has its limits, as we observed in the case of TRW-Credit.Data, two state law-enforcement networks, and with respect to the sharing of tax-return information by IRS. In each of these instances, managers of the central system admitted that the expulsion of a participating unit would be an extreme act and felt that firm control over participants would come only with time.

More Large Record Systems

Where large-scale governmental and private programs were thought important enough, they were managed successfully during the half century before computers by clerical help using manual filing techniques and unit-record equipment. In 1950, for example, the Social Security system handled more than 200 million quarterly earnings reports; the Internal Revenue Service processed 89 million income-tax returns; Retail Credit Corporation had records on over 40 million persons which it used for commercial credit and investigative reporting; and R. L. Polk handled lists including the names of 40 or 50 million Americans for the use of advertisers. Furthermore, some of the large-scale government programs enacted after computers arrived—such as Medicare—would have probably been instituted (with modified procedures) even if computers had not been available.

Nevertheless, large data bases and special data communication networks have emerged in the past decade that would be highly difficult or even impossible to manage without computers. If computer processing were not available, a system such as California BankAmericard could not be operated profitably with its current number and type of cardholders and volume of transactions, especially with its ability to satisfy current account-status inquiries. The move by the FBI from a manual file and mail distribution system for the bulk handling of wanted-persons information to a national, high-volume, fast-response system similarly depended on the availability of real-time computers. One social research project we visited was keeping extensive research files on almost 500,000 people who were high school students in 1960, the year in which the data were gathered from over 1,100 secondary schools across the nation. This very large sample is maintained for the use of researchers, some of whom wish to take a population of interest today (e.g., successful college graduates) and "follow back" to look at the data gathered on some of them in 1960. In the American Council of Education profile, we saw that a large file (over 300,000) is not only maintained, but information on individuals in it is updated periodically. Though there were certainly some large research files in the precomputer era, a project of this scale would not have been feasible then.

A good example of the computer's role in creating new information systems is the so-called ALPS project (*Automatic License Plate Scanning*) with which police in New York City and the New York State Identification and Intelligence System have been experimenting through pilot and demonstration projects for the past five years. The project's components would include a very large file of wanted-car license-plate numbers, to be put onto the NYSIIS computer; television cameras mounted at the toll booths of state highways, tunnels, and bridges; and a radio-activated display device placed in police patrol cars. As vehicles stop at a toll booth, the camera would scan the license plate and send the number it recognizes to the state computer. If a "hit" were made with the stolen-car file, or other files that contain the license plates of wanted persons or other subjects "of law-enforcement interest," a message and the license number would be radioed to the patrol car, which would then move out to apprehend the vehicle or to take other designated action before the car moved much past the toll booth.

While this system is not yet in operation and remains a demonstration project, the point for our purposes is that such a large scale surveillance system depends essentially on a combination of computer and communication technology. Whether it should be created and, if so, what limits should be set on its scope and use, are obviously questions for society to determine; but society would not have been presented with such a choice had computers not arrived.

Having examined five important changes in record-keeping that have been stimulated by computerization, we turn next to the questions of accuracy and security of information in computerized systems.

Accuracy of Information

It was quite clear across our 55 site visits that managers believe some errors to be inevitable in any large-scale record system, and that those executives and officials who are caught up in the extensive reorganization of human and machine record-keeping practices occasioned by computerization regard some errors in the creation and debugging of new data-processing systems as equally inescapable. In managerial perspectives, the key task is to keep such errors at the lowest acceptable level and to establish procedures for rectifying errors—procedures which will prevent mistakes in judgment which might hurt the organization (e.g., granting a loan to a bad credit risk) and through which the organization can avoid strong customer or public discontent.

There is a fundamental conflict, however, between the managerial perspective on record error and that of the individual. Talk about "acceptable" levels of error is hardly satisfactory to the individual if a mistake adversely affects his benefits, rights, or opportunities, and if there are not direct and reasonable ways to correct such errors. According to recent public opinion polls, many Americans report that they have had direct experience with "computer errors"—factual mistakes in their records or in various kinds of notices, bills, and payments that are ascribed to "the computer" rather than traditional clerical inaccuracy.[1] The issue of how computerized record systems compare to manual ones in the generation and dissemination of erroneous information has been a central part of the civil-liberties debate over record-keeping.

Our framework for analysis of this problem evolved out of observations at our 55 sites and can be summarized under six headings.

1. Accuracy of information should be seen as an issue separate from (though obviously related to) that of the *interpretation* of facts that go into a decision. Basically, the accuracy of personal records involves four elements: the proper identification of the individual being reported on (is this the right John Q. Jones?); the correctness of each objective fact (is he really nine months in default on a bank loan and was he once convicted of grand larceny?); the completeness of reporting about any critical situation (if he did refuse to pay the bill, does the record show that the merchandise he received was damaged?); and the timeliness or currency of the information (how close to the time of decision are the most recent reports about his outstanding loans, debts, or judgments?). Though the degree of importance attached to each of these four elements will vary according to the kind of judgment being made about the individual, they are the key elements of the accuracy problem in organizational record-keeping.

---

[1] We discuss the most recent of these surveys in Appendix B below, pages 479-485. In a 1971 survey, 34 percent of a nationwide sample reported that they had had "problems because of a computer."

2. Factual errors can take place at each of the four basic stages of information handling—the collection of the information, its reduction to recorded form, its processing within the organization, and its dissemination to the evaluator. Often, of course, some of these stages will be duplicated two or three times between collection and use, as in the case of an item of credit information which is generated and recorded initially within a bank, reported to a credit bureau and recorded once again, reported to another customer of the credit bureau and written down still another time, until, finally, it appears with related items of credit information on a form in front of a credit officer about to make a decision.

3. How many errors take place in the record system and how uniformly these will be corrected before individuals are judged on the basis of inaccurate information will depend on a blend of factors relating to the organizational setting. These include the type of information being gathered, the means used to obtain it, the degree to which the individual himself verifies the information in the collection stage, the time and money the organization expends to ensure accurate recording and processing, the individual's ability to audit the record before it is used or to contest it at some point before the decision of the organization becomes final, the degree of secrecy or openness involved in the use of the records, and any legal requirements governing the maintenance and use of the information for decision making.

4. Record systems vary in terms of the individual's ability to ensure that information in his own record is timely, complete, and correct. First, there are files in which the information collected and used is fully reported to and audited by the individual himself, as with bank statements, charge account summaries, and utility bills. This would include records, such as Social Security earnings reports, which the individual has a right to monitor at any time, but typically does not do so until he is ready to claim a benefit.

Second, there are files in which some or even most of the record is disclosed to the individual but a certain portion is withheld as confidential. Examples would be an employee's annual performance rating and personnel record, in which almost every organization will keep secret some aspect of the supervisor's judgment or opinion as to promotability, and educational records, where certain teacher and staff evaluations are not revealed.

Finally, there are files in which virtually no part of a report or record is made available to the individual, and where he may not even know that a report has been made at all. Familiar examples of this situation are law enforcement intelligence records, credit and preemployment reports furnished by commercial reporting agencies before passage of the Fair Credit Reporting Act, reports done for organizations that are considering a new appointment of an executive but have not informed him that he is under consideration, and most medical and psychiatric records. (Of course an individual can go to court to seek access to some of these records and may gain entry in his case, but the organization does not open the file as a matter of policy.)

5. Those organizations in which individuals know about, see, and can challenge their own records are likely to have more accurate records in the final stages of use than those which operate in secret, depending upon informants, observations, and other documentary records as sources of information about the individual. This general rule will obviously have some exceptions, as where an intelligence system is extremely professional, verifies its information from several sources before recording it, and prizes the accuracy of its data so highly that it spends substantial time and money on quality controls at each stage of its recording and dissemination process. However, the self-interest of individuals is such that they will detect errors in the records they are allowed or entitled to see, and the awareness that this is so has become an increasingly important part of public debates over record systems and civil liberties in the past decade.

6. Surprising as it may seem, very few organizations in the precomputer era did systematic studies of or could describe with solid data the error rates in their record systems, the effects of mistakes on the quality of their decisions, or the improvement in accuracy they would achieve for a given amount spent on increases in staff or revised procedures. The notion of "muddling through" applies more directly to the handling of accuracy problems than to any other aspect of record-keeping. Accepting the presence of some errors as an inevitable aspect of clerical procedures, each type of organization evolved its distinctive ways of recognizing when record errors had become "a problem" and of devising some means to minimize, correct, or adjust to the situation. Where an increase in consumer complaints raises the specter of significant loss of customers, for instance, a business establishment may respond with both a public-relations effort and some new procedures for correcting mistakes. Similarly, commercial customers may complain to a reporting agency that its credit and investigative reports are "getting worse and worse," leading to efforts to improve the "product." Where the setting is governmental, laws may require corrective procedures or impose sanctions in the

interest of the citizen. Legislatures may bring pressure on an agency to maintain more accurate records so as to avoid dispersing undeserved benefits. In some cases managers are aware that there is little correspondence between the "problem" detected and actual changes in the accuracy of typical records in their files.

Our emphasis during site visits was on defining the manual-era conditions in each organization, tracing this forward to initial computerization, and examining conditions under the current computerized and manual operations. It should be stressed that we did *not* conduct any independent studies of error rates. Our sources of information were the managers and employees interviewed at each organization, literature about the field or industry, any legislative or regulatory inquiries that might have been made, and discussions with computer applications specialists in each area.

Our first finding is that informants do not believe computerization has led to an overall decrease in the accuracy of personal records; in many organizations, they believe it has produced substantial *increases* in accuracy, compared to the way the same file was maintained under manual procedures. We noted four main reasons for this effect.

1. In order to convert large manual files to tape or other electromagnetic storage, most organizations inspected their manual records to see whether the content and format of data collection documents were satisfactory; whether the items called for on the forms were being provided as consistently and as quickly as they were supposed to be; and whether incompleteness or lateness of information was considered a problem for either decision-making or public relations reasons.

Some organizations turned up few error problems in their review of the manual records, especially if they had been through a somewhat similar effort in converting the file earlier to punch-card storage for EAM processing. But in most of the organizations we visited, data conversion studies did uncover substantial inaccuracies in the manual records. For example, the FBI found that 38 percent of the existing warrants were outdated or invalid, and similarly high rates of incomplete or inaccurate records were discovered by the New York State Identification and Intelligence System when it converted existing state summary criminal history records. The New Haven, Connecticut, Controller's Office, which handled that city's data processing operation, found the records of various city departments to be "in terrible shape—materials were missing from records, inconsistencies had crept in (such as a person being listed as born on a date two days before he was recorded as committing a crime), and a variety of sloppy oversights in the recording of data had taken place."

In such instances, organizations faced the decision whether to ignore the inaccuracies uncovered in the manual files and try to improve accuracy in the new computerized entries, or to expend time and money to correct the manual records before converting them. The key factor in this decision was usually how critical the historic manual records would be in future decisions made with the computerized file. For many organizations we studied, such as law-enforcement agencies using summary criminal-history records and credit bureaus relying on past payment performance, bankruptcies, and court judgments, the precomputer records are heavily relied on in making present evaluative judgments. Thus many of the organizations threw out incorrect records that were not vital and brought those they considered essential up to sufficient levels of accuracy *vis à vis* proper identification, completeness, and record consistency. This was done even though it sometimes led to serious delays in data-conversion schedules; the New York State Identification and Intelligence System fell several years behind in its computerization program, in large part because of record-correction work.

Other factors also contributed to the decision to devote resources to improving the accuracy of manual records before computerization. In some cases, conflicts in individual identification had to be resolved before records from different sources or files could be merged, or a new identification number could be assigned to each record holder. In other instances, managements had not been aware of how much error had existed in their manual records, and the airing of the situation led them to move promptly to "regain" the level of accuracy at which they had thought they were working.

The basic point is that had there been no move to computers, the histories of these organizations suggest strongly that they would have continued to make the errors discovered in their manual records, at least until some other outside force such as new standards of legal liability or citizen access to records forced a reexamination of accuracy levels.

2. Managers were emphatic in reporting that once their computer systems were operating, they were able to avoid or correct errors in ways that had not been possible previously. At Mutual of Omaha, the manual system had called for many accuracy checks to be made before a new entry was posted to their policy record. Many of these checks were simply ignored under pressure of time

in the clerical days; with the computer system, checks are performed automatically.

Today, computer systems within IRS make it possible to check every return for arithmetical mistakes. While errors are discovered (and corrected) which taxpayers have made in the government's favor, the principal impact of this new program has been to increase tax revenues, since taxpayers have always been more likely to make mistakes which benefit themselves.

3. Several other features available in computer systems also contributed to an increase in accuracy. Because computerized systems lead to faster recording of information, records were generally more up-to-date in the computerizing organizations we visited, from credit bureaus, airline reservation systems, and college registrar offices, to law enforcement information networks, welfare entitlement records, and medical laboratory reports.[2] We also found organizations that had programmed their systems to require that all the elements of a record be filled in before it is lodged in the computer file, or which had created a "tickler" procedure to remind field units to supply the missing items at some later time. Both procedures led to more complete records than had been typical under manual procedures.

Computerization has *not* had a major effect on the *substantive correctness* (as contrasted with the completeness, logical consistency, or currency) of the information initially put into the record. In many cases organizational employees obtain information about individuals through observation, interviews with third parties, and examination of documents. When these sources are used, mistakes in description, personal bias by the individuals interviewed, and inadequate coverage of sources can take place just as they did in the precomputer era, and the resulting accounts will be carefully preserved, errors and all, by the computerized system. Among computer personnel, this fact has been memorialized in warnings about the "GIGO effect"—Garbage In, Garbage Out.

Alongside this first finding as to the increased accuracy brought about by computerization goes a second and equally important one. Computerization introduces some special kinds of

---

[2] In some batch-processing operations, such as one county welfare department we visited, computerization did not improve record update time but did enable the organization to handle an increased volume of record transactions in the same period of time. Other batch-processing systems we saw increased both transaction volume and update speed.

error possibilities that deserve very careful attention in any discussion of accuracy.

As we made our site visits, managers and data-processing employees frequently prefaced our conversations about accuracy by remarking that any computerized record system that still depends on human beings in its operations—in system design, programming, making data entries, and operating peripheral equipment—is bound to produce some errors. The complexity and newness of computerized systems and the relative inexperience of organizational personnel in using these tools and techniques virtually ensures that mistakes will be made, and managers at every site were able to supply us with examples from their own experience. Though increasing experience and sophistication were seen as leading to greater control of these kinds of human-machine interface mistakes, no manager we talked to believed that they could be eliminated entirely.

More important for our purposes, managers were quite candid in adding that certain kinds of errors being made in computerized record systems would probably not take place, or at least not on the same scale, in manual systems. "When the computer screws up," one official at New Haven remarked, "it screws up big." First, programming mistakes can result in important errors being made across entire huge files. At one credit bureau, thousands of credit histories showing excellent financial performance were designated as unsatisfactory through a mistake in software instructions during data conversion. In one Eastern state (not New York), the state motor-vehicle department inadvertently dropped about 25 percent of the registered vehicles from an official list furnished to municipalities for the purpose of making up local property-tax assessments, with some loss in tax revenues before the mistake was discovered. We learned of examples of mistakes also in the running of computer operations at Kaiser-Permanente in the unintentional overwriting of tapes containing medical records with other data. Finally, electrical interruptions, power fluctuations, mismatched components, and other equipment failures can cause errors as data are being processed in the central computer hardware or passed along communications lines. Some of these errors may be of a type that will produce mistakes in the records being handled at that moment.

Among those we talked to, there was a general belief that the kinds of errors that humans or machines create in computer systems are more noticeable and are therefore more likely to be corrected in time than those that take place in manual record-keeping. "Precisely because the computer does screw up big," the New Haven official quoted earlier continued, "you can almost always put your finger on it when it happens. You couldn't always do that in the manual system." And in some cases computer errors can be corrected as "easily" as they were made. In the case of the misclassified credit records, the massive mistake was corrected by writing simple instructions for the computer to make all the "D" ratings read "A" as they should have been.[3]

Our two principal findings about accuracy of records can be summarized as follows: computerization has in many cases reduced omissions from standardized records and increased logical consistency and/or timeliness of the records that are converted to machine-readable form; many computerized operations keep their records more accurate in these respects by software and personnel supervision. But human and machine errors are still possible and present in computerized systems, with some kinds of mistakes capable of affecting very large numbers of individual records. Even when these mistakes are noticed, very important damage may have been done in the elapsed time to the rights and interests of those persons affected. And computerization has not affected the substantive correctness of the facts about people collected at the source. The conclusion we draw, therefore, is that society must assume that there can be inaccuracies in the records maintained in both manual and computerized systems.

Since reduction of errors in either manual or computer operations is usually a matter of spending money for improving data collection, monitoring recording procedures, and setting up correction mechanisms, a critical factor is whether the organization regards avoiding "occasional" mistakes in individual records as worth the costs involved. The mistakes in billing and collection procedures that many Americans have encountered are examples of inaccuracies that have been considered (until recent civic and government pressures) "tolerable errors" rather than anything most organizations were willing to correct by altering basic software programming as to billing and dunning cycles or bringing more humans into the complaint process. In the end, therefore, it will be up to customers, clients, employees, and the public regulatory process to set the outer boundaries of acceptable and unacceptable error in each type of record system and for each sphere

---

[3] We asked our survey respondents to comment on the computer's impact on the accuracy of personal records. Their responses are discussed in Appendix A, pages 433-436 below.

of organizational life. This is especially clear where individuals and organizations disagree about the importance of a given error. Mistakes that are relatively unimportant in one decision context may loom large where records have been shared and are being used for some entirely different purpose. Police investigators may be unconcerned if many of their arrest records contain no note as to disposition. But where these records are used in the hiring process, their inaccuracy in this regard may take on an entirely different meaning for the individuals whose jobs are at stake.

Information Security

Information security involves an organization's efforts to ensure that only authorized persons obtain access to confidential or secret information in its files. It thus partakes of the larger problem of providing system security, preventing the loss, alteration, or compromise of data through natural disasters, machine failures, deliberate destruction, fraud, theft, or accidental human error. Since many of the same techniques required to protect proprietary information or financial transactions from being seen by unauthorized persons are used to protect confidential personal data, there is significant overlap in the consideration of these two spheres. However, our focus in the course of site visits was on the issue of disclosure of information about individuals, in keeping with our project's concern with the civil-liberties impact of computers. While the principal focus of the privacy-and-records debate has been upon the *disclosure policies* of organizations, the issue of an organization's ability to exert effective controls over those disclosures it defines as improper has come up repeatedly.

Obviously the problem of information security existed long before the arrival of computers. However, some commentators have warned that computerization seriously aggravates the problem of protecting confidential information in large organizations. They cite the fact that information which was once scattered in various locations is usually brought into central storage at the computer facility, providing a single convenient target for attack. Because large amounts of confidential information are now stored compactly on computer tapes or disks, it is said that taking these away or copying them is an easier way of obtaining large amounts of personal data than when the same records took up a room full of filing cabinets. Where an organization's computer system is on-line, it has been said that the presence of many remote terminals creates more opportunities for outside intruders or unauthorized employees to get information from the central data base than would have been feasible from manual record rooms. And it is suggested that unless special precautions are taken, such unauthorized inquiries can be made without systems managers knowing that the records have been scrutinized. Moreover, as with paper records, computer records can be copied without altering the original stored copy.

In reply, it has been argued that even though the problems of information security have been significantly altered by computerized operations, they can still be controlled effectively through the application of proper security measures. The result of these views and replies has been to lodge the issue of security for confidential information high on the agenda of debates over computer databanks.

We examined procedures for information security at our 55 site visits, particularly to compare conditions in these organizations before and after computerization. Before presenting our observations, three findings about the general effects of computerization on record-keeping should be recalled from earlier discussions:

1. Because some sizable files and operations in every organization we visited remained entirely in manual form, because the information considered most confidential and sensitive in each type of organization has not generally been put into computerized files, and because a great deal of the data in computerized files is also maintained in various hard-copy forms (data-entry forms preserved in the originating office, computer print-outs distributed to users and management, long-term microfilm files, etc.), information security in today's computerizing organizations involves the protection of a mixture of eye-readable and machine-readable records, automated and manual procedures, and communication links which range from messenger service and voice telephone to teletypes and computer-to-computer links.

2. Every organization visited had at least a few files that were considered confidential by their managements, such as certain personnel files or customer records that represent valuable proprietary resources. Beyond this minimum, however, our 55 organizations differed widely in the extent to which their activities involve information that managers, record subjects or American society regards as personal or confidential. At one end of the scale

were a few organizations whose basic files were regarded as highly sensitive, and were covered by strict legal or administrative rules of confidentiality, as with the U.S. Census Bureau, a psychiatric hospital, and the Mormon Church. At the opposite end of the scale were some organizations which deal almost entirely in information that American law and social norms regard as a matter of public record. The New York State Motor Vehicle Department, a city clerk's office, and a county tax assessor's department illustrate this situation.

Between these sparsely populated poles, the great majority of our 55 organizations maintain files with different levels of confidentiality. Some of their constituent units or divisions handle highly confidential records, some maintain files of minimum confidential status, and others have only public-record data in their files. Law-enforcement agencies, for example, have central record offices maintaining patrol, case-report, and arrest records that are usually open to press and individual inspection. Particular bureaus such as "rackets" or "auto theft" have confidential files dealing with investigations in progress. And special intelligence units maintain entirely secret files, even to the extent of limiting disclosures from them to other intelligence units within law enforcement. Several social science research centers we visited had some files with identified information that were kept under tight confidentiality controls, while other research records, especially those stripped of identifying data, were open to all interested scholars. In still another large survey research center, fully identified questionnaire returns were left virtually unprotected (at one point sitting on an outside loading dock) in the belief that no one was interested in browsing through them, much less trying to locate information on specific individuals.

3. Finally, organizations have generally carried over into their computerized operations whatever rules as to confidentiality and data sharing they had in the manual era. Where no rules existed, or where sharing of information in violation of the formal rules went on without serious efforts at control, these conditions continued after computerization. Only in rare instances had there been legislative intervention that altered the precomputer rules, as with the federal Fair Credit Reporting Act.

Based on these findings, we approached the question of information security in computerizing organizations with the perspective that "adequate safeguards" could not be studied in the abstract. What was adequate would depend on the specific context: how sensitive was the personal information collected (and

did managers and record subjects agree about the sensitivity of the
data); what rules of confidentiality and data-sharing were set by
law or social expectations; how attractive was this information to
outside intruders and what attempts had been made in the past to
secure unauthorized access to it; and how far did the organization's activities or its various techniques of data handling make its
confidential information vulnerable to attack?

Our first discovery was that no person we asked in 55
organizations reported to us an instance in which unauthorized
access to a computer file of personal data had been obtained in his
organization solely through technical means and without inside
information or assistance. We also asked whether they had heard
about any episodes of intrusion by outsiders into computerized
files taking place in organizations similar to theirs—other banks,
law-enforcement agencies, credit bureaus, welfare agencies, etc. No
specific episodes were reported. In addition, we talked to security
specialists from several computer manufacturers, software houses,
and consulting firms, asking the same question. One of these,
Robert H. Courtney, manager of data security and privacy for
IBM's System Development Division, had visited hundreds of
computer installations during the past five years, talking to installation managers about security breaches or problems they were
encountering. None of these experts could recall an instance where
complete outsiders had, without inside knowledge or aid from a
cooperating employee, gained unauthorized access to computerized files to obtain information about individuals contained there.

We cannot dismiss the possibility that file intrusions have
occurred without being detected. But in every instance of unauthorized access that we have been able to corroborate, there was
use of inside information or cooperation by the organization's
employees. Our purpose in focusing on intrusion into files by
outsiders acting alone is to point up the difference between what
we found and the fears which civil libertarians have expressed.

One major explanation for this fact is that the most confidential and sensitive information about people in each organization is still kept largely in manual files; thus the payoff in personal
data from attack on computerized records is not yet great in most
organizations.[4]

It should also be remembered that much of the confidential

---

[4] This clearly applies only to personal information; many organizations
have extremely valuable proprietary information in their computer files. (A
few cases involving former employees obtaining proprietary information from
the computer systems in which they had worked will be discussed later.)

information in computerized files is shared as a matter of policy or law with outside agencies or organizations. This takes place when managers consider the purposes to be socially justified, profitable, or where it is "worthwhile" for them to sell the data or trade them in order to maintain good relations with other organizations. Law-enforcement agencies are given information about specified individuals by banks, insurance companies, credit bureaus, educational institutions, etc. Information about credit, employment, education, and medical histories are shared among organizations making decisions in those spheres. In short, very few organizations seal off their identified information the way the Census Bureau must by law. Thus information that powerful organizations regard as vital to their operations is more often than not available by direct inquiry to other organizations which hold it; stealthy intrusion into files is unnecessary.

Furthermore, we noted that even where legal or organizational rules forbid certain kinds of information sharing, informal exchanges in violation of the rules have been a standard practice in areas such as law enforcement, personnel, and credit. When outsiders can secure information through a cooperating employee within the organization, this will obviously be preferred to the risk and much greater expense of a technological assault on the files.

Finally, while only a handful of the 55 organizations we studied were using elaborate technological measures to safeguard information in their computerized files from unauthorized access, computer software and system operations provide some significant barriers to unauthorized intrusion by those who do not know the procedure specific to a given system. Even a highly skilled expert in computer systems, unless he knows how a particular system operates and how its programs have been set up, cannot simply step up to a terminal and get information out. He will have to probe to discover the rules of the system, to see what software modifications have been made specifically for that record-keeping operation, etc. When probes of this kind are made, they often disrupt things and will affect the system in ways that will alert its operators. Thus the element of customizing that is involved in each organization's arrangement of its computer system and software provides impediments to outside intruders that produce some important inhibiting effects.

This discussion leads directly into our second principal finding about information security in our 55 sites. During the past decade, violations of information confidentiality in these organizations have been accomplished primarily from manual files and were carried out by employees of the organization holding the records or of cooperating organizations sharing access to a central file. The kinds of incidents involved have been illustrated in the profiles. At the Social Security Administration, the two episodes where employees gave confidential information to outsiders involved data taken from manual records. The New York City policemen who illegally sold information about arrest records and other criminal-history elements to various commercial reporting agencies and large employers during the late 1960s obtained their information from the hard copy maintained at the New York City Police Department, not by directly querying the computerized files of the New York State Identification and Intelligence System or the FBI's National Crime Information Center. (However, NYPD manual files are updated through regular inquiries to NYSIIS and NCIC.)

Third, the few instances we heard of in which information from computerized files had been improperly obtained all involved employees or former employees of the organizations maintaining the files. One employee at TRW-Credit Data Corporation was fired when he was detected changing some derogatory items in his own credit record, and a former employee was found using the authorization code of a TRW customer that he had learned about during his TRW employ to obtain credit reports and charge their cost to that customer's account. Police and probation officials in one Western county had cooperating employees from the welfare department obtain address information about welfare clients from the computerized social services index. The use of the Kansas City Police Department's ALERT system by two participating local police departments to perform criminal-history checks for local employers and landlords illustrates a breach by employees of an agency participating in a computer network. To give a final example, a systems programmer employed in one state income-tax department went to the computer center at night to obtain information about salaries and incomes which he sold to firms which gave him names to check out for credit purposes.

In one case that we learned of a group of systems programmers were employed to develop the computer operations of a state tax agency. Later, several of these programmers moved to the state attorney general's department to do similar systems work. When they heard officials at the law enforcement agency remark how valuable it would be if they could search income tax records in their investigations—an access that was limited by state law to certain specified cases and with controlling procedures—the programmers (knowing all the routines and controls of the tax system) obliged their new employers by dialing into the state income tax files for the desired information.

Lastly, there have been penetrations of computer systems by insiders interested in something other than personal records (e.g., to steal proprietary computer programs or to disturb the system as a prank). It is clear that these insiders could have gained unauthorized access to personal data as well. But the current availability of most items of personal data through access to manual files makes it unlikely that computer systems would be penetrated for this purpose alone. In the future, however, if computer systems become more attractive as sources of personal data, the likelihood of unauthorized access for this purpose will increase.

At the majority of the 55 organizations, we found information security to be a decidedly low-priority item when compared with the problems of physical security and theft. Managers who had once put their computer center behind glass walls and displayed its operations as an attraction to visitors became alarmed during the late 1960s over bombings of computer installations by radical groups, occupations of computer centers for political protest, and deliberate destruction of computer tapes and other records. Managers were also concerned over more frequent instances of money theft by employees through manipulation of computer programs, thefts of proprietary information and software programs, and the pirating of valuable computer time. In many instances, protection of computerized files against such threats of physical attack or unauthorized appropriations served at the same time to give confidential personal information increased protection from outsider intrusion and from some forms of unauthorized use by insiders. In such instances, however, managers were clearly spending money and devoting organizational effort because they saw physical security and theft as the "real" problems.

Stemming partly from this outlook, we found that the great majority of these organizations, including those with highly confidential information, were using physical security measures as their first line of defense, supported sometimes by sophisticated technological measures. The major security measures include locked doors to the computing center, guards and identification measures, and sign-out procedures for computer tapes and disk packs, etc.; some personnel integrity checks for employees working in the computer facilities; and minimum software procedures (such as terminal identification codes for on-line systems). Very little was being done in the way of requiring the identification of terminal users, employing scrambling or other data-transformation techniques on data being communicated over phone lines, or similar measures.[5]

Because identified data move outside a large number of organizations for processing elsewhere, some mention of security protections in computer service bureaus is in order here. In the course of our project work we visited two commercial service bureaus. In addition, many of our other site-visit organizations either made use of service bureaus or themselves supplied data-processing services for other organizations. Banks we visited took on the job of billing and financial record-keeping for local physicians and dentists; a hospital computer system handled medical record-keeping for a group-practice health plan. And several organizations, such as a major manufacturing firm, had their identified individual records processed in a commercial establishment.

While such processing arrangements do not represent data "sharing" for use by the processing organization, questions of data security are clearly present. In examining the security of an organization's record system, the service bureau it uses must be thought of as an extension of that system. While a number of attempts to intrude into the files of computer service bureaus—some successful—were reported to us, we heard of no instances in which violations of confidentiality resulted. The attempts were in all cases by employees or former employees of the service bureaus or their users and were directed at such things as obtaining free computer time or achieving access to proprietary financial data or programs.[6]

Though we are aware that not all service bureaus operate in this fashion, the two that we visited make it a matter of policy not to learn very much about what kind of processing work users are doing with their computer time. The idea behind this policy is that it helps to convince users who may be processing sensitive proprietary data that service-bureau employees would not have easy access to such data as they were being stored or processed—

---

[5] Responses of our survey respondents concerning the physical and technological safeguards they employ for computerized files are discussed in Appendix A, pages 441-444 below.

[6] One example that we heard about on several site visits and which was reported in the press involved the alleged theft of a computer program from a service bureau (Information Systems Design). An employee of another service bureau managed to gain remote access to the ISD computer and obtain a print-out of the proprietary set of instructions. He had learned the identification number of an ISD customer and used that to "call" the ISD computer and ask it questions. (As reported in *Computerworld*, November 10, 1971.)

since they would have to make some special effort to learn the details of the programs set up by users.

The security precautions which commercial service bureaus reported to us reflected greater concern about protection of proprietary information and programs than about protecting the confidentiality of individually identified records. Both reported that their customers had not expressed much concern about the latter.

An example of the gap between information security goals and organizational performance was disclosed recently when the State Comptroller's Office conducted an audit of the New York State Identification and Intelligence System, one of the organizations in our site-visit group.[7] NYSIIS was created by the state legislature in 1965 to apply new technology to the sharing of critical identification and intelligence information among the 3,600 agencies of criminal justice in the state—police, prosecutors, courts, correctional institutions, and probation and parole agencies. Manual fingerprint and summary criminal history files were taken over by NYSIIS from its predecessor (the Bureau of Identification). The bulk of the criminal-history records were then gradually converted to machine-readable form; the fingerprint-matching process—which is still done by hand—was speeded up through establishing a file of general fingerprint classification numbers on a computer, which can be rapidly searched to produce a list of possible matches.

In 1967, NYSIIS opened a facsimile transmission network by which user agencies throughout the state can transmit copies of fingerprints to NYSIIS headquarters in Albany in 15 minutes, and NYSIIS can reply with a criminal history (rap sheet) on high-priority requests in several hours. Previously, it took 10-14 days to complete such an inquiry and response. By 1971, NYSIIS had computerized 2 million criminal-record fingerprint classification numbers, and approximately 400,000 criminal histories. NYSIIS has also pursued several research projects, such as an Organized Crime Intelligence Module (presently in wholly manual files), an experiment to develop better identification of personal appearances by witnesses, and a system for apprehending stolen vehicles through camera scanning of license plates and rapid checking against a computerized file listing the plate numbers of stolen vehicles. However, the fingerprint identification and summary

---

[7] Report No. AL-St.-29-71, *Audit Report on Financial and Operating Practices, New York State Identification and Intelligence System*, Office of the Comptroller, State of New York, 1971.

criminal-history programs have the only operative computerized files presently at NYSIIS.

Because of its serious attention to issues of privacy and security and its promulgation of administrative rules embodying policies more advanced in civil-liberties orientation than those of most other law-enforcement agencies at the time, NYSIIS won considerable praise during the 1960s and early 1970s from such civil-liberties spokesmen as Sen. Sam Ervin, Jr., and Congressman Cornelius Gallagher. Its security and privacy protections were widely imitated by other local, state, and national law-enforcement agencies as they moved into computerization, and it was a subcommittee of Project SEARCH headed by NYSIIS Director Dr. Robert R. J. Gallati that proposed a model code for security and privacy to govern any interstate criminal-history network that might be established.

However, the State Comptroller's Audit found significant areas "in which privacy, civil rights and civil liberties have not been protected in a manner consistent with" NYSIIS' goals and state law. Furthermore, the report concluded that NYSIIS security procedures were "inadequate" in controlling access to information, providing physical security, maintaining personnel integrity, and in computer software measures. Since the Comptroller's Office criticism highlights the kind of political, organizational, and technical issues involved in providing information security in a computerizing system, even in an organization with a history of active concern for civil-liberties protections, the key conclusions of this report are worth noting.

1. The audit found that "personnel of the United States Army and Navy regularly perform searches of NYSIIS records for histories of individuals who are enlisting in these branches of the armed forces." The military personnel "have access to the overall NYSIIS file," and there "is no check to assure that their search is restricted to enlistees only." While the auditors acknowledged that this arrangement with the military dated back as a practice to the days of NYSIIS's predecessor agency, the report noted that Article 21 of the state law creating NYSIIS did not include the army and navy among the criminal-justice agencies authorized to use the system. The auditors recommended that access should not be provided unless and until the law is amended. Furthermore, the auditors noted that letting military personnel search the records themselves, rather than to have this done for them by NYSIIS

employees, "appears to be in direct conflict" with NYSIIS's policy to "optimize the protection of individual privacy."

2. New York law requires an individual who is arrested and fingerprinted to file an application if he wants to expunge that record when no conviction results; if he does not do so, the arrest record is retained and can be circulated to NYSIIS users. As part of its 1967 System Development Plan, NYSIIS proposed to purge such records automatically where no conviction was obtained. However, this would require an amendment of state law, and the auditors criticized NYSIIS for not sponsoring legislation "which would enable it to operate consistent with the posture of privacy that it specified" in its statute and system plans.

3. The audit noted that "improper disclosures of information" from NYSIIS files of information on about 2.1 million persons with criminal histories or those fingerprinted for clearances for state licenses and employment (another 2 million persons) "could tend to compromise confidential criminal-justice activities or to jeopardize an individual's rights." Visits by the auditors to the user agencies showed that "thousands of employees at the 3,600 user agencies" are presently allowed to initiate inquiries and get information back, and the report recalled that the New York City police officers convicted in 1971 for selling information from that department's records to commercial users made use of files updated from NYSIIS. Therefore, the auditors called on NYSIIS to use its authority to "establish and enforce constraints as to persons having access to NYSIIS-disseminated data."

4. The NYSIIS security program called for background investigations, clearance levels, and training programs. The auditors found that clearance levels had not been installed to govern employee access to various segments of the records and that a formal training program of adequate scope had not been instituted.

5. The 1967 NYSIIS system development plan called for an identification code to be required to obtain information from any file; thus, even if a person obtained access to the computer illegally, he could not secure information unless he knew the code. The auditors found that the identification code was being used only for NYSIIS programs with Project SEARCH, and not in its intrastate files, and called for provision of the code as a basic element of security for the computerized files.

Other parts of the Comptroller's Office report on security

and privacy went into matters of building security, personnel identification devices, and communications security, and a recommendation was made that NYSIIS seek legal measures to forbid unauthorized disclosure or use of information by employees of user agencies, with penal sanctions.

In one sense, the comptroller's report represented a critical look at how far NYSIIS was living up to the civil-libertarian promises and policies that it had voluntarily promulgated, and on which its reputation rested. However, in many of its criticisms, the Comptroller's Office (an influential executive agency and one independent of the governor's control) was calling for tighter restrictions on "buddy system" sharing than state law currently specifies, as well as stricter controls over the practices of politically powerful user agencies, and changes in state law to allow automatic expungement of arrests-without-conviction records. Many of NYSIIS policies were in direct conformity with state law, though the auditor criticized them for conducting operations in those ways. If the auditors recommendations win editorial and legislative support, NYSIIS would then be in a position to live up to some promises that it realistically lacked the power to impose before some signal of public or legislative support.[8] As for NYSIIS' failure to provide identification codes for all its access programs, this is generally explained by NYSIIS personnel as a procedure that they believed in (and had recommended); however, with the system running far behind schedule in its processing of fingerprints and responses to inquiries, this had seemed a costly and time-consuming matter to the hard-pressed system managers, at least until the comptroller's report called attention to it.[9]

Looking over our discussion of information security, we can summarize our findings and observations as follows:

1. We found no instances of complete-outsider intrusion, solely by technological means, into computerized files to obtain information content, and very few examples across 55 organizations of unauthorized disclosure or use of computerized records by employees. We found far more examples of information breaches from manual files, reflecting their presently greater value in confidential information. What were sometimes seen in public

---

[8] In fact, following the audit, NYSIIS ceased allowing military personnel to search NYSIIS files for record data on enlistees, referring the military departments to FBI files instead. When complaints were made by the military, NYSIIS officials cited the comptroller's audit.

[9] For NYSIIS' full reply to the Audit, see statement of Robert R. J. Gallati, before N. Y. State Ass. Comm. on Gov't. Ops., Mar. 23, 1972.

discussions as breaches of security frequently turned out to be sharing of data authorized by law or organizational policy, but disputed by various critical groups, or sharing that was being done as part of the informal information buddy system because of the general public's lack of knowledge or concern over the matter.

2. With a few exceptions in organizations with unusually strong confidentiality concerns, most organizations we studied have not been convinced that unauthorized persons want their information about people badly enough to try to get it without permission. As a result, the information security measures taken by computerizing organizations have, thus far, been distinctly minimal, or have been bonuses from data-security measures directed at problems of physical security and theft of valuable property.

3. Although no system operating in the active world of government, commercial, and private life can be made permanently and completely safe, there are available techniques for providing far more security for information in computerized files than are presently being used. The strong impression that we drew at our site visits was that whether organizations would give the staff attention, spend the money, and accept the constraints on system operations that security measures generally require will depend primarily on outside pressures, especially the attitudes of regulatory agencies and lawmakers on how important it is to assure confidentiality of information in various sectors of record-keeping.

Part IV

Future Directions in Computer Technology

Elements of a Technological Forecast

Though our concentration in this study has been on how organizations are currently using computers in their record-keeping activities, we cannot apply our findings to the discussion of public policy without considering future directions in computer technology. The past 25 years have witnessed the development of steadily more powerful and versatile computer and communication systems, with larger storage capacities, faster access to stored data, and devices which make data input and output cheaper and available in more varied formats. There have also been dramatic reductions in the cost of performing computations. The adoption rate of these innovations has been, on the whole, extremely rapid during the last two decades. Factors such as the federal government's sponsorship of advanced computer systems for military and space programs, strong economic pressures for automating various operations in the world of large government and private organizations, skillful marketing by the computer industry, and a public opinion generally receptive to the provision of better material and social services through computers have all contributed to the growth of a highly responsive user marketplace.

Given this pattern of rapid innovation and utilization, policymakers concerned with civil liberties in record-keeping must assume that the computer field will be a dynamic technological environment in the future. A legitimate question to be raised about our research is whether or not there are technological changes waiting around the corner which—in marked contrast to developments of the past 25 years—would significantly reduce the civil-liberties protections individuals receive in organizational record systems. What is needed, therefore, is an informed forecast of the direction that technological innovation is likely to take in the years ahead, how such new capabilities would be likely to affect patterns of organizational record-keeping, and what impact these changes might have on civil-liberties interests.

Two important issues arise at the outset in making such a technological forecast—choosing the time span to be covered and identifying some of the social factors that will affect utilization of technological advances by record-keeping organizations. We consider the next five to eight years to be the forecasting period critical for current public policy discussions. Informed public discussion needs a "surprise-free" estimate of technological change and utilization for the middle and late 1970s. And, so that public debates will not be warped by unrealistic fears, it is especially important to have a description of what is *not* likely to happen in the next five to eight years. Our forecast is therefore framed in terms of what can be anticipated with some confidence for the remainder of the 1970s.

The second problem in framing a forecast involves a specification of the social factors that will affect the utilization of computer technology for record-keeping. As we have noted, many commentaries on the databank problem have drawn upon announcements of new technological capabilities in technical papers or demonstrated under laboratory conditions, under the assumption that such capabilities would be quickly installed in the computer systems of the commercial and governmental world. The assumption has been that technological possibilities invariably become organizational realities, unless an aroused public opinion forces the passage of prohibitory legislation holding back the tide of technological determinism.

Our site visits to advanced computerizing organizations disclosed a very different pattern of utilization, however. Innovative organizations moved quickly to install some of the improved methods of processing personal records made possible by successive generations of computer systems. However, many techniques shown in laboratory demonstrations or in highly special organizational environments (e.g., NASA) proved far more difficult to use than had been assumed. In the case of building central databanks, for example, we saw how problems of organizing complex data bases and providing the flexible software desired proved more difficult or more costly than the organizations had expected.

We also saw that a great deal of existing technological capability has not been adopted widely in the organizational world, especially to create the kind of databanks most feared by civil libertarians. For example, there is not the slightest doubt that it is *technologically* possible today, especially with recent advances in mass storage memories, to build a computerized, on-line file containing the compacted equivalent of 20 pages of typed information about the personal history and selected activities of every man, woman, and child in the United States, arranging the system so that any single record could be retrieved in about 30 seconds. It follows automatically that omnibus citizen files could be built today to cover all residents in a given state, county, or city, or that such a comprehensive personal file could be created for 5, 10, or 20 million particular individuals on whom a governmental authority or commercial enterprise wanted to keep records.[1]

To use less global examples, there is nothing technologically that prevents American Airlines today from arranging its SABRE II reservation system to retain past traveler information for years and make it available to investigators; or for American Express to program its computer systems to produce detailed purchase histories for each cardholder for as long as he has been using American Express; or for the Massachusetts Institute of Technology to create a computerized file into which every student's academic, financial, medical, extracurricular, and other records are consolidated.

That such changes have not come about cannot be laid to inadequacies in the computer technology of 1972. Rather, the manner in which organizations adopt computer technology has been shaped by three major controlling factors: organizational goals and priorities; the presence of administrative and political constraints within organizations; and the sociopolitical environment in which the organization exists.

Organizational Goals and Priorities

The simplest explanation of why the kinds of technological possibilities just illustrated have not been embraced in the organizational world is that such ventures do not reflect the existing goals and priorities of organizational leaders. Creating the kind of on-line, permanent record system that would meet the needs of a criminal investigator is neither a business necessity nor a profit-making

---

[1] It should be noted that the public's concern over such giant databanks focuses on developments that are not as likely in the 1970s as the interconnection of separate computer systems within a single organization or between organizations. Given linking techniques already available, and if the problems of common personal identifiers, compatible record formats, and appropriate software instructions for the desired use could be worked out among participating departments or organizations, there would be no need to specify a mammoth central processing unit to operate such data systems.

opportunity for American Airlines or American Express; thus their computer systems are not organized to do so. Further, there is no evidence to suggest that pressure has come from law-enforcement officials for organizations to modify their systems to serve government's investigatory needs.

Most administrative decisions about students at MIT today do not require an examination of the student's total record; reorganizing the various departmental or school record systems to produce such a comprehensive single file is therefore not among MIT's present plans, and we did not encounter plans for such a comprehensive file at other colleges and universities.

Similarly, there has been no program by the executive branch of the federal government, or of any state, to create an all-encompassing administrative file on each citizen in those jurisdictions. Even the construction of a national data center for statistical purposes, an idea advocated by consultants and Bureau of the Budget officials in 1966-67 and based on consolidating information from the personal records of individuals in various federal agencies, was never officially endorsed by the Johnson administration and has not been proposed by the Nixon administration. Within the statistical and research community itself, several scholars have suggested that the goals of such a databank could be better achieved through ad hoc studies that do not depend for their success on a massive central statistical file.[2]

Whatever may be the desires of some individuals within major record-keeping organizations (research or marketing staffs, management science specialists, etc.), and whatever recommendations may be offered by some manufacturers and software consultants, the organizations we studied generally moved to take up technological innovations only when these promised to advance what leaders saw as high-priority business opportunities or pressing governmental program needs.

Intraorganizational Constraints

Where organizational leaders do want to pursue an important activity or program through an advanced computer application, our site visits documented how often administrative and political problems within organizations can hold back such developments. Typical constraints include heavy initial financial costs; disruptive effects upon ongoing operations that usually accompany data

---

[2] As a most recent example of this criticism, see *Federal Statistics: Report of the President's Commission* (1971), Vol. II, Chapter 1.

conversion or reprogramming; securing agreement in large organizations or within fields on personal identifiers, record terminology, and general file content for unified data bases; resolving the problems of organizational policy that must be clarified to write effective software (especially in databank approaches); arranging reorganization of functions and powers among subunits; and dealing with conflicts between data-processing-oriented members of management and those that are hostile to approaches along these lines. Our profiles showed this blend of factors leading some organizations (such as New Haven) to abandon or postpone indefinitely an advanced computer application, while others (such as Santa Clara County) had to stretch out the timetable for their advanced databank projects. These actions thus slowed down the spread of on-line central databanks into local governments.

Social and Political Conditions

Even though a particular organization or all organizations in a given field might want to exploit a particular technological capability, and even if the intraorganizational factors are favorable, the social and political milieu must be one that allows or encourages such innovation. In the case of governmental agencies, this includes support from key interest groups and general public opinion, an absence of direct or indirect legal prohibitions, legislative approval, and the availability of funding. In the case of business enterprises, there must be cost reduction or market opportunities, customer acceptance, and an absence of legal restrictions such as antitrust laws or regulatory-agency bars. Private, nonprofit organizations must have a similarly open legal situation and a favorable outlook from relevant constituencies (such as the medical profession and funding sources for advanced medical-record applications).

The key point to note is that these organizational and sociopolitical factors provide pathways and barriers that affect the reception of technological innovations. Our site visits showed some record-keeping sectors in which conditions have moved technological advances very rapidly into operating systems. For example, national concern about crime and strong public support for law-enforcement record-keeping activities, the availability of major funding for computerization through the Law Enforcement Assistance Administration, and the active stimulation of this market by computer manufacturers and systems consultants led to rapid and extensive utilization of computer technology and communications in law enforcement during the late 1960s and early '70s—facsimile transmission, on-line storage, large terminal networks, and, most recently, satellite communications. Banks also represent an area of rapid utilization. The cash resources available for capital investment, the heavy crush of paper transactions requiring drastic remedies, the objective character of the basic records to be automated, the business need for swift credit authorizations in loan and credit-card business, and similar factors made banking an early starter, continuing innovator, and receptive future market in the area of computer technology.

On the other hand, the medical-record area has been slow to move into advanced computer utilization for personal recordkeeping and will probably remain so in the near future. With funds for direct patient care and new facilities scarce, there are severe shortages of money to expend on the development of automation projects; many problems of record standardization (because of differences over the terminology to be used in describing symptoms and diseases); and considerable resistance among doctors to moving computerization beyond its present housekeeping and lab report focus. While many developments in the 1970s can be imagined that would alter this situation—from enactment of national health insurance to creation of a computerized "health catastrophe" record for every individual to assist in emergencies away from home—hospitals and medical records would have to be on the lower end of a scale indicating readiness for utilization of computer technology in record-keeping.

Recognizing that the technology will not surge out into an organizational and sociopolitical vacuum, we can turn now to a discussion of likely trends.

Technological Prospects for the 1970s

In forecasting technological changes that might affect the input-tooutput cycle of record-keeping, we have relied primarily on a combination of sources: interviews with computer manufacturers and consultants, our site-visit discussions with organizational managers and data-processing specialists, leading forecasting studies that have been published or privately circulated,[3] and an analysis of technological trends prepared by a panel of the Computer Science and Engineering Board as part of a report on library automation.[4] It should be noted that we have framed our forecast in the broad terms that are of interest to policymakers and the public, rather than going into the details that would be of interest to technical specialists.

To begin, let us recall the different points in the record-keeping process at which new computer capabilities might have some impact. New technology could conceivably improve the present means of entering data at source points, putting them into machine-readable form, keeping them in various forms of storage (on- and off-line), programming the manipulation of stored data, improving access time for update and retrieval, and providing various means of displaying and distributing data output. Reducing the cost of performing each of these functions is perhaps the most important aspect of technological innovation, and could affect significantly the willingness of managements either to computerize presently manual operations or to alter the way in which computer applications are now organized.

Input

Improved direct-entry input devices will be developed and used more widely. These include key-to-tape peripheral devices, which allow magnetic tape—on reels or in cassettes—to be prepared directly from a keyboard without the usual intermediate step of producing punched cards. Optical scanning methods represent another technique by which data from typed or written forms are converted to magnetic tape or punched-card storage without resorting to keyboard operations. Some forecasters believe that voice input devices to computers may be developed by the end of the 1970s.

---

[3] Particularly helpful have been the forecasting studies of Auerbach Corporation, Arthur D. Little, Inc., International Data Corporation, and Frost and Sullivan. For a very recent summary of anticipated trends, see F. G. Withington, "The Next (and Last?) Generation," *Datamation* (May 1972), pp. 71-74.

[4] Information Systems Panel of the Computer Science and Engineering Board, National Academy of Sciences, *Libraries and Information Technology: A National System Challenge* (Washington, D.C., 1971).

The more likely input developments will reduce considerably the costs for large-volume data entry, as has already been demonstrated at organizations such as the Internal Revenue Service and the Bureau of the Census, where a great deal of incoming data must be converted to computer-readable form within very short periods of time. These are not totally new devices, and development will take the form of "getting the bugs out," e.g., reducing the level of recognition errors in the optical scanning process at the same time that the range of type fonts and variations in hand lettering that the equipment will read is broadened. Data entry for some large record-keeping operations will therefore become faster and cheaper.

Storage

Larger memory storage capacities are being developed which will allow organizations to place much greater volumes of data into direct-access storage for on-line operations than has been feasible before. New ways of recording and entering data (e.g., via laser beam) will allow data to be packed together far more tightly, and thus more cheaply.

The first few production models of very large (mass) storage devices are being delivered principally for use in control systems within industry and NASA. Such units could be used to relieve storage problems for some existing high-volume, on-line record-keeping operations. This development also encourages organizations that want direct access to large files to move to on-line operation, by reducing present costs of such storage. However, mass memory systems require new systems and software approaches by organizations adopting them, and this requirement leads some experts to predict a slow entry of the very large mass memory devices into the general marketplace.

Configuration Arrangements

More flexible options will be available for arranging the configuration of computer systems. Particularly important will be an array of relatively low-cost "minicomputers"[5] which could be used for self-contained record-keeping applications. There will also be improved capacities for linking more terminals into on-line systems

---

[5] There is no precise definition of a "minicomputer." Dr. Ruth Davis, Director of the Center for Computer Sciences and Technology of the National Bureau of Standards, suggests as a rule of thumb that minicomputers are those that cost less than $50,000.

than it is presently cost-effective for many organizations to do. Remote terminals are expected to increase in number from about 200,000 in 1970 to 800,000 in 1975, while stand-alone mini-computers are expected to increase from their present level of 40,000 to 150,000 by 1975.

Greater flexibility of computer configurations makes it difficult to envision the way record-keeping systems will look in the late 1970s. With an expanded range of options, some organizations will become more decentralized in their record-keeping activities, using minicomputers for a variety of relatively low volume, self-contained record-keeping operations. Others will elect to use large, multiterminal centralized systems. A decision might be made, for instance, to maintain the particularly sensitive intelligence files of a state police department as a completely self-contained unit on a minicomputer, rather than as one of many on-line files in the central system. Other organizations may shift large parts of their data processing to commercial service bureaus, which would offer low-cost terminal access to central computing facilities.

System Reliability

It is expected that computer systems will become increasingly reliable during the 1970s. For instance, systems will experience shorter periods of "down time" during which they cannot be used, they will come with a greater array of time-tested programs, and "intelligent" input terminals will continue to reduce input error problems. Coupled with the availability of a greater array of network or minicomputer "backup" arrangements, this increased reliability will affect what configurations are developed and whether or not paper files are considered technologically necessary as backup. In developing hospital systems, for instance, much discussion has surrounded the need for some fail-safe system if the primary working medical record is put into on-line storage for video display at bedside or the nursing station. The greater flexibility and reliability of available systems may therefore allow computer applications to go forward that are not being made today for such reasons.

Software and Data-base Management

Considerable improvement is expected in the system software of computers—programs such as the operating system, data-base manager, communication manager, and language processor that manage what goes on within the machine. The present difficulties in applying these subsystems are expected to be relieved as system software is made more automatic and easier to use. This will enable management to get computer systems to do more effectively what they are desired to do.

However, when it comes to applications software—the instructions that govern what data should be stored and how they should be processed and weighed to accomplish organizational objectives—there is less agreement among forecasters. Some experts believe that there will be much better general-purpose software for managing large data bases and, beyond that, movement toward management information systems (MIS) that will allow the separate files in today's data centers to be unified into responsive data bases for greatly improved operations and management decision making. However, other specialists point out that these applications depend for their success on better understanding of business, social, and political processes and relationships, as well as major administrative reforms within organizations. Our experience in watching organizations grapple with the complexities of translating broad policy objectives and weak cause-and-effect theories into the applications software for databank and MIS projects makes us lean strongly toward the skeptical side in this area.

Availability of Computers

The development of low-cost minicomputers and inexpensive terminal links into commercial time-sharing services will also greatly increase the availability of computing for small organizations. With terminal rentals starting at just over $100 per month and minicomputers of respectable performance available for purchase at less than $10,000, stored files and computing power can become cost-effective for the corner grocery store, the local retail credit bureau, or the private detective's office. By way of comparison, it should be noted that minicomputers typically have more storage and computing capacity than the large second-generation computers on which many advanced organizations designed their initial record-keeping applications. As a result, the range of record-keeping options open to organizations beginning their computerization with a minicomputer is far greater than that available to organizations in the '50s and early '60s. Many such services will be provided by time-sharing networks, though it is difficult to estimate how large these networks will be, and users' costs will depend on the extent of the market that develops.

Communications Systems

Cheaper and more highly specialized communication systems for data transmissions, both for user-to-computer and computer-to-computer purposes, will develop during the 1970s. These will range from improved microwave channels assisted over long distances by satellites, to the use of cable-television (CATV) channels and possibly to laser communication networks.

Like the development of transistors and solid-state devices, communications networks not specifically developed for computer systems may nevertheless have a profound effect on EDP as they are adopted for computer-to-computer or human-to-computer communications. In the case of CATV, experts agree that there is great potential for distribution of information of all types through local channels, with estimates that anywhere between 5 and 20 million such connections will be in place by 1980.

Output Devices

More flexible and less expensive computer output technology will be developed in the 1970s. The computer will more frequently be used as "support" for microfilm or microfiche systems—sorting and preparing these hard-copy media through computer-output-to-microfilm (COM) devices.[6] Display terminals and low-speed printer terminals are expected to appear in much less expensive versions. There will also be continued improvement in the speed and reliability of facsimile transmission systems.

Behind these widely predicted trends for electronic data processing in the 1970s lies a general conviction among industry leaders that users are not seeking machines to do radically different things than they do at present. What users want, as our site-visit interviews confirmed, are cost-effective ways to obtain the appropriate storage and computing capacity when and where they need it. Factors such as the heavy investments that major computer manufacturers have in existing hardware and the heavy costs of reprogramming which usually accompany shifts to a new generation of hardware are also expected to reinforce the emphasis on gradualism for the next few years. The central conclusion about which technological forecasters are in high agreement is that the next five to eight years are expected to be primarily a period of improving existing computer and communication technology

---

[6] *Libraries and Information Technology, op. cit.*, p. 75.

and increasing the user's capacities to manage these tools; it will not be a time of radical new departures in hardware design, software programming concepts, and communication systems such as the EDP field experienced in moving from first- to third-generation computer systems between 1958 and the mid-1960s.

There may well be some dramatic advances in particular aspects of the technology, such as erasable laser storage or laser communication networks—two developments receiving much discussion in the field today. But as far as their record-keeping implications are concerned, even such breakthroughs will still represent advances that would have the same effects on civil liberties as the more modest technological developments we have predicted. To see why, let us turn to the question of civil-liberties impact.

Civil Liberties Implications

None of the technological advances that we have been discussing will bear directly on the central *privacy* issue: should a given piece of personal information be collected and stored at all by the organization. Nor will technological changes control the question of how information in organizational records should be used to make allocative judgments about particular individuals or groups of people. These will continue to be sociopolitical and legal issues.

As a general matter, computerized record-keeping will spread much more widely during the 1970s under the forecast we have made. Many more organizations will acquire their own computers; estimates are that there will be 500,000 computers (including minicomputers) at the close of the 1970s, compared to the 90,000 now in use. The use of time-sharing and service bureau computer facilities will also increase, and this is an important indication of growth in computerized record-keeping to be considered alongside the number of computer units by itself. For organizations which have no computer applications, it is likely that financial housekeeping operations will be the first target for computerization. Equally likely, however, is that newly computerizing organizations will move from housekeeping to file automation in a shorter span of time than was true of organizations in the '60s. This will produce computerization at a faster rate of development.

Even where an increasing number of computerizing organizations incorporate new developments into their data-processing systems, organizational record-keeping in the '70s will, in ways relevant to civil liberties, look very much like those of the late '60s. There will continue to be complex mixtures of manual and computerized files and procedures, though the proportion of computerized records in most large organizations will increase. In addition, the most subjective and sensitive records in each type of operation will likely remain in manual form, and enormous problems in developing the software for complex data-base transactions will continue to exist.

Unlike the 1960s, however, almost all new record systems created to carry on large-scale programs in government, business, and private organizations in the 1970s will be planned from the outset as computerized systems, and will therefore be geared directly to computer and data-communications approaches. Welfare reform proposals introduced by the Nixon administration in 1970 and 1971, for instance, were designed around computer capabilities, and the existence of extensive computerized record systems at the state and federal levels.

Finally, information exchanges among organizations will increasingly be computerized. As a result, expectations as to what information one organization can realistically call on another to supply (for industry or functional-area cooperation, or to comply with regulatory or law-enforcement authority) will increasingly be based on the capacities of computerized record systems.

If there were in the offing some computer developments which would produce EDP systems far different from those we have today, it would be extremely difficult to anticipate the civil-liberties implications of record-keeping applications. But assuming that computer technology develops along the lines we have set out, we can usefully explore the effect these developments are likely to have on record-keeping practices and civil-liberties protections. To do this, we return to the basic questions about computers and civil liberties that we addressed in our site-visit findings, and reexamine these in light of our technological forecast.

1. Will these develoments in computer technology lead organizations to collect more extensive personal data about individuals than they have done until now? We noted that certain technological constraints (physical and cost limits on core storage, high costs of keyboarding for data conversion, etc.) had the serendipitous effect of creating a pressure on managers to limit the amount of information they collected or converted from existing files for their computerized files. Though most of the organizations we studied did not feel they needed to collect more information,

there were some which did want to do so, and there are many new programs or services developing for which organizations must decide how much personal information they need to collect and store. Clearly, some previous technological constraints will be lessened by the advances that have been predicted. However, there are other costs that will continue to place economic constraints on data collection, such as the cost of new procedures for gathering data which are not already being collected, the cost of added processing time, and costs of print-out and display. Even more important, the "record reviews" by organizations to examine what items of information should be computerized are likely to be continued and even made more intensive as protests over civil-liberties issues in various record systems become more prominent in the public and legislative arena. Our site visits showed that such sociopolitical factors are becoming increasingly important to organizations considering what information ought to go into law-enforcement files, medical records, employment histories, and the like. Thus forseeable technological developments of the 1970s may lead to some relaxation of economic pressures against increased data collection, but this does not promise to have a revolutionary effect in light of the other factors we have noted.

2. Will there be even greater sharing of confidential information than previously? To the extent that information has not been shared in the past because of physical difficulties or high costs in conveying data from one organization to another, or among departments of a large organization, the technological trends we have noted will greatly relieve such limitations. The kind of faster and more comprehensive networks for information exchange that we saw evolving in law enforcement, airline reservations, and credit reporting will become even easier and cheaper to construct in the next five to eight years. As a result, there will be even more need, from a civil-liberties standpoint, to define which exchanges of identified information should be permitted among organizations, when the individual's consent must be obtained for such transfers, and how to ensure that only authorized uses are made by the secondary recipients of personal information. This may well be the most important effect of technological progress during the 1970s, and deserves serious attention now from policymakers.

3. Will it be more difficult to provide adequate security for confidential personal information in computer systems as they develop during the 1970s? With more sensitive information being added to the computerized segment of organizational record systems, the value to unauthorized persons of penetrating security

clearly becomes much greater. Also, the fact that more organizations will be storing their confidential files off their premises, in time-sharing and service-bureau computer centers, means that security must be provided at those sites and in data transmission, as well as at the terminals and for the files of the primary organization. These developments will require that security measures be taken commensurate with the attractiveness of the information stored, the guarantees of confidentiality given to record subjects, and similar factors.

Perhaps the best way to characterize the future shape of the security issue is to say that, at the least, greater computerization adds more automated files and data-transmission lines to the security problems that organizations with confidential information already had and will continue to have in the 1970s in protecting their manual and automated files, telephone conversations, and other information processes from intruders. Furthermore, our studies show that significant sectors of American opinion believe that confidential information should be given more protection in many areas of record-keeping in the future than the public required before computers came along. There is also considerable pressure to control the information buddy system of unauthorized sharing that has recently become an object of national civil-liberties concern. If such security is demanded, and if organizations allocate money, personnel, and managerial attention to the task, the technological trends we have noted would not, per se, lead to a lower level of security. If the protective interventions are not made, organizations will be less able to fulfill their promises of confidentiality than they have been, simply because there will be more points of leakage in the total data system.

Another point about security needs to be made here. Our findings indicate that much personal information is already shared widely and readily by the individual himself and by the organizations which maintain records on him. If, in response to public concern, court rulings, legislative actions, etc., information which is now openly shared is declared confidential, this may increase the pressure for unauthorized access, as the demand for black-market data grows. As a result, record systems which do not have a security problem today—because they share data willingly—may come to have one in the future.

4. Will it be more difficult in the next five to eight years to provide individuals with notice of files kept about them and an opportunity for access to the contents of their record as appropriate in a given field? Again, nothing in the technological changes

we have forecast suggests that this will be the case. The basic factor that will govern whether the individual enjoys a meaningful right of access will continue to be organizational policy or legal regulations, not whether the record is on a typed card, a minicomputer file, stored on a magnetic bubble memory, or placed in a time-sharing system.

Taken as a whole, our technological forecast suggests three major conclusions:

1. Managers will have at their command increasingly powerful and more flexible tools with which to pursue policies through the collection and use of information.

2. Organizational, legal, and political factors will continue to be the dominant forces that shape how technological options are applied to record-keeping and decision making about people. No greater degree of technological determinism lies ahead than we have seen thus far in the history of computerization.

3. As more and more organizational record-keeping becomes computerized, and as important new record systems are developed, it will become critically important that the standards and procedures that are being applied more efficiently by these computerizing organizations are faithful to democratic goals, especially individual rights to privacy and due process.

By their very nature, of course, forecasts of technological impact can be misleading unless used with care and continually modified as events unfold. It is always possible that particular innovations will occur that stand apart from the larger trends we have predicted for the near future. And there is as well the problem of quantitative changes cumulating into important and unforseen qualitative change. For example, when most of the record systems in most of the government and private organizations in the United States are computerized, and if substantial progress were to be made in standardizing record content and personal identifiers across organizations in major fields of personal record-keeping, such conditions might produce a set of attitudes concerning the collection and use of information in 1980 that would differ significantly from that of today. Critical in such a situation would be how the law and public policy had operated while these technological and organizational developments had been unfolding.

Such problems of forecasting, even for the short range, argue that the assessment of technological changes, and of the sociolegal conditions that shape their reception by organizations, must be a continuous process, not an occasional affair. In 1972, American society does not have in government, industry, or the academic community the proper monitoring systems for tracing and publicizing these changes, especially as they affect civil-liberties interests. As the rate of computerization increases, however, and as an even greater diversity of systems come into operation, the creation of mechanisms for the regular reporting and assessment of such developments will become a necessity if we are to have informed public policy.

Part V

Implications for
Public Policy

In turning to the public policy implications of our research, it is useful to quote from the project proposal our mandate for this analysis:

> The Study would focus on the public policy problems that arise because of the movement of organizations to develop and use computerized databanks containing sensitive information about individuals and social groups. It would explore alternative methods for producing safeguards for the citizen's right to privacy and his interests in due process, as these would be redefined and specified in the context of public and private databanks. In addition, the question of forms of public review and accountability to ensure the operations of such safeguards would be a central part of the study.

The basis for this policy analysis was to be an empirical investigation of three main questions: (1) How are computers being used by governmental and private organizations to collect, process, and exchange information about individuals? (2) What effect is such computer use having on the way organizations use records to make judgments about the individual's rights, benefits, and opportunities? (3) How has the development of computerized record systems affected the rules of privacy and due process that prevailed in the same field of record-keeping in the manual data-processing era?

In undertaking its investigation, the project began with two explicit premises about the role of information in a democratic society. We assume that the collection and intelligent use of considerable information about people, events, and social processes is necessary in a complex society, especially one in which people expect a high level of social and public services from government, extensive goods and services from private business and industry, and a wide range of cultural, educational, and civic services from private associations. We also assume that the collection and use of personal information, particularly when it is relied upon heavily to determine the rights, benefits, and opportunities of individuals, has to be conducted in conformity with the constitutional protections that American society provides for its citizenry. Setting a balance between these two valuable interests of society requires, as it always has, the application of law and organizational policy to arrive at sensitive, area-by-area judgments.

From our empirical studies, we sought to identify those areas of organizational record-keeping in which current uses of computers, and public concern over such use, might prompt policymakers in a democratic society to reexamine whether the rules and practices for protecting citizen rights in computerized and manual record systems are still adequate. Our research into managerial EDP plans for the next five years and our forecast of technological trends for the 1970s was done to help identify civil-liberties problems that are likely to become more serious in the near future, and thus to require some anticipatory attention by policymakers now.

Following these guidelines, our approach to drawing policy implications will be to identify a set of priority areas for civic attention, discuss various approaches that our studies lead us to believe would provide meaningful safeguards for privacy and due process in the major areas of record-keeping that we have been discussing, and to analyze the effects that developing such policies might have on the use of information in the organizations affected.

Our purpose, then, is to help develop the agenda for public discussion of the databank issue. We have tried to supply concrete illustrations of policies that would respond to the issues that emerged from our site-visit findings, the opinion surveys, and our technological forecasts. We have not taken it as our charge to develop finished proposals for administrative or legal action, or to offer suggestions for the entire range of civil-liberties issues that our studies have covered. That will be the work of many more years, by many groups and institutions.

With this explanation of our goals in this chapter on policy implications, we turn first to an analysis of what our findings suggest about the meaning of the databanks-and-civil-liberties problem as a sociopolitical issue.

Broad Significance
of Our Findings

In our site-visit findings, we drew three major sets of conclusions about the effects of computerization on personal record-keeping.

1. First, computer usage has not created the revolutionary new powers of data surveillance predicted by some commentators. Specifically, the great majority of organizations we studied are not, as a result of computerizing their records, collecting or exchanging more detailed personal information about individuals than they did in the precomputer era. They are not sharing identified information more widely among organizations that did not carry out such exchanges in the precomputer era. And individuals are not receiving less due process in computerized data systems than law and practice mandated in each field of record-keeping when decisions were made using manual files.

2. Second, computerization is definitely bringing some important increases in the efficiency of organizational record-keeping. The most important of these are the production of more complete and up-to-date records; faster responses to inquiries; more extensive use of information already in the files; more extensive networks for interorganizational exchange of data; and the creation of some large data bases that would not have been feasible without computers. As a result, organizations are able to carry out record transactions more swiftly and effectively through computerized data systems.

3. However, even where these increases in efficiency are taking place, organizational policies which affect individual rights are still generally following the precomputer patterns in each field of record-keeping. Where an individual's right to privacy, confidentiality, or due process had been recognized in the past, these rights have been carried over into the computerized systems; where organizations did not afford these rights with respect to a given area of record-keeping previously, such policies have generally

been continued after computerization. And in those instances where new legal measures or public pressures have led to an extension of individual rights in particular areas of record-keeping, computerized systems have been as responsive as manual systems in putting such changes into effect.

Going beyond the site-visit findings, our forecast of technological trends in the 1970s indicates that there is very little likelihood that new developments will drastically alter the way in which organizational goals, institutional limitations, and legal and social constraints shape the reception and use of new computer technology. We anticipate more flexible and reliable computer systems, and greater ease in carrying on data exchanges between computerized systems. It is the increased feasibility of data sharing, and not any significant changes in either privacy or due-process interests, that will be the most important effect of advances in computer technology during the next eight years.

These being our basic findings, some readers might conclude that the issue of databanks and civil liberties is not a matter of pressing importance for public policy at this time. Our research showed that there was considerable misunderstanding on the part of many experts, the press, legislators, and the general public about what computers were actually being used to accomplish. Given our findings, however, one could conclude that society should allow the managers of governmental, commercial, and nonprofit organizations to continue adapting their computerized systems to the existing civil-liberties rules in their particular field. This would leave a few particularly sensitive computerizing systems, such as the criminal-history system of the National Crime Information Center, as possible candidates for new legislative rules.

This is not the conclusion that we draw. What is critical for putting our findings into the proper policy context is to realize the moment in American national life at which computers arrived, and the significance of this timing for the question of legal intervention.

First of all, by the 1950s American society had already become a record-based social system. Individuals in our urban, industrialized, and mobile society had their basic opportunities and rights heavily determined by formal organizations—in education, employment, credit, government licensing, social services, etc. As our profiles showed, such judgments were based to a considerable extent on the production and use of written records, and on networks of cooperative information sharing among the organizational gatekeepers. As this credential system became even more important in controlling judgments about people in the 1950s and early 1960s, it raised to a critical level many older, unresolved issues of civil liberties in record-keeping, such as the circulation of derogatory-information lists in government and private industry and the use of records without the individual's knowledge or his right to examine their contents.

The maturing of the "records-and-liberty" issue was hastened by a number of major social trends that, like the development of credential-based gatekeeping itself, had nothing to do with computers. As we need hardly labor here, the 1960s and early '70s have been a time of widespread challenges to the authority, goals, programs, and procedures of the established public and private institutions. Survey research studies, for example, show the percentage of respondents expressing basic trust in American national government dropping from 71 percent in 1958 to 62 percent in 1962 and then to 37 percent in 1970.[1] Such erosions of customary faith in government have been paralleled by a climate of disaffection within churches, labor unions, universities, businesses, and other institutions of national life.

It was in this general setting that credential systems became an object of wide-ranging protest in the 1960s. There were protests against both the open and disguised preferments that were given to whites over blacks and other minorities and to the well-to-do over the poor. Not only was discrimination attacked but programs of positive compensation were demanded to overcome the economic, social, and political damage that had been done by long-standing policies. Many criteria of individual evaluation also came under attack, such as reliance on the results of what were criticized as "culture-bound" intelligence tests, and personality-adjustment tests that were felt to measure social and religious conformity. As for sociopolitical disqualifications, there were demands that information about the exercise of lawful political dissent, cultural nonconformity, and homosexual preferences should no longer be used to bar otherwise qualified individuals from basic opportunities and rights. By the early 1970s, such criticisms had been voiced in every major area in which large-scale organizations made controlling decisions about people.

---

[1] "Election Time Series Analysis of Attitudes of Trust in Government," Center for Political Studies, Institute for Social Research, University of Michigan, Fall, 1971. See also B. R. Roper and J. Heinig, "Is America Off on the Wrong Track?" *Los Angeles Times*, July 18, 1971; and A. H. Cantril and C. W. Roll, Jr., *Hopes and Fears of the American People*, New York, 1971.

The challenges came from a highly diverse set of critics. Some spoke on behalf of groups long discriminated against under the American social system, such as blacks, other minorities, and the poor. Some spoke for new sociopolitical movements drawing heavily on the white middle classes, such as consumer-rights groups, sexual liberationists, the youth culture, and women's-rights movements. Still others voiced positions associated with traditional civil-liberties organizations or even conservatively-oriented constitutional fundamentalism. Some of the spokesmen attacked the alleged injustices of the credential system not to call for reform but to seek revolutionary changes in American society. Others sought to reform the system to make it more responsive to their group needs and so that they might win a larger piece of the economic and political pie. Still others accepted the goals of the system but sought to make it live up to its professed ideals of merit selection, equality of opportunity, and respect for individual differences.

With such different and often conflicting social objectives, it was obvious that the challengers did not represent a single social movement. But most of them had what might be called a negative unity. They were contesting major aspects of the white, middle-class, achievement-and-conformity-oriented credential systems that were accepted by the majority in the 1950s and doing so in the name of deep-seated American principles—equality, due process, and individual liberty.

Since organizational record systems were the typical means of applying the standards that were being challenged, these increasingly became a focus of protest. These included challenges to the use of arrest records to limit the employment opportunities of ghetto residents and political activists; to Selective Service records as the supply instrument of the Vietnam War; to the U.S. Army Intelligence Command's development of files on civilian protest movements in the late 1960s; to seizure of the bank records of political groups by legislative committees and law-enforcement agencies for investigative purposes; to the maintenance of local, state, and federal police intelligence files on militant groups; to the presence of investigative reports on the personal lives and sexual behavior of employees in the files of government and private employers; to social research files about radicals and other "deviant" groups; to medical and psychiatric records dealing with the commitment of patients and other mental-health issues; and to records kept by schools and universities about the personal and political behavior of students.

The procedures by which these standards were applied in record systems also became a target of protest groups. Organizations such as schools and universities which traditionally used informal and paternalistic administrative procedures have been challenged by student rights groups demanding formal hearings whenever disciplinary actions are instituted. Persons receiving welfare aid, living in public housing, or receiving other public assistance have insisted that these government benefits should not be refused or terminated unless due process is observed. Consumer groups and civil-liberties organizations convinced Congress that commercial reporting agencies should no longer be allowed to disseminate evaluative information about millions of consumers and employees without each individual receiving notice that a report was used to deny him credit, employment, or insurance, and having available a procedure for contesting its accuracy and completeness. Secret investigative files, such as the army's files on political activists and many police department "antisubversive" records, were also assailed as improper, partly on the ground that no system existed for public review of what kind of information was collected and how it was being used.

While it is beyond the scope and mandate of our study to pass judgments on the positions expressed in these various protests, we did consider it important to gather information on how widely such views were held in the American population. In Appendix B, we analyze the available public opinion data dealing with civil-liberties issues in record-keeping. The overall conclusion suggested by these materials is that concern over privacy and other civil-liberties interests in record-keeping characterizes a far larger segment of the population than would be represented solely by civil-liberties activists or political radicals. On the basis of three national surveys and half a dozen polls of more specialized populations, we find that invasion of privacy, as a general issue, is a matter of concern by about one-third of the American public. Among youth groups, as reflected by the 1971 White House Conference on Youth and a national survey of college students in the same year, concern over invasion of privacy is more widespread than in the general population. For example, 83 percent of the respondents in the college poll agreed with the statement that "People's privacy is being destroyed."

As for record-keeping specifically, 62 percent of those polled in a national survey stated that they were "very" or "fairly" concerned about the information that some organizations were keeping about people in their files. As one studies opinion-poll responses to questions about specific areas of record-keeping, from credit reporting to police surveillance of radical groups, it becomes clear that the public is, for the most part, rather sophisticated in distinguishing between data collection it considers legitimate and that which it thinks is improper, with indications that the judgment turns on issues such as who will have access to the information, how it will be used, and what safeguards will be present.

It was while these debates over the use of records were unfolding in the 1960s that the public first became aware of the scientific and technological marvels of surveillance—the microminiaturized listening and watching devices that increased the capacity to keep persons under physical surveillance; the projective personality tests and emotion-sensing devices that could be used to put individuals under psychological surveillance; and the computer systems which threatened to multiply the capacity of organizational authorities to collect and manipulate information about the individual's personal history and daily activities.

Caught up by these concerns, the public moved in the late 1960s and early '70s to the kind of misunderstandings about what computer usage was currently doing to civil liberties that we analyzed in part three. For a time, the computer was treated in a good deal of public discussion as the essential villain of the piece, and there was talk about forbidding or regulating "computer databanks" as the basic remedy for the privacy-and-record-keeping problem.

From the brief historical and social analysis that we have noted, however, it is clear that debates over the uses of records and manual databanks would have become a major issue in American society even if computers had never been invented. What is being challenged are the standards and procedures being used to make judgments about people, at a time when the national social consensus is severely strained and when many new definitions of individual liberty and equality are being urged upon the legal system.

However, the reality is that computers *did* spread through the organizational world in the 1960s, and are being used more widely every day. Setting aside the incorrect assumptions and unfounded fears of many commentators on computerization, the fact is that computers have led to the creation of more effective interorganizational data networks and larger data bases than would have been feasible in the precomputer era. Computerization is encouraging greater standardization of record formats in many areas, and helping to move more complete information about individuals more swiftly through major records systems in the organizational world. Thus record systems that, as manual operations, would have been the subject of public debate are now being discussed—quite properly—in terms of their faster and more efficient computerized procedures. But, while computerization has proceeded with great speed in the past decade, there has *not* been a similar acceleration in the development of new legal rules responding to demands for greater rights of citizen access to records, specification of limits on data collection, and rules controlling the sharing of personal data among organizational entities.

There are many explanations for the dearth of new legal rules to govern the computerizing systems. Not every claim to privacy or due process deserves automatically to be ratified into law. There are complex questions of law and policy involved, and a complicated new area—computer technology—for judges, legislators, and regulatory-agency commissioners to comprehend. Furthermore, most managers, used to operating with the old standards and procedures and generally believing that they are still quite proper, are prone to make only minimal changes in behalf of civil-liberties claims unless they are directed to go further by law or official regulation.

While these realities may explain in part the slow development of new legal protections, they do not present a persuasive case for continuing this situation. We are in the midst of a major social redefinition of our organizational goals, standards, and procedures. Ours is a society that has always expected law to define and guarantee basic citizen rights, and the scope of what American society regards as *rights* and not privileges has been widened dramatically in the past decade. The time is therefore right for the consideration of new legislative and judicial measures to regulate the use of information systems, and for a variety of administrative and private actions as well. It is to the definition of a basic approach for such new policies, and an agenda of priorities for civic attention, that we now turn.

Defining Civil-Liberties Issues

We have emphasized already that it is the civil-liberties aspects of organizational record-keeping that represent our mandated focus, not the broader sociopolitical questions. The latter involve major issues of our time, such as changes in the distribution of wealth and political power, the direction of our foreign and military policies, new social welfare and work programs, relations between whites and nonwhites, the reshaping of urban life, evolution of new life styles, etc. In a very real sense, the evolution of new standards and procedures for making judgments about individuals that will command general support in the nation will come only with the emergence of new political consensus on such matters, a development that may or may not take place in the near future. For those who see a sharpening of the present social and political crisis as the only course that will bring the changes they seek, defining rules to protect individual rights in the existing organizational world may seem a useless, even counterproductive activity.

However, it has been a tenet of American constitutionalism that the protection and enhancement of civil liberties is *particularly* important in times of social and political crisis. It is through the full protection of dissent and the securing of effective due process that civil libertarians believe American society can rearrange its sociopolitical institutions with the greatest fidelity to democratic will. This notion does not rest on the premise that the transition will be peaceful since such changes in established power and position do not take place without focused strength and political force from, and significant confrontation by, the movements for change. But the civil-liberties position is that repression of dissenters is not only morally wrong in a democratic society but also likely to produce antidemocratic outcomes such as the development of fundamentally repressive institutions, the spread of violent revolutionary groups, and the thorough alienation of large segments of the population.

How the main lines of a civil-liberties approach would be applied to the databank problem can be illustrated by returning to the three aspects of individual rights in record systems that we have been using throughout this report—privacy, confidentiality, and due process.

1. First, in terms of privacy, a general policy should be to extend the zones of personal and group freedom from compulsory data collection so that matters that ought not to be considered in making decisions about individuals do not become part of the formal records at all. In this sense, privacy is the primary civil-liberties issue, since both confidentiality and due-process questions disappear if the data are not gathered in the first place, or once they are destroyed. Not only should the need for and relevance of specific items of personal data have to be established in positive

terms but serious consideration should be given to whether some entire record-keeping programs deserve to be continued at all; this was the basic question raised about the army's domestic intelligence watch over civilian political activity in the late 1960s.[2] A further consideration where the need for collecting data is at issue is whether records should be retained beyond their period of likely use for the purposes for which they were originally collected.

A related but more complicated question concerns the continued existence in files of information which is no longer supposed to be used for making decisions about individuals. Many cumulative records about individuals in various sectors of the organizational world are filled with facts and evaluations set down in an earlier time, under a different sociopolitical ethos. In this setting, it is not enough to say "from now on we will not. . .''; steps need to be taken to remove from historical records in high schools, colleges, commercial reporting agencies, law-enforcement files, and other organizations the personal information previously gathered about political, racial, cultural, and sexual matters that would not be put in the files under present rules. To the extent that evaluators today have such records to consult, especially for decisions that are not visible to the individual, the presence of such information represents a dead (and improper) hand from the past.

2. A second principal civil-liberties policy would require the provision of greater rights of access by individuals to the records maintained about them. This speaks to several strands of the current challenges—to those who are presently weak or powerless members of society and need to be assured with their own rights of inspection that the programs affecting them are fairly administered; to those members of minority groups who want assurance that the formal policies of racial, religious, and sexual equality that have been declared by law are really being carried out by organizations; and to those citizens such as criminal offenders, drug addicts, mental patients, etc., whose opportunity to contest the records used to make judgments about them in custodial or punishment-centered institutions may well be a way to help develop the kind of new humanistic and participative settings that rehabilitation will require.

3. Finally, new rules for data sharing and confidentiality need to be fashioned. We saw that sharing of information about individ-

---

[2] See "Federal Data Banks, Computers and the Bill of Rights," *Hearings before the Subcommittee on Constitutional Rights of the Committee on the Judiciary*, U.S. Senate, 92d Cong., 1st Sess., 1971.

uals among various organizational realms has been widespread, often goes on unknown and unconsented to by the individual involved, and is sometimes in direct violation of the promises of confidentiality under which he had supplied the information originally. We noted the worthy social objectives that are cited in support of such information sharing, and some of these may well survive a full public policy discussion of when information should or should not be shared. But a full-dress and open consideration of these boundaries of confidentiality is what public policy requires at a time when computerization is circulating personal data more swiftly and efficiently and will be able to do so with even greater cost-effectiveness in the later 1970s. To the extent that American citizens come to believe that organizational employees and managers have a greater loyalty to the "buddy system's" definition of the need for sharing than to the promises made to individuals within each realm, and set by law, we will be setting the stage for serious troubles in the coming years.

We will return to a more complete analysis of these three civil-liberties areas shortly. Our goal here was to show how they relate to the sociopolitical debates over databanks, and why it is essential under our constitutional traditions that we address these issues of policy seriously in the coming years.[3]

Some Preliminary Observations

Some of our studies and findings shed useful light on current proposals for control of databanks, by suggesting where it would be either unrealistic or unwise to apply certain approaches. For example, given the great diversity of record-keeping goals, practices, and content that we have shown to characterize organizational life; given the fact that not all record-keeping systems present the same issues of civil liberties; and given the fact that the social balance between individual privacy claims and organizational needs for information shifts markedly from one record-keeping area to another, and through different periods of national life, it appears clear to us that no single law, constitutional amendment, or court decision can cope with the tremendous diversity of issues and settings, and the uneven readiness for

---

[3] We asked our survey respondents to comment on what needs for new administrative, legal, and technological safeguards they see as important. Their responses are discussed in Appendix A, pages 453-458 below.

corrective action, that make up the current databank problem. Such total solutions are not worth pursuing. There are some important policy actions covering broad segments of record-keeping that may be called for, and we will discuss these shortly. But a healthy skepticism toward all-at-once remedies is strongly suggested by our studies.

Some commentators have also suggested that it would be helpful to create a national study commission on the computers and civil-liberties problem, to make recommendations for public policy. We do not think this would be a useful step. We already know the present impact of computerization and have a picture of what is foreseeable in the near future; our need at this point is to initiate new laws and other civic interventions that will bring organizational practices into line with new social values and civil-liberties claims, and will resolve record-keeping issues of long standing in several fields.

During the recent databank discussion it has been proposed that a special supervisory institution be created at each level of American government to oversee the creation of all computerized systems so that proper civil-liberties safeguards will be installed. Any government agency automating its files would have to disclose its plans to the supervisory body, establish its need to gather the personal data involved, and demonstrate the adequacy of its confidentiality, access, and security procedures.

If the supervisory agency were really given the power to decide whether departments could computerize or not, what personal information they "needed" and would thus be allowed to collect and share, and how they were to use information to make evaluative decisions about the individuals covered by their programs, the agency would be exercising enormous power. Realistically, it would have to be set up to reflect existing political forces, with its appointees reflecting many interests other than those of civil liberties. Even if it were given a strong mandate to pay attention to issues of privacy, confidentiality, access, and security, there is no guarantee that its decisions would be any more sensitive to these interests than the executive agencies, congressional committees, and courts that would consider these questions under existing governmental practices.

However, where there are special projects in which government is consolidating information in multiagency databanks, or in jurisdictionwide information systems projects, some combination of citizen advisory group and ombudsmanlike official deserves serious attention. Such an approach was recently adopted in

Wichita Falls, Texas, which is trying to develop a "total unified information system" of the central databank type under a federal grant from the Department of Housing and Urban Development. As part of its obligation to formulate a "data access control plan," the city passed an ordinance in February 1972 creating a "Data Access Advisory Board" of five members appointed by the mayor and confirmed by the city's board of aldermen, and the position of "data registrar," defined as a city employee "of substantial responsibility" to be appointed by and report directly to the city manager. Information "identifiable to any particular person" is to be released only to someone with a "legitimate need to know" such information. The data registrar is authorized to receive and pass on requests for release of information beyond that which it is "normal routine" for city departments to share or which is "information that has been traditionally available to the general public." If requests are granted, the data registrar must keep a record of each, including the name of the party requesting it, date, purpose, etc.

The Data Access Advisory Board is empowered to "advise" the registrar and aldermen "regarding controls and policies affecting release of information," in "establishing criteria to determine the 'need to know' test" and to "consider any expansion of the data base which will result in acquisition and storage of data not previously maintained by the city." The ordinance also gives any person "on whom data is accumulated" the right to review his record and "correct any inaccurate data," with "any questioned data frozen with respect to dissemination for a reasonable time until the accuracy or inaccuracy . . . is established." Special rules are specified for release of information from the departments of vital statistics, police, fire prevention, and public health.

Another approach was taken in one specific area—law enforcement—in a municipal ordinance passed by Berkeley, California, in December 1971, creating a citizens' committee to supervise privacy and security aspects of a microfilm criminal-history record file being set up by city police under a federal grant. The City Council resolution limits the system to recording convictions or guilty pleas for 11 specified serious crimes; excludes "unverified data such as that emanating from intelligence sources"; gives the individual a right to inspect his record and a procedure for challenging its accuracy or completeness; and generally limits access to the system to criminal-justice personnel and to defense counsel or the Public Defender for the defendant involved in any single case. A citizens' Committee on Records, Access, Privacy, and Retention is created to review and approve the initial procedures created and to make special audits of the system's operation every six months. (The committee is required to include one member of the police department, one city council member, one civil-liberties representative from the local American Civil Liberties Union chapter, one member of the "general public," and one person possessing expertise in computer science, but not an employee of the city.) The ordinance provides that no information from the Berkeley police file shall be "integrated into any computerized information exchange system" until the City Council obtains "a detailed list of technical and administrative safeguards for individual privacy and security" in that system and the council gives express approval to the exchange.

Outside the areas where special files or central databank projects might prompt such controls, the importance of considering civil-liberties issues when automation of files is being planned and installed suggests that some form of continuing legislative review of executive-agency computerization deserves consideration. For example, government operations committees or judiciary committees of the federal, state, and local legislatures might well create standing subcommittees that would take computerization and civil-liberties protections as a subject of continuing inquiry. With a legislative resolution authorizing a review of all automation of personal-information files, and provision of adequate funds and staff to ensure the necessary skills for such a subcommittee, such bodies could require appearances by executive agencies planning to go forward with major computer applications. The plans could be studied to make sure that the issues of minimizing intrusive questioning, providing adequate confidentiality and security measures, and affording individual access to records for challenge and correction had been properly weighed by the executive agency. Witnesses from public interest groups and affected segments of the population would also be able to participate in the hearings. It is true that reviews of this kind now take place, with varying degrees of formality, in the authorization and appropriations committee hearings of legislatures, and in occasional inquiries by constitutional rights committees (such as Senator Ervin's 1971 hearings). But if one recognizes that computerization of files and development of new computer applications are going to be continuing, expanding aspects of government agency activity in the coming years, there is much to support the view that legislatures should have standing committees to pay steady, expert attention to the civil-liberties aspects of this process.

To mention one last preliminary topic, the project looked at foreign experience with computerization in almost two dozen nations, to see whether significant rules or institutions for dealing with civil-liberties interests in computerized record systems are evolving that might serve as models for adaptation to the American scene. The results of our survey are reported in Appendix C. We found that computerization of government and private record systems is going forward actively in many of these countries, but there have been no *national* laws or major court decisions as yet redefining individual rights in computerized record systems. Some local statutes have been enacted, study commissions are at work in several nations, and proposals for protection of citizen rights are under active consideration in the legislatures of almost a dozen countries. But the situation in 1972 is that there are no models of national legislation for the United States to look to; countries such as Britain, Canada, France, West Germany, Sweden, and others are at precisely the position that the United States finds itself in the mid-1970s: moving from recognition of a significant problem to the formulation of policies to cope with it wisely and effectively.

Areas of Priority
for Public Policy

In the remainder of the chapter, we take up six areas of priority for public policy. In the first three, we discuss possible measures by courts and legislatures that would increase safeguards for due process, confidentiality, and privacy in record systems; while the discussions involve issues that would generally apply whether the record systems are computerized or manual, the analysis concentrates on civil-liberties problems that are growing particularly acute as a result of computer usage. The remaining three areas of priority we treat involve increasing technological protections for computerized information systems, use of the Social Security number as a universal identifier, and new institutions for the management of sensitive record systems.

The Citizen's Right
to See His Record

In this section, we review the reasons why giving an individual the right to see and contest his record has become more important in the past decade, what role the courts may play in defining for individuals a constitutional right of access, and legislative approaches that might be taken to provide an effective general right of access in government files.

Under American law, an individual does not have a *constitutional* right to see and contest the record about him contained in an agency file unless it is brought into a formal proceeding affecting his legal rights. He might be given various opportunities for access to his record by the statute setting up a particular government program, or as part of a general public-record statute designating the government files open to any member of the public. Or he might be given an opportunity to examine all or part of his file as a matter of the agency's own administrative rules. On the other hand, statutes or administrative rules might explicitly deny the individual a right to see his own file in a particular agency or type of government program. Such restrictions have been upheld by the courts in the interest of protecting secret sources of information, ensuring frank evaluations by professionals, and on similar grounds. Furthermore some reports about the individual or some information drawn from a file maintained about him by a government agency can be used in an official proceeding without being disclosed to the individual because they have been designated as "confidential" by rule of the hearing body or by statute. Examples include the presentencing and probation reports about convicted persons prepared for judges, the reports of prison officials used in parole proceedings, and reports from caseworkers used in adoption and welfare proceedings. The courts have upheld such closed-file policies, reasoning that protection of the identity of informants or the need to foster frank disclosures by reporting sources had to take precedence in such instances over the individual's right to know the contents of such reports about him.

Closed-file policies have come under increasing attack. Organizations reflecting the interests of many consumers, women, students, the poor, minority groups, servicemen, and others are asserting that decisions affecting their rights and interests should be made with more disclosure of the facts which entered into the decision and the criteria that were applied. Demands for individual access also arise from a lessening of faith that professionals always make objective decisions in the best interests of their clients in fields such as welfare, probation, clinical psychology, psychiatry, and education. Where groups challenging the prevailing social and political leadership are involved, and where decision makers are operating in public bureaucracies under tremendous pressures of time and limited fiscal resources that may preclude the best profesfesional procedures, the claim to access assumes pivotal importance.

There has also been increased concern in American civic life about the mere *holding* of information about individuals in organizational files. Not all actions against or in the interests of individuals are accomplished through formal proceedings in which existing legal rights of inspection can come into play. It is assumed that if inaccurate, incomplete, or biased information is in an individual's record, it can be used without his or her knowledge for decisions by government and private organizations which have access to the files. In matters such as promotion and assignment to jobs, discretionary prosecutive decisions (whether or not to seek an indictment in law enforcement), selection of individuals for services or benefits in supplemental and pilot government programs, and in many other situations the content of an individual's record can be examined by evaluators; their decisions may have important consequences, totally without the person's knowledge of the role which information in the record has played.

Concern has also been focused on giving individuals greater knowledge about the *circulation* of their individual records within government or between government and private agencies, even though no formal proceedings may have yet arisen, as when fingerprints and "rap sheet" information are routinely forwarded from local police agencies to the FBI immediately after arrest but before disposition of a case.

The growing pressures for the establishment of individual access rights have already produced changes in administrative practice and law. We saw that law-enforcement agencies such as the FBI and many state and local police departments have moved (usually under pressure from the courts and civic groups) to provide individuals with a right to inspect their summary criminal-history records and to question the accuracy and completeness of these. The passage of federal and state fair credit reporting acts in the past two years gave individuals a right to be told the contents of commercial reports that have been used to deny them credit, insurance, or employment and established procedures for rectifying errors in such reports, or noting the existence of disputed items of information. Ensuring individuals access to their records is therefore a major priority for public policy. The central questions, of course, are who should define such a right of access, what should be its scope and limits, what procedures should be set for its exercise, and how can its proper enforcement be ensured?

POSSIBLE ROLES FOR THE COURTS IN DEFINING NEW ACCESS RIGHTS

Courts may well extend constitutional due-process requirements to cover some important aspects of the right-to-access issue. In 1971, a case presenting such an opportunity came before the U.S.

Supreme Court.[1] Mrs. Catherine Tarver was receiving welfare support from the Department of Social and Health Services of the state of Washington, under the Federal Aid to Families with Dependent Children (AFDC) program. Her caseworker prepared a highly critical report, which included derogatory comments about Mrs. Tarver, allegations of child neglect, and a recommendation that she be permanently deprived of the custody of her children. Because Mrs. Tarver was hospitalized, custody was temporarily taken over by the juvenile court, but a subsequent hearing in that court produced a decision "exonerating" Mrs. Tarver and leaving her in custody of her children. (Another caseworker told Mrs. Tarver that the file contained false information about her.)

Neither Mrs. Tarver nor her lawyer ever got to see the caseworker's report that was presented in juvenile court. The report remained in the files of the Department of Social and Health Services, a "confidential and privileged" document to be used for "purposes directly connected with the administration of public assistance."

Mrs. Tarver asked the department for a hearing to learn the contents of the report and remove false information from it. This was refused. She then brought suit in state court, with aid from the local American Civil Liberties Union, alleging that the report would be consulted by caseworkers and other welfare officials, and was available to other state agencies in the social services field with whom she might have dealings. Her argument was rejected by the Washington state courts, on the ground that state law did not permit hearings in such hypothetical cases.

When the case was carried to the U.S. Supreme Court, only two of the four justices required to accept the case for hearing voted to do so; this action left standing the state court ruling. However, the decision did not constitute a Supreme Court approval of the state decision, and what is useful for our purposes is the opinion by Justices Douglas and Brennan explaining why they thought the case should have been reviewed.

Justice Douglas began by noting that "The ability of the government and private agencies to gather, retain, and catalogue information on anyone for their unfettered use raises problems concerning the privacy and dignity of individuals." Noting that "the problems of a computerized society with large databanks are immense," the Justice stated that the Tarver appeal presented the fundamental issue of "what mechanisms ought there to be for

---

[1] *Tarver* v. *Smith*. 29 L. Ed. 2d 1966 (1971).

correcting factual errors?" In her case, "The one thing perfectly clear from this record is that petitioner has no rights under state law to a hearing to correct the reports even if they are total lies. And it appears petitioner will never be informed prior to transmittal of her file to the various 'authorized' groups."

To the state's arguments that welfare officials will know that the report is only an opinion, that the juvenile court decree is also in the file, and that the file "will be treated confidentially," Justice Douglas replied that the agency would still be making decisions as to whether Mrs. Tarver is a person likely "to benefit" under Work-Incentive Programs by consulting a case file containing a report that Mrs. Tarver alleges to be false. Denying Mrs. Tarver a hearing in this circumstance, Justice Douglas said, raises "an important question of procedural due process . . . under the Fourteenth Amendment. For petitioner's right to continued assistance—an important property interest—cannot be reduced or terminated without notice and an opportunity to be heard." For Justices Douglas and Brennan, this raised a question of "national importance" that they felt the Court should have considered.[2]

The denial of certiorari in the *Tarver* case does not necessarily mean that Justice Douglas' position was rejected by the Court's majority; it may have been the cloudy state of the facts developed in the lower court, or other special factors, that led seven justices to decline to hear this particular case. What the *Tarver* case suggests to us is that lower and appellate courts have an important role to play in the development of new individual access rules. As test cases are brought by guardian groups, the courts can—and should—redefine the existing law governing agency and legislative

---

[2] Justice Douglas might have cited Franz Kafka's account of how secret records are retained after one official proceeding has delivered an acquittal. In *The Trial*, "K," who has been arrested for a crime but not told the nature of the charge, asks a friend what would take place among the "courts" of the novel after an "ostensible acquittal" might be obtained.

"The whole dossier continues to circulate, as the regular official routine demands, passing on to the higher Courts, being referred to the lower ones again, and thus swinging backwards and forwards with greater or smaller oscillations, longer or shorter delays. These peregrinations are incalculable. A detached observer might sometimes fancy that the whole case had been forgotten, the documents lost, and the acquittal made absolute. No one really acquainted with the Court could think such a thing. No document is ever lost, the Court never forgets anything. One day—quite unexpectedly—some Judge will take up the documents. . . ." "And the case begins all over again?" asked K. almost incredulously. "Certainly," said the painter.

The Trial, by Franz Kafka, pages 198-199. Copyright 1937 and renewed 1965 by Alfred A. Knopf, Inc.

definitions of file confidentiality. The ideal rule would declare that hearings on the accuracy of records must be afforded, as a matter of due process, when a record is preserved by government agencies in a situation where there are continuing determinations of an individual's rights and benefits, and where the individual can show that there are grounds to believe that his record contains inaccurate information. Such a ruling would have a salutary effect on the legislative process (by prompting legislators to reconsider access and hearing rules) and on administrative practice (since agencies would know that the courts would be reviewing denials of access to one's file along due-process lines).

The adoption of such a position by the courts is by no means certain, of course, and it would take time to develop as test cases were brought and carried through appeals. Furthermore, while the courts could specify situations in which rights of access and contest could not be constitutionally denied, it is not their function to work out the necessary details as to scope, procedures, and safeguards for such access in executive agencies and departments. This suggests that legislation still needs to be the immediate focus of policy action, even if assistance is forthcoming from the courts.

LEGISLATIVE TREATMENT OF ACCESS RIGHTS

We saw in the profiles that each field of organizational life has evolved distinctive traditions as to the files that are open to individual access and those the contents or even the existence of which are kept from him.[3] With a growing concern that these boundaries unduly favor organizational goals and convenience over the due-process interests of the individual, two main legislative approaches have recently been proposed to redefine those boundaries. One is to lay out new access rights in statutes specific to particular fields of government activity or private record systems. We saw this in passage of the state and federal fair credit reporting acts, and this approach is illustrated in pending congressional bills to permit an individual to see his arrest record in any federal or federally aided law-enforcement agency.[4] The other approach would have a comprehensive statute enacted at the federal, state,

---

[3] In this regard, see also the analysis of our survey findings, pages 437-439 below.

[4] H.R. 13315 (Congressman Edwards), 92d Congress, 2d Session, 1972; the "Arrest Record Security and Privacy Act."

or local level to give individuals a general right of access to records held about them in all agencies of government in that jurisdiction, with some exceptions and under designated procedures. Bills of this sort have been proposed recently in Congress[5] and the state of California.[6]

Both approaches require legislators to appreciate the consequences of giving—or not giving—individuals greater rights of access than they now have. Thus our discussion centers on what the findings of our study lead us to suggest to policy makers considering these issues.

First of all, our studies of organizations suggest that *files* are the appropriate unit for defining access rules, not *agencies*. In general, it helps to speak of three general classes of files based on the *uses* to which the information in them are put. *Administrative* files are those used to service, license, regulate, or prosecute specific individuals. *Research* files are used to produce reports for planning, policy evaluation, or general scientific studies and not for decisions about specific individuals. (They may contain either statistical or identified data.) *Intelligence* files are closed (secret) records used for investigative purposes, either compiled preparatory to a decision whether to prosecute or take other administrative action, or as part of long-range monitoring of activities which the agency defines as being "of law-enforcement interest."

Although there may be a few government agencies as a whole that compile identified records on people which the legislature might decide to exempt entirely from access rights (the CIA for example), these are very few. For example, because individuals should have rights of access to their summary criminal-history records, access statutes must include such files; the fact that some of these records are held by the FBI ought to make no difference. The same policy would be true for military agencies, the Treasury Department, state police forces, or local waterfront commissions.

Secondly, the concept of access involves three elements of protection for the individual: *notice* (whether he is informed that a record about him exists); *inspection* (whether he can learn the contents of the record if he wishes to); and *challenge* (whether he can obtain a formal hearing and make higher appeals to contest the accuracy, completeness, or appropriateness of the informa-

---

[5] H.R. 9527 (Congressman Koch) and S. 975 (Senator Bayh), 92d Congress, 1st Session, 1971; the "Citizen's Privacy Act."

[6] A. B. 2643 and A. B. 2933, California Assembly, 1971 Regular Session.

tion). It is helpful to discuss the key issues and possible measures that might be taken on each of these matters.

Notice

It has been suggested that legislation require all government agencies at the federal, state, and local levels to send a notice to each individual on whom they presently have a record, notifying him of its existence. Given the report of a Senate subcommittee in 1967 that there were 3.1 *billion* person-records on individual citizens in federal files,[7] we should realize that such a requirement for federal agencies alone would produce a blizzard of paper.

Such legislation would be even more catastrophic if legislators were to adopt another frequently mentioned suggestion, that the individual be sent a notice by government agencies each time a new piece of derogatory or unfavorable information were added to his record. The implementation of such proposals would entail great expense, severe logistical problems and, more importantly, might not at all serve to keep the citizen well informed about the creation and use of records in government. As a practical and political reality, for instance, investigative and intelligence files would most probably *not* be included; as a result, there would be little protection for the individual if these sensitive files were misused. Further, receipt of periodic notices concerning entries to 10 or 20 administrative files might prove more confusing than informative for the individual. Finally, we have seen many times in the course of the privacy debate of the past ten years that the record-keeping agency and the individual concerned may not share the same concept as to what information is "derogatory"—especially in cases where the personal data can move outside the organization which collected them in the first place.

Instead of these unrealistic and unnecessarily cumbersome procedures, we think two vital steps might be taken for keeping the citizen usefully informed. First, a Citizen's Guide to Files could be compiled and issued free of charge (or at a very small fee) by every jurisdiction of American government. This Guide to Files would contain a listing for every government agency, specifying the nature and content of each of its files containing information about individuals; the statutory authority for its maintenance; the class and number of persons covered; the types of information contained in it; the uses to which the file is put; whether identified

---

[7] *Government Dossier: Survey of Information contained in Government Files*, Subcommittee on Administrative Practice and Procedure, Committee on the Judiciary, U.S. Senate, 90th Congress, 1st Session, 1967.

information from the file is shared and, if so, with whom, and under what authority; whether the individual has access to all or part of his record in the file; and similar information. The emphasis in such a booklet would be on clearly written, detailed descriptions so that sensitive files of information would not be masked by the general nature of a description or lost in a trailing "et cetera." Files on individuals maintained by regulatory agencies and congressional committees would also be covered.

To ensure its effective initial preparation and regular updating, the Guide ought to be produced under the supervision of a legislative committee at each level of jurisdiction, such as the Government Operations Committees of the Congress. Having this done by the legislature would provide the necessary legal and political bases for ensuring executive-agency compliance.

In considering whether the Guide would list files about individuals held by investigative and intelligence agencies, we start with the principle that at least a general description ought to be required for every file about individuals kept by agencies of a democratic government. There may be a few files so sensitive that notice of their very existence would harm the national interest; to deal with those rare instances, a procedure could be established to have the legislative committee in charge of the Guide make a determination as to whether such was the case, on petition by the executive agency involved and in a closed proceeding. Unwarranted attempts at secrecy would thus be opened to challenges from legislators as to the need for the file itself and for closing it off from public view.

The great value of a general Guide to Files is that it would provide the citizen with a thorough, detailed, and nontechnical directory of the record systems that contain information about him, and the general rules under which it is being held and used. If the Guide were to be distributed by public groups and in schools and colleges, it would supply Americans with some extremely useful indications of how government action affects them directly. In an age of record-keeping, it would go a long way not only toward showing the citizen that legislatures were performing their duty to keep executive government in the open but would also provide a means for seeing to it that executive agencies were conducting their record-keeping operations about the citizen under law, and subject to public review.

The second step needed to provide citizens with better notice is to redesign government data-collection forms so that the individual learns several critical pieces of information at the time that he is asked to supply data about himself. Forms or accompanying instruction sheets could note whether supplying the information is mandatory or voluntary, the authority under which the information is collected, what use is to be made of the data, how they would be kept, with whom they would be shared, and what rights of access the individual has to examine his record in that file. There seems no reason why this kind of information should not be included on annual income-tax forms, Social Security application forms, on a form given out at the time of arrest and fingerprinting, or when a person begins receiving welfare assistance. Such a general summary could be given in a few lines and would not represent either an administrative burden or a financial cost of any consequence. Citizens could be referred to the Guide to Files for more detailed information.

Encountering on a form even a brief statement concerning other agencies with whom data from the form might be shared would serve to remind the citizen about the existence of files in these agencies. Legislatures concerned with the citizen's right of notice could provide that individuals would not be required by law to supply information to any government agency on a form which did not have such information on it.

Inspection

The general principle that should guide the inspection aspect of access legislation is that any record about an individual which is consulted by government officials in the determination of the individual's rights, opportunities, and benefits under a government program should be open to inspection. The value of such an initial principle is that it provides a means of distinguishing *administrative* files (which would be open to inspection) from those held and used solely for *intelligence* or *research* purposes (where inspection would not be automatically granted). Why we set the general principle and why it is limited to administrative files deserves careful explanation.

Where an individual knows that there is a record maintained about him (that is, where the fact of the particular record's existence is not itself secret, as in surveillance files), resistance to allowing rights of inspection generally proceeds on one of three grounds: that the organization needs to protect itself from being observed by its record subjects, that the reporting and evaluation process will be damaged if individuals are allowed access, or that the individual himself might be hurt in some way by what he might learn from his own file.

Though managers and employees generally want to be fair, they have an almost instinctive desire to do as much of their "background" or "kitchen" work as possible free from the pressures on the organization that arise when individuals can see what went into the file and how it was used. Behind the formal definition of how decisions are made in any government agency or private organization are the realities of imperfect procedures and unspoken value orientations of the clerks, officials, and professionals, who stand as organizational "gatekeepers" where rights and benefits are determined. Where high-volume processing of clients or citizens is involved, the organization may not be concerned with achieving fairness or accuracy in every single case, even though there may be an overall concern that the rate of unfair decisions be kept to some minimum. Because they know that errors inevitably creep into the collection and recording of information, that all the formal requirements for completing each record cannot always be met, and that judgments about individuals are really made on a combination of formal records and the intuitive feelings of experienced personnel, organizational managers want to define themselves which records or parts of records individuals should be allowed to see.

Where this desire is all that supports denial of inspection, we think the individual's right to see his own file is the superior claim in a democratic society. An access law should start with a presumption against accepting an agency's classification of a whole file or of specific items in a record as being closed to the individual himself, with the agency bearing the burden of proving that some specific public interest justifies denying access.

We encountered two such alleged interests for refusing inspection today: the need to encourage frankness in reporting or evaluation, and the need to protect the individual himself from learning information about his status or condition that could harm him. Though these are genuine concerns, and we have no difficulty in thinking of occasional situations in which they ought to be accepted as paramount by legislators, their importance has been greatly overstated in many evaluative situations, producing procedures that leave individuals with feelings of powerlessness and the conviction that government authority is fundamentally arbitrary. This is particularly observable where individuals are in various forms of legal custody (prisoners in jails, juveniles in detention houses, persons committed as mental patients) or in dependent relationships to the authorities (children in schools, persons on welfare, residents in public housing projects).

The need to foster frank reporting and evaluation has been the basis for insulating record subjects from probation and parole reports, welfare and adoption caseworker reports, certain medical records, evaluations by teachers and professors, personnel appraisals by supervisors, and many other kinds of commentaries about the individual. At a minimum, it ought to be possible for legislators to require government agencies to set up their manual records or provide computer software so that at least the objectively verifiable portions of such now wholly secret reports could be made available to individuals. Information such as personal and employment history, military service, civic activities, criminal record, and other matters which, if inaccurately reported, could seriously damage the individual in an evaluative proceeding could thus be inspected by the individual, since these items would be separated from the more subjective opinions and comments of officials and professionals.

Some movement to open formerly secret files is already in evidence. To give one example, presentencing reports forwarded to courts by probation officers have traditionally been withheld from the individual defendant and his lawyer. The policy has been based on the desire to protect sources of information, to avoid harming family and friendship relationships when such persons supply information, and to prevent the defendant from being hurt by the revelation of psychiatric evaluations. Reliance is placed upon the training of the probation officer as a professional to know how to report and evaluate the data. However, the trend recently has been to extend access at least to the defendant's lawyer and to the defendant himself where he is acting as his own counsel. Arguments supporting this trend stress that sentencing is a vital part of the judicial proceeding affecting the individual's rights; that allowing access can lead to the clarification or refutation of factual allegations; that even though *some* probation officers are professionals, others are not, and that even professionals can misunderstand situations and introduce various kinds of bias into their accounts of the defendant's character and activities; that what are sometimes called "therapeutic" settings in fact bear greater resemblance to custodial or punishment settings in which adversary proceedings are more appropriate than reliance on more informal procedures; and the hope that "the caseworker relationship will be strengthened if the defendant can see that everyone is being aboveboard with him. Understanding the reasons underlying the probation officer's recommendation and court's order may be the first step in the treatment process."[8]

Legislatures considering the provision of such access rights will have to look at each record-keeping situation to see whether the reporting of facts and opinions that is needed for decisions about individuals would be badly retarded or whether it would simply go forward in some more careful ways that would not seriously weaken the evaluative process. Even as an experimental matter, we think the importance of increasing due-process protections for the individual argues for the provision of greater access in many now closed areas, with society looking on to see whether anything truly harmful results. For example, spokesmen for most credit bureaus and investigative reporting agencies were adamant in telling congressional committees in the 1960s that their sources would dry up if the legislature allowed the individuals affected by such reports to find out what their records contained. While the state and federal fair credit reporting acts have been in operation only about a year, banks, insurance companies, personnel departments, and other users are obviously finding ways of making judgments on the basis of the information now available to them.

As for withholding reports on the ground that the individual would be harmed by knowing certain things about himself, this seems a paternalistic concept that ought to be severely limited in application. During our site visits, we continually encountered situations in which this was given as the justification for withholding a key report that determined an individual's benefit, opportunity, or right. Preinsurance investigators argued that an applicant should not be told of an incurable or very serious disease that was uncovered in the medical exmination and reported to the insurance company. The widow of a miner killed by black lung disease was told that she could not see her deceased husband's medical file (in a Social Security claims proceeding) because it might show, for instance, that he had had a venereal disease and this fact would upset her. The results of psychological evaluations and other testing done on mental patients, children in schools, prisoners in jail, and individuals in many other types of institutional settings have been said to be potentially harmful if revealed to individuals who, not understanding the terms used, might have their self-images gravely affected.

---

[8] Benson Schaffer, "The Defendant's Right of Access to Presentence Reports," *Criminal Law Bulletin*, Vol. 3. No. 10 (1971), pp. 671-678.

We believe access could still be provided in such cases, if not to the individual himself, then surely to his own doctor, lawyer, parent, or other selected representative. Where necessary as a result of such access, the reports could frame their statements in clear English rather than professional jargon, or define and explain specialized terms, and be careful to provide qualifying remarks about any speculative hypotheses employed. Again, we can imagine instances in which the withholding of a professional report may be so clearly in the interest of the individual himself that access should not be granted. But the basic thrust of the law should be to open records to the individual's own inspection, not to ratify the wide denials of such access that exist today.

In some cases, adopting a right of access may serve to drive records and decision-making processes "underground." Where organizational managers believe strongly that records must be kept or decision criteria employed without an individual's knowledge, informal exchanges of information may develop in direct violation of law or formal administrative rules. The telephone and the social engagement may be used even more widely than they already are for collecting or sharing sensitive information. But we should not fail to set formal access rights because we know that some informal processes may arise as a result, especially where part of the goal is to prevent the *formal* recording and official circulation of certain kinds of information. In some cases, it may well be better to allow derogatory information to circulate by word of mouth than to allow it to lodge unknown and unseen by the individual reported on in the permanent record.

Along the same lines, there are also situations where the problem can be substantially reduced although not solved altogether. We may forbid businesses, for instance, to use arrest records in the process of making employment and promotion decisions. Some of the firms which formerly used such reports may deem it necessary to continue this practice and will use illegal means to get the information. But due to the inconveniences involved and after some salutary enforcement proceedings, most of the organizations will conclude that it is not worth their while to get involved in illegal transactions.

It has been suggested that inspection rights might become a liability to the individual if the record keeper assumes that the individual is responsible for the accuracy of his file, and if information is taken as "confessed to" if the individual does not come forward to see or contest it. Again, this ought not to be a roadblock to giving access. Organization officials and authorized recipients of the record should simply be told by a printed notice that the accuracy or completeness of a record is not to be assumed from the fact that an "open records" policy exists unless it is officially recorded that the individual has, after notice of the consequences, declared his record to be correct.

Several other key problems relating to inspection rights need to be considered. We said earlier that research files maintained solely for the purpose of producing aggregate and group data should not be included in access laws. Our assumption is that the individual cannot be harmed in any way through such a file when his data are not individually identifiable. If it is necessary to retain identifiers on records in such files, in order to update them with additional information at a later time, for instance, this presents important confidentiality and security problems, but not matters relating to access. As a general matter, of course, the individual should know what kind of research files are created out of administrative files to which he contributes information and should, in most circumstances, have a real choice as to whether to participate in research which requires additional data from him.

As a general principle, intelligence files would also be excluded from provisions for individual access. However, legislators must be careful to control how freely agencies are allowed to define a record system as serving intelligence rather than administrative functions. For instance, if the New York State Identification and Intelligence System makes its organized-crime intelligence file operational, uses could be made of it which would not be merely intelligence activity as we are conceiving it. Job applicants for the state liquor authority could be checked through its files, for instance, to see whether or not they had an "organized-crime background." Such a use of the files would be of a clearly administrative nature once the information was communicated outside the intelligence unit, and access rights to the information so supplied should then be provided.

Other minimum protections for individuals about whom information is recorded in intelligence files might also be devised. For example, a person who believes that his name has been put improperly into an intelligence file, as by mistaken identity, might be given a chance to raise that issue before an administrative agency or court empowered to call the investigative unit into a private hearing and raise the mistaken-identity question.

Another provision relating to intelligence files might deal with the issue of information "leaks" and the highly damaging results of government-press cooperation in violation of confidentiality or secrecy laws. Information from federal investigative files has leaked its way into the hands of "investigative reporters" favored by government officials, who then publish the gist (or even quote from) the files in stories about citizens. Because of the protections against libel actions given to published reports dealing with public figures, such individuals are left without effective remedies. The individual has not been prosecuted or regulated by government, so the intelligence file has not been made "administrative" and therefore subject to discovery procedures or cross-examination as to its sources or contents. The only relief available today is disciplining the agent who made the leak, if he can be found and if he does not turn out to be a high government official or the chief of police.

One way to deal with this practice would be to include in a citizen's access statute the provision that, should any part of an intelligence file maintained by government under secrecy provisions be made public, the individual obtains a right to inspect in full the record from which such published reports were prepared, subject to court review to protect undercover agents or similar special sources, with the opportunity to contest in some tribunal the validity of the information.

A final word about inspection. At least where government files are concerned, we think inspection should mean the right of the individual to see a copy or display of the actual record in full, and to obtain an official copy of it for a nominal fee. Having an official describe the contents of the record to the individual but not let him examine it himself (as is done under the Fair Credit Reporting Act) does not meet the test of openness or provide the psychological sense of having satisfied oneself about what is really there.

Challenge

Once inspection has occurred, an individual should be given by law a proper succession of remedies for contesting the accuracy, completeness, or propriety of information he finds there. Where his position is not accepted by the record keeper, the first formal proceeding would be an administrative hearing provided by the agency. Appeals from agency decisions ought to go, we suggest, to a Board of Citizens Access Rights created by each level of government to hear appeals from the various agencies. Such a board should be made up of representatives from the executive branch, the legislature, and the public. Final appeal would be to the courts.

To be responsive to citizen rights while not unduly impeding vital programs of government, such statutes would obviously have to fashion careful definitions and procedures. But it is a fact of national life that citizens *are* worried about what information government has about them and how it is used; the provision of access rights would meet those concerns with genuine reform. After an initial flurry we suspect that only a very small number of persons would be likely to seek access to their record in any given period, and this does not seem an unbearable burden for government to pay to foster greater trust among its citizenry. Furthermore, achieving the degree of openness and visibility that such access laws would create would be a good way for a democratic society to work on the sociopolitical issues involved in its allocative processes. For example, disguised or hidden criteria as to race, sex, political or cultural beliefs, and other discriminatory standards have been declared improper by recent legal enactments; with due-process protections, individuals will be better able to see whether such criteria are really being rejected in practice.

While subtle discrimination in decision making is not easily observed, access by the individual to his own record can be an important step in the discovery process. The very existence of a document concerning the political activities of an applicant in the files of an organization which is not supposed to be taking such matters into account may be an important fact for the individual to have in the cause of trying to figure out how decisions about himself were made. Similarly, the discovery that an item of information was reported by a commercial preemployment reporting agency may be an important step in determining what information was actually *used* by the employer for his decision. (In many cases, of course, access by the individual to his own file is not the critically important protection. To deal with discrimination on the basis of sex or race, for instance, statistical studies are often required.) While we have limited our analysis to government files, believing that these should have immediate priority, passage of access laws in this realm could have a pronounced and positive "ripple effect" on record-keeping policies in the private sphere as well. They could serve as models for legislative or regulatory-agency action covering the private sector in the same reciprocal way that enactment of the fair credit reporting acts in commercial reporting has helped point the way for new access laws in the public sector.

We have had nothing to say about computers as such in this analysis of access rights. This reflects one of our clearest findings:

officials using computerized record systems are at least as capable as the managers of manual systems of following legal and administrative directives as to notice, inspection, and challenge. Indeed we assume that computer technology could be used in many positive ways to enhance the civil-liberties goals set out here: to compile and update the Citizen's Guide to Government Files; to keep the notification clauses on government data-collection forms up to date; to make it easier to separate those parts of records legally open for access from those that are closed by law; to keep track of data sharing from each record, where this is required; to make data available to legislators, guardian groups, the board of access rights, and the courts on refusals of each agency to grant individual rights of access; and in many other ways to supply information resources to those concerned with seeing to it that the citizen access laws are vigorously administered.

Rules for Confidentiality and Data-Sharing

In the area of confidentiality and data sharing, we begin with a discussion of trends in judicial supervision of this aspect of government record-keeping. Then, to illustrate the importance of these issues being carefully and fully considered in the legislative process when new record systems are created, we present a case study of pending national welfare reform proposals, followed by some observations about other record systems that also merit legislative attention regarding confidentiality rules.

As in the due-process area, we can expect the courts to become more active during the next few years in examining sensitive record systems to see whether they have proper rules as to confidentiality and data sharing. We saw in the FBI profile that the federal district court in the *Menard* case took explicit note of the computerization of arrest and conviction records that was going forward in the FBI's National Crime Information Center. Judge Gesell cited the added efficiency brought by computerization as a factor which deepened the necessity for insisting that proper standards of data sharing and confidentiality be ratified by Congress and that more effective security controls over misuse be provided, if the system were not to raise grave questions about violation of the citizen's personal rights. He did not suggest that the danger to civil liberties was caused by computerization. But the ongoing development of NCIC helped convince Judge Gesell that Congress ought not to let the system continue its forward march without explicit consideration of the standards and safeguards under which arrest and conviction records would be disseminated.

The outlook of the *Menard* case embodies our basic recommendation as to the policies needed to protect confidentiality in record systems. It will no longer be acceptable in a society that wants organizations to keep the promises of confidentiality they have made—or that the law has demanded—for officials to manage inadequately regulated and controlled record systems. Our findings documented the existence of organizational data sharing in violation of law or organizational rules, information "buddy system" exchanges that were either tacitly approved by the record-holding organization, or achieved in clandestine fashion by employees and outside parties.[9] Where the fault lies with insufficiently clear or detailed policy directives, these must be reformulated. Where the fault is with inadequate administrative supervision and enforcement mechanisms, those must be revised. And where technological safeguards are required to give effect to those confidentiality rules, society has a right to insist that safeguards be installed appropriate to the dangers involved.

This will clearly require a system-by-system, agency-by-agency analysis of confidentiality and data-sharing policies, with legislatures and courts looking over the shoulders of government officials and private record keepers to see that the responses are adequate. To demonstrate the kinds of issues that must be considered, we have selected one problem as a case study, the development of national welfare reform legislation and the record-keeping problems that this promises to present.

During the period 1968-72, proposals to reorganize welfare programs in the United States were a major concern in the White House, Congress, and legislatures at the city and state level. Three major proposals were debated in this period, a Nixon administration bill, a more liberal Democratic version offered by Sen. Abraham Ribicoff, and a more conservatively oriented measure sponsored by Sen. Russell Long. As of early June 1972, it was not clear whether any one or a mixture of these proposals would be enacted by the ninety-second Congress, but there was a consensus that

---

[9] See the FBI, Kansas City, New York Motor Vehicle Department, and Santa Clara County Profiles, as well as the discussion of data sharing in part three.

some form of national welfare reform program would be passed by Congress before much longer.

Under the administration bill, some 10.5 million persons who are not currently receiving assistance under any federal program would be eligible for welfare, increasing the total rolls to approximately 26 million. Social Security and Medicare benefits would be increased, with income support for those who fell below a new federal income minimum. Major assistance programs for the blind, the aged, and the disabled would be shifted from HEW to the Social Security Administration. The current Aid to Families with Dependent Children (AFDC) program would be revised, placing some 2.6 million families with an adult able to work or receive training under an Opportunities for Families Program to be administered by the Department of Labor. HEW would administer a Family Assistance Plan for another 1.4 million families (primarily mothers with young children).

The administration bill would "federalize" the welfare function to a substantial degree, particularly where record-keeping and the determination of eligibility are concerned. Two broad principles would underlie the administration's approach:

Work Requirements

The benefits of many welfare recipients would be tied to eligibility for and willingness to work. Mothers with children over six years of age, and all others over 16 and neither disabled nor in school, would either have to work or be registered for training and job placement with the Department of Labor. The decision as to ability to work would be made by the Labor Department, not county or state welfare workers. Those refusing to work, to register for training, or to accept treatment if found to have alcohol or drug problems would have their benefits cut off. For many poor persons, the work-eligibility features of either the administration or Long proposals would mean involvement in a new federal program in which their employment status and work-related characteristics would be monitored by federal authorities.

The Enforcement Perspective

In both the administration and the Long proposals, there is strong emphasis on catching those frequently called "welfare cheaters." The principal means of achieving "tight" enforcement would be through centralized determination of eligibility and a verification of both the recipient's identity and his answers on detailed application forms through record checks with other government agencies and third-party sources. This would represent a major change over the "declarative method" used in some states and for Medicare, in which only a small sample of the declarations of need filed by applicants are checked in order to keep the level of fraud within acceptable limits, and would also go further than the so-called "prudent person" approach recently enacted in New York, which calls for verification of those applications which show inconsistencies or gaps in the information presented.

The administration bill includes a broad provision requiring the heads of all federal executive agencies to supply whatever information is needed so that, for instance, routine checks on reported income for the past year could be made through IRS and the files of the Social Security Administration, and on whether the applicant is receiving benefits under programs of the Veterans Administration, Department of Labor, Railroad Retirement Board, Bureau of Indian Affairs, unemployment offices, etc.

Recipients in many categories would be required to submit quarterly reports of income, and it is proposed that these be routinely checked against the quarterly reports SSA requires from most employers. If an applicant is more than a month late in filing his quarterly report of income, benefits for him would automatically cease. As an additional precaution, it is proposed that many recipients be required to reapply for support every two years.

Each adult or child in the various programs would have to have a Social Security number or be assigned one. The Social Security Administration would tighten its number-issuing procedures by requiring applicants to produce birth certificates for themselves and all members of their families; from these, it is suggested that information such as place and date of birth and father's and mother's names might be lifted for future reference and possible checks against other records. It would be a federal criminal offense to supply false information to the SSA in order to mislead as to one's identity. As part of a special emphasis on getting both parents to support their children, current efforts to locate deserting parents (e.g., through IRS and SSA records) would be expanded, and it would become a new federal offense to cross state lines in order to avoid supporting a family.

The administration proposal anticipates computerized eligibility and payment files, and a team in HEW was at work in 1971-72 doing advance planning for a computer-assisted system. Given quarterly reports of income, the requirement that many recipients reapply every two years, extensive record checks with other agencies, and central disbursement of funds, a manual system would be almost impossible. Some combination of central processing centers linked via communication lines to terminals in field offices is envisioned, with a move some time in the future to on-line terminal operations for checking eligibility and entering changes in benefits.

Civil-liberties Implications

With records on more than 26 million people, a federalized welfare program with the features described above would represent the largest record system on the nation's poor and its minorities, with as much as 40 percent of the nonwhite and Spanish-surname populations included. It is clear that the basic philosophy of such a program will be a major determinant of civil-liberties problems likely to result from its administration. For example, Senator Ribicoff's proposals would alter the administration system to operate primarily through a declaration process, would reduce the size of the record on each individual, decrease the frequency with which information has to be obtained from those covered, and limit the extent of data sharing for enforcement purposes. Overall, this would lessen the scrutiny to which many of the 26 million persons covered would be subjected.

If an enforcement-oriented bill were passed, major civil-liberties issues would need to be considered. The administration bill provides that the heads of all federal agencies would supply information about individuals as this is necessary for the program's operations. Whether any information should be obtained from law-enforcement sources or from Internal Revenue Service files beyond that necessary to verify reported income is not specified. Rather than leave such issues to administrative decision, the demands to be made on various federal record systems deserve to be specified in advance, thus raising openly the appropriateness of certain data exchanges.

Another issue is the confidentiality of personal data once it has been entered on the recipient's welfare record. In terms of their use for investigative surveillance, the records of the new welfare program would be a potential resource unprecedented in scope, drawing together for the first time in central files up-to-date identifying, location, and other information presently scattered in local, state, and federal files. Whether law-enforcement officers would have access to these administrative files for investigations unrelated to administration of the welfare program deserves to be specified by Congress.

Personal information in the system will include income, assets, work history, benefits received, job training reports, paternity, alcoholism and drug-addiction reports, family-planning services received, allegations of child abuse, charges of fraud, etc. While it is unlikely that all this would be lodged in a central federal file, consideration needs to be given as to how queries from various federal, state, and local officials would be controlled, monitored, and audited in the approval centers or local offices. Also, need-to-know limitations on access to personal data within the new program's administration (by clerks, caseworkers, social workers, officials, etc.) should be required.

Another civil-liberties issue is how long data on a given individual or family should be retained. If welfare reform does succeed in getting people off welfare in the long run (as the administration suggests that it can), will participants have to fear damage in the future from release of records concerning this period of their lives? For instance, will future employers have access to information in job training or work placement files, and will they be allowed to know that a given individual received welfare assistance at one time?

There are also due-process questions. When relying on a large record system—computerized or not—when should benefits be cut off without a hearing, in reliance on the accuracy of the record system? The administration bill does not provide for hearings before terminating benefits in cases where a quarterly income report is not received in time. Senator Long's plan would cut off the benefits of an entire family without hearings where an administrator decided that the head of the family had "refused" work. In both cases, the absence of a hearing raises serious due-process questions.

Civil-liberties issues of this kind were *not* systematically addressed in any of the congressional hearings during 1970-72. The resultant bills, now under consideration, contain broad authorizations for data collection and sharing that would create one of the largest, most sensitive, and highly computerized record systems in the nation's history. Questions of civil liberties, particularly those concerning confidentiality, data sharing, and due process, ought to be of constant concern throughout the congressional hearings, drafting, amendment, and enactment processes. The fact that they have not been should be a warning that we might build large-scale record systems without installing explicit protections consistent with civil liberties interests.

Beyond the national welfare system there are several other government programs whose data sharing and confidentiality pro-

visions need legislative attention. The FBI's computerized criminal-history exchange under NCIC is an obvious candidate. Several
measures are already pending in Congress to set basic standards for
privacy and security for all state and local law-enforcement information systems funded under federal Law Enforcement Assistance
Administration grants.

    On the private side, the time would appear auspicious to
consider legislation that would define the rights of various investigative agencies (tax authorities, law enforcement, legislative committees, etc.) to obtain account records in travel and entertainment company files, credit and bank card files, customer accounts
in banks, and the growing number of "less-check" and "less-cash"
payment mechanisms that are being experimented with throughout the country.[1] If the confidentiality of these files is to be
respected (and there are also questions of associational privacy
where the accounts of political and religious organizations are
involved), there ought to be far more explicit policies to protect
civil liberties than now obtain. Today, whether or not a request by
a government agency for delivery of these records is met depends
on a decision by the organization that holds the records to provide
some restrictions on behalf of the individual record subject—
decisions as to questioning the scope of the government inquiry,
whether to insist on a subpoena or a court order, whether to
notify the record subject before complying, etc. Within the next
five to eight years, an increasing portion of the travel, entertainment, purchasing, credit, and financial transactions of the middle
and upper economic groups in America will be recorded in one of
the handful of master money cards that are expected to emerge
from the current competition among card systems. This development will make the individual's account record more comprehensive and a very inviting target for investigators of all kinds. With
that rise in sensitivity and attractiveness ought to go legislative
enactments spelling out retention and destruction policies, confidentiality rules, and procedures for protecting individual rights
when outsiders seek to obtain access for what are asserted to be
lawful and necessary purposes.

---

[1] For a report of the American Civil Liberties Union's campaign asking
banks to formulate policies and procedures to protect the confidentiality of
customer accounts, see *American Banker*, May 19, 1972.

Limiting Unnecessary
Data Collection

Deciding what personal information ought to be collected or acquired at all—the privacy question—is the broadest challenge to organizational authority and programs and is probably the hardest of the three civil-liberties interests on which to derive public policy based on a broad national consensus. Our discussion treats the general problem of defining criteria for making privacy decisions, examines prospects for judicial action in this area, and then examines legislative options by discussing, as examples, proposals for bills to protect government employees' rights of privacy, to control the sale of government name lists to commercial advertisers, and to limit the dissemination of arrest records to private and government employers.

American society has seen the necessity to impose restrictions on organizations which collect information in order to make discriminatory judgments on the basis of religion, race, nationality, and most recently as to sex. When we move beyond these, however, and the civil-liberties claim is made that certain other personal information is not truly relevant to a given decision, the policymaker must decide how he can judge what is a relevant piece of information for a national security investigation, or bearing on credit, parole, scholarships, employment suitability, etc.

Courts and legislatures are in something of a quandary where such decisions are concerned. On the one hand, it is difficult for them to justify the substitution of their own judgments for those of managers and experienced professionals in the organization whose practices are being challenged. This problem is particularly acute where the claim to privacy is that some personal characteristic ought not to be considered at all in determining a given benefit or opportunity and the public policymaker may be faced with forbidding organizations to determine such vague but important qualities as reputation, character, morality, loyalty, or talent. On the other hand, civil-liberties claims are important and are often put forward with strong and plausible challenges to the arguments of record keepers. Particularly where it is clear that within the same field or industry there are open differences of opinion as to the need for certain types of personal information, there can be little justification for courts and legislatures to accept uncritically the claims to data of some managers and officials.[2]

Some commentators have urged that the Supreme Court formulate and declare a general constitutional right of privacy from unreasonable surveillance. This could be lodged directly under the First Amendment, representing an unexpressed premise of the Founding Fathers as to the conditions required for free expression that must now be made explicit because of the increased technological and organizational capacities for keeping citizens under surveillance.

The advantages in having such a comprehensive right formulated, from a civil-libertarian standpoint, are that it would provide something of a constitutional thumb on the scale when courts were weighing the declared needs of government agencies to extract or compile sensitive personal information against the individual's claim to privacy. Useful as it might be, the effect of specific constitutional protection should not be overestimated. Courts would still have to consider, in each given type and form of government record system, whether the collection and use of the personal information was reasonable. It is not at all clear, in thinking about the judiciary's role in dealing with computer databank problems, that anything really far-reaching would be gained by judges weighing the conflicting interests under a new, generally stated First Amendment right of privacy, rather than continuing to treat privacy as a vital instrumentality for achieving expressly protected rights of free speech, press, assembly, association, and religion.

Moreover, some pessimism about the judiciary's willingness to place *constitutional* limits on government or private record systems must be derived from the recent history of court decisions about record-keeping. During the past decade, no U.S. Supreme Court ruling has dealt with individual rights to privacy and due process in record-keeping systems. Among the lower federal and state courts, there has been a relatively small number of rulings dealing episodically with these issues. One group of decisions, weighing government's need for information against protests on civil-liberties grounds, has found that the government record-keeping programs were constitutionally sound. In this group, we

---

[2] In the course of deliberation surrounding passage of the federal Fair Credit Reporting Act, it became clear that some insurance companies and employers believed strongly in the need for information of the type produced in reports by the Retail Credit Company and similar firms; but it was equally clear that many other insurers and employers saw no need for such reports.

have rulings that upheld the compulsory decennial census against persons alleging a right to refuse cooperation on personal privacy grounds,[3] and that rejected a challenge to the New York State law requiring fingerprinting and a check of criminal records for all employees in the New York brokerage industry.[4] Similarly, the New Jersey Supreme Court refused to strike down police collection and storage of detailed personal information about individuals who might engage in future civil disorders, where there had been no concrete showing that such activity created a "chilling effect" on the exercise of First Amendment rights.[5] Courts have also refused to order state motor-vehicle departments to stop selling registration lists to direct-mail advertising services, rejecting the claim that this leads to an unwarranted invasion of privacy.[6] And the courts upheld the Internal Revenue Service's demand that Credit Data Corporation provide IRS with personal credit histories, as long as specific records were called for by subpoena and a reasonable fee was paid for their provision.[7]

In other cases, the courts have upheld individual claims to protection of constitutional rights over the claims of necessity by government. Several decisions have directed local police departments to destroy particular dossiers of political information that had been collected by improper surveillance of political activity or through improper questioning of persons held under arrest.[8] Other rulings, for example, have ordered law-enforcement agencies to stop preserving or circulating records of arrests for particular defendants that did not result in convictions.[9]

What is critical to note about these two streams of judicial decisions is that the broad programs of government administrative, intelligence, and statistical activity tend to be upheld as reasonable, or at least as activities with which the judiciary does not feel

---

[3] *United States* v. *Rickenbacker*, 197 F. Supp. 924 (S.D., N.Y. 1961), *aff.* 309 F. 2d 462 (2d Cir. 1962), *cert. den.*, 371 U.S. 962 (1963).

[4] *Miller* v. *N.Y. Stock Exchange*, 306 F. Supp. 1002 (1969); 425 F. 2d 1074 (1970); *cert. den.*, 398 U.S. 905 (1970).

[5] *Anderson* v. *Sills*, 56 N.J. 210, 265 A. 2d 678 (1970).

[6] *Lamont* v. *Commissioner of Motor Vehicles*, 269 F. Supp. 880 (1967); *Chapin* v. *Tynan*, 158 Conn. 625, 264 A. 2d 566 (1969).

[7] *U.S.* v. *Davey*, 426 F. 2d 842 (2d Cir. 1970).

[8] *Holmes* v. *Church*, 70 Civ. 5691 (S.D.N.Y., June 14, 1971); *Avirgan* v. *Rizzo*, 70 Civ. 477 (E.D.Pa. 1970).

[9] See, for example, *U.S.* v. *McLeod*, 385 F. 2d 734 (5th Cir. 1967); *U.S.* v. *Kalish*, 217 F. Supp. 968 (D. Puerto Rico, 1967); *Morrow* v. *District of Columbia*, 417 F. 2d 728 (1969); and *Eddy* v. *Moore*, 9 Crim. L. Rep. 2463 (Wash. Ct. App. 1971).

ready to interfere on constitutional grounds. It is abuse in the
conduct of such programs that the courts have generally inter-
vened to control.

It may be that the courts are growing more sensitive to the
possibilities for misuse that arise when large-scale official record
systems filled with sensitive data are created, and personal records
are to be disseminated widely within various government circles as
a central feature of such operations. The *Menard* case on distribution of FBI NCIC records for nonlaw-enforcement use may be
such a response. Such increasing sensitivity could lead to stricter
supervision of the way major government record systems are
operated. But it does not seem realistic to expect the Supreme
Court to strike down major government record systems in the near
future on grounds of privacy. Rather, the court can be expected to
scrutinize government record-keeping to demand that legislative
and administrative schemes are sufficiently defined that they do
not abridge the First Amendment rights of speech, press, association, and assembly, which constitute the traditional pillars of a
citizen's right to political privacy. While civil-liberties groups will
press for constitutional limits to be placed on police surveillance
(including record-keeping) that intrudes into First Amendment
areas, a realistic estimate is that the courts will rule against such
broad claims, or decline to hear the cases at all, or decide them in
ways that protect civil-liberties interests on narrower grounds.

When we shift to private record systems, which are not
covered by the constitutional guarantees that limit government
powers, the role of the courts in the privacy sphere is likely to be
very limited. Only in a few areas, such as commercial reporting
services, have the courts reviewed private information-gathering
and record-keeping activities. Even here, though juries have recently made some large libel awards to persons who were injured by
dissemination of false reports and who could show gross negli-
gence by the reporting agency in the preparation of the report, the
courts have severely narrowed libel and defamation remedies in
the interest of protecting freedom of speech and the press. Furthermore, lengthy and expensive litigation by individuals did not
provide the systemwide reforms that were needed; it was this
reality that led to passage of the state and federal fair credit
reporting statutes in 1970-72. While the courts will be influential
in reviewing the application of legislative regulations created to
protect consumer and citizen rights in private record systems, the
limited scope of the state common-law right-to-privacy action and
the absence of any "due-process" guarantee in private law suggest

that the courts will play a secondary part in the evolution of basic civil-liberties protections in the private sphere.

Turning from judicial to legislative treatment of privacy interests, there are certain similarities to be expected in the way legislators are likely to respond to this issue. We saw in the congressional and state legislative debates over fair credit reporting statutes that due process—giving individuals notice of reports, a right to learn their contents, and a procedure for challenging them—was chosen as the basic approach for dealing with the civil-liberties issues raised by the activities of commercial reporting agencies.[1] Legislators during 1970-72 rejected the proposals by consumer and civil-liberties groups which would have defined and limited the types of information that could be collected at all for credit, preemployment, or preinsurance inquiries, and specified the investigative methods that should and should not be used. Essentially, the legislators chose to bring the investigative and evaluative process into greater visibility, believing that this would give sufficient publicity to the kinds of personal information used in decisions for one of two outcomes to result. First, the personal information being collected for credit, insurance, and employment decisions might be shown, in the newly visible processes of commercial reporting, to be in line with legislative and public notions of what it is appropriate for these industries to collect in making their business and personnel decisions. The due-process mechanisms might also have induced the user industries to reconsider what personal information they really need and led to evolution of a common feeling between the industry and the general public as to the information it is appropriate to collect, given a concern for civil liberties.

A second possible outcome is that the visibility given to commercial reporting agency practices might disclose intrusive investigations that the public would not accept as legitimate, either because there is insufficient guarantee that errors can be avoided, or because the information sought is regarded as inappropriate to the credit, insurance, or employment decision being made. In this case, legislators might use the documentary evidence

---

[1] We should emphasize that the particular due-process mechanisms adopted in these acts did not go as far as many civil-liberties spokesmen had urged. For example, the individual still does not get to inspect the actual record held about him or to see the report as it was transmitted; he is merely told about its contents by a representative of the commercial reporting agency. Another aspect of the due-process scheme that has been criticized is that the individual does not have an opportunity to see and contest a report *before* it is transmitted.

built up under fair credit reporting act cases to draw up new substantive privacy boundaries, acting then with the conviction that they had a better grasp of the area involved and its impact on citizen rights than if they had tried to set such privacy boundaries in 1970-72.

An example of legislation attempting to set boundaries on the collection of personal information is a proposed right-to-privacy act for federal employees. Hearings before the Senate Subcommittee on Constitutional Rights in 1966 had disclosed that some federal agencies were collecting sensitive personal information through techniques that raised serious questions of privacy, and these practices had evoked protests from the major unions and professional associations representing federal employees. Believing that these abuses were not being dealt with effectively through executive self-regulation, the subcommittee chairman, Senator Ervin, introduced a bill in 1966[2] (with 55 cosponsors) which listed a series of improper information-gathering practices that would be forbidden by law. These include requiring a federal employee "to disclose his race, religion, or national origin" or that of his forebears, or to submit to either a "psychological test" or a "polygraph test" that is "designed to elicit from him information concerning his personal relationship with any person connected with him by blood or marriage, or concerning his religious beliefs or practices, or concerning his attitude or conduct with respect to sexual matters." A three-member "Board on Employees' Rights" would be created to "receive and investigate written complaints" from any person claiming to be affected by violations of the act; to hold hearings, issue cease-and-desist orders, and pursue other remedies against officials found to be violating the act. (The bill exempts the FBI, CIA and National Security Agency from its operations.)

The employee's right to privacy bill passed the Senate three times since 1966, twice by unanimous consent and once by a 90 to 4 vote, and the bill has enjoyed widespread support from labor unions, the press, and civil liberties groups. However, it has not been passed by the House of Representatives. In House testimony, spokesmen for the executive branch in both the Johnson and Nixon administrations took the position that the bill would provide unnecessarily strict limits on executive personnel management. They also argued that the undesirable practices that had

---

[2] The bill is now numbered S. 1438, 92d Cong., 1st Sess., 1971. For the hearings, see *Privacy and the Rights of Federal Employees*, Hearings before the Subcommittee on Constitutional Rights of the Committee on the Judiciary, U.S. Senate, 89th Cong., 2d Sess. 1966.

been highlighted at the 1966 Congressional hearings had already
been eliminated or brought under proper controls through executive self-regulation.

Although there can be disagreement among reasonable men
over particular provisions of the employee's right to privacy bill,
some specification of types and forms of data collection that are
improper in personnel administration and the identification of
zones of personal life that should not be investigated by federal
agencies represents the kind of measure that needs serious consideration at each level of American government if privacy rights are
to have a proper legislative foundation and if effective independent review mechanisms are to be provided.

There are quite a few other areas of organizational record-
keeping in which privacy questions could be addressed by legislators. For example, our profile of R. L. Polk discussed the
complaints raised about the sale or provision of names from government files to the mailing-list industry. We also noted the response of the Direct Mail Advertisers Association (DMAA) in providing a mechanism by which individuals can get their names
removed from the output lists of those DMAA members who subscribe to the DMAA service. For many persons, this does not
resolve the basic privacy issue: when individuals give information
about themselves to government agencies for one purpose, usually
under legal compulsion to report, should their names, addresses,
and data about their occupations, ownership, military service, or
other activities be made available to organizations that would use
the information for purposes that these individuals consider intrusive?

In a time of major problems of housing, education, crime,
race relations, pollution, and peace, it may seem a disturbingly
trivial matter to worry about government records leading to the
receipt of mail advertisements that some individuals do not want.
But the issue symbolizes something we cannot afford to ignore—
how do we make the individual's informed consent a more respected and controlling feature of life in organizational society? Our
approach to this problem should not be to make matters confidential which have long been considered open for public access; rather
it should be to find a way to accommodate those who feel their
privacy intruded upon by such direct-mail practices.

The provision of entire government name lists to commercial
users offers an opportunity to use computer technology to serve
individual consent, if policymakers appreciate how to require this
to be done. If the collecting government agency agreed (or was
required by law), a single check-box on its data-collection form

could allow the individual to indicate whether he wanted such uses made of his name. Then, any government agency that is presently allowed by law to sell lists of names from its administrative files would simply make a pass through its computer files, make up a new tape or print-out of those who had given their consent, and furnish it to the advertisers.

In this way, almost everyone ought to be satisfied.[3] The government agency would obtain revenues to help reduce its operating costs. Individuals who do not want to get such mail do not get it. Those who enjoy getting advertising are not denied it because a few persons claiming to speak in the high name of civil liberties wish to prevent such practices entirely. And the information suppliers and advertisers get that best of all commercial mailing situations—a pretested list of persons who will be less likely to throw the mail item, unopened, into the wastebasket. Were this principle of individual choice to be adopted at the local, state, and federal levels for all sale or distribution of personal information from government files, what has been treated as a Gordian knot could be cut at a stroke.

It might be observed that this idea has been applied in a limited fashion already in the federal statute that allows an individual to notify the Post Office that he does not want to receive sexually oriented mail. The law then requires mailers of such material to purchase the lists of objecting individuals and purge those names from the mailer's files.

As an illustrative case study of policy questions in the privacy sphere, we turn to the problem of arrest and conviction records, the use of which we examined not only at the law-enforcement agencies and central databank projects we visited but also at various organizations outside law enforcement, from criminal and civil courts to the personnel departments of corporations and government civil service agencies. In order to focus sharply on the *privacy* aspect of such record-keeping, we will confine our discussion to the use of *arrest-only* records. In these, either the disposition of the case is not noted or the outcome of the arrest has been in favor of the individual (usually because the charges were dropped or dismissed, the defendant was acquitted, or a conviction was reversed on appeal). It is in such cases that clear

---

[3] Mailing-list industry spokesmen have expressed their concern that the wording of the question about consent might be unfairly "anti-advertising" or that many individuals would check "no" without realizing the consequences. These concerns seem to go to the fair administration and publicizing of the system, however, not its basic merits.

privacy questions arise as to whether it is appropriate to use the criminal record for decisions about licensing and employment.

As we saw in the FBI profile, local and state police have maintained arrest and conviction records on a permanent basis for more than half a century, and a manual network for circulating nationally the records on file with the FBI has been in operation since the 1920s. By the 1950s and '60s, several aspects of this local and national record-sharing system had become clear to students of law-enforcement and employment practices:[4]

1. Law-enforcement agencies believed that it was necessary to keep permanent records of arrests even when they did not result in convictions, for use as leads in later investigations or as information deemed necessary by prosecutors and courts. Although inadequacies in the record-keeping procedures of courts and police agencies frequently resulted in no information being recorded about the disposition of arrests, criminal record bureaus did not find it practical to segregate such incomplete records or to withhold them from users of the system.

2. By the late 1960s, of the 7.5 million arrests being made annually, 1.3 million were never prosecuted and another 2.2 million resulted in acquittals or dismissal of charges,[5] leaving 3.5 million arrest-only entries lodged yearly in the national criminal record network.

3. Included among the arrests that did not result in conviction were a considerable number of cases involving political dissidents, "hippie types," civil-rights activists, and others whom many police officers regarded with suspicion and were quick to charge with criminal offenses. Furthermore, round-up arrests for investigative purposes were so widespread in ghetto areas that a presidential commission estimated a 90 percent probability that a black urban male would be arrested at least once in his lifetime.[6] Courts

---

[4] A voluminous literature has apppeared on this topic in the past few years. As examples, see H. S. Miller, *The Closed Door: The Effect of a Criminal Record on Employment with State and Local Public Agencies*, U.S. Department of Labor Manpower Administration study 81-09-70-02, February 1972; Report of the Committee to Investigate the Effect of Police Arrest Records on Employment Opportunities in the District of Columbia (1957); Note, "Maintenance and Dissemination of Records of Arrest Versus the Right to Privacy," *Wayne Law Review*, Vol. 17 (1971), p. 995; and the extensive literature cited in the Hearings before Subcommittee No. 4, House Judiciary Committee, on H. R. 13315, 1972.

[5] *Crime in the United States*, Uniform Crime Reports, Federal Bureau of Investigation, Washington, D.C., 1969.

[6] *Task Force on Science and Technology*, President's Commission on Law Enforcement and the Administration of Justice, Appendix J, at p. 216 (1967).

took judicial notice of such improper police practices in several cases involving exclusion from jobs because of criminal records.[7]

4. The general practice was for "criminal offender" records (including those involving only arrest) to be made available to government licensing agencies, private employers, and government personnel departments. Sometimes this was authorized under local or national law. Even where it was not, however, or where such disclosure was forbidden, it is well documented that police personnel in most large cities did perform "record checks" for influential corporations and private employers.[8]

5. When employers obtained "criminal record" information, studies showed that the great majority of them used an arrest-only record not as the occasion for checking further into the nature and circumstances of the arrest but as grounds to reject automatically the job applicant in favor of others without any "criminal" record.[9] The result has been, as one commentary noted, that millions of persons are prevented from getting "jobs, licenses, homes, credit, or admission to schools because of their 'records,' " giving rise to the question whether crime rates and recidivism may be increasing in part because people are being "forced into crime by their inability to escape . . . reports of acts that they have never been proved to have committed. . . ."[1]

While these aspects of the use of arrest-only records were beginning to receive wider attention in civil-liberties circles and in the press, computerization of state, local, and federal arrest and conviction files was going forward. In some cases, important progress was made during the data-conversion process in complet-

---

[7] *Gregory* v. *Litton Systems, Inc.,* 316 F. Supp. 401 (C.D. Calif. 1970); *Matter of Smith and Vasquez,* 310 N.Y.S. 2d 617 (Fam. Ct. 1971); *Carter* v. *Gallagher,* Decree of U.S. Dist. Ct., D. of Minnesota, March 9, 1971.

[8] See the discussion of the sale of such information by officers of the New York Police Department in the New York Motor Vehicle Department profile; for a recent case in a suburb near Washington, D.C., see "Officer Demoted for Selling Data," *Washington Post,* March 12, 1971. *The Report of the Committee to Investigate the Effect of Police Arrest Records on Employment Opportunities in the District of Columbia* (1967) found that influential employers in Los Angeles, San Francisco, Chicago, Boston, and New York were often able to obtain records despite regulations or policies to the contrary.

[9] Miller, *The Closed Door, op. cit.*; E. Sparer, *Employability and the Juvenile Arrest Record* (Center for the Study of Unemployed Youth, New York University, 1966); Hess and LePoole, "The Abuse of the Record of Arrest Not Leading to Conviction," *Crime and Delinquency,* Vol. 13 (1967), p. 494; "Discrimination on the Basis of Arrest Records," *Cornell Law Review,* Vol. 56 (1971), p. 470.

[1] Statement of the American Civil Liberties Union, before Subcommittee No. 4 of the House Judiciary Committee, on H. R. 13315, April 26, 1972.

ing arrest records that lacked dispositions, and in persuading those agencies responsible for supplying disposition information (with manual procedures) to improve their performance. But even in the most highly computerized law-enforcement agencies, many incomplete records remained, and the circulation of reports on arrests that resulted in acquittals, dismissals, etc., was continued as a matter of policy.

The growth of a national computerized network for sharing arrest and conviction reords coincided with an increase in the proportion of government licenses and jobs for which "criminal record checks" are now required. For a sizable portion of the population, perhaps as many as 10 million persons, employment opportunities are seriously limited today because of the official distribution by law-enforcement agencies, on a nationwide basis, of the fact that they have been arrested. Questions about the propriety of such distribution were raised in the courts during the 1960s, as we saw in the FBI profile. Individuals were allowed to have records of arrests expunged when they were acquitted, charges were dismissed, etc., with one court stressing that keeping such records was "contrary to the public interest in helping deprived youths climb out of the poverty ghetto."[2] Many of these court rulings cited invasion of privacy as a major ground for ordering expungement. We also saw that a federal court in the *Menard* case directed the FBI to cease disseminating criminal records to those outside the law-enforcement community.[3] The court's opinion stated that "accusations not proven [and] charges made without adequate supporting evidence when tested by the judicial process . . . should not be indiscriminately broadcast under governmental auspices." Because of the "increasing complexity of our society and technological advances" in the dissemination of arrest data, the court said, there is "a pressing need to preserve and to redefine aspects of the right to privacy to ensure the basic freedoms guaranteed by this democracy."

However, as we have seen, Congress has temporarily authorized the FBI to continue disseminating criminal records to government licensing agencies and certain private employers. Furthermore, the *Menard* case and other recent decisions[4] indicate that

---

[2] *Matter of Smith and Vasquez, op. cit.*

[3] *Menard* v. *Mitchell*, 328 F. Supp. 718 (1971).

[4] See particularly *Spock* v. *District of Columbia*, D.C. Ct. App. No. 5860, October 20, 1971, refusing to expunge arrest records of demonstrators even when the arrestees are exonerated of wrongdoing or charges are dismissed.

the judiciary basically regards the question of whether arrest and conviction records should be made available to private and public employers to be a matter for *legislative* rather than judicial decision. Civil-liberties groups have argued that the right not to be harmed in one's employment and licensing opportunities by an arrest record "rises to constitutional dimensions" because the presumption of innocence until proved guilty makes any official promulgation of arrest information a violation of the rights to privacy and due process of law.[5] While this viewpoint may come to be accepted in the future it has not yet been adopted by the Supreme Court; thus the current center of attention is on the state and federal legislatures, where bills to control the use of arrest records are now pending.[6] It is these proposals that we wish to examine more closely.

The first principle to work from, we believe, is that circulation of arrest-only records should not be permitted *unless* a case can be made, with solid supporting evidence, that a person arrested but not convicted of a crime is more likely to be a poor employee, misuse his license privileges, or engage in some misconduct relevant to his work than someone from the same socioeconomic class and educational background and subject to the same on-the-job supervision who has never been arrested. Because there is evidence that most employers automatically reject applicants with arrest-only records, thus harming the employment opportunities of many persons who were formally found to be innocent, the burden of establishing the predictive value of arrest-only records should be on those who support their dissemination beyond law-enforcement agencies.[7]

If this burden of proof is not met, or if the legislature should

---

[5] See Statement of American Civil Liberties Union, before Subcommittee No. 4, *op. cit.*

[6] In Congress, S. 2732, sponsored by Senator Burdick, would provide for nullification of arrest-without-conviction records upon application by the individual; H. R. 13315, sponsored by Congressman Edwards, would provide for expunging arrest-without-conviction records automatically after two years for individuals who have no prior felony convictions, and would prohibit dissemination of arrest information to nonlaw-enforcement agencies. At the state level, Illinois in 1971 passed a law forbidding employers to obtain arrest records, either by asking an applicant about his arrest record or by asking him to sign a waiver so that official record sources could be examined. Illinois Fair Employment Practices Act, Public Act No. 71-1552, September 17, 1971.

[7] Clearly, the question of arrest-only records ought to be dealt with as part of a broader examination which would cover as well the use of criminal conviction records—within and outside law enforcement. Many of the same privacy questions are relevant to the use of both types of records.

decide that the claim to privacy is the superior one to protect, it will take carefully detailed legislation to carry out such a policy and enforce a ban on the use of arrest-only records in the employment and licensing areas. If law-enforcement agencies are allowed to preserve arrest-only records for their own investigative purposes, while dissemination to employers and similar users is forbidden, there must be effective controls in the local and national computerized systems to ensure that leakage to employers and other private users does not take place as it has in the past.[8] Furthermore, any statute would have to control the use by employers of alternative sources of information, such as directly questioning applicants about arrest records or using commercial reporting services which search newspapers and other nonlaw-enforcement sources.

Between the present system and a ban on the use of arrest-only records in employment and licensing decisions lies what might be called a minimum "due-process" approach to legislative action. Based on the premise that employers and licensing agencies should have the right to know if a person has ever been arrested and to weigh this fact in their decisions, the records would be disseminated; however, any applicant would have to be informed that arrests are taken into account and, if he has a record, there would have to be a right for him to review its accuracy, to make sure that it is complete, and to correct any errors.[9] He might also have a right to add a statement of reasonable length to the record explaining the arrest from his own viewpoint; this explanation would then have to be circulated along with the arrest record.

Which of these legislative approaches ought to be adopted, and what safeguards would be needed to make that policy effective, are matters that are currently under debate, and which lie beyond the scope of our discussion here. Our point in treating arrest records as an example is to stress that a democratic society should not allow arrest records to be collected and circulated nationwide with increasing efficiency without considering directly the actual social impact of their use in the employment and licensing spheres, and without examining the possibility that dissemination beyond law-enforcement agencies represents an official

---

[8] A first—and by no means easy—step in this direction would be to deal with the problem of updating millions of criminal files so that arrest-only and conviction records can be distinguished from one another.

[9] This position was developed by Donald E. Santarelli, Associate Deputy Attorney General, in testimony before House Subcommittee, No. 4, *op. cit.*, March 23, 1972.

stigmatization of the citizen that ought to be either forbidden by law, or closely regulated. In this reconsideration, legislators should also recognize that computerization may offer opportunities for greater control over records under whatever policy is adopted, and more effective monitoring of compliance than was available in manual systems.

As in the case of allowing individuals access to their own records, the consequences of new privacy-oriented policies for record-holding organizations themselves may not be entirely predictable. But given our sense from site visits and a number of empirical studies that many individuals can be hurt under current policies for the use of arrest-only records, it would seem only appropriate to approach the question of organizational needs for data in the spirit of experimentation. When persons stigmatized by past criminal arrest are denied jobs and licenses at the point of application, there is little opportunity to test long-standing assumptions about what an arrest record means. If there are indeed important ways that society would suffer in the employment and licensing of individuals who have arrest records, these dangers can only be uncovered (and weighed against the protection of individual rights) through experience.

Technological Safeguards
for Information Systems

Our profiles and findings have indicated that the primary civil-liberties issues raised by the uses of computers are not matters of information security to be resolved by technical specialists but are instead policy choices as to privacy, confidentiality, and due process. Thus no "technological fix" can be applied to the data-bank problem. Computer specialists are needed to inform policy-makers about the technical options available to accomplish civil-liberties objectives in computerized information systems and the costs in money and efficiency that would be incurred in seeking a given level of protection. But social policy must precede technique, and our discussion in this section registers such a priority for the social, legal, and administrative problems.

Our report has already stressed the confusion that exists in both the technical and nontechnical literature about "security and privacy" protections for computer systems; we invite readers to recall the discussion in part three about security in record systems, since this is the source of our policy recommendations here.

The basic definitions we noted are worth restating briefly, however. *Privacy*, we suggested, is independent of technological safeguards; it involves the social policy issues of what information should be collected at all and how much information should be assembled in one information system. *Confidentiality* is the central issue for which technological safeguards are relevant. Where an organization has promised those from whom it collects information that unauthorized uses will not be made by persons inside or outside that agency, making good that promise of confidentiality requires record security controls in both manual and computerized files. Finally, *due process* is a policy matter in which organizations define individual rights of access to files; both administrative and technological measures are then needed to carry out such policies effectively.

Using these concepts, what technological safeguards should computerizing organizations be considering today? It seems clear that any organization with confidential personal information to protect must adopt a "total record system" approach, covering both manual and computerized files and processes; focusing on the computerized pieces of the system alone would be ineffective. Furthermore, no minimum set of technological safeguards can be specified in the abstract for computerized files in all types of organizations; the level of protection required will always depend on the nature of the organization; its mission, policies, and structure, and on the specific manual and computerized elements which comprise its data-processing system. Considering a general set of technological safeguards, as some commentaries have done, is like trying to design a safe craft without knowing what medium it will travel in, its intended speed, whether it will have 10 or 1,000 passengers, and whether the principal risks it will face are snowstorms or guided missiles.

Whatever the organization and its data-processing system, of course, it cannot be made absolutely safe, even by adopting the extreme approaches used by government establishments for securing classified files. Furthermore, it would hardly advance civil liberties in this country if, in the name of protecting confidential files, civilian government agencies and private organizations were to adopt the authoritarian environments and intrusive personnel policies used by defense and intelligence agencies to safeguard their information systems.

Policymakers must also realize that installing technological safeguards does not come cost-free to organizations, to the clientele they serve, or to society. Such measures have costs in money, time, and efficiency; some of the measures being discussed as desirable for organizations to adopt would involve considerable sums. For this reason, estimating the likely threats to the confidentiality of personal data must be approached in a realistic fashion, not only by organizational managers but by the legislators, civic groups, and outside observers who will make judgments about what organizations ought to do in these regards. The best predictor, until new experience proves otherwise, is what violations of confidentiality took place in the manual record systems in any given area. For example, in the law-enforcement community, leakage by insiders of criminal records has taken place. In the social welfare area, information from client records has been furnished to police officials in violation of stated confidentiality policies. Information from medical records has been leaked by hospital employees. It is these historic types of violations that ought to set the framework for the safeguards built into computerized systems, not hypothetical images of intelligence agents using computer specialists to carry out sophisticated raids on databanks. There may be some databanks that require such elaborate protections, but they will be few.

It is beyond the scope of this report to describe and analyze the inventory of existing devices and techniques from which organizations can select in making up an appropriate package of physical security and technological measures. Publications such as the IBM booklet, *The Considerations of Data Security in a Computer Environment*, have been prepared for computer users. Handbooks, technical papers, and special seminars have been developed to discuss these problems. There are also some consulting organizations available to do security analyses and recommend programs of safeguards.

What seems clear is that adequate computer technology already exists to provide both the hardware and software protections that are needed to afford effective levels of security for personal data in the kinds of record systems we have been considering. To give several examples of particular relevance to civil-liberties issues, much more could be done by computer manufacturers to put record-field access control features into the software operating systems of computer systems, so that users could exercise greater control over the authorization tables that govern access to the data base for each user. Similarly, much more could be done by software developers to provide the programs for real-time monitoring against unusual volumes of use or unusually low yields of "hits," in order to warn system managers about what may be unauthorized uses or improper "browsing" in sensitive files.

To pursue these technological capabilities, however, the first task remains the formulation of policies as to privacy and confidentiality, which would then define the quality and extent of the technological safeguards needed for a given field of record-keeping or particular organization. From this can come the "user demand"—in the form of organizational specifications to manufacturers and software developers and legal requirements set out for systems to follow—that would cause the hardware manufacturers and software developers to turn technological capacities into available and workable products. Unless there are economic and political incentives for them to do so, however, development and production work is not likely to be undertaken.[1]

Both managers and policymakers should be aware that the payoff in sensitive personal information to be obtained by insiders violating confidentiality rules and outsiders breaching system security is going to increase in the coming years. More comprehensive information about people will be collected in the kind of large-scale record systems that are growing up, such as the omnibus charge-card systems and national welfare assistance programs described earlier. Furthermore, as more organizations make use of the low cost and flexible services that are available in commercial time-sharing facilities, more high-payoff targets such as the membership and contributor lists of various kinds of organizations will be appearing in time-sharing systems, requiring more attention to the security problems in multiple-user commercial facilities than this area has received thus far.

This analysis of technological protections draws on our conception of the responsibilities that society ought to assign to the computer industry. Computer manufacturers, systems designers, and computer professionals cannot decide what rights to privacy, confidentiality, and due process individuals ought to have in

---

[1] In May 1972, IBM announced that it was initiating a five-year, $40 million project to develop "security options" for computer users "that are as near as we can come to the limit of the art." Pilot work would proceed at four data-security centers, three "in highly qualified user installations" and one within IBM itself, with the results of these studies "shared in the public domain." Measures would be examined for both hardware and software protections. Speech of T. Vincent Learson, Chairman of the Board, IBM Corporation, Spring Joint Computer Conference, May 16, 1972. For immediate reactions from various computer users, see *Computerworld*, May 29, 1972, pp. 1-2.

relation to organizations, either as a general principle or as applied to each realm of record-keeping. That is for the organizational managers to propose and for law and public opinion to decide. Suggestions that computer societies might undertake to certify record systems as having the "necessary safeguards" are well-intentioned but flawed proposals; they confuse the testing of a system's performance under stated specifications with the setting up of those specifications, which we have shown to involve questions of power, liberty, and social allocation, issues on which computer professionals are fellow citizens, not experts.

Similarly, suggestions that computer manufacturers should be required to install "necessary safeguards" in their machines before they leave the factories betray a basic lack of understanding about computers and their uses. What user organizations and the public do have a right to expect of computer manufacturers is accelerated development of hardware and software measures that would enhance the user's ability to carry out confidentiality policies; production of such devices or dissemination of such techniques as options to users; studies of user successes and failures in this regard; and dissemination of such research and studies (with proper safeguards for protecting the confidential or proprietary information throughout the user community and the public arenas. As such devices or techniques are developed, policymakers should consider whether any of these should be mandated for systems of a particular kind by legal enactments or regulatory rules.

The Social Security Number as a Universal Identifier

In our profile of the Social Security Administration, we noted that (contrary to some belief) there is no congressional bar to using the number assigned for Social Security record-keeping in other government or private record systems. In fact, executive orders and legislative concern over efficiency and costs have led to the adoption of the number in many major federal record systems (IRS, VA, the military, FAA, Civil Service Commission, etc.), and the number has increasingly been adopted as an identifier in the record systems of local and state government agencies, commercial organizations, universities, and other private bodies. We have also described the heavy pressures in Congress and the state legislatures to use the Social Security number in all welfare programs, as a means of detecting fraud and controlling program operations. Finally, we noted that the position of the Department of Health, Education, and Welfare and the Nixon administration has been essentially one of postponing any general decision about how the Social Security number should be used in our society.[2]

The uses made of the Social Security number have led various critics, such as Senator Ervin, to urge that deliberate measures be taken to halt the trend. The concern is that having the number as identifier in more and more files on individuals will make it cheaper and easier for organizations to exchange data among themselves and to merge the records from files of different agencies, departments, and organizations into central databanks. It is also feared that having the number would help outsiders, both authorized and unauthorized, to locate and extract the records of given individuals more easily from various record systems than if each organization maintained its own unique identifying number system.

To analyze the policy choices involved, we should start by recognizing that having the Social Security number in each departmental file or organizational record system is not essential to the merger of files, although there is no doubt that its use would make such mergers easier and more economical. In computer systems particularly, files can be combined by working with whatever common identifiers already exist in the various files (name, address, birthdate, mother's maiden name, etc.) and writing computer programs to extract this information from each record, either for a temporary display or to make up a new permanent record. Secretary of HEW Richardson was right when he said that halting the spread of the Social Security number would not prevent organizations (especially those with computerized files) from con-

---

[2] In February 1972, Secretary of HEW Richardson established an Advisory Committee on Automated Personal Data Systems. The committee's appointees are drawn from a wide range of university, business, and government institutions. Their mandate includes (1) analysis of the civil-liberties implications of automated record systems, "with special emphasis on . . . systems which, though not used or supported by the Department, use or might use the Social Security number. . .;" (2) general consideration of both administrative and technical safeguards which might be employed in automated data systems; (3) consideration of means for redressing harm done to individuals from the use of automated data systems; and (4) an analysis of policy governing use of the Social Security number and consideration of "prohibitions, restrictions or other qualifications on the issuance and use of the Social Security number which now exist or which might be imposed as a means of inducing the adoption of safeguards. . . ." The committee is to submit its final report to the Secretary of HEW by December 1972.

solidating or sharing data when they felt this to be necessary, and worth the expense. Such impediments would have to flow instead from deliberate organizational and legal policies. Thus no one should enter a discussion of the Social Security number thinking that barring its further spread would prevent most organizations from assembling records in a way that was highly intrusive or from exchanging data with other organizations in violation of confidentiality. The added cost and inconvenience involved where Social Security numbers are not available could range from minimal to enormous, depending on the compatibility of the files being merged; the acceptability of the costs of merger or exchange will vary with the resources of the organization.

Those who favor allowing the use of the number to spread or deliberately adopting it as an official national citizen identifier point to the fact that many countries with at least as much dedication to civil liberties as our own—Norway, Sweden, and Israel, for example—assign numbers to each of their citizens and have not thereby produced databanks and other record systems that trample on individual rights. Thus it is argued that we should recognize that a national numbering system is inevitable, and not only allow but encourage the use of the Social Security number for identification purposes. In so doing, supporters of this position suggest, we can obtain the economies in the exchange and merger of records that would arise from such use, greater accuracy of identification for persons with common names, and perhaps make more simple and convenient the citizen's everyday dealings with organizational record systems. Attention to the problem of record privacy abuses could be focused where it is appropriate: on the setting of policy for the gathering, use, and sharing of identified data.

Our conclusion from studying the databank problem and public reactions to it[3] is that this would be a bad moment in our national history to adopt such a policy. We have seen that most large-scale record systems in this country are not yet operating with rules about privacy, confidentiality, and due process that reflect the updated constitutional ideals and new social values that have been developing over the past decade. We also saw that protest over the way organizations actually conduct their decision making about people is a major facet of the sociopolitical struggles of our era. Regardless of the actual usefulness of a national personal identifier in increasing the efficiency of record-keeping

---

[3] See Appendix B.

processes, many dissenting and minority groups in the society would view the establishment of such an identifier (or its informal equivalent) as a giant step toward tightening government control over the citizen for repressive purposes.

We have argued in this section that we are at a point in the public debate over databanks and civil liberties where we can—and must—move forward to resolve both long-standing and newly rising issues. Many important problems in this sphere can be effectively resolved. But to develop sensitive policies will require that a minimum level of trust be maintained between American citizens and their government. Under these conditions, adopting the Social Security number officially as a national identifier or letting its use spread unchecked cannot help but contribute to public distrust of government.

Given the cleavages in the nation today, the levels of distrust in government already present, and the fears that a national administration might take repressive actions in response to disorders or political crises, we should join nations such as Great Britain, Canada, and France that are not moving to change historic policies against the establishment of a citizen numbering system at this time.

There are limits on the steps we might reasonably expect the Congress or HEW to take in support of a position which rests principally on the *symbolic* significance of a government act. Legislation to prohibit the number's use beyond the federal government, for instance, is highly unlikely. But, at the very least, the administration might *refrain* from establishing a formal national identification system. In addition, we see three positive steps which the administration might take in the direction of limiting the number's steadily increasing use.

By law, all federal agencies which establish new record systems must now adopt the Social Security number as an identifier. Congress could repeal this legislation, on the ground that *all* aspects of important new record systems should be subject to examination as to their civil-liberties implications and as to citizen reaction to their various features. As with computerization itself, the process of establishing new record systems or changing old ones in executive agencies ought to become more visible and deliberate.

As a second positive move, the administration might see to it that no steps are taken to "tighten up" the issuing of Social Security numbers unless such moves are necessary for the administration of SSA's own programs. Social Security could be discouraged from cooperating in any special or extraordinary way with nonfederal organizations wishing to adopt the number as an identifier. These moves, which could be handled administratively within HEW, would have the effect of making the account numbering system less attractive to organizations which have not already adopted it.

Finally, the establishment of a national citizen identification system—formally or through enhancement of the Social Security number—should not go forward on the basis of decisions internal to HEW or SSA. With the exception of ad hoc treatment on the floor or in hearings convened for some related but different purpose, the question of a national identifying number has been given relatively little treatment in Congress. It ought to receive the fullest possible public airing and discussion in the legislature.

Special Agencies for Sensitive Data

The creation of information trust agencies whose function it would be to manage certain bodies of particularly sensitive personal data offers an intriguing possibility for the future. The essential purposes to be served are these: to have the files managed by officials without line-agency responsibility for using the data; to encourage the passage of legislation that would install citizen rights at the center of such an agency's administrative concerns; and to provide a physical and administrative setting that encourages independence in the conduct of these custodial responsibilities. The typical situation in which such an information trust agency would be created is where there are many participating users in a data system, where the user agencies have some different and even competing institutional and social interests, and where misuse of the data could result in serious harm to the individuals whose records are being stored.

An example of an area in which such an agency might be created is law enforcement. There have been arguments for many years that it is not in society's best interest to have the Federal Bureau of Investigation manage the collection and preparation of uniform crime statistics for the nation. As a line agency whose reputation and appropriations depend on how policymakers and public opinion view the incidence of crime and the effectiveness of the FBI in dealing with it, the FBI cannot be wholly disinterested. Furthermore, the priorities that the FBI sets for data collection and the formats used in classifying crimes may meet the needs of police agencies but may not be fully responsive to what courts, probation agencies, correctional agencies, the legal profession, and students of the criminal-justice process desire in a criminal-justice statistical service. For these reasons, it has been recommended by some leading law-enforcement spokesmen and legal experts that this function be placed in an independent federal bureau, along the lines of the Bureau of Labor Statistics.[4]

To this function of keeping crime statistics one would add management of the national criminal-history segment of the FBI's National Crime Information Center. It makes a certain amount of good sense to have the FBI keep fingerprint cards and run the national warrant-and-wanted system with which NCIC was begun. This is a police apprehension function, the data stored are highly objective and very limited in scope, and the operational interests of the various federal, state, and local police agencies are basically similar. Summary criminal-history records, however, have far more information in them; the users include prosecutors, courts, probation, parole, and correction agencies, whose interests as to what should be stored and how it should be disseminated are not identical with those of the police agencies; and the management of this system by the national investigative arm of the Justice Department inevitably links the system to the policy outlooks and reputation of both the FBI and the Justice Department. As the future of the FBI and the nation's law-enforcement activities are considered by Congress in the post-Hoover era, such an idea deserves careful consideration.

To be sure, creating such agencies would trade one set of political and institutional constraints for another. Though an information trust agency would not have line responsibilities (to apprehend, prosecute, sentence, or parole in the enforcement area; or to make medical diagnoses or decide on the admission of students for graduate school—other areas in which such agencies might be envisaged), it would still have to be responsive to the interests of the various influential user agencies which depended on the system for information. If the new agency drew its political strength from the chief executive's office (the President, governors, mayors, or county executives), it could become an instru-

---

[4] See, for example, Hans Zeisel, "The Future of Law Enforcement Statistics: A Summary View," in *Federal Statistics*, Report of the President's Commission, 1971, Vol. II, pp. 540-43, and sources cited there.

ment for his notions about program priorities and citizen rights in the field involved; this might or might not be an advantage over the civil-liberties perspectives of line agencies in a given field. There would also be dangers that such agencies might develop along the lines of the independent regulatory commissions, which have tended to have such sympathy for the fate of the private industries under their jurisdiction that regulation in the public interest has frequently suffered.

These are genuine concerns. What would make the difference is whether an information trust agency was established with a clear legislative mandate to be a "guardian" institution; whether the civil-liberties guarantees were clearly stated in legislative policy, rather than left to the discretion of the new agency's managers; and whether supervisory boards were set up to bring civic groups and public representatives into the management of the agency in ways that rarely take place when line agencies set up their "user committees." If conditions such as these were created, the new type of agency might discharge its duties in ways more protective of constitutional rights, yet without sacrifice to larger social interests, than we are likely to achieve by automatically pouring our new large-scale record system into the existing institutional vessel.

Other Areas of Action

There are many important avenues for dealing with databank issues that we have not treated among the six priorities that we chose to highlight. In a sense, each major institution and process of the American political system will be needed to play a creative part—guardian groups speaking for minorities, civil liberties, and consumers to bring test cases and to press for better legislation; legislative committees to make visible the practices of government agencies and private organizations; interagency committees in executive branches to address the civil-liberties issues in record systems as they are being planned; federal fund-granting agencies to set civil-liberties standards when they give grants-in-aid for building computer systems in fields such as law enforcement, education, and social services; advisory groups on privacy to play meaningful roles in specific agencies with sensitive record systems;

professional groups to formulate codes for record-keeping practices in their fields; private foundations to underwrite wide-ranging studies of record-keeping practices and civil-liberties problems; and the media, to keep the issue high on the public agenda while learning themselves how to distinguish between fantasies and realities in this field. Each one of these aids to the formulation of sound public policy could be treated at length, with examples of leading contributions in each area that should serve as models for far greater effort.

Though we cannot take the time to do that here, there is one final avenue for action that has a special claim to attention. In most writing about the dilemmas of life in a highly organized, technological age, the individual person is portrayed as almost helpless before the accumulated power of technocracies. Compared to some points in history when men lived in highly decentralized settings, in highly autonomous (but authoritative) family units, and when there were relatively weak local and national political authorities, it is unquestionable that individuals today pay a greater price in organizational handling and processing to get the mixed benefits of urban civilization.

While this is the basic reality, many organizations can be affected by the refusal of individuals to cooperate in what are seen as offensive information-gathering activities. Research and survey organizations depend on the willing cooperation of subjects. Business organizations are subject to customer and client preferences, including their attitudes on what information they consider it appropriate to provide and how they want the organization to handle it once collected. Universities must create a willingness by students to provide personal information that goes beyond necessary administrative data. In addition, both government agencies and private organizations cannot ignore out of hand the sentiments of those professional employees within the organizations who carry out the major programs. While there is little concern about sporadic complaints,[5] managers treat more seriously the possibility that individual complaints represent the beginnings of a trend toward noncompliance with some aspect of their record-keeping. Even where information is required to be given by law, many managers were frank in saying to us that it would be bad public relations to

---

[5] The matter of managerial perception of levels of complaint is discussed in Appendix A below, pages 446-453.

have to bring about prosecutions or that the costs of enforcement would be prohibitive if enough individuals failed to comply.

We do not want to romanticize the individual's options here. Refusing to give information will require an individual to be inconvenienced, at the least; to risk losing a benefit or opportunity; to spend his own time and money pursuing his claim; and perhaps even to defend his principles in a criminal trial. Yet the advancement of civil liberties has always depended on the willingness of individuals to run such risks and pay such prices to assert their principles; such dedicated conduct—even on the part of relatively few individuals—often affects courts and other governmental agencies when they weigh personal claims against the information needs of society in a given context.

Furthermore, the American legal system has some encouraging aspects for such action, including the assertion of principle by employees of the government. For example, a social worker in Alameda County, California, Benny Max Parrish, declined to participate in a large-scale, surprise inspection of the homes of county welfare recipients in 1962. He asserted that such raids were unconstitutional invasions of a right to privacy that is not surrendered by persons on welfare. He was dismissed for insubordination and failure to follow orders. The Supreme Court of California, in a 1967 opinion, ordered Parrish reinstated with back pay, on the ground that the early morning raids *were* unconstitutional searches and seizures.[6] What is most significant for us in the *Parrish* case was the court's reiteration of the constitutional principle that a government employee cannot be punished for insubordination when he refuses to carry out what the court, on review, finds to be an unconstitutional order.

Obviously, if every employee in government were to decide for himself and act on whether each program he was involved in was unconstitutional, there would be chaos. A presumption of legality does—and should—attach to governmental programs as a general matter. But there is just enough play in the system, under the *Parrish* doctrine, to allow those government employees who believe that constitutional rights to privacy and due process are being ignored, and that their own professional norms of confidentiality and client service are being violated, to generate a good deal of creative challenge to authority.

---

[6] *Parrish* v. *Civil Service Commission of Alameda County*, 66 C. 2d 260, 425 p. 2d 223 (1967).

A Concluding Note on Men and Machines

If our empirical findings showed anything, they indicate that man is still in charge of the machines. What is collected, for what purposes, with whom information is shared, and what opportunities individuals have to see and contest records are all matters of policy choice, not technological determinism. Man cannot escape his social or moral responsibilities by murmuring feebly that "the Machine made me do it."

There is also a powerful tendency to romanticize the precomputer era as a time of robust privacy, respect for individuality in organizations, and "face-to-face" relations in decision making. Such Arcadian notions delude us. In every age, limiting the arbitrary use of power, applying broad principles of civil liberties to the troubles and challenges of that time, and using technology to advance the social well-being of the nation represent terribly hard questions of public policy, and always will. We do not help resolve our current dilemma by thinking that earlier ages had magic answers.

Computers are here to stay. So are large organizations and the need for data. So is the American commitment to civil liberties. Equally real are the social cleavages and cultural reassessments that mark our era. Our task is to see that appropriate safeguards for the individual's rights to privacy, confidentiality, and due process are embedded in every major record system in the nation, particularly the computerizing systems that promise to be the setting for most important organizational uses of information affecting individuals in the coming decades.

Appendix A

Report on a Survey
of Managerial Opinion
on the Impact of Computers
in Record-Keeping

The findings discussed in part three cover what we have called "high technology" systems: organizations that are among the most advanced in their field in applying computers to keeping records about people. To probe how far these conclusions could be generalized to the mainstream of organizations in each field, our project developed a survey questionnaire that was mailed during the winter of 1970 and the spring of 1971 to managers of 2,121 organizations across the nation. Treating respondents as competent observers of record-keeping in their own organizations, we asked questions about the computer's impact on specifically designated files within each organization. In all, anonymous responses were received from managers of 1,541 organizations in 14 different fields. Since the survey was an exploratory one, specially tailored to supplement the other types of data collected for our project, we should explain its concept and execution carefully.

SURVEY OBJECTIVES AND METHODS

Three considerations shaped our survey work. First, to allow our findings to have broad relevance for policymaking, we sought to cover as many important areas of personal record-keeping as possible. Thus, we did broadly focused exploratory work rather than conducting a definitive study of one or two fields.

Second, even with this broad focus, limitations in both time and budget forced us not only to restrict our coverage of record systems more than we would have liked, but also to limit the extent to which the questionnaire was tailored to record systems in different fields.

Finally, we knew from our site-visit experiences that a survey questionnaire is an inappropriate instrument with which to undertake *in-depth* work on computerization in record systems. We could not hope to reproduce the full picture of record-keeping practices and policies obtained from on-site interviews and documentary analysis. Thus, we had to select features of the computer's impact that could be obtained by responses to a mail survey.

Selecting Organizations for Study

Since we did not have the resources to study a sample of organizations from each of the approximately 25 fields in which our site visits were conducted, we eliminated those fields for which a survey would provide us with the least new information. For example, we excluded manufacturing establishments because we knew them to have little in the way of computerized records on people (apart from very "thin" files in payroll or personnel). For religious bodies, local credit bureaus, and private elementary and secondary schools, we knew that so few are using computers that we could not produce a sample of computerized systems large enough for meaningful analysis. Similarly, we saw no way in which even a centrally placed official, such as a mayor, data-processing director, or county executive, could answer a single questionnaire meaningfully for all of the departments in his jurisdiction; thus no whole government jurisdictions were surveyed. Since we had conducted full site visits to most of the federal civilian, nonclassified agencies maintaining important records about individuals, we did not include these in our sample.

With these exclusions, we selected ten functional areas of governmental and private activity. Half of these involve record-keeping by governmental organizations—covering law enforcement, welfare, primary and secondary education, taxation, and motor-vehicle regulation. Because jurisdiction is an important determinant of both policy and EDP development, we drew separate samples of city, county, and state law-enforcement agencies; local public school districts and state education departments; and county and state welfare agencies.[1] In two fields—hospitals and higher education—we defined populations that included both governmental and private organizations, on the assumption that there were not enough differences in record-keeping rules and practices to warrant dividing them along jurisdictional lines. Three fields of private profit-making activity were selected—banking, life insurance, and health and accident insurance. This produced a total of 14 organizational populations—unusually broad coverage for a single survey effort, but fitting our purposes. Random samples were drawn from current (and as far as we could determine, complete) lists of organizations available through trade and professional associations and in published directories.[2]

---

[1] See footnote d to Table A-1.

[2] An attempt was made also to sample social science databanks and departments of health at city, county, and state levels. No complete samples were drawn, however, when it became clear that there would be too few

We had no way to identify in advance which specific organizations in each area had computer applications in important "people files." As a result, we defined populations so as to be certain of obtaining a sufficient number of computerizing organizations in each sample. We knew that organization size is related to computer use, with larger organizations more likely to employ EDP. Thus we drew our samples of government agencies from cities with populations over 50,000 or counties of over 250,000, and we sampled from among local school districts with more than 10,000 pupils. In populations containing a small number of organizations, the entire membership was sent a questionnaire. Thus, the 49 state law-enforcement and state motor-vehicle agencies in the continental United States were included. In the larger populations, sample sizes were determined on a statistical basis, within general limits set by costs.

Within these boundaries, the sample in each field contains organizations that vary considerably in their number of employees, clients and customers, or subjects; the size of the files they maintain; and the degree of computerization. As a result, the survey populations differ markedly from the advanced and generally large organizations we studied in each field. For example, two of the three banks we visited had checking-account files on more than 5 million customers; however, 74 percent of our bank survey respondents report they have fewer than 50,000 checking-account customers, and almost 50 percent have less than 500 such accounts.

Our site visits were for the most part made to organizations which started their computer development earlier than most others in their field and have remained in the forefront of EDP development. Each of our survey samples, however, as we expected, contains some organizations which computerized early, some which moved with the mainstream, and some which developed their first applications quite late. Among hospitals, for instance, 57 percent report no computer applications to any central medical-record files prior to 1968; 30 percent report initial applications in this area between 1960 and 1967; and 13 percent report an "early start"—prior to 1960. Thus we have a broad range of

social science databanks for us to work with and that we could not appropriately specify a file of interest common to all departments in the health department field.

We should also note that, by using directories we ignored some small organizations that were without official status or professional recognition. Thus unaccredited colleges were not included in our target population or in the source list.

Sample Size and Return Rate for Each Organizational Field

Type and Approximate Number of Organizations in the Field		Number of Questionnaires Sent Out (Our Target Sample)	Return Rate, Percent
Banks (commercial)	14,000	300	60
Health/accident insurance[a]	55	55	46
Life insurance	2,000	300	53
Colleges and universities (junior, senior; county, state, and private)	2,300	301	93
Hospitals (city, county, state; voluntary, proprietary)	7,000	300	70
City law enforcement[b]	330	139	96
County law enforcement[c]	275	80	60
Regional welfare	275	101[d]	
Local school districts[e]	22,000	300	74
State education	50	49	78
State welfare	50	49[d]	
State law enforcement	50	49[f]	84
State motor vehicle	50	49	77
State taxation	50	49[g]	86

[a]Companies which handle *only* health and accident policies.

[b]Cities with populations over 50,000 were sampled.

[c]Counties with populations over 250,000 were sampled.

[d]Federal welfare programs, such as Aid to the Blind, are administered locally by county welfare departments in most states and by local offices of the state social service department in others. Federal funds are channeled to each state through the *head offices* of state social service departments, and while these offices may keep identified records on welfare recipients in the state, their primary function is to monitor the program administration of lower-level state and county welfare offices. Because of their differences in function and jurisdiction, we had hoped to draw separate samples of state head offices and county departments in the welfare area. State head offices were easily sampled; but through an error, a few questionnaires intended for *county* departments went to *local state offices* instead. As a result, we received responses from 61 organizations which identified themselves as "state welfare" agencies. We should have received at most 49. This error had two consequences:

1. On the returns we have no way of distinguishing between state head offices and state offices which administer welfare programs on the local level. Thus our category "State Welfare" consists mostly of state head offices, but includes a few local state offices as well.

2. We cannot compute a response rate for either county or state head-office departments, though we estimate it to be 80 percent for the county departments and 71 percent for the state departments.

[e]Local public school districts with 10,000 or more pupils were selected.

[f]Only state agencies in the continental U.S. were included.

[g]Forty-seven of the 50 states have individual income taxes, and it is the files from such taxes that we asked about.

computer experience represented in our survey, against which to explore our findings from visits to the advanced organizations.[3]

The response rate (table A-1) was quite satisfactory by customary research standards and by comparison with other mail surveys of computer utilization conducted in particular fields. Our combined responses (1,541) represent a return rate of 72.6 percent. Returns for each category, ranged from 46 percent (health and accident insurance companies) to 96 percent (city police departments). In 12 of the 14 fields, the response rate was 60 percent or more. In no case did we feel the responses were so low as to preclude the simple analysis we intended.

Questionnaire Content

We were reluctant to ask managers for appraisals of the computer's overall impact on record-keeping in their organizations, since our experience on numerous site visits was that such general questions were very difficult to answer carefully—and all too easy for the respondent in a hurry to answer in glib fashion. We concluded that general questions about the computer's impact on all of the personal files in the organization would produce virtually meaningless responses, given the complexity of record systems typical of most of our respondent organizations. To attempt to overcome this problem by asking managers to complete a questionnaire on each of several record systems in their organization would have all but guaranteed a low response rate jeopardizing confidence in analyzing the sample data.[4] Thus, we asked our survey respondents to tell us about the impact of computerization on a single

---

[3] As we saw in part three above, not all those organizations which made early starts remained on the leading edge of computer development in their fields. However, it is likely that among the "early starters" in each of our survey samples there are some advanced organizations of the type which were the focus of our site visits. See pages 417-419 below.

[4] Our site visits showed that compiling a complete and realistic portrait of record-keeping, computerization, and civil liberties practices in any large organization was a complicated matter. It required highly detailed, interactive questioning; interviews with a considerable number of managers and specialists from different parts of the organization; and resort to documentary research into some important matters about which managers did not have information at hand, or may never have considered as matters of policy. Furthermore, computer applications and civil liberties practices often differed substantially from one record system to another within each organization. We concluded that to ask about the "general extent" or "general impact" of computerization for "all the files in your organization" would almost inevitably have produced results with little real meaning. Bank respondents, for instance, might have answered questions about computer impact with savings,

set of records (e.g., on "current personal-checking-account holders" in banks). Working from our site-visit materials, we selected
files in which civil-liberties issues have typically been raised, which
are central to the operations of that type of organization, and in
which there was a likelihood that some computerization had
occurred. With respect to each type of organization, we assumed
that the sets of records we defined are fairly consistent in content
and handling across organizations in that area. In table A-2 the
designated files are listed, along with the proportion of organizations reporting computerization in these areas.

We asked 23 questions, some with two or more parts.[5] We
began with a few questions to identify the type of responding
organization; the person who would complete the questionnaire;
the number of employees, clients and customers, and "subjects"
on whom the organization maintained records; and whether or not
computerized records were maintained on any of these individuals.
The remainder of the questions dealt with the records we had
specified for each type of organization in the cover letter which
accompanied the questionnaire. We first asked a series of questions
about due process, data sharing, and the frequency of complaints
about information policies for these records, whether they were
computerized or not. In the remainder of the questionnaire we
asked those organizations which reported computer applications
to these records about various aspects of the computer's impact on
the use of the designated file.[6]

Respondents

Questionnaires were mailed to the chief executive or top official in
each organization, and they were asked to note the title of the

loan, checking, payroll, personnel, or charge-card files in mind; our findings
for banks then, would have reflected a meaningless conglomeration of responses about the computer's impact on different files.

[5] A copy of the questionnaire appears at the end of this Appendix. We
have keyed all of the charts that follow to the questions in the survey
instrument.

[6] The reader will see that we have not discussed the response distribu-
tions for each field, on each question. Instead, we have provided charts in
which the results of each field are presented. The general reader should note
that two problems make percentage comparisons among the fields perilous at
some points. First is the fact that the number of cases on which percentaging
was done in any one chart varies across the fields from 17 to 280. This makes
"eyeball" comparison difficult, since a small difference looks much bigger
where the percentage base is small (25 cases, for instance) than where it is
considerably larger (200 cases, for instance). Second, we do not have uniform
response rates on each question. This makes interpretation difficult, even
though we have noted the nonresponse rate for each.

Percent Reporting Computer Applications to Designated Sets of Records
(Question 4)

Type and Number of Organizations Reporting	Designated Records	Percent Reporting Computer Applications to These Records
Banks (179)	Current personal-checking-account customers	64
Health/accident insurance (25)	Current health and accident policyholders	84
Life insurance (159)	Current life policyholders	80
Colleges (280)	Registrar's records on current and previous under-graduates	64
Hospitals (211)	Centrally held medical files on previous in-patients	24
City law enforcement (133)	Central records ("rap sheets") on arrest/conviction/criminal history	20
County law enforcement (48)	Central records ("rap sheets") on arrest/conviction/criminal history	35
Regional welfare (62)	Persons or families currently receiving payments under OAA, AFDC, AB, APTD, or general-assistance programs[a]	44
Local school districts (223)	Permanent pupil records on past and present elementary- and secondary-school students	55
State education (38)	Academic records on current and previous elementary- or secondary-school students	63
State welfare (61)	Persons or families who have received or are receiving money payments under OAA, AFDC, AB, or APTD programs[a]	82
State law enforcement (41)	Central records ("rap sheets") on arrest/conviction/criminal history	39
State motor vehicle (38)	Individuals who are or were state-licensed to operate a motor vehicle	87
State tax (43)	Past or present income tax-payers	97

[a]The abbreviations refer to federal "categorical" programs of Old Age Assistance, Aid to Families with Dependent Children, Aid to the Blind, and Aid to the Permanently and Totally Disabled.

individual actually completing the form. In 35 percent of the returns, the official to whom we addressed the questionnaire made the reply. In another 40 percent of the cases, it was turned over to the data-processing managers for reply. In the remaining cases, the person responsible for a specific set of records (such as college registrars or medical-record librarians) completed the questionnaire.

In asking these respondents to judge the computer's impact on specific record-keeping activities, we were treating them as reliable observers of record-keeping in their own organizations and as individuals able to comment on policy questions. This is obviously an approach which requires caution since managers may feel obligated to provide an answer even when they are not sure about some aspect of the computer's impact; they might also be inclined to offer self-serving responses. By asking for information about as narrow a range of record-keeping activity as possible and providing for "don't know" responses at some points, we hoped to encourage careful replies and to invite managers, where appropriate, to display their *lack* of knowledge about the computer's impact.

Although the survey asks for no information of a personal nature from respondents or about illegal practices, some of the questions were sensitive in that answers might reflect badly on the organization, or be thought to do so, leading managers to answer such questions in what they assumed were socially desirable directions. To elicit the frankest possible answers, therefore, respondents were specifically asked *not* to identify themselves or their organizations.

Presentation of the Survey Data

We have in effect conducted 14 separate surveys, using the same questionnaire for each. At no point in the sections that follow below do we refer to all organizations or offer statements about response distribution based on the total number of respondents. If we did the latter, we would be mixing the responses from 62 county welfare departments, 159 life-insurance companies, 280 colleges and universities, etc., and combining answers to questions relating to different sets of files. While it is somewhat awkward in literary terms to report the results of 14 surveys simultaneously, the total set of respondents is simply not a sample of any known or functionally unified population and for this reason has virtually no meaning as far as an analysis is concerned.

We did not collect the data with which to make distinctions

within fields as to the number of individuals affected by a given record-keeping practice or policy. Clearly, a few hundred very large organizations in a field may affect a far greater proportion of record subjects than all of the remaining thousands of organizations put together (e.g., in banking). How evenly record subjects are distributed across organizations varies considerably from field to field, and none of the results which follow can be used to estimate what proportion of clients, customers, or citizens in a given field may be affected by specific policies or practices of data collection, sharing, or use.

THE SURVEY RESULTS AND THEIR INTERPRETATION

Readers will note from table A-2 that there is considerable variation in levels of computerization among the 14 types of organizations. One-fifth of the police departments in large cities, for instance, have computerized some aspect of their "rap sheet" files; more than half the colleges and universities have computer applications to student files held by the registrar's office; and virtually all state tax departments have computerized some files on past and present income taxpayers.

From table A-3 we can see also that there is much variation among the organizations surveyed in the year at which they developed their first computer application to the files we specified. From the mid-1950s through 1962, for instance, "early starters" in several fields developed computer applications to the personal files we asked about. More than one-third of the insurance companies, the state tax and motor-vehicle agencies, and the regional welfare departments report some computer applications to these files by 1962. In contrast, less than 20 percent of the state law-enforcement agencies and education departments report any computer applications to rap sheet or student record files prior to 1962, and only 6 percent of the banks report applications to checking-account files prior to that date.

Rapid development continued to some fields through the mid-1960s, as we see by the fact that 75 percent of the state tax and motor-vehicle agencies, regional welfare departments, and insurance companies had their first applications to the files we specified by 1966. For others, such as state and city law-enforcement agencies, colleges and local school districts, more than 40 percent of the development in each field has occurred since 1967.

In further contrast, one-third of the hospitals and 58 percent of the city law-enforcement agencies had *no* applications to the designated files prior to 1969.

Looking further at table A-3 it is also clear that no single pattern of development characterizes all 14 fields. Among the largest school districts in the country (each one in our sample had at least 10,000 students), 12 percent report computer applications to their permanent pupil records prior to 1960; the same proportion, however, report that they first computerized these files in 1969 or 1970. We find a slightly different pattern among hospitals, where most of the development in computerized medical records (58 percent) appears to have occurred in the past four years, but 14 percent of the institutions report that they had some application in this area much earlier, by 1960.

It is by no means obvious that those organizations which moved early into computerization are today "leaders" in the application of EDP to record-keeping tasks. Some early starters, we know, were not successful in moving beyond their initial steps, and "late" starts on the part of organizations in the same field may represent the kind of careful management which catapults an organization into the forefront of computerization in its field, if only because they began with the advantages of third-generation equipment. Further, we should note that, having sampled from among large cities, counties, and local school districts, table A-3 exaggerates the proportion of organizations which began their computer applications to the designated file early in each of these fields.

In all but two fields (hospitals and regional welfare departments), a majority of the managers report that data processing for the specified file is done on their own in-house computer system. This is the case for more than 80 percent of the state tax, motor-vehicle, and law-enforcement agencies and the insurance companies. Some organizations in each field (at least 14 percent) make use of a service bureau or other outside computer facility, either for all of their processing on the designated files or for some of it. The use of outside computer facilities is particularly pronounced among regional welfare departments (59 percent) and hospitals (63 percent).

Of the organizations in each field which had computer applications to the designated file, we asked a series of 17 questions. One set of these probed the quantity and nature of data in the computerized file compared to that in the manual record system.

Table A-3

Year of First Computer Application to Designated Files[a]

Type and Number of Organizations Reporting Computer Applications	When First Used Computer System to Store and Process Records in the File (Cumulative Percentages).[b]						No Answer
	Before 1955	1955-58	1959-62	1963-66	1967-68	1969-70	
Banks (115)	0	5	20	65	85	100	0
Health/accident insurance (21)	5	15	35	72	91	100	0
Life insurance (126)	0	18	43	77	91	98	2
Colleges (179)	0	8	19	54	81	100	0
Hospitals (51)	4	12	25	46	69	100	0
City law enforcement (27)	7	11	18	50	78	96	4
County law enforcement (17)	0	0	12	18	42	100	0
Regional welfare (27)	8	27	61	84	92	100	0
Local school districts (122)	3	7	22	57	85	98	2
State education (25)	0	0	17	62	83	100	0
State welfare (50)	10	18	28	64	78	100	0
State law enforcement (16)	0	0	19	55	73	98	2
State motor vehicle (33)	3	9	36	69	93	99	1
State tax (42)	7	10	40	73	88	97	3

[a]Those files to which we specifically directed respondents' attention in answering our questions. See table A-2, page 405.
[b]E.g., of the 115 banks in our sample which report computer applications to the file we designated (personal-checking-account records), none had applications to this file prior to 1955. By 1966, 65 percent of the banks in our sample had computer applications to this file.

We turn to the results of these questions in the next section and to examination of the other items on computer impact in the subsequent five sections.

The Quantity and Nature of Data

We noted in our discussion of the site-visit findings that many civil libertarians believe that computerization enables managers to accumulate a greater store of information on each individual than was possible through manual record-keeping methods. Our survey indicates considerable differences from field to field on this matter. Asked first about general increases in data collection over time, many managers reported no increases in data collection since computerization. At the same time, at least one-third of the managers in each field (more than 60 percent in some fields) report that they are indeed collecting more information on each individual since computerizing the files we asked about. (See table

Table A-4

Reported Increases in Data Collection Over Time
(Question 17a)

Type and Number of Organizations with Computer Applications	*Percent Reporting That They Are "Collecting More . . . Data on A Given Individual Than Before Computerization"*[a]
Banks (115)	56
Health/accident insurance (21)	43
Life insurance (126)	32
Colleges (179)	59
Hospitals (51)	65
City law enforcement (27)	37
County law enforcement (17)	41
Regional welfare (27)	33
Local school districts (122)	47
State education (24)	67
State welfare (50)	64
State law enforcement (16)	38
State motor vehicle (33)	49
State tax (42)	62

[a]Less than 3 percent in each field report that they are collecting *less* data on each individual since computerization.

A-4.) The mixed results on this question present a picture not very different from that we drew out of the site visits.

But these responses do not tell us much about how managers perceive the computer's role where there were increases, since changes in record keeping may have occurred simultaneously with computerization that were not in any sense caused by it. Respondents reporting increases were asked in addition if "computerization of these records *directly* affected the amount of data being collected per record." (See table A-5.) While in each field some-

Table A-5

**Percent Reporting the Computer
Directly Responsible for Increased Data Collection
(Question 17b)**

Type and Number of Organizations with Computer Applications	Percent Reporting Both That They Are Collecting More Data on a Given Individual Since Computerization, and That "Computerization of These Records Directly Affected the Amount of Data Being Collected Per Record":	No Answer (to One or Both Questions), Percent
Banks (115)	52	0
Health/accident insurance (21)	40	0
Life insurance (126)	36	3
Colleges (179)	56	2
Hospitals (51)	64	0
City law enforcement (27)	32	3
County law enforcement (17)	35	0
Regional welfare (27)	29	4
Local school districts (122)	42	4
State education (25)	54	0
State welfare (50)	60	2
State law enforcement (16)	19	5
State motor vehicle (33)	47	3
State tax (42)	57	3

what fewer managers were willing to accept this specification, the results remain substantially the same: many of our survey respondents report that increases in the amount of data collected on a given individual are a direct result of computerization.

If we accept this finding at face value, it conflicts with our site-visit finding that, though some organizations have experienced increases in data collection over time, very few managers attribute such changes directly to computerization. We cannot rule out the possibility that among the mainstream of organizations in some fields the computer has had such an effect. But our site-visit findings suggest several clarifications of the way computers can be seen as causing such changes; on the basis of these we suggest that the meaning of this set of survey findings is not at all clear.

First, our use in the questionnaire of the phrases "more data" and "amount of data" fails to distinguish among dimensions we developed later in our project, in clarifying our site-visit findings. We saw in part three that these include *frequency* of update, changes in the *type* of data gathered, increases in the *number* of *items* per record and the introduction of whole new *programs* of data gathering. A "more data" response from one organization may refer to the actual addition of new types of information to a standardized individual record; for another organization, however, the same response might reflect a situation in which computerization has simply prompted more uniform gathering of data which had been collected only haphazardly in the manual era.

Second, our respondents may have confused the computer's impact on the greater *use* of data from individual records with its effect on the collection of *new* items of information; we may have asked managers to make a comparison between manual and computer records which is difficult given their orientation to the use of records. Whether or not a given item of information was actually present in the manual record may be a matter of little significance to managers—compared with the importance of changes in *the amount of information available* for making decisions. The computer's impact in making more available that information which is in the record may have led some respondents to report an actual increase in data collection.

Third, responses to an additional question asked of those who reported a direct computer impact on data collection leave in doubt the matter of how managers interpreted the word "direct." Presented with concrete examples of what we defined as direct and indirect computer effects on data-gathering programs, managers in all fields were able to distinguish between the computer's

Table A-6

Direct and Indirect Computer Impact
(Question 17c)

Of those managers who said that computerization had directly affected the amount of data being gathered per person, we asked the following: "Which would you say is the *primary* reason for increased data collection: (*a*) increased collection, storage, and processing capability of computer; or (*b*) changes in organizational objectives or programs and/or increasing government requirements for collection or reporting information?"

Type and Number of Organizations	Number[a] Reporting the Primary Reason to Be:	
	Increased Computer Capacity	Changes in Programs or Requirements
Banks (60)	42	18
Health/accident insurance (8)	6	1 (no answer: 1)
Life insurance (34)	22	12
Colleges (98)	47	51
Hospitals (34)	17	17
City law enforcement (9)	3	5 (no answer: 1)
County law enforcement (6)	4	2
Regional welfare (8)	4	3 (no answer: 1)
Local school districts (53)	30	23
State education (13)	9	4
State welfare (15)	5	10
State law enforcement (3)	2	1
State motor vehicle (16)	7	9
State tax (24)	14	10

[a]For more than half the fields there were 16 or fewer respondents. Rather than offering percentages on so few cases for these fields, we have not shown percentaged responses for *any* field.

larger storage and retrieval capacity *per se* as a reason for undertaking greater data collection on each individual, and instances in which the computer played a role in program changes or the setting of increased government reporting requirements, but was not the prime mover behind such changes. (See table A-6.) Responses to this question suggest that, in the previous question, some managers described as direct a computer impact which we think of as indirect. Thus for example, half the hospitals which report a direct computer impact on the amount of data collected go on to suggest that the primary reason for the increase is that new programs or government reporting requirements had been established. In several fields this question was relevant for only a small number of organizations (fewer than 15), and we will not therefore attempt to draw conclusions about differences between fields on this item.

Overall, this set of findings indicates that many among our survey respondents believe that the computer has, in some sense, directly resulted in an increase in the amount of data collected per record. Our difficulty in interpreting what the responses mean points up the need to pose with care questions as to what changes in data collection are "associated with" computerization. As in advanced organizations, the computer rarely stands alone as an agent of change in complex organizations and is almost always embedded in policy and social settings which affect its use.

When we move beyond the sheer size of the individual's computerized record to consider the nature of personal data to be found within it, the general thrust of our survey findings is more clearly similar to that of the site-visit results. We asked managers to compare the content of their computerized and manual records on the same individuals, and to agree or disagree with three separate statements that reflect what we found in advanced computerizing organizations (table A-7). Since the questions were not equally successful in eliciting meaningful results, we will discuss each one separately below.

Judging from the relatively low rate of nonresponse, the question on "narrative" data seems to have been the clearest of the three—perhaps representing the least sensitive issue to respondents. In most of the organizations, the computerized files we specified contain relatively little personal data in narrative form— though some (e.g., medical records or welfare files) may contain coded information which was derived from narrative reports. At least 72 percent of the managers in each field report that the more narrative information on clients, customers, and citizens is still kept in manual form. College registrar offices for example, may maintain recommendations on students but they do not generally put narrative detail from such documents into their computer

Table A-7

Where Is the Most Narrative, Sensitive, and Subjective Information Stored?
(Question 23)

Type and Number of Organizations with Computer Applications	Percent Agreeing That:		
	"The more narrative and lengthy information is still kept in manual form"	*"The more sensitive and confidential information is kept in manual form"*[a]	*"The more subjective (opinion based) information is still kept in manual form"*[a]
Banks (115)	72	44	61
Health/accident insurance (21)	76	59	76
Life insurance (126)	91	76	73
Colleges (179)	84	71	76
Hospitals (51)	77	63	58
City law enforcement (27)	88	76	76
County law enforcement (17)	88	75	56
Regional welfare (27)	96	73	77
Local school districts (122)	87	83	87
State education (25)	74	47	68
State welfare (50)	100	69	78
State law enforcement (16)	87	60	67
State motor vehicle (33)	87	40	43
State tax (42)	93	50	57

[a]Nonresponse rates approximate the proportion of negative responses to the item. For example, 71 percent of college respondents say manual files are more sensitive, but only 15 percent say that manual files are *not* more sensitive. Presumably the remaining 14 percent who did not respond could not decide which files were more sensitive because "sensitive" is too ill defined or because the contents of the manual and computerized files are too heterogeneous to permit a judgment. The same applies to the item on "subjective" information.

files. State motor-vehicle departments which maintain accident reports typically do not computerize narratives from these.

A majority of managers in most (11 out of 14) fields also suggest that the more "sensitive and confidential" information is kept in manual, rather than computerized, form. This finding fits well both with the preceding one and with our site-visit observations, but is marred by the difficulty we had in getting across the concept of "relative sensitivity" clearly. As a result, there were as many nonrespondents as there were those who answered "no" on this item—complicating even some simple comparisons. On the whole, however, the sensitivity of records and whether or not they are narrative in character are related phenomena as far as computerization is concerned. In the site visits to advanced organizations, we noted that the information considered by managers to be most sensitive and confidential was more likely to be narrative in character. As a result, it was less likely to be computerized given the additional cost often associated with computerization of lengthy English text or the reduction of narrative data to codes which retain the necessary detail and meaning. We also noted that, beyond these technical difficulties, a special effort was made in some organizations to keep sensitive information off the computer because managers felt that computer storage was less secure.

However, we can see in the banking and state motor-vehicles responses that this finding with respect to sensitivity has to be related directly to the specific files we asked about. Fifty percent of the bank managers in our sample report that the most sensitive information on checking-account customers is *not* in manual form. Given the nature of such files, this reponse is quite understandable, since managers might well regard the account-balance and account "activity" information on checking customers to be as sensitive as anything held in the manual checking files on them. Had we asked instead about computerization in the loan departments their responses would probably have been different, since sensitive information used in making decisions about loans—credit and employment information and the results of interviews with loan officers—are typically not computerized.

In motor-vehicle agencies also, 50 percent of the officials reported that the most sensitive information on drivers licenses is *not* in manual form. This response is also understandable, since for most licensees, information which may be regarded as sensitive—on convictions, accidents, revocations, and disabilities—is computerized. While there may be manual files containing more sensitive information (as in the medical complaint and hearings files at the

New York State Motor Vehicle Department), these typically pertain only to a small proportion of the licensees. In addition, at least *summary* information from even these sensitive manual files is almost always on tape. Thus, while the detailed medical reports on a disability are not computerized, *some notation* of the disability will be in the computer files; and while the full conditions surrounding a conviction and license revocation may be spelled out only in manual files, the revocation and reasons for it will be noted in the computer record. For all practical purposes in such organizations then, the information in computerized files *is* as sensitive as that in their manual counterparts.

At least 56 percent of the managers in most of the fields (13 out of 14) also agreed that "the more subjective (opinion-based) information is still kept in manual form." This question as well was marred by a high nonresponse rate, and it is clear that this item was not well constructed—especially for those organizations which have relatively little "opinion-based" information in the files we designated (such as in checking-account and state motor-vehicle files). Further, there are files such as those in medicine in which diagnoses may be entered into the computer files, while other opinion-based but less certain information—such as a physician's working notes or hunches—does indeed remain off the computer. Our question was not suited for so fine but important a distinction.

Consolidation and Integration of Information in Computerized Files

At the beginning of the questionnaire, we asked managers to estimate for us how much of their total information on employees, clients, customers, and other persons they have computerized. No one said that "all" the information in their files is on computer, and fewer than 40 percent of the managers in ten fields answered that "most" of their information on employees, clients or citizens is computerized. The exceptions occurred in four fields where computerization has been particularly far-reaching—state motor-vehicle and tax departments, life-insurance companies, and welfare departments at the state level.

In most organizations, this pattern holds for *all* files. Even in the most highly computerized record systems (e.g., payroll files in many organizations and checking-account records in banks), some manual files are still retained and used. For the files we specifically designated, at least three-quarters of the managers in each field report that they have manual records as well on the same individuals, and that these manual files are not simply duplicates; not all of the information in these files has been computerized.

Given this picture of "mixed media" record systems and the utter lack of overall data integration we observed in the most advanced computer systems, our survey results from a question on the integration of records were at first puzzling. In five fields, at least 70 percent of managers agree that the computer has *not* enabled them to pull together, in one record, "all of the information your organization collects and records about a given individual." But between 40 and 60 percent of the managers in nine fields report that computerization *has* resulted in this integration of information into a single record. (See table A-8.) We think, however, that the results in table A-8 are not credible, since they contradict what managers report at other points in the survey and because it is likely that respondents were led by the wording of the question to report greater integration of records than had in fact occurred as a result of computerization.

As we noted above, at two different points in the survey most of the managers report that they have not computerized records on all of their employees, clients, and citizens, and that for any single category of record subject, there are manual files containing information which is not duplicated in the computer system. We cannot square these findings with the results in table A-8 without assuming some misunderstanding.

We intentionally phrased the question in an extreme fashion, reflecting one aspect of the public fears expressed about computerization. In the midst of items relating to specifically designated files, this question required an answer in terms of *all* the data typically maintained on a given individual in the organization. Some respondents obviously caught this shift and answered appropriately. Very probably, however, many others answered with the same specific set of records in mind to which we had forced their attention for most of the questionnaire. For example, some university respondents may have answered with only the records of the registrar in mind, rather than with respect to *all* the records maintained by the university on each student. Without taking the term too strictly, "all" of the data on students maintained and used regularly by the registrar's office may be on computer in some colleges; but this is not the kind of integration of records we were asking about or concerning which civil libertarians have raised alarms.

The assertion by this solid minority of managers that com-

Table A-8

Data Integration Arising Out of Computerization

Type and Number of Organizations with Computer Applications	Percent Agreeing That the Application of Computer Technology in Their Organization Does Not Enable Them to Pull Together, in One Record, All of the Information the Organization Collects and Records on a Given Individual	No Response, Percent
Banks (115)	74	2
Health/accident insurance (21)	53	0
Life insurance (126)	58	1
Colleges (179)	63	0
Hospitals (51)	59	0
City law enforcement (27)	52	7
County law enforcement (17)	41	0
Regional welfare (27)	74	0
Local school districts (122)	57	3
State education (24)	46	0
State welfare (50)	70	0
State law enforcement (16)	81	0
State motor vehicle (33)	58	0
State tax (42)	72	2

puterization had led to organizationwide data integration is so far outside our site-visit experiences, and beyond even the exaggerated management and computer literature, that we have to treat it as reflecting an error rather than as new and important information. With this set of results disregarded, our survey findings about data integration support the notion that the kind of "total" integration many civil libertarians fear has not yet occurred in most organizations, be they small and new to computers or the largest and most advanced computerizing institutions.

Individual Rights of Access

In all but one field (hospitals) a majority of the managers say that individuals *do* know that their records exist in the organization and can examine at least some of the data in these. Further, it appears that in most organizations computerization has not led to changes in the extent to which managers either restrict or allow an individual access to his files.

We asked the managers in each field about individual access to the designated files, whether they were computerized or not (table A-9). With the exception of hospitals, a majority of managers in each field report that individuals both know that the particular records exist and can examine at least some of the data in them. However, in all but four fields, a majority of organizations restrict access to these records in some degree; an individual cannot examine all of the data in his record.

Beyond these uniformities, the findings reflect the diversity of record-keeping policies and traditions among organizations. Life-insurance companies and state welfare agencies, for instance, are more likely to report that an individual does not even know that his file exists. What accounts for this in the former is the fact that most life policy files tend not to be active; except for paying premiums, the individual may have little contact with the firm and may give little thought to what kinds of records his life-insurance company retains concerning him. State welfare files may be invisible to the individual in another way. Many central state agencies have no direct contact with clients—maintaining records on individuals only for regulatory and evaluation purposes, while the active files remain at the state field offices (or in the county departments) which actually administer the programs.

The organizations most likely to report that individuals have access to *no data* in their own records are hospitals (54 percent) and regional welfare offices (42 percent). There is considerable variation *within* fields here—reflecting both differences in state law on access to medical records, for instance[7] and county administrative practice. The same kind of differences were seen on our site visits.

Bank managers and officials in state education, tax, and motor-vehicle departments are most likely to report that the individual is allowed to examine *all* the data in his file. Differences

---

[7]Some of the hospitals in our sample are psychiatric institutions. Even where state law permits access to *medical* files, no patient access to psychiatric files may be allowed.

Table A-9

Individual Access to Records
(Question 6)

Type and Total Number of Organizations Responding to the Survey	Percent[a] Reporting That the Individual Can Examine All, Some, or None of the Data in the Specified Records on Them:			Individual Does Not Know That the Record Exists, Percent	No Response on This Item, Percent
	All Data	Some Data	No Data		
Banks (179)	51	27	7	8	7
Health/accident insurance (25)	48	28	16	8	0
Life insurance (159)	20	33	20	25	2
Colleges (280)	46	47	5	1	1
Hospitals (211)	18	24	54	3	1
City law enforcement (133)	27	44	28	1	0
County law enforcement (48)	21	29	38	4	8
Regional welfare (62)	10	42	42	3	5
Local school districts (223)	30	56	9	4	1
State education (38)	55	24	8	8	5
State welfare (61)	13	38	21	25	3
State law enforcement (41)	37	27	27	5	4
State motor vehicle (38)	68	29	3	0	0
State tax (43)	56	29	5	5	8

[a]Percentages may not add across to 100 because of rounding.

among fields on this question reflect the content of the records we designated. Checking-account files, academic records on primary and secondary school students, and driver's-license files each contain data that the individual himself supplied, and they do not typically contain employee evaluations or the kind of third-party data which might threaten the organization's interests if revealed to the individual.

Three sources of distortion probably affected responses to this item. First is the likelihood that, even in this anonymous survey, managers exaggerated the extent to which individuals really have access to their own records. A second (and possibly offsetting) problem with this question is that we used the term "examine" to describe individual access to records. Some organizations will tell individuals about the content of files on them, but will not let them actually examine the record. If managers took this term literally, our results may underestimate somewhat the level of access which individuals actually have. It is difficult to estimate the effect of these problems on responses for any particular field. Finally, even though we asked the managers of each type of organization about a fairly specific set of records, variations in access practices *within* each field may reflect differences among organizations of the same type as to what they include in the records we designated. Thus college registrar office files which contain no confidential recommendations are more likely to be open for examination by the student than those which do contain confidential documents.

We compared access policies in computerized and noncomputerized files. In some organizational realms it appears that the individual is allowed greater access to computerized records than to those which are not computerized. In other fields, the reverse seems to be true.[8] But the differences were small and there were too few cases involved in these comparisons to make firm statistical statements possible. We can say without doubt, however, that the survey produced no clear indication that computerization has the effect of *reducing* the individual's access to important files.

This finding was confirmed by the recollections of managers in organizations which had computerized the specific files we asked about. An overwhelming majority (over 80 percent) of the managers in each field report that no "new rules concerning the individual's right to examine his record" had been issued since computerization. As in the case of the site visit organizations, access rules have been carried over from manual to computerized systems—whether these rules were restrictive or protective of individual civil liberties in this area.

---

[8] Among colleges, for instance, 53 percent of the 179 institutions with computer applications to undergraduate files in the registrar's office allow the individual to examine all the data in such files, while 39 percent of the 101 colleges without computer applications in this area allow such access.

Among life-insurance companies, on the other hand, 19 percent of the 126 firms with computer applications to files on current policy holders allow them access to all data in the files, while 29 percent of the 33 firms with no such applications allow the customer access to all his records.

The Accuracy and Completeness of Individual Records

The managers surveyed report both that computerization turns up errors in the manual records, and that computer processing itself involves some new occasions for errors.

Questions about the accuracy of files were not always answered with ease on our site visits. As expected, our question ("Has conversion of these records to computerized form led to detection and correction of factual errors which previously existed in manual records?") was marked by a relatively high rate of "don't know" responses—as high as 47 percent. This confirms in part what we saw in the site visits: in many organizations little is known and few, if any, studies are done.

This is also an area in which computerizing organizations differ in their computerization experience. The location and detection of errors that is so prominent an aspect of some computer conversion efforts is virtually absent in others. The extent to which this corrective process takes place depends on such factors as the resources an organization is able to devote to it, the susceptibility of a given file to errors, the level of error which is tolerable given the organization's goals, and whether the computer application is being developed out of paper files or from files which have previously been converted to cards for EAM processing.

Even with the high rate of "don't know" responses from some types of organizations, at least 63 percent of the managers in 9 of the 14 fields report (table A-10) that errors were detected and corrected in the computer conversion of the designated records. For banks, colleges, city and county law-enforcement agencies, and regional welfare departments, the results were less clear, since many respondents in these fields report that they do not know whether or not detection and correction of errors occurred.

Because it is possible that the kind of errors discovered in the process of computerization may have trivial civil-liberties implications, we asked managers whether the corrections they made in computer conversion concerned items which are typically important in making decisions about the individuals. For all but two types of organizations, a majority of the managers who report that computerization led to detection and correction or errors in personal records also report (table A-11) that these errors were important. A substantial proportion of the managers in the three commercial fields report that the errors detected in their checking

Table A-10

Record Accuracy and Computerization
(Question 16a)

Type and Number of Organizations with Computer Applications	Did Conversion of the Designated Records to Computerized Form Lead to Detection and Correction of Factual Errors Which Previously Existed in Manual Records?			
	Yes, Percent	No, Percent	Don't Know, Percent	No Answer, Percent
Banks (115)	60	27	13	0
Health/accident insurance (21)	86	4	10	0
Life insurance (126)	89	4	7	0
Colleges (179)	50	28	22	0
Hospitals (51)	65	7	28	0
City law enforcement (27)	52	14	33	1
County law enforcement (17)	41	12	47	0
Regional welfare (27)	52	11	37	0
Local school districts (122)	63	10	26	1
State education (24)	63	12	25	0
State welfare (50)	82	6	12	0
State law enforcement (16)	100	0	0	0
State motor vehicle (33)	88	3	9	0
State tax (42)	77	7	15	1

and insurance files were of "little or no importance," perhaps reflecting the use of checking-account records and life-insurance policy files more for bookkeeping than for making decisions about individuals. Government agencies, on the other hand, more frequently report as of "considerable importance" the errors discovered in converting tax, motor-vehicle, and welfare files.

We noted in the course of our site visits that conversion to computer storage and processing carried with it some new possibilities for error which might affect the accuracy of personal records. While most of these errors (of commission or omission, substantive

Table A-11

Importance of Errors Discovered through Computerization
(Question 16b)

Type and Number of Organizations Discovering Errors through Computerization	Were the Corrections Made on Record Items Which Are Important in Making Decisions About the Individuals on Whom Records Are Kept?				
	Yes, Considerable Importance, Percent	*Yes, Marginal Importance, Percent*	*No, of Little or No importance, Percent*	*Don't Know, Percent*	*No Answer, Percent*
Banks (68)	25	34	37	4	0
Health/accident insurance (18)	50	11	39	0	0
Life insurance (115)	23	27	48	2	0
Colleges (100)	37	33	22	7	1
Hospitals (38)	18	44	24	13	0
City law enforcement (15)	33	40	20	7	0
County law enforcement (8)	(4)[a]	(1)	(1)	(2)	0
Regional welfare (17)	35	29	12	24	0
Local school districts (80)	36	49	11	4	0
State education (15)	40	40	13	7	0
State welfare (44)	41	39	14	6	0
State law enforcement (16)	25	44	19	12	0
State motor vehicle (31)	52	26	6	16	0
State tax (32)	75	13	6	6	0

[a]Where fewer than 15 cases were involved, results were not percentaged.

errors in content, misidentifications, etc.) do not differ from those in manual systems, the new equipment and processes involved require new solutions to accuracy problems. In addition to carrying many of the same types of error forward, as we noted, computerization also carries with it some kinds of error unique to electronic data processing. A majority of the managers in seven fields agreed (table A-12) that they have encountered problems in

Table A-12

The Computer as a Source of Error
(Question 16c)

Have There Been Significant Problems in Maintaining
Accuracy of Computerized Records—Problems Which
Were Not Present in the Manual System?[a]

Type and Number of Organizations with Computer Applications	Yes, Significant Problems, Percent	Yes, Marginal Problems, Percent	No, Problems of Little or No Importance, Percent	Don't Know, Percent	No Answer, Percent
Banks (115)	3	14	77	4	2
Health/accident insurance (21)	5	33	62	0	0
Life insurance (126)	9	18	71	3	0
Colleges (179)	16	47	34	2	1
Hospitals (51)	6	28	63	4	0
City law enforcement (27)	11	26	52	7	5
County law enforcement (17)	24	24	39	8	5
Regional welfare (27)	26	33	36	7	0
Local school districts (122)	15	53	26	4	2
State education (24)	29	29	42	0	0
State welfare (50)	44	30	20	8	0
State law enforcement (16)	19	44	38	0	0
State motor vehicle (33)	24	42	27	6	3
State tax (42)	18	31	41	8	2

[a]Percentages may not add across to 100 because of rounding.

maintaining the accuracy of computer records "which were not
present in the manual system." In five types of government
organizations (state welfare, state motor vehicle, regional welfare,
state education, and county law enforcement) between 24 and 44
percent of the managers report that the accuracy problems were
"significant" rather than "marginal."

Computerization and Confidentiality

Each of the 14 types of organizations shares identified data from its files with outside persons or agencies. Some share as a matter of routine, e.g., government agencies such as motor-vehicle departments and law-enforcement organizations. Others share on an ad hoc basis only: banks respond to occasional inquiries from law-enforcement agencies or from legislative committees about checking accounts. At least 60 percent of the managers in 10 of the 14 fields we surveyed report that they regularly[9] make identified information from the designated files available to some outside individuals and groups. Between 16 percent and 48 percent of the banks, insurance companies, and state tax agencies report the same.

A clear majority of the managers and officials in each field say that their organization has formulated a policy—written or unwritten—covering such disclosures (see table A-13). The degree to which such policies have been formalized varies considerably among the responding organizations. Private commercial firms appear least likely to have written policies; in fact, 20 percent of the health and accident insurers, 18 percent of the life insurers, and 11 percent of the banks report that they have formulated no policy at all on the matter of disclosures from their files on customers, and less than 30 percent in each field report *written* policies. In contrast, over 70 percent of the welfare departments and state tax and state motor-vehicle agencies report *written* policies. This is not a matter of choice for individual welfare agencies; for the files we asked about, there are formal regulations on disclosure handed down by HEW.

Of equal importance to civil liberties is whether or not policies are communicated to the individuals about whom records are stored. At least 25 percent of the organizations in 9 of the 14 fields report (table A-14) that "an explicit statement" of their policy on disclosure is "almost *never* communicated" to the individuals whose records they maintain and use. Insurance firms and law-enforcement agencies stand out in this regard. Colleges and regional welfare departments are more likely than others to communicate their disclosure policies regularly. A majority of man-

---

[9] We did not ask managers to distinguish between "regular" and "occasional" sharing of data from their files. In fact, we simply asked whether or not they shared data. But follow-up on some of our respondents indicates that most (quite appropriately) took our question to mean "share on a regular basis."

Table A-13

Policy on Disclosures of Information
(Question 7)

Type and Number of Organizations Responding to the Survey	*Is There a General Management Policy Regarding Disclosures from the Designated Files?*			
	No Policy Has Been Formulated, Percent	Unwritten Policy, Percent	Written Policy, Percent	No Answer, Percent
Banks (179)	11	55	25	9
Health/accident insurance (25)	20	56	24	0
Life insurance (159)	18	65	15	2
Colleges (280)	5	46	46	3
Hospitals (211)	10	29	60	1
City law enforcement (133)	4	46	49	1
County law enforcement (48)	13	42	44	1
Regional welfare (62)	0	23	74	3
Local school districts (223)	5	49	43	3
State education (38)	13	47	34	6
State welfare (61)	5	12	80	3
State law enforcement (41)	5	32	56	7
State motor vehicle (38)	3	24	71	2
State tax (43)	2	12	81	5

agers in ten of the fields, however, report that they discuss their disclosure policies "at times . . . as the need arises."

Computerization does not seem to affect these dimensions of data sharing policies. When we compared the responses from organizations which had computerized the designated files with those which had not, we found that computerizing organizations do not report regular data sharing from these personal records with any greater frequency. Furthermore computerization does not appear to have significantly affected either the degree to which disclosure policies are formalized or the degree to which

Table A-14

Communication of Disclosure Policies
(Question 7)

Is an Explicit Statement of the Policy on Disclosure Communicated to the Individuals Whose Records Are Maintained in the File?

Type and Number of Responding Organizations with Disclosure Policy	Almost Never Communicated, Percent	Discussed at Times, Percent	Regularly Communicated, Percent	No Answer, Percent
Banks (144)	29	55	8	8
Health/accident insurance (17)	45	50	5	0
Life insurance (127)	58	35	2	5
Colleges (258)	12	62	24	2
Hospitals (187)	22	64	14	0
City law enforcement (127)	49	47	4	0
County law enforcement (42)	44	54	2	0
Regional welfare (58)	10	67	18	5
Local school districts (205)	24	60	11	5
State education (31)	26	39	32	3
State welfare (56)	30	36	21	13
State law enforcement (36)	42	53	3	2
State motor vehicle (36)	22	69	8	1
State tax (40)	31	51	15	3

such policies are communicated to those on whom records are kept.

Like the issue of "more" data collection, the question of "how much" or how "widely" an organization shares identified information from its files is complicated. In the sites studied, computerization had indirectly affected the data sharing of some organizations (1) when government agencies set reporting requirements in the knowledge that computerization made provision of the requested information feasible, and (2) as new programs were established or expanded in part because of the advantages represented by computerization.

A majority of the managers and officials in only three fields surveyed report (table A-15) that "the increased retrieval capacity after computerization" has led them to "furnish more *identified* information about individuals in this file" to a government agency. While the question we used had to be worded in a very general fashion, these results confirm our impression that the role of computerization in encouraging new reporting requirements and programs has been a highly selective one. Law enforcement, wel-

Table A-15

Does Computerization Affect Data Sharing?
(Question 20)

Type and Number of Organizations with Computer Applications	Percent Saying That They Do Furnish More Identified Information About Individuals in This File to a Government Agency (Executive, Legislative, or Judicial; Federal, State, or Local) as a Result of the Increased Retrieval Capacity After Computerization	No Answer, Percent
Banks (115)	8	2
Health/accident insurance (21)	24	0
Life insurance (129)	11	10
Colleges (179)	18	0
Hospitals (51)	22	8
City law enforcement (27)	22	10
County law enforcement (17)	47	1
Regional welfare (27)	37	5
Local school districts (122)	13	1
State education (24)	33	0
State welfare (50)	52	0
State law enforcement (16)	50	0
State motor vehicle (33)	64	0
State tax (42)	36	2

fare, and state motor-vehicle departments are most likely to report this indirect impact of computerization. This probably reflects the computer's role in some relatively new programs at the federal level, such as the National Driver Registration Service (which we discussed in the New York State Motor Vehicle profile). Note that the "new" sharing encouraged by computerization in some of the organizations we visited represented more frequent sharing of personal data, rather than any expansion of the class of legitimate users. Note also that our question does *not* tap increased sharing with private organizations as a result of computerization.

A majority of managers in 9 of the 14 fields agreed that computerization has resulted in greater sharing of *statistical* data (in which individuals are not identified) from the designated files. This increase is most frequently reported (table A-16) by managers in government systems. This pattern fits well with what we heard from the government officials we visited, who described to us demands being made on them for statistical reports—demands they felt would never have been made were it not for the assumption that their computer systems would permit easy compliance.

Such sharing generally represents little threat to individual civil liberties, as noted in part three. But there may be serious problems where individual identities can be deduced from the statistical data. The statistical exchanges reported in the survey reflect the fact that managers are often more interested in statistical summaries than in information on individual cases. But as such interorganizational exchanges have developed and become widespread, they may have generated some civil-liberties concern among those who assumed that computerization "naturally" leads to the sharing of identified information. There is nothing in our data to suggest that this is the case; the character of the data and whether or not records on identified individuals are shared depends not on the computer's capacities but on organizational needs and legal and policy considerations.

In part three, we noted that another aspect of confidentiality in personal record-keeping is the ability of the organization to keep its records secure from unauthorized access. We suggested that good security did not necessarily protect confidentiality, since *deliberate* sharing of data by organizations has been the greatest threat to confidentiality. We also pointed out that even the best intentioned confidentiality policies could be ineffective where security did not match the threat of illegitimate penetration

Table A-16

Does Computerization Affect the Sharing of Statistical Data?
(Question 21)

Type and Number of Organizations with Computer Applications	*Percent Saying That They Do Furnish More Statistical (Unidentified) Data About Individuals in This File to a Government Agency as a Result of the Increased Retrieval Capacity After Computerization*	No Answer, Percent
Banks (115)	24	3
Health/accident insurance (21)	19	0
Life insurance (126)	14	0
Colleges (179)	53	10
Hospitals (51)	47	0
City law enforcement (27)	56	7
County law enforcement (17)	59	0
Regional welfare (27)	70	0
Local school districts (122)	48	0
State education (24)	83	0
State welfare (50)	84	0
State law enforcement (16)	81	0
State motor vehicle (33)	88	0
State tax (42)	80	2

of the files. With this set of concerns in mind, we asked the managers about the security of their computerized files.

As might be expected from our site visit findings, physical and administrative protections are reported (table A-17) more frequently than technological ones. In 10 of the 14 fields, more than 60 percent of the managers report some control of physical access to the files, such as door locks or badges for access to the computer room. Similarly, over 50 percent of the managers in 10

Table A-17

Technical and Administrative Safeguards
(Question 19)

A number of countermeasures have been proposed to prevent access to computerized records by unauthorized persons. Do you use any of the following for the designated file?

(a) Control of physical access to the file (e.g., door locks, badges for access to computer room).
(b) Hardware/software security measures (e.g., cryptographic encoding, passwords, terminal identification code).
(c) Personal integrity checks (e.g., special investigation of operating personnel; bonded employees).
(d) Audit logs or other data-monitoring methods.
(e) Procedures and rules for disposal of data (e.g., destruction of print-out or tapes).
(f) Other, please specify.

Percent Reporting the Following Security Safeguards:

Type and Number of Organizations with Computer Applications	Control Physical Access	Hardware/ Software Measures	Investigate Personnel	Audit Logs	Destroy Discarded Data	Other
Banks (115)	64	32	69	62	75	3
Health/accident insurance (21)	67	33	48	67	67	0
Life insurance (126)	55	25	41	48	51	3
Colleges (179)	67	30	16	28	52	3
Hospitals (51)	67	18	29	26	29	6
City law enforcement (27)	67	44	48	41	63	4
County law enforcement (17)	53	41	41	41	41	6
Regional welfare (27)	63	26	26	26	48	0
Local school districts (122)	54	29	23	34	50	4
State education (24)	42	33	8	29	71	8
State welfare (50)	60	22	32	44	72	0
State law enforcement (16)	63	63	69	69	44	0
State motor vehicle (33)	82	58	39	42	57	3
State tax (42)	77	39	62	59	85	8

of the 14 fields report that they have procedures and rules for disposal of data, such as destruction of print-out or taped data which are no longer needed. In contrast, less than 50 percent of the managers in 12 of the 14 fields report that they use hardware/software security measures such as cryptographic encoding, passwords, audit logs, or other methods of data monitoring.

The "Need" for Computers

Managers responded to two questions which speak both to the continuing nature of computerization efforts and to the character of computer applications already accomplished. In the first, we asked managers to note whether computerization of the designated records had had any of the following three effects on their organization: (1) "Improvement in routine, large-scale operations"; (2) "Generation of more timely or complete reports to management"; or (3) "Direct improvement in policy planning by top management." (See table A-18.)

Even taking into account the bias introduced by the order of these items in the questionnaire, the differences between (1) and (3) are striking. At least 70 percent of the managers in 13 of the 14 fields report that the computer has improved large scale data handling operations. Between 46 and 86 percent of the managers in each field report that the computer caused better management reporting. However, in only two fields (health and accident insurance firms and state motor-vehicle departments) did a clear majority of the managers report direct improvement in policy planning.

There is some circularity in our questioning here, of course, since the files we designated for many organizations are among those of highest volume and subject to routine processing. We did not ask about the *overall* impact of the computer in each organization or about its effect on those files which are by definition closer to the policy and planning function.

The pattern of impact may differ for computer applications to *other* files in the same organizations. But these responses partially confirm what the site visits and an increasing number of knowledgeable commentators suggest: with very few exceptions the computer has figured more in the support of routine operations than it has in management decision making which affects individuals. Furthermore, what we have called "file automation" (part three) has not generated, by intent or as a serendipitous effect, substantial changes in policy-making capability.

Second, we asked managers to describe how they perceive

Table A-18

Overall Computer Impact
(Question 13)

		Percent Reporting the Following Computer Impact:		
Type and Number of Organizations with Computerized Files	*Specified Files*	*Improvement in Routine, Large-Scale Operations*	*Generation of More Timely or Complete Reports to Management*	*Direct Improvement in Policy Planning*
Banks (115)	Personal checking	86	77	44
Health/accident insurance (21)	Current policyholders	86	86	57
Life insurance (126)	Current policyholders	91	79	45
Colleges (179)	Registrar's file	77	70	28
Hospitals (51)	Central medical records	71	84	39
City law enforcement (27)	Rap sheets	70	78	48
County law enforcement (17)	Rap sheets	59	46	29
Regional welfare (26)	Current recipients	74	59	44
Local school districts (122)	Pupil records	76	71	35
State education (24)	Pupil records	79	71	33
State welfare (50)	Past and present recipients	78	70	40
State law enforcement (16)	Rap sheets	75	50	31
State motor vehicle (33)	Licensed operators	94	70	58
State tax (42)	Past and present taxpayers	87	64	49

their overall needs for the computer. With respect to the designated files, they were asked to select either: "We could not manage a file of this size or complexity without the computer" or

"The applications have had relatively little impact on our use of this file." Their answers reflect the "permanence" of computer applications, *especially* in those fields most subject to the press of high-volume operations, such as motor vehicle, tax, and welfare departments, and in the insurance area. In 7 out of 14 fields, more than 60 percent of the managers report that they could not manage the files without the computer.

In five of the remaining fields, responses are split about evenly between those who could not manage without it and those for whom the computer is only a useful improvement. Where a substantial proportion of managers report that they could manage the designated file without the computer, as is asserted by 63 percent of the city law-enforcement agencies and 49 percent of the local school districts, we have no way of knowing whether such responses came from organizations with very limited computer applications, or from systems for whom the promised benefits of more extensive computer applications failed to materialize. Very few respondents were ready to discount the computer's impact completely (table A-19). In only three fields (city, county, and state law enforcement) did more than 5 percent of the managers say that the computer had had little or no impact on their handling of rap sheet files. County agencies stand out in this regard (28 percent), but the small number of cases here (17) make this result difficult to assess.

Had we asked about computer applications in less sensitive files, the perceived "indispensability" of the computer might well have been greater for several categories of organizations. For instance, had we probed computer applications in hospital billing or university payroll operations, rather than the more civil-liberties-relevant files on patients and students, a far higher proportion of respondents might well have reported that they could not manage this high-volume record-keeping without the advantages of EDP. This is not to suggest that their perception must be accepted as true, but rather to recall our site-visit judgment that managerial perceptions of computerization are tied to *specific* record systems.

Managers' Awareness of Complaints from Record Subjects

In each of the 55 advanced computerizing organizations we visited, some managers were not even aware of certain civil-liberties issues and problems and in some cases had little knowledge of some aspects of their own record-keeping. Managers sometimes

Table A-19

Is the Computer Indispensable?
(Question 14)

Percent Reporting the Following Computer Impact to the Designated Files:

Type and Number of Responding Organizations with Computerized Files	Could Not Manage Without Computer	Useful Improvement But Could Do Without	Relatively Little Impact	No Answer
Banks (115)	51	45	4	0
Health/accident insurance (21)	67	33	0	0
Life insurance (126)	65	32	1	1
Colleges (179)	49	47	3	1
Hospitals (51)	53	45	2	1
City law enforcement (27)	26	63	11	0
County law enforcement (17)	53	19	28	0
Regional welfare (26)	74	26	0	0
Local school districts (122)	49	49	2	0
State education (24)	63	33	4	0
State welfare (50)	78	22	0	0
State law enforcement (16)	50	44	6	0
State motor vehicle (33)	85	15	0	0
State tax (42)	87	13	0	0

constructed policies on the basis of assumptions about the concerns of customers, clients, or citizens, but few of the organizations we visited had made any special effort to obtain information which might test such assumptions. This was particularly evident where record use and data-sharing practices were not visible to record subjects or where the latter were reluctant to provide the kind of feedback to managers which might reflect their civil-liberties concerns. We touched upon some aspects of the problem of "awareness" in the survey findings presented above. Some managers, for instance, report having no policy whatsoever on disclosure of personal information from the files we designated. This suggests that the matter of disclosure has not become an important issue or problem for these organizations. We suggest further that the relatively high nonresponse rates for items probing the accuracy of records may reflect a lack of awareness in this area similar to that which we encountered at some of the advanced site-visit organizations.

The volume of complaints from individual record subjects is not a source of high awareness and concern for most managers (table A-20). Our survey results on this specific question suggest very clearly three conclusions from the site visits: that managers do not receive what they consider to be "frequent" complaints about their record-keeping practices; that they are often not in a position to know the nature or number of complaints made; and that data on the sheer number of complaints an organization receives are very difficult to interpret in any meaningful way.

Managers were asked to describe the frequency with which they received complaints "on grounds of privacy, against the *collection* of any item of information in the designated file." Similar questions were posed covering complaints about *disclosure* of information and about the individual's right to examine his own file. Further, respondents were asked to specify the level of complaint from employees, record subjects, civic and community groups, and government agencies.

No matter what the issue, almost no respondents report "frequent" complaints about their policies from any source (tables A-20 through A-22). While many managers report that they have received "occasional" complaints on one or more of the issues we specified, in 10 out of the 14 fields more than 50 percent say that their organization never receives complaints from any source, on any issue; for the private firms this is reported by more than 70 percent of the managers. Complaints on each issue are reported to come more frequently from clients, customers, third parties, and employees than from civic groups and government agencies. In general, organizations report receiving fewer complaints about access to records than about the collection of specific items of data or the disclosure of data. Taking into account the temptation to underreport such events—even on an anonymous questionnaire —the results still confirm our sense that managers do not see what

Table A-20

Complaints About the Collection of Data
(Question 8)

Percent Reporting "Occasional"[a] Complaints Against Collection of Any Item of Information in the Designated File:

COMPLAINT SOURCE

Type and Number of Organizations Responding to This Survey	Individuals	Employees	Civic, Community, Professional Groups	Government Agencies	Don't Know[b]	No Answer[b]
Banks (179)	16	3	2	2	8	14
Health/accident insurance (25)	16	4	4	4	14	13
Life insurance (159)	18	4	3	1	9	6
Colleges (280)	28	10	7	6	9	14
Hospitals (211)	20	8	7	4	4	9
City law enforcement (133)	38	11	19	5	7	8
County law enforcement (48)	42	17	19	0	9	14
Regional welfare (62)	37	21	19	2	11	9
Local school districts (223)	21	23	14	6	11	15
State education (38)	21	5	5	16	19	12
State welfare (61)	30	21	21	15	24	5
State law enforcement (41)	17	7	15	2	18	15
State motor vehicle (38)	55	8	24	8	16	17
State tax (43)	29	7	12	2	5	11

[a]Very few respondents in any field reported "frequent" complaints from any source; we have combined the "frequent" and "occasional" responses. "Never" responses are not presented in this table; they are described briefly in the text.

[b]We have averaged the "Don't know" and "No answer" rates for the different complaint sources.

Table A-21

Complaints Concerning Disclosure of Information
(Question 9)

Percent Reporting "Occasional"[a] Complaints Against Disclosure of Information from the Designated File to People Outside the Organization:

COMPLAINT SOURCE

Type and Total Number Organizations Responding to This Survey	Individuals	Employees	Civic, Community, Professional Groups	Government Agencies	Don't Know[b]	No Answer[b]
Banks (179)	23	4	2	1	10	14
Health/accident insurance (25)	8	8	4	4	10	8
Life insurance (159)	6	3	1	0	10	7
Colleges (280)	26	10	7	5	13	14
Hospitals (211)	23	13	7	4	7	8
City law enforcement (133)	43	12	16	8	12	8
County law enforcement (48)	33	15	19	2	13	13
Regional welfare (62)	31	18	16	3	13	11
Local school districts (223)	22	23	9	4	12	15
State education (38)	16	5	13	18	16	13
State welfare (61)	26	23	25	20	27	5
State law enforcement (41)	27	7	17	2	15	12
State motor vehicle (38)	53	8	26	5	19	15
State tax (43)	29	2	2	7	17	13

[a]Very few respondents in any field reported "frequent" complaints from any source; we have combined the "frequent" and "occasional" responses. "Never" responses are not presented in this table; they are described briefly in the text.

[b]We have averaged the "Don't know" and "No answer" rates for the different complaint sources.

Table A-22

Complaints About Individuals' Access to Their Own Records
(Question 10)

Percent Reporting "Occasional"[a] Complaints About the Adequacy of Practices Covering an Individual's Ability to Examine His Own Record:

COMPLAINT SOURCE

Type and Total Number of Organizations Responding to This Survey	Individuals	Employees	Civic, Community, Professional Groups	Government Agencies	Don't Know[b]	No Answer[b]
Banks (179)	9	3	1	1	8	15
Health/accident insurance (25)	8	0	4	0	10	3
Life insurance (159)	8	3	1	1	8	5
Colleges (280)	19	8	4	4	9	14
Hospitals (211)	37	10	12	7	6	7
City law enforcement (133)	34	10	17	4	12	6
County law enforcement (48)	27	8	8	2	14	13
Regional welfare (62)	32	16	16	2	10	10
Local school districts (223)	25	27	13	5	11	15
State education (38)	11	3	5	8	18	13
State welfare (61)	21	13	12	8	32	5
State law enforcement (41)	17	7	17	2	9	12
State motor vehicle (38)	29	8	18	11	19	14
State tax (43)	17	5	7	12	4	10

[a]Very few respondents in any field reported "frequent" complaints from any source; we have combined the "frequent" and "occasional" responses. "Never" responses are not covered in this table; they are described briefly in the text.

[b]We have averaged the "Don't know" and "No answer" rates for the different complaint sources.

they define as civil-liberties complaints against record-keeping practices surfacing frequently within their organizations.[1]

Examination of these findings also confirms that complaint levels are difficult to measure and that differences between fields are not easily interpreted. As we noted in the site-visit findings, the visibility of complaints to management is subject to several important forces. In many organizations, for instance, low-level employees serve as a screen to keep managers from encountering complaining customers, clients, or citizens. In organizations which are both large and decentralized, headquarters management (e.g., those who answered our questionnaire) may not be aware of the level of complaint in the branch offices, unless civil-liberties questions have become important matters for central policy or public relations action. Some managers must be aware of this lack of knowledge because in some cases the proportion answering that they "don't know" whether or not complaints have been received is as high (or higher) as that reporting that they receive complaints.

In addition, managers may not at all see complaints from various sources as being a *civil-liberties* matter—even if they are defined that way by record subjects or others who complain. Complaints may instead represent practical economic or political matters to the record keeper.

Our site-visit and survey findings about complaints do not of course tell us how satisfied individuals are with the civil-liberties protections afforded them in record systems. Where record-keeping practices are of low visibility (as in insurance) or where individuals feel that they have been harmed but are not in a position to "make waves" (for example, welfare clients and those with police records), the level of complaint may well not reflect the feelings of those on whom records are kept. However, complaints need not be of high volume to be of high concern. Individual complaints worry profit-making organizations, for instance, when they are seen as a *prelude* to a mass of complaints which may spell loss of customers or other "trouble." More important still are instances in which the individual invokes the aid of courts, legislatures, regulatory agencies, civic groups or other powerful bodies to press his complaint. Such challenges to record-keeping policy and practice have been rare. But where they involve sizable

---

[1] Note that we asked specifically about complaints which record subjects and others couched in civil-liberties terms ("on privacy grounds. . ."). This may have discouraged the respondent from reporting complaints based on other grounds.

damage suits or raise the specter of regulatory action they assume an importance for managers far greater than their number might suggest.

A comparison of the level of complaints against computerized files with the level of complaints against manual files reveals no pattern that is consistent across the fields of organizations. Within most fields, our sample sizes are too small to reveal any significant difference at all. Though somewhat more complaints against computerized than manual files might have been expected from popular literature, either the difference does not exist or our survey is not sensitive enough to pick it up.

Managers View the Future

Another dimension of managerial awareness shows through as one examines managers' views of future needs for civil-liberties protections in record-keeping. Our survey findings are mixed but generally reflect the dominant impression we obtained from the site visits. Managers in most of the fields surveyed are satisfied with the balance they have struck between individual civil-liberties and organizational needs. They do not see a need for more physical safeguards, or clearer internal administrative rules. Further, they wish to avoid legislation in the privacy and records area which would alter current arrangements. However, many managers do report the need for changes which might better protect their organizations or their clients. Many also express support for legislation which, by clarifying the balance to be struck, would take them out of current controversies.

Through a single question on the survey, we touched three areas of potential change. In effect, we asked managers to appraise the adequacy of their own physical arrangements for civil-liberties protections in the designated files, their own internal rules, and the current laws on collection and disclosure of the kinds of information involved in these records.[2] (See tables A-23–A-25.)

The findings are clearest for commercial organizations. At least 70 percent of the managers in each of these fields report that current physical safeguards, internal administrative rules, and ex-

---

[2] This question was marred by a high nonresponse rate from managers in several fields, primarily law enforcement, education, and welfare agencies. Follow up on respondents suggest that some managers found it difficult to answer what they regarded as a complicated question with the relatively simple response alternatives we provided. We have therefore been cautious in interpreting differences among these types of organizations and the other respondents.

isting legislation are adequate, given their understanding of the "balance between organizational needs and the individual's interest in the confidentiality of his record." This finding is quite understandable in light of our site-visit experiences: managers in commercial organization were not at all ashamed of their record-keeping practices and believed that they are providing an appropriate level of administrative and physical protection for the civil liberties of those on whom they keep records. Out of this sense, and from a predictable tendency to protect their own autonomy, they see no need for new legislation in the privacy and records area.

The fact that we directed respondents' attention to the designated files also helps to understand these results. The checking-account and insurance files we asked about in the commercial area are not of the type which have aroused a great deal of controversy in their respective fields. Civil-liberties concerns in the insurance area, for instance, have been raised principally with respect to personal investigations and information gathering for the underwriting process itself; little has been said about unauthorized disclosures from the files of life or health and accident customers. Further, many of the managers in each of these three fields probably answered in the knowledge that a sweeping piece of legislation (the Fair Credit Reporting Act) had just been passed and would soon go into effect—covering civil-liberties protections in many of their files. Close as they were to the experience of considering the impact of this bill, it is understandable that they would not see a need for more legislation.

Our findings are much more mixed for fields such as welfare, local school districts, and county law-enforcement agencies, where civil-liberties issues have surfaced in the record-keeping areas we asked about. Less than 55 percent of the managers in these fields report satisfaction with current physical, administrative, and legislative protections. While managers we visited were not very concerned about the problems of unauthorized access to personal records, some felt that they "could do better" in providing physical safeguards for information on clients, customers, employees, and others. This is also the opinion of between 30 and 40 percent of the survey respondents in colleges, state welfare departments, regional school districts, and both city and county law-enforcement agencies (table A23).

Turning to the question of the adequacy of internal rules, we see that in no field do more than 38 percent of the managers perceive a need for "new and more detailed organizational rules to

Table A-23

The Need for More Physical Safeguards
(Question 11)

Type and Total Number of Organizations Responding to This Survey	*Percent Reporting That, Given Their Understanding of the Balance Between Organizational Needs and Civil-Liberties Protections in the Designated Files:*		
	We Need Additional Physical Safeguards on Collection, Storage, and Distribution of Information in This File	*Our Physical Safeguards Are Now Adequate*	*No Response*
Banks (179)	21	70	9
Health/accident insurance (25)	8	84	8
Life insurance (159)	11	79	10
Colleges (280)	35	52	13
Hospitals (211)	28	63	9
City law enforcement (133)	37	54	9
County law enforcement (48)	40	48	12
Regional welfare (61)	27	52	21
Local school districts (223)	38	46	16
State education (38)	32	55	13
State welfare (61)	38	54	8
State law enforcement (41)	32	59	9
State motor vehicle (38)	26	61	13
State tax (43)	33	57	10

cover collection and use of data in this file" (table A-24). In all 14 categories of organizations, managers appear more certain of the adequacy of their current administrative rules than of current physical safeguards and laws. This probably reflects the attitudes we encountered in many of the site-visit organizations: managers feel that they are doing "the best we can" administratively; if

Table A-24

The Need for More Administrative Safeguards
(Question 11)

Percent Reporting That, Given Their Understanding of the Balance Between Organizational Needs and Civil-Liberties Protections in the Designated Files:

Type and Total Number of Organizations Responding to This Survey	*We Need New and More Detailed Organizational Rules to Govern Collection and Use of Data in This File*	*Our Present Rules or Practices Are Adequate*	*No Response*
Banks (179)	12	70	18
Health/accident insurance (25)	4	92	4
Life insurance (159)	8	84	8
Colleges (280)	23	66	11
Hospitals (211)	21	75	4
City law enforcement (133)	29	63	8
County law enforcement (48)	27	50	23
Regional welfare (61)	37	48	15
Local school districts (223)	38	53	9
State education (38)	34	56	10
State welfare (61)	30	67	3
State law enforcement (41)	17	73	10
State motor vehicle (38)	26	66	8
State tax (43)	14	76	10

their record-keeping does pose some civil-liberties problems, the fault lies somewhere "outside" their own policy-making sphere—in the wider society, or in technical matters which had to do with the manner in which policies were implemented, not with the nature of the policies themselves.

The general reluctance of managers to "invite" legislation

Table A-25

The Need for New Legislation
(Question 11)

Percent Reporting That, Given Their Understanding of the Balance Between Organizational Needs and Civil-Liberties Protections in the Designated Files:

Type and Total Number of Organizations Responding to This Survey	We Believe That Constructive Legislation Would Be a Definite Help in This Area	No New or Amended Legislation Is Needed to Clarify the Existing Balance Between Information Needs and Privacy	No Response
Banks (179)	17	70	13
Health/accident insurance (25)	12	80	8
Life insurance (159)	17	76	7
Colleges (280)	36	57	7
Hospitals (211)	32	59	9
City law enforcement (133)	43	50	7
County law enforcement (133)	29	48	23
Regional welfare (62)	40	45	15
Local school districts (223)	40	49	11
State education (38)	24	66	10
State welfare (61)	31	64	5
State law enforcement (41)	32	59	9
State motor vehicle (38)	37	58	5
State tax (43)	14	81	5

affecting their practices is reflected in table A-25. In 9 of the 14 fields, fewer than one-third of the respondents suggest that they "believe that constructive legislation would be a definite help in this area." Managers are most likely to report such a need in fields where issues of privacy and confidentiality have surfaced prominently as "problems" in recent years—in law enforcement, welfare, state motor-vehicle departments, and local school districts.

Comparing the responses of managers who answered concerning a computerized file with answers concerning noncomputerized files, we found no significant differences on any of the three questions.

SUMMARY

Some of the survey results we have reported are quite clearly in line with our findings about the impact of computerization on personal records in the advanced organizations which were the object of our site visits. With respect to some kinds of potential computer impact, however (for instance, on the amount of information collected on each record subject), many of our survey respondents report an effect of computerization which quite decidedly we did *not* observe in the course of our site visits. For still other questions of computer impact (for instance, the matter of data integration), the survey produced ambiguous results, reflecting the failure of our instrument to communicate clearly the questions we had in mind.

On the whole, our experience with this survey convinces us that valuable information about the effect of computerization on record systems (or for that matter about record practices themselves, irrespective of the issue of computerization) is extremely difficult to gather through use of a mail questionnaire. It is our sense that increases in the length of the instrument or a reduction in the number of fields covered would do little to resolve the very basic problems of this approach. The questioning of managers about record-keeping practices and the complex matter of the impact of technological change is not, in the long run, economically accomplished at long distance with a standardized instrument. The study of "mainstream" organizations in each of the fields covered by our site visits would no doubt be valuable; our survey results tell us at least this much. But differences between the computer's impact on record-keeping in the advanced organizations we visited and its effect on personal records in smaller, less advanced organizations in the same fields are likely to be discovered only through detailed study of the latter organizations, with a full range of interview, documentary, and public record data available.

NATIONAL ACADEMY of SCIENCES

PROJECT ON COMPUTER DATABANKS

SURVEY QUESTIONNAIRE

Most of the questions refer to the file of records specified in the cover letter. Please furnish information with respect to this file alone, unless a question indicates that some other file is of interest.

Definitions

Individual's Record. A set of one or more consecutive units of information on a single identified individual (e.g., an employee's history of employment or a payroll record).

File. A collection of related records treated as a unit, e.g., a file on all employees in the organization.

Manual Files comprise hard copy records (including microfilm) which are maintained and accessed by hand.

Electronic Accounting Machine (EAM) Files include records which are typically accessed and manipulated by using electro—mechanical devices such as card sorters, tabulating machines, collators, etc.

Computerized Files refer to individuals' records which are maintained in card, tape, disc, drum, or core storage, and are manipulated by a computer.

DIRECTIONS FOR MARKING

- Use only soft black lead pencil (No. 2).
- Do NOT use ink or ball-point pen.
- Make heavy black marks that completely fill the circle.
- Erase completely any marks you wish to change.
- Make no stray marks on this questionnaire.

1. Who will complete this questionnaire? (Please mark all that apply).

The person to whom the questionnaire was sent . . . . O
The data records manager or data processing manager . . . . . O
Others (please specify) ⟶ . . . . O

NCS-S344A (Series T)

2. Please mark the <u>one</u> category which best describes your organization.

Bank . . . . ○
College/University . . . . ○
Hospital . . . . ○
Information supplier. . . . . ○
National Religious Body . . . . ○
Life Insurance . . . . ○
Health and Accident Insurance . . . . ○
Social Science Data Bank . . . . ○
Travel/Entertainment Cards & Reservations . . . . ○
Industrial or Manufacturing. . . . . ○

City Law Enforcement . . . . ○
City Welfare . . . . ○
City Data Processing Center . . . . ○

County Law Enforcement. . . . . ○
County Health. . . . . ○
County Welfare . . . . ○
County Data Processing Center. . . . . ○

Local School District/System . . . . ○

State Law Enforcement. . . . . ○
State Health . . . . ○
State Welfare. . . . . ○
State Education . . . . ○

State Motor Vehicles . . . . ○
State Taxation. . . . . ○

Federal Regulatory Agency. ○
Federal Cabinet Agency. . . . . ○

3. Do you maintain any records on individuals in the following categories? (Please mark all that apply)

Number of Employees (Present, full—time employees at all levels in your organization)

1–100 ○   100–500 ○   500–1,000 ○   Over 1,000 ○

Number of Clients and Customers (e.g., present clients, customers, patients, students, policy holders, etc.)

None ○   1–500 ○   500–2,000 ○
2,000–10,000 ○   10,000–25,000 ○   Over 25,000 ○

Number of Subjects (e.g., prospective clients or customers; persons upon whom credit, criminal and arrest records are held; auto registrants and licensees; research subjects; etc.)

None ○   1–500 ○   500–1,000 ○
1,000–10,000 ○   10,000–100,000 ○   100,000–1 million ○
Over 1 million ○

4. Do you maintain <u>computerized</u> records on any (none, some, most, or all) of your employees, clients/customers and subjects? (Please mark one response in each row.)

```
        None
        Some
        Most
        All
```
Ⓝ Ⓢ Ⓜ Ⓐ Employee
Ⓝ Ⓢ Ⓜ Ⓐ Client/Customer
Ⓝ Ⓢ Ⓜ Ⓐ Subject

Given the total information on each employee, client/customer, or subject, how much of this information is in <u>computerized</u> form? (Please mark one response in each row.)

```
        No Information
        Some Information
        Most Information
        All Information
```
Ⓝ Ⓢ Ⓜ Ⓐ Employee
Ⓝ Ⓢ Ⓜ Ⓐ Client/Customer
Ⓝ Ⓢ Ⓜ Ⓐ Subject

In this section, would you please answer each of the following questions about the <u>file designated in the cover letter.</u>

5. Please indicate the approximate number of individuals on whom records are maintained in this file.

1–1,000 . . . . ○   50,000–100,000 . . . . ○
1,000–5,000 . . . . . . ○   100,000–500,000 . . . . ○
5,000–10,000 . . . . . ○   500,000–1 million . . . . ○
10,000–50,000 . . . . ○   more than 1 million . . . . . . ○

6. As a general rule, can the individual examine his own record or a copy of his record from the file? (Please mark only one response)

The individual does not know the record exists . . . . . . ○
Can examine <u>all data</u> in his record . . . . ○
Can examine <u>some data</u> in the record . . . . ○
Can examine <u>no data</u> in his record . . . . ○

7. Do you ever make individually identified information from this file available to persons or organizations outside your own?

Yes ○   No ○

Is there a general management policy regarding such disclosure? (Please mark only one response)

No policy has been formulated . . . . ○
Yes, we have an unwritten policy. . . . . ○
Yes, we have a written policy. . . . . ○

(Continued in next column)

460

7. (Continued)

If yes, is an explicit statement of the policy communicated to the individual whose records are maintained in this file? (Please mark only one response)

Almost never communicated . . . . ○
Discussed with individual at times, e.g., as the
need arises . . . . ○
Regularly communicated to the individual . . . . ○

8. Have members of the following groups ever complained, on grounds of privacy, against the <u>collection</u> of any item of information in this file? (Please mark one response in each row)

```
          ┌─── Never
          │┌── Occasionally
          ││┌─ Frequently
          │││┌ Do Not Know
```
Ⓝ Ⓞ Ⓕ Ⓓ Individuals on whom records are kept
Ⓝ Ⓞ Ⓕ Ⓓ Your own employees
Ⓝ Ⓞ Ⓕ Ⓓ Outside professional, civil or community groups
Ⓝ Ⓞ Ⓕ Ⓓ Government agencies (Federal, state or local)

9. Have members of the following groups ever complained, on grounds of privacy, against <u>disclosure</u> of information in this file to people outside your organization? (Please mark one response in each row)

```
          ┌─── Never
          │┌── Occasionally
          ││┌─ Frequently
          │││┌ Do Not Know
```
Ⓝ Ⓞ Ⓕ Ⓓ Individuals on whom records are kept
Ⓝ Ⓞ Ⓕ Ⓓ Your own employees
Ⓝ Ⓞ Ⓕ Ⓓ Outside professional, civic or community groups
Ⓝ Ⓞ Ⓕ Ⓓ Government agencies (Federal, state or local)

10. Have members of the following groups ever complained about the adequacy of your organization's practices regarding an individual's ability to examine his own record? (Please mark one response in each row)

```
          ┌─── Never
          │┌── Occasionally
          ││┌─ Frequently
          │││┌ Do Not Know
```
Ⓝ Ⓞ Ⓕ Ⓓ Individuals on whom records are kept
Ⓝ Ⓞ Ⓕ Ⓓ Your own employees
Ⓝ Ⓞ Ⓕ Ⓓ Outside professional, civic or community groups
Ⓝ Ⓞ Ⓕ Ⓓ Government agencies (Federal, state or local)

11. Given your understanding of the balance between organizational needs to collect information and the individual's interest in the confidentiality of his record, please indicate which of the statements (a or b) in each set best applies to the file under consideration.

a. No new or amended legislation is needed to clarify the
existing balance between information needs and privacy ○
b. We believe that constructive legislation would be a
definite help in this area . . . . ○

a. We need new and more detailed organizational rules
to govern collection and use of data in this file . . . . . . ○
b. Our present rules or practices are adequate . . . . ○

a. We need additional physical safeguards on collection,
storage and distribution of information in this file . . . . ○
b. Our physical safeguards are now adequate . . . . ○

THE FOLLOWING QUESTIONS REFER TO COMPUTER-IZED RECORDS IN THE FILE DESIGNATED BY THE COVER LETTER. IF YOU DO <u>NOT</u> USE A COMPUTER SYSTEM FOR THIS FILE, PLEASE STOP HERE AND RETURN THE QUESTIONNAIRE TO US AT YOUR EARLIEST CONVENIENCE.
THANK YOU FOR YOUR COOPERATION.

---

12. When did you <u>first</u> use a computer system to store and process records in the file?

Before 1955 ○	1963–1964 ○
1955–1956 ○	1965–1966 ○
1957–1958 ○	1967–1968 ○
1959–1960 ○	1969–1970 ○
1961–1962 ○	

13. What have been the effects on your organization of computerizing this file? (Please mark all that apply)

Improvement in routine, large scale operations . . . . ○
Generation of more timely or complete reports to
management . . . . ○
Direct improvement in policy planning by top
management . . . . ○

14. Which of the following statements best describe your experience with computer applications to this file? (Please mark only one response)

We could not manage a file of this size or complexity
without the computer . . . . ○
The applications have provided a useful improvement
in operations, but we could continue service on this
file without the computer . . . . ○
The applications have had relatively little impact on
our use of this file . . . . ○

461

15. **Who generally operates the computer system for handling records in the file? (Please mark all that apply)**

We have our own in-house computer system . . . . ○
We generally use a service bureau or other outside computer facility . . . . ○

16a. **Has conversion of these records to computerized form led to detection and correction of factual errors which previously existed in manual records?**

Yes ○   No ○   Do not know ○

16b. **If yes, were the corrections about items important in making decisions about the individuals on whom records are kept? (Please mark only one response)**

Yes, considerable importance . . . . ○
Yes, marginal importance . . . . ○
No, of little or no importance . . . . ○
Do not know . . . . ○

16c. **Have there been significant problems in maintaining accuracy of computerized records, which were not present in the manual system?**

Yes, significant problems . . . . ○
Yes, marginal problems . . . . ○
No, problems of little or no importance . . . . ○
Do not know . . . . ○

17a. **For this file, are you collecting more data or less data on a given individual than before computerization? (Please mark only one response)**

More data per individual is collected . . . . ○
About the same amount of data per individual is collected as before . . . . ○
Less data per individual is collected . . . . ○

17b. **If more, has computerization of these records directly affected the amount of data being collected per record?**

Yes ○   No ○

17c. **If your response to 17b is yes, which of the following conditions would you say is the primary reason for increased data collection? (Please mark only one response)**

Increased collection, storage, and processing capability of computer . . . . ○
Changes in organizational objectives or programs and/or increasing government requirements for collection or reporting information . . . . ○

18. **Have any new rules concerning the individual's right to examine his record in this file been issued since you began using a computerized record system?**

Yes ○   No ○

(Continued in next column)

18. **(Continued)**
If yes, do you see this change as being a <u>direct</u> result of computerization of the records?

Yes, Direct result . . . . ○
No, Not a direct result . . . . ○

19. **A number of countermeasures have been proposed to prevent access to computerized records by unauthorized persons. Do you use any of the following for this file?**

	Yes	No
Control of physical access to the file (e.g., door locks, badges for access to computer room)	○	○
Hardware/Software security measures (e.g., crytographic encoding, passwords, terminal identification code)	○	○
Personal integrity checks (e.g., special investigation of operating personnel; bonded employees) . .	○	○
Audit logs or other data monitoring methods	○	○
Procedures and rules for disposal of data (e.g., destruction of printout or tapes)	○	○
Other, please specify	○	○

DO NOT WRITE
OUTSIDE BOX

20. **Do you furnish more <u>identified information</u> about individuals in this file to any government agency (executive, legislative, or judicial; Federal, state, or local) as a result of the increased retrieval capacity after computerization?**

Yes ○   No ○

21. **Do you furnish more <u>statistical</u> (unidentified) data about individuals in this file to any government agency as a result of the increased retrieval capacity after computerization?**

Yes ○   No ○

22. **Does the application of computer technology in your organization enable you to pull together, in one record, all of the information your organization collects and records about a given individual?**

Yes ○   No ○

23. **With regard to the individuals on whom you maintain records in the file designated by the cover letter, do you maintain any other information, <u>in manual form</u>, on the same individuals?**

Yes ○   No ○

If yes, how would you compare the information kept in manual form with the information in computerized form?

	Yes	No
The more subjective (opinion based) information is still kept in manual form . . .	○	○
The more narrative and lengthy information is still kept in manual form	○	○
The most sensitive and confidential information is kept in manual form	○	○

Thank you for your cooperation. Please return the questionnaire in the envelope provided.

Appendix B

Public Opinion Surveys on Computers, Privacy and Record-Keeping

This Appendix examines opinions of Americans on the following three questions:

1. At the most general level of concern, how does the public react to invasion of privacy as an issue?

2. What does the public opinion literature reveal about the way in which people balance individual claims to privacy and due process against organizational claims about the necessity for data collection and the use of restrictive administrative procedures?

3. How does the public view the computer as a source of privacy and record-keeping problems?

No extensive set of public opinion studies on these three questions exists. However, an interesting though small number of national, regional, and special opinion surveys have been done during the past few years, diverse in focus and uneven in quality. It is these materials that we have drawn together.

The very nature of the privacy issue creates some special difficulties when opinion research is done. Privacy is a very amorphous topic, and something to which almost everyone pays allegiance in the abstract; the Friends of Big Brother Society is not a prominent group in our national life. But many people have not had direct experience with the kinds of record-keeping problems being asked about. Where opinion issues are not salient to the public, its reactions are difficult to evaluate. Further, individuals frequently do not know about record-keeping practices which do directly affect them. This problem becomes even more acute where computerized systems are involved; individuals may not know whether a given record system is computerized—to say nothing of having sufficient information to judge the computer's impact on their own records. These factors do not rule out obtaining insight into public opinions on privacy and computers by survey research, but this absence of public experience must be taken into account in analyzing the data.

GENERAL PUBLIC CONCERN OVER PRIVACY AND RECORD-KEEPING

There have been no nationwide polls in which researchers have probed opinions on the full range of privacy issues in American life. However, three recent national opinion samplings have included several questions on privacy and privacy-related topics.

In 1970, Louis Harris Associates, the well-known polling organization, included a question on privacy among several other political and social opinion items on a questionnaire administered to a national cross-section sample.[1] Each respondent was asked, "Do you ever tend to feel that sometimes your sense of privacy is being invaded or not [sic]—that people are trying to find out things about you that are not any of their business?" Thirty-four percent said "yes," 62 percent said "no," and 4 percent were "not sure." While this suggests that invasion of privacy is not seen as personally affecting a majority of American adults, it shows that privacy is an issue on which a substantial minority do feel concerned. Projecting roughly from the Harris sample, one in three Americans would describe himself as the object of some practices which invade his privacy; and this is a segment of the American population far larger than the civil libertarians, political radicals, and others with special interests who might be expected to register such an opinion.

Less direct evidence on general public concern over privacy comes from an item included in a study of public attitudes toward computers, sponsored jointly by the American Federation of Information Processing Societies (AFIPS) and *Time* magazine. Lengthy phone interviews were conducted with a national sample of a thousand adults in the summer of 1971.[2] About midway through the interview, in which other items about privacy and computers were covered, respondents were asked: "Nowadays, some organizations keep information about millions of people. How do you feel about this—are you very concerned, fairly concerned, or not too concerned at all?" Sixty-two percent replied that they were "very"

[1] This was what the Harris organization refers to as an "amalgam" survey, containing questions on the war in Vietnam, labor strikes of national importance, politics, confidence in the President, etc. It was conducted in the summer of 1970, and 1,362 adults comprised the sample.

[2] *A National Survey of the Public's Attitude Toward Computers.* A national probability sample of 1,001 adults (over 18) was drawn from telephone households in the continental U.S. Half-hour phone interviews were conducted with a randomly selected member of each household. We present results from this survey in more detail later.

or "fairly" concerned about the information being kept; 36 percent reported being "not too concerned at all."[3]

Despite this concern about record confidentiality and the way in which powerful organizations use the personal information in their files, it is difficult to discern from the survey materials just where privacy and related issues stand relative to other matters which capture national public attention. Responses to one national survey, conducted for the Retail Credit Company by Opinion Research Corporation, give us some clues to this matter.[4] Respondents in 1970 were asked which of ten subjects they had "heard or read most about in recent months."[5] Twenty-three percent included "invasion of privacy" and 33 percent noted "wiretapping/bugging by government" in their list of mentions. Seven of the eight remaining topics received significantly greater mention, including "high automobile insurance rates" (65 percent), "chemical additives/preservatives in food" (61 percent) and "low-quality public education" (44 percent). Asked to choose which "two or three" of the issues they "most feel something should be done about," no more than 44 percent of the respondents singled out any one issue. Most frequent choices were chemical additives in food, (41 percent), high auto insurance rates (44 percent) and low-quality public education (30 percent). Invasion of privacy and wiretapping/bugging were mentioned by 9 percent and 6 percent of respondents, respectively, as among the two or three problems it is most important that something be done about. In this survey, the privacy-related items were the most abstractly worded of the issues presented to respondents, and their answers suggest a tendency of respondents to treat as most important those matters which strike closest to home. How much the results might have differed if more specific privacy items had been defined. such as an individual's right to see his credit report, is difficult to estimate.

---

[3] Throughout Appendix B, unless otherwise noted, we omit the percentage of "no answers" for a given question. Where the figures we present do not total 100 percent, "no answers" account for the remainder.

[4] *Investigations Relating to Insurance, Job and Credit Applications: A Nationwide Study of Public Attitudes.* This survey was conducted for the Retail Credit Company by Caravan Surveys, a division of Opinion Research Corporation. Personal interviews were conducted with a probability sample of 2,034 men and women 18 years of age and older living in private households in the continental U.S.

[5] (1) Misleading packaging/labeling grocery products; (2) Chemical additives/preservatives in food; (3) Overcharged/poor auto service/repair; (4) Warranties/guarantees of no value/not honored; (5) Overcharging for drugs/pharmaceuticals; (6) Invasion of privacy; (7) DDT in food; (8) Wiretapping/bugging by government; (9) High automobile insurance rates; (10) Low-quality public education.

A number of surveys of special populations also confirm that privacy-related issues are a matter of solid minority concern. When the Transportation Institute, a joint labor-management research body, sponsored a conference on privacy in Washington, D.C. in the spring of 1971, those attending were informally polled on a number of privacy-related issues.[6] A version of the 1970 Harris Poll question on privacy was put to those who elected to take part in the poll. As might be expected of those attending a conference on privacy, 61 percent answered that they did indeed believe that their privacy was being invaded by "people trying to find out things that are not any of their business." Fourteen percent said no and 19 percent were not sure. In response to another question, 84 percent said that they believed the individual's privacy is "less secure now than it was ten years ago."

Even in this gathering of high privacy concern, however, only about one-third of the respondents felt that privacy is one of the three most important policy issues in "comparison with other policy issues facing America today."

In the fall of 1971, following the widespread publicity given to the U.S. Army's collection of information on civilian protest groups and to Sen. Sam Ervin's hearings on political surveillance, a mail survey on constitutent opinions was conducted by Congressman David Obey of the Seventh Congressional District of Wisconsin, a district that swings between liberal and conservative voting patterns. Ten thousand returns were received from a mailing to 100,000 residents. One of the questions on the survey asked, "Do you think there has been more of a tendency recently for the government to infringe unnecessarily upon the average American's privacy than there was ten years ago?" Sixty-seven percent of those returning the questionnaire said yes; 30 percent felt it was "the same," and 3 percent felt there was less infringement.

College students were surveyed in a 1971 study conducted for the John D. Rockefeller III Foundation.[7] Sixty-four percent

---

[6] This poll is reported in Transportation Institute, *The Privacy Battleground* (Washington, D.C., 1971). Those attending were not systematically sampled, but approximately 30 percent of the participants filled out a 12-page questionnaire at some point during the three-day conference; 132 persons responded including 36 labor union officials and blue-collar workers; 33 officials from federal and state executive or legislative bodies; 60 persons from business, professional, academic, student, and civic sectors. In age, the 132 respondents divided into 21 percent between 18 and 29 years, 43 percent between 30 and 50 years, and 35 percent over 50 years of age.

[7] *The Changing Values on Campus: Political and Personal Attitudes of Today's College Students.* This survey was conducted for the John D. Rockefeller III Foundation by the firm of Daniel Yankelovich, Inc., in 1971.

of the respondents said that they value privacy highly. Among seventeen aspects of life which students rated in terms of their personal importance, privacy was among the five most frequently cited as being "very important." Eighty-three percent of the student respondents in this survey also agreed with the statement, "People's privacy is being destroyed."

From a recent conference comes still another reflection of national youth opinion. In April of 1971, the Nixon administration convened the decennial White House Conference on Youth. The 918 youth delegates were carefully selected to represent youth between 14 and 24 years of age, reflecting the racial, sex, educational, and occupational characteristics of this segment of the national population. Proportionate representation was given to youth in the military, in college, in high school, vocational schools, working, and unemployed. The youth delegates were then divided in cross-sectional fashion into task forces on major issues facing American society. The Task Force on Legal Rights and Justice adopted a resolution on "Invasion of Privacy" which set the problem this way: "The practices of collecting confidential information have become uncontrollably widespread in this country. Such information is passed among and by commercial institutions, including insurance agencies, credit bureaus, loan companies, banks, promotional sales forces, etc., without the individual's consent. We believe in many cases this constitutes an invasion of privacy." The task force resolution also deplored the "diminution of civil rights" caused by "surveillances by various government agencies of the activities of politicians, political candiates, and politically active citizens, and those considered radicals (whether to the left or the right of the political spectrum)." The "offending agencies" responsible for such privacy invasions, the task force concluded, "have inadequate, unrestrictive regulations placed on them, leaving the individual with very little means of redress to correct injustices which may result from these practices." The task force then went on to specify a set of remedies including greater access for the individual to records about himself and greater public control over the record-keeping activities of commercial firms and government agencies such as the FBI.

More systematic information comes from a 1970 study com-

Interviews were conducted with 1,244 students at 50 colleges. Stratified random sampling was applied to the entire population of two- and four-year colleges and universities in the U.S. Once institutions had been selected, quota sampling was employed as a method for selecting respondents by years of college completed, sex, and race.

missioned by the Harvard Program on Technology and Society. As a pilot study on the public's perceptions of technology, 201 interviews were conducted in three towns in the Greater Boston area, selected for their mix of income, education, occupations, and urban-rural settings.[8] Four privacy-related questions were put to the respondents. Sixty percent agreed that it is wrong for credit bureaus "to have a lot of information about people's finances"; a somewhat smaller proportion, 43 percent, agreed that the government "knows too much about personal life"; and 27 percent said that they worry about their phone being tapped. Later in the same interview the following question was put to the respondents, intentionally constructed to present the "databank" issue in an extreme form:

> As you know, the government now collects different kinds of information on people, such as income tax, census, Social Security records, criminal records, and military records. There has been some talk of the government using computers to establish a national databank—a computerized file which would combine all of this information in one place. Those proposing this see it as a way of increasing efficiency; critics say that it would be an invasion of privacy. Would you personally favor or oppose such a development?

Fifty-six percent of the respondents said that they would oppose the development of such a databank; 31 percent supported the idea and 12 percent were not sure how they felt on this issue. Asked to explain their response, almost all of those who were opposed to the idea of one big national databank offered some version of "invasion of privacy" as a reason for their opposition.

BALANCING PRIVACY RIGHTS AND INFORMATION NEEDS

What we see in these national and more specialized polls is a solid minority sentiment that people feel their privacy is being eroded

---

[8] In the communities of Belmont, Cambridge, and Maynard, random samples of 41, 140, and 20 were selected, for a total of 201 respondents. The survey was conducted by David Armor, Sherwin Feinhandler, and Karen Sapolsky of Social Systems Analysts, Cambridge, Mass. For a more extended discussion, see Irene Taviss, "A Survey of Popular Attitudes toward Technology," *Technology and Culture*, forthcoming January 1973.

in some respect. But as we look more closely at some of these survey results, we find that when they are given a chance, people ask "Why?" or "What will it be used for?" when confronted with a question about record-keeping. And when such questions become more specific, individuals distinguish rather carefully among appropriate and inappropriate collection, use and sharing of information. And because people have different experiences with respect to record-keeping in organizations, privacy and confidentiality tend to mean different things to different people.

This complexity of opinions in concrete situations can be seen from pretesting interviews conducted as preparation for the Harvard Program's survey. A version of the "one big databank" question reproduced above was discussed with thirteen individuals. While we cannot take this set of depth interviews as representative of the total population included in the final survey, there is no commonsense reason to believe that the full sample of survey respondents would have been less thoughtful in their responses if they had had a chance to discuss the questions asked of them. The framers of the databank question, as we noted above, deliberately chose to put the issue in terms of the most sweeping and national proposal—the one big federal data dump—and to use this question to get a reading on the public's basic fears about a federal "big brother." In these relatively unstructured interviews, the first reaction of most of the 13 respondents was to ask what the information in the databank would be used for, whether only the government would have access to it, and whether the government didn't have all of this information already. Able to specify certain limiting conditions, the final comments of almost all those interviewed in the pretest were either in favor of or not opposed to the hypothetical national databank. More important than the question of whether they supported or rejected the national databank idea is the fact that among the respondents there were wide differences in their reasons for support or opposition. Whether they correctly perceived the possible consequences of such a databank or not, all had specific reasons for either supporting or rejecting the idea; what may have been an ideological initial response quickly dissolved, with very little suggestion on the part of the interviewer, into a complex set of opinions.

One woman concluded that she wouldn't mind the central federal databank "if it were to be used by the government." A man replied, "Probably to some people it would be harmful. They wouldn't want certain things found out about them, but I don't see where it really would be harmful . . . if they wanted to find out the information anyway, they could." Another man said that his answer would depend on who would have access to it. He didn't favor letting credit reference people see it, but thought it would be a "more efficient" way for government to operate. Another man was strongly positive in his response, saying, "I think that's a good idea . . . Sometimes they try to find out information and it takes them days and everything gets all mixed up. The way records are kept now, it's unbelievable. People can't find anything. This way, all the information would be in one place and that's it." When asked by the interviewer whether it would bother him that the databank would have the information, he said, "Oh, no. I have nothing to hide."

Typical of the less enthusiastic responses was that from a man who said, "Well, they have all this information . . . [and] if they're going to put it all together, there's nothing we can do about it. But I don't want to be known by my Social Security number. I have a name. No one else has this name. I'd like to have this name until I die, and I don't want to be known by a Social Security number." Another critical response came from a man who felt he was ambivalent about the issue. "I don't know if I would like just anybody who wanted to push a button to pick me out and get me." When asked whether he would approve if only the government had the right to use the information, he replied, "I don't have too much faith in them right now; if it was different I would." He said, "There are certain things that have to be known about people," and that government needed to know about the "types of people" in the country to deal with the situation.

The 201 respondents in the full survey were also asked about the process that might be used to set up such a big federal databank. For a series of technological and social programs, respondents were asked to specify who they believe *does* make decisions on each program today and who they think *should* make such decisions. On the issue of "creating a databank" the responses were as shown in table B-1.

Consolidating these figures, it seems that 15.1 percent believe that individuals and popular participation control the decision today, but that 53.6 percent think that the decision *should* be made through such popular processes. Conversely, while 68.1 percent think the President and Congress now make the decision to create databanks, only 35.5 percent think they *should* make this decision. In both the "do" and "should" categories only 7 percent think this is a matter for "experts" to decide.

Measured through this question, the privacy issue appears

Table B-1

Who Creates National Databank?

	Who Does?	Who Should?
Individual	3.8%	5.7%
Public opinion poll	4.3	10.3
Direct vote	7.0	37.6
President	18.4	13.9
Congress	49.7	12.6
Elected state representatives	2.7	1.6
Elected local representatives	.5	—
Experts	7.6	6.7
Industry	3.8	2.1
Military	2.2	.5
	100.0%	100.0%

quite strong, in the sense that the public feels a need to control this much-talked-about government record system. Compared with the other issues respondents were asked to judge, the databank issue generated the largest discrepancy between the respondents' views of who does and who should make technology-related public policy decisions. It was also the only one of the ten issues tested on which more than a third of the sample felt that the decision should be made by direct citizen vote. Other issues on which more citizen decisions were believed desirable were the guaranteed annual income and the installation of nuclear power plants. Overall, the sample wanted Congress to have less power than they believe it now exercises in eight of the ten issues.

We see the same tendency to make rather fine distinctions in the treatment of more specific questions put to participants in the 1971 Transportation Institute Conference on privacy. We noted above that an informal sampling of members turned up the kind of high concern about privacy that one would expect in the course of a conference on that topic. But given more specific questions, respondents were quite selective by area and issue in drawing their balances between claims to personal privacy and claims to information by society or organizations.

On technology, for example, 30 percent felt that the effect of general technological change on the individual American had been mostly beneficial, 37 percent "about equally beneficial and harmful," 21 percent "mostly harmful," and 12 percent were uncertain. When asked to what extent personal privacy should be "legally protected" in criminal investigations, 21 percent checked "only if it does not hamper law enforcement," while 60 percent favored this course "even if it should enable some criminals to escape prosecution." (On this question, 16 percent were "uncertain" and 2 percent did not answer.)

Majorities also favored law-enforcement agencies maintaining records of persons convicted of crime (89 percent) and sharing these with other law-enforcement agencies (78 percent), but 77 percent opposed making such records available to credit bureaus and 82 percent would place a similar restriction on preemployment reporting agencies.

Majorities favored state telephone tapping under court order in cases involving danger to human life (83 percent) and "organized crime networks of gambling and extortion" (59 percent), but opposed the use of taps to investigate "traffic in marijuana" (56 percent). Sixty-three percent felt that the U.S. Attorney General should "under no circumstances" tap telephones or conduct room monitoring without obtaining a judicial warrant, even when dealing with "groups conspiring to overthrow the government." (Thirty-four percent supported such use, with 3 percent uncertain.)

In terms of an individual's access to records kept about him, 59 percent felt that an individual should know "in all circumstances" that a file has been opened on him by a government agency that passes judgment on him concerning some benefit, opportunity, status, or right. Only 28 percent preferred the answer that this should be done "as a general right, except for special circumstances, such as during criminal investigations." (Five percent would follow such a rule "in no circumstances," and 10 percent were "uncertain" on this matter.)

At the height of press and congressional protest over the FBI's surveillance of white and black political organizations, the George Gallup polling organization did a representative national cross-section telephone survey of 522 persons. From this survey, we note what rather frequently crops up in the public opinion literature on privacy: that where law enforcement is concerned the public is highly supportive of police agencies and displays little concern about intelligence and administrative law enforcement records. Rating the job J. Edgar Hoover was doing as head of the FBI, 70 percent judged it to be "good" or "excellent"; 11 percent said "fair"; and only 6 percent said "poor" or "bad." Rating the FBI itself, 49 percent said that they were "highly favorable"; 31

percent said they were "moderately favorable;" 11 percent reported a "neutral" reaction; and only 4 percent rated the FBI "unfavorably."[9]

Turning to the public's evaluation of particular FBI activities, 35 percent of the respondents said that it had "not done enough" with respect to "keeping files on many people regardless of whether they are suspected of illegal acts" while 20 percent said that what the bureau was doing was "about right." Only 27 percent said that the bureau had "gone too far."

Interesting throughout this poll was the high level of indecision evidenced. Over 20 percent were undecided concerning the use of telephone taps and informers at political rallies; and one-third answered "don't know" when asked the following question: "Some people say that political protestors are not being dealt with strongly enough. Others say that the constitutional rights of political protestors are not being respected. What is your opinion?" Forty-six percent of the sample would have protestors dealt with "more strongly" and 21 percent say that the rights of protestors are "not respected."

Congressman Obey's poll of constituents gives us still another example of the complexities of privacy as a public opinion issue. Even though the questions were worded in a way that would encourage pro-privacy responses, almost one-third of the respondents said that the U.S. Attorney General should be allowed to wiretap without a court order and almost half said that they were not opposed to military surveillance of the political activities of private citizens and public officials.

Further evidence of the public's selectivity on record-keeping issues comes from the Opinion Research Survey conducted for the Retail Credit Company. This poll did not raise as issues the kinds of problems which sparked the privacy-and-records debate over commercial reporting agencies during the 1960s (accuracy of information, lack of due process, the use of irrelevant criteria in credit decisions, etc.). As a result, it came up with a picture of opinions more supportive of business practices than might have been the case if these issues had been presented. Even so, we see that public responses are not uniform when very specific matters of record-keeping are involved. Asked whether life-insurance companies have a right to investigate applicants for insurance, 92

---

[9] In the survey of college students for the John D. Rockefeller III Foundation, almost 40 percent of the respondents said that the FBI as an institution is in need of fundamental reform (39 percent) or should be "done away with" (10 percent).

percent agreed that "health and medical history" were legitimate matters of investigation. Agreement dropped to 66 percent, however, with respect to the propriety of investigating "financial integrity" and to 58 percent for "personal habits and character."

What these poll results suggest to us is that underneath the concern over confidentiality which many people have and the solid minority concern about "invasion of privacy" as a general theme lie opinions which are at least varied and at some points reflect inner conflict on the part of the respondents. Questioned in sufficient detail, many in the public have opinions on the relevance of different criteria for making decisions about individuals, on the relative need for different types of government record-keeping and surveillance activities, and on conditions appropriate to setting up and safeguarding public record systems.

Some of these differences on specific items reflect the fact that there are real dilemmas present in setting the balance between the information needs of organizations and the rights of individuals. A large portion of the public is at some points worried for instance about *both* dissent-out-of-control *and* the abuses of surveillance systems, and believes *both* that businesses have a need for information *and* that there are abuses where credit, preemployment, and preinsurance investigations are involved.

Differences among people on specific record-keeping issues obviously have something to do with differences in the real-life experiences people have with privacy, confidentiality, and due-process problems. The general public evidences least concern about the civil liberties of those groups in the population with which it has trouble identifying and in situations where individuals are least able to envision themselves as the subjects of record-keeping abuses. For some kinds of events (e.g., arrests) we know without public opinion polls that only a minority of Americans and their families have experienced the accompanying record-keeping, and that fewer still have encountered civil-liberties problems with their records.

In the Harris poll mentioned earlier, a question on actual experiences with invasion of privacy was included. While 34 percent had said that they felt their privacy was being invaded, no more than 19 percent of the respondents checked any one item on the following list (table B-2) which had many items phrased in terms of violations the respondent had experienced personally.

For our purposes, it is significant that "computers which collect a lot of information about you" was one of the two items that drew the largest positive response (19 percent), along with

Table B-2

Personal Experiences with Privacy Invasions

Violation of Privacy By	Is Violated	Not Violated	Not Sure
Computers which collect a lot of information about you	19%	71%	10%
Business which sells you things on credit	19	76	5
The government when it collects tax returns	17	79	4
People looking in your windows	17	80	3
People listening into your telephone conversations	15	81	4
People overhearing your conversations with other people	15	81	4
The government when it takes a census	14	84	2
Employment interviewers	11	83	6
Neighbors who gossip about your family	10	86	4
Public opinion polltakers	10	86	4
The government when filling out Social Security cards	8	86	6
Hotel and motel phone operators	6	80	14
People over you in your work	5	90	5

credit inquiries by businesses. But more important is the fact that for those concerned about privacy, no one problem appears to represent the one-third concerned respondents.

When participants in the Transportation Institute Conference were asked to check from a list of items relating to privacy those they had personally experienced, 73 percent said that they had encountered "billing or accounting errors from organizations that used computerized procedures." This was by far the most common experience shared by the respondents. The next most reported experience concerned "intrusive questions" on compulsory government forms (47 percent) and on credit applications (45 percent). Twenty-six percent reported being "photographed at political meetings," and 14 percent reported instances in which an "erroneous report of some kind" was used to deny them employment, a license, or some benefit.

Most of the polls we have been discussing do not show wide differentiation in opinion along age, sex, race, or income lines. Privacy, in the several different aspects tapped in this collection of polls, does not appear to be an issue which is the special concern of men over women, young over old, or rich over poor. There are occasional differences along some of these dimensions, but only along the lines of education do any consistent (though relatively small) differences in general privacy concern or opinions on specific practices appear. This probably reflects the fact that those with greater education usually have more contact with news media, and that the news media and other sources of information about public issues represent an alternative source of "experiences" with privacy violations. Since violations of privacy rights are not everyday events for most people, the added exposure through the media which more highly educated people receive may produce a higher level of concern.

We have little data concerning those who live on the fringes of society. Public opinion polls—even very well-conducted ones—typically underrepresent the poorest segments of the population and, through noncooperation and their relatively small numbers, the most radical groups on the left or right. Yet the views of those who live on the fringes of the society politically and economically are of considerable importance in any estimation of privacy concerns, since they are so often the "victims" of intrusive practices. Further, those we have incarcerated in prisons and mental hospitals represent populations whose experiences with record-keeping and with privacy in "total" institutions make it important that their views be added to those of "the public."

To summarize our analysis thus far, we have seen from the results of three national samplings and from polls of more specialized populations that invasion of privacy, as a general issue, generates strong concern on the part of a one-third minority of the American people. It is not the issue which people see as most pressing (especially when they are asked about it as a general matter). When individuals are asked about more specific aspects of privacy and records problems, we see that (1) their responses are not uniform and show considerable difference in level of concern from issue to issue, and (2) a "practical" streak appears as individuals pick and choose among the record-keeping practices they see as necessary and the way these are balanced with the protection of individual liberties.

PUBLIC OPINION ON PRIVACY AND COMPUTERS

All of the features of public opinion on privacy which we have described in the foregoing show clearly in public perceptions and feelings on computerized record systems. Let us start by looking again at the survey work of the Harvard Program on Technology and Society.

Overall, the thrust of the survey, according to an analysis done by a scholar at the Harvard Program, was as follows. It

> revealed that whatever their discontents with what might be called "the quality of life" most people do not hold technology responsible. On the contrary, the sample viewed technology as being generally more beneficial than harmful. They rejected the view that technology has made life too complicated and expressed little desire to "return to nature!" Expressions of malaise and alienation were considerably more frequent among the lower status and less educated groups in the sample. The higher status and better educated groups tended to be more content with life and to express more support for technology.[1]

Most people saw both benefits and harms in technology, and while there was considerable ambivalence in many areas, the majority of those interviewed gave technology "a favorable evaluation." Ninety-four percent agreed that machines have made life easier, 76 percent said that overall, "technology does more good than harm"; and another version of the same question later in the interview drew 83 percent agreement that "technology is more beneficial than harmful."

Asked to evaluate several different technological efforts, strong majorities favored fluoridation and genetic research, but 78 percent expressed concern about pollution, 52 percent were in opposition to development of the SST, and 42 percent were against the ABM. These figures suggest that the public sees some particular uses of technology as questionable policies for the nation and are not committed to every technological venture. In ranking seven federal spending programs according to "highest priority," the respondents put programs for welfare, crime preven-

---

[1] See Irene Taviss, *op. cit.*

tion, mental health, pollution control, and urban housing ahead of national defense and the space program.

An interesting question was also asked about the individual's feelings of "satisfaction" or "dissatisfaction" in his dealings with the large organizations that make up so much of American life today, and with which technology is so strongly identified. Respondents registered high satisfaction for their dealings with banks, utilities, supermarkets, and department stores, while the heaviest dissatisfaction was registered for state and federal governments.

A series of questions were asked about computers as an example of technology, with 87 percent agreeing that computers have increased efficiency in government and business. However, 73 percent also agreed with the statement that "the problem with government and big business is that they have reduced individuals to a set of punched holes in an IBM card."

Respondents with differing levels of general knowledge about technology were compared on the question of whether or not people generally benefit from computers and automation, and differences in opinion became apparent. Twenty-eight percent of those measured to be relatively low in technological information believed that people generally benefit from computers—as compared with 62 percent of those with a moderate level of general knowledge about technology and 50 percent of those judged to have a relatively high knowledge about technology. These differences are not necessarily a result of education alone; it may be that some combination of education and occupation accounts for differences in attitudes towards computers. Throughout the study, these two factors showed up as important.

When asked more specifically who benefits from and who is harmed by various technological developments, many respondents felt that the results of developments like computerization haven't yet filtered down in direct ways to most individuals. Only 52.3 percent said they themselves benefited, though 82.9 percent saw "business people" benefiting and 87 percent felt scientists benefited; 50.8 percent said "people in general" and 48.5 percent "working people" benefited.

The reader will recall our discussion of the one-big-databank question. A majority of respondents were opposed to establishing a single large federal file on citizens and suggested that if it were constructed at all, the more popular participation in the decision, the better.

The AFIPS Study

For our purposes, the best of the public opinion surveys on privacy and computers was that conducted by the American Federal of Information Processing Societies (AFIPS) and Time magazine.[2] It was administered in the spring of 1971—at the height of press and congressional concern about FBI surveillance activities (as revealed in the stolen Media, Pennsylvania, FBI documents) and during the course of Senator Ervin's hearings on federal databanks and military surveillance of civilian groups.

Respondents are generally approving of computers and their effect on the quality of life; but it is also clear that they are not prepared to accept every laudatory platitude about computerization and they see some real dangers in this technology. To get a sense for their general familiarity with and reaction to computers, four questions in the AFIPS survey dealt with individual experience with computers. Forty-nine percent of the AFIPS national sample reported that at some time they have had a job which "required some contact with a computer—either directly or indirectly—such as receiving or giving information that a computer has something to do with." Only 15 percent report, however, that their job required them to "have some knowledge of how a computer system works."

Reporting on a very different kind of experience, 34 percent of the AFIPS respondents said that they had had some "problems because of a computer." Most frequently mentioned were "problems with billing." The survey probed further on this matter to ask whether respondents had ever had trouble getting a mix-up with a bill corrected. Twenty-four percent of all the respondents said that they had had such a problem at one time or another; most said further that the trouble in getting the bill cleared up was mainly "the fault of the company's personnel" rather than "the fault of the computer."

AFIPS respondents were asked for their opinion "overall" as to what effect "the use of computers has had on life." Seventy-one percent reported that use of computers has made life "somewhat" or "much" better; 15 percent felt that life is somewhat or much worse; only 5 percent said that the computer had had no

---

[2] See note on page 466 above. Distribution of respondents by age, sex education and income was close to that of the U.S. as a whole. By political orientation (self-description), respondents were liberal (22 percent), middle of the road (37 percent), and conservative (34 percent).

effect on the quality of life. (Nine percent did not answer or said that they didn't know.)

Presented with a list of alternatives, respondents were asked what kinds of things they believed computers were being used for. Credit-card billing, preparing bank statements and "compiling information files on U.S. citizens" were mentioned by more than 90 percent of the respondents; 64 percent said that they thought that computers were being used for "keeping track of criminals." Least mentioned of all was the use of computers for "surveillance of activist or radical groups" (54 percent). Such a question does not provide us with any sense for how widespread the public believes these uses of the computer to be. Respondents were about as likely to mention "automatic control of factory machinery" as they were to say "medical diagnosis," and "sending mail advertisements to the home" was mentioned with about the same frequency as "teaching children in school." In all four cases, those with higher education and incomes were more likely than other respondents to note these as current uses of the computer—a reflection perhaps of higher exposure to the media and of the fact that few distinctions are made in what is said and published concerning the difference between experimental work, pioneering attempts at computerization, and well-established uses of the computer.

As we saw in the case of the Harvard survey, general questions, examined alone, can mask very specific fears and complaints. Thirty-eight percent of the AFIPS respondents (including some who found the overall effect of computers to be good) said that "Computers represent a real threat to people's privacy." (A majority disagreed, and 8 percent either did not answer or said that they did not know.) Where the AFIPS survey turns to examine people's feelings about uses of the computer, we begin to observe the same pattern noted in our discussion of public opinion on record-keeping: the structure of opinions as to what should and should not be done grows more complex. Respondents were asked to evaluate a list of record-keeping activities and decide which should be increased, which should be decreased, and which should remain the same. High support was evidenced for increasing the computer's use for keeping track of criminals (78 percent), gathering and analyzing census data (70 percent), medical diagnoses (74 percent), and vote counting (66 percent). Support was less firm but still in the majority range for increases in computerized credit-card billing systems (52 percent) and credit reference checks (52 percent), surveillance of activist or radical groups (56 percent) and "compiling information files on U.S. citizens" (50 percent).

Respondents called for *decreases* in the use of computers in the case of "matching people for dating" (14 percent), and "sending mail advertisements to the home" (63 percent). On items such as surveillance and compiling files on citizens, respondents of higher education and income were less likely than other respondents to support an increase in the use of computers.

Following along the same train of questioning, the AFIPS survey asked respondents to say what items on a list "should or should not be kept in a central computerized information file." As might be expected from the foregoing responses, at least 70 percent of the respondents approved of keeping police, medical, school, tax, credit rating, and employment records in a central computer file. Less support appeared for salary (54 percent), political activity (50 percent), and information about "the brands of products people buy" (46 percent).

Scattered throughout the AFIPS survey were questions about beliefs as to what effects computers were having on record systems, civil liberties, and the quality of life. More than 60 percent in each case agreed that life is better because of computers and that there are many things we can do today that we would not be able to do without computers; that computers have helped raise our standard of living and that the development of "large computerized information files will help to make our government more effective." At the same time, at least 50 percent of the respondents said that computerized files may be used to destroy individual freedom or that because of such files, "too many people have information about other people," that people are becoming "too dependent" on computers, and that "computers are dehumanizing people and turning them into numbers."

The AFIPS survey found that a substantial segment of the American public was also worried about the accuracy of information held in computerized files. But even here wide divergencies of opinion are apparent. Seventy-seven percent *dis*agreed with the statement "Computers always give accurate information," though 81 percent believe that " 'Computer mistakes' are really mistakes made by people who use computers." Forty-two percent believe "There is no way to find out if information about you that is stored in a computer is accurate," and 39 percent believe "It is very difficult to correct computer errors"; yet 49 percent of the respondents said that "Computers are more reliable than people."

If the opinions of AFIPS respondents generally favor the use of computers in society now and in the future, there is also high agreement that the government should be more concerned in the future about regulating the use of computers. Asked how concerned they think the government *is* about regulation, 61 percent answered "very" or "fairly" concerned. Asked about how concerned the government *should be*, 84 percent said that it should be concerned.

As in the case of the public opinion materials on privacy issues in general, education seems to play some role in the formation of opinions on the computer's role in society and record-keeping. As was pointed out in the Harvard Survey, those with more education appeared more likely to see technology in a basically positive light. However, the more educated respondents in the AFIPS survey also seem to display a greater concern for the potential damage to civil liberties that the computer might do. This suggests that the computer-privacy issue represents an "elite" concern, probably dependent on greater awareness of this new issue by those following media discussions of it. The demographic elements also suggest that middle- and upper-class groups concerned about the effects of more complete and consolidated records on their business, civic, or political lives are more likely to be concerned than those who are poorer, and have traditionally been subject to more direct controls and discriminations than those deriving from organizational record-keeping. For the poor especially, privacy problems may be very real, but given the range of other problems which have to be faced, privacy may not be an issue of immediate importance.

Privacy concerns are in part then rooted in structural features of the society and to some extent in actual experiences with record-keeping. Privacy and confidentiality are elite issues at least in the sense that one must exist in a sufficiently stable and unthreatened existence for record-privacy problems to take on some importance.

There are a number of dimensions of the privacy debate which the available public opinion materials do not begin to reveal. It is extremely difficult, for instance, to judge the extent to which concern about privacy issues changes over time. It is our sense that concern is indeed growing. But this is a conclusion reached from immersion in the debate itself and from assumptions as to what forces affect public opinion, not from empirical research.

Along similar lines, most of the available poll data does not let us know how deeply held the opinions we have been examining tend to be. We have yet to see the large-scale empirical study of what privacy means to people—a study which would have to probe much deeper than the opinion poll is usually designed to do. Because our focus has been on computers and record-keeping practices, we have touched only in passing on the important psychosocial dimensions of privacy (and intrusions upon it) as an experience.

It is quite possible that the psychological aspects of privacy complaints and fears are particularly important when it comes to public attitudes on computers and organizational record-keeping. Despite the relatively accepting public environment in which computers have developed over the past decade and a half, we saw throughout the profile reports that many protests have been raised about the computerization of record systems. In some of these cases, the panic button was pushed by mistake. But other protests were less a matter of error than they were instances of the privacy issue becoming a surrogate for deeper questions of power and values in American life.

One of the pioneering studies of public reactions to computers was conducted in 1963 by Robert S. Lee. From his interviews with 3,000 persons nationwide he concluded that a simple "pro" or "con" model of public opinion *vis à vis* the computer is inappropriate. His findings were that "popular reaction to the computer is organized around two basic ideas—that the computer is a beneficial tool of man, and that it may be a superhuman thinking machine that downgrades man's previously unique significance in the order of things." These findings suggested to him that, when held by the same individual, such potentially conflicting orientations to the computer can produce an ambivalence which is not conducive to the forming of simple, clear opinions. Further, he suggests that "the computer as an object of social perception functions to a certain degree as a Rorschach blot or TAT card. It is a complex and ambiguous stimulus; how individuals perceive it and give meaning to it depends very much on their fundamental values, on their personality dynamics and on their basic orientations toward life."[3]

---

[3] Robert S. Lee, "Social Attitudes and the Computer Revolution," *Public Opinion Quarterly*, Vol. 34, No. 1 (Spring 1970).

Appendix C

Databank Developments
in Other Nations

In considering what policy measures might be taken in the United States, one might usefully inquire whether other nations engaged in computerization of record systems have developed measures to assure citizen rights that might be adapted to the American situation. To explore this possibility, extensive materials were gathered during 1969-72 covering Great Britain, Canada, and most of the twenty-one other nations that make up the Organization for Economic Co-operation and Development (OECD).[1] Site visits to British central and local governments and to organizations in the private sector in Britain were conducted in 1970 and 1972, and close liaison was maintained with several national study projects (as in Canada) that have been conducting empirical investigations into databanks and civil liberties. Materials were also obtained from the United Nations Commission on Human Rights, which has been collecting information about the effects of technology on individual liberties throughout the world.[2] The following are the trends most relevant to the discussion of American policy alternatives.

1. During the past decade, file automation in the public sectors of OECD nations has proceeded in many of the same subject-matter areas of administrative, intelligence, and research record-keeping as in the United States. A 1971 *Inventory of Data Banks in the Public Sector*, compiled by OECD,[3] shows automation of personal records going forward (with varying emphases by

---

[1] The 23 members of OECD are Australia, Austria, Belgium, Canada, Denmark, Finland, France, the Federal Republic of Germany, Greece, Iceland, Ireland, Italy, Japan, Luxembourg, the Netherlands, Norway, Portugal, Spain, Sweden, Switzerland, Turkey, the United Kingdom, and the United States.

[2] See, for example, General Assembly Resolution 2751 (XXV) of 15 December 1970, and Commission on Human Rights Resolution 10 (XXVII) of 18 March 1971, and the reports of the Secretary General dealing with "Human Rights and Scientific and Technological Developments" (A/8055, XXV session) and Addendum of 29 December 1970.

[3] Directorate for Scientific Affairs, Computer Utilization Group, OECD, Paris, 1971 Edition. See also U. Thomas, *Computerised Data Banks in Public Administration: Trends and Policy Issues*, OECD Informatics Studies, Paris, 1971; K. Lenk, *Integrated Data Bases in Public Administration*, OECD Directorate for Scientific Affairs, Computer Utilization Group, Paris, April 7, 1972; R. Pipes, *Toward Central Government Computer Policies, ibid.*, May 5, 1972.

country) in fields such as law enforcement, driver licenses, taxation, welfare, social insurance, employment job banks, public employee personnel files, and census and social statistics. In addition, as a result of their distinctive constitutional and administrative traditions, many of these nations are engaged in computerizing personal record systems that have no parallel in the United States. These include national population registers, based on files of residence registration or citizen identifying numbers; central indexes of various groups in the nation (such as subscribers to state-owned telephone systems, owners of radio and TV sets, secondary and university students, debtors to central government banks, etc.); and files used in special governmental programs (national disease registers, regional medical patient records, central land-ownership registries, etc.).

2. Computerization of these public record systems during the past decade has generally followed the patterns of development we described for American systems in part three (internal housekeeping, file automation, databank and MIS projects, etc.). Computerization also reflects the emphasis on high-volume, routine, objective records noted and seems to be having the same specific effects on record-keeping practices described in part three (more complete and up-to-date records, etc.).

While the United States entered the 1970s several years ahead of even the most advanced OECD nations in operating on-line, random-access systems and creating databank projects of the Santa Clara County type, both on-line systems and experimental databank projects are now spreading rapidly at the local and central government levels of many OECD countries. The presence of national citizen numbers in some of these nations has encouraged efforts to link various record systems in databank applications. Projects for databanks in municipal government, for national research studies, and for national medical or social welfare purposes are in the planning or implementation stages in many of the OECD countries.

3. In keeping with social trends throughout the industrialized nations, there have been significant public discussions in most of the OECD countries during the past few years over potential threats to privacy arising from the growth of personal record systems in the public and private sectors, and the additional powers of data consolidation and utilization made possible by computerization. Press stories, resolutions by legal and political

groups, and parliamentary debates have occurred with increasing frequency.[4] Two main conclusions have been drawn:

a. First, the existing law as to personal privacy, especially as it relates to the collection and use of personal information in public or private record systems, has been found to be highly fragmentary. A survey done for the Computer Utilization Group of OECD concluded as of 1971:

> [I]n most countries there exists no clear legal definition of privacy. The legal notion, insofar as it exists, derives from general legal principles. Rather than providing a positive expression of an individual's right to privacy, the law in most Member countries consists of specific prohibitions, dispersed widely throughout the body of the law: for example, prohibitions concerning eavesdropping, tampering with the mails and defamation. In no country are there yet prohibitions dealing specifically with invasion of privacy by data banks.

However, most countries have some legislation safeguarding the confidentiality of personal information held in government files.[5]

b. As a result of this realization, national commissions have been set up in almost a dozen of the OECD nations, with mandates to gather factual information about the progress of automation involving personal records, study the present and impending state of the art, and present recommendations as to legal measures that ought to be taken. Some of these government commissions are looking exclusively at the computerized databank problem, while others are considering this as part of a larger examination of privacy-and-technology issues. The initial reports of most of these bodies are scheduled to appear in 1972-74.[6] Some important multinational studies that include treatment of databanks and civil

---

[4] For two recent books dealing with these questions, see B. C. Rowe (ed.), *Privacy, Computers, and You* (London: National Computing Centre Limited, 1972); and E. Samuelson, *Statlige databanker og personlighetsvern* (Public Data Banks and the Privacy Problem) (Oslo: Universitetsforlaget, 1972). See also "L'Informatique et les Libertés," *Problèmes Politiques et Sociaux*, No. 55 (January 15, 1971).

[5] G. B. F. Niblett, "Digital Information and the Privacy Problem," OECD Informatics Studies, Paris, 1971, p. 41.

[6] The report of Sir Kenneth Younger's Committee on Privacy was scheduled to appear in England in July of 1972, as was the Report of the Privacy and Computers Task Force of the Departments of Communications and Justice in Canada.

liberties are also being done by various groups, ranging from the International Commission of Jurists and the Council of Europe to the OECD, the UN Commission on Human Rights, and the Nordic Council.

4. As of mid-1972, there has been no *national* legislation in any OECD nation dealing with the civil-liberties aspects of *computerized* record systems. Bills of varying kinds to define rights of privacy or create supervisory institutions over databanks have been introduced in the parliaments of several countries, such as Canada, Great Britain, France, and West Germany, but none of these has yet been enacted. In addition, the OECD survey published in 1971 found that there have not been any court decisions dealing specifically with computerized record systems,[7] though there have been rulings dealing with confidentiality of information in government or private record systems in general.

There has been one piece of legislation enacted at the state (*"Land"*) level in the Federal Republic of Germany that is worth noting. A "Data Protection Act" passed by the state of Hesse in 1970[8] (and since then passed in two other West German states as well) sets out regulations governing protection of data and the rights of the individual in "all records prepared for purposes of automatic data processing" in the state. The creation of databanks and information systems is expressly authorized for state government. Protection of data against inspection or alteration by unauthorized persons is mandated to be carried out "by appropriate staff and technical arrangements"; employees of ADP installations are forbidden to reveal confidential information; an "aggrieved party" may demand "rectification" of stored data that is "incorrect." Whoever makes data covered by the act available to unauthorized persons commits a criminal offense. Statistical data may be published from databanks when there are no "individual details concerning natural or legal persons and permitting no such details to be inferred," and when "there is no legal prohibition against it

---

[7] Niblett, *op. cit.*, pp. 42-43. "There are no reported cases dealing directly with computerized information systems. But in 1965 the Swedish Supreme Administrative Court held that the principle laid down by the Freedom of the Press Act, viz., that every Swedish citizen should have free access to official documents, should apply also to computer stored information."

[8] Data Protection Act, State of Hesse, Federal Republic of Germany, 7 October 1970, reprinted in Niblett, *op. cit*, pp. 47-51.

nor any important public interest to prevent it. As a rule, public interest shall not stand in the way of the Land Parliament's right to information." The act creates an elected Data Protection Commissioner to ensure that its provisions are met. He is instructed to "observe the effects of automatic data processing on the operations and powers of decision" of agencies, "inform the responsible control authorities of any infringements committed," and "shall initiate measures for improving data protection." "Every person shall be entitled to apply to the data protection commissioner if he considers his rights to have been infringed by the automatic data processing [by state agencies]." An annual report by the Commissioner to the State Parliament and Prime Minister is required, and the first report has just been published.[9]

5. Those experts who have been studying comparative national reactions to the databank issue are firm in stressing that the regulatory approaches that will be adopted will have to arise from the particular (and often very different) legal and political traditions of the individual countries or regions represented. As the Head of the OECD Science Resources Division noted:

> The problems . . . are seen differently in different countries according to the cultural, social and legal traditions. In the Anglo-Saxon countries, for instance, there is no residents registration as is normal in France or Germany, where nobody thinks that such registration inhibits fundamental rights. Sweden and Italy have serious objections to giving Ministries of the Interior (which supervise the police) responsibilities of coordinating databanks, whereas in France or Germany there are no objections raised so far.[1]

To this must be added the differences between countries such as Sweden or Israel, which have national citizen numbers and identification cards, and those such as Britain, Canada, or the United States, in which such official numbers have never been accepted. And the German administrative tradition which made the Data Protection Commissioner a ready instrument for dealing with issues of data confidentiality would raise serious issues in nations

---

[9] Erster Tätigkeitsbericht des Hessischen Datenschutzbeauftragten vorgelegt 31. März 1972.

[1] Peter Menke-Glückert, letter to Alan F. Westin, September 24, 1969.

where notions of parliamentary responsibility or separation of powers would raise problems about giving such an official meaningful powers.

The general conclusion that we draw from this review of foreign experience is that most of the other industrialized nations with active computerization are at work in the mid-1970s at just the problems of definition and development of protections for the citizen's individual liberties in record systems that now confront the American people.

Appendix D

Site-Visit Letters

Typical Letter
Arranging Site Visits

NATIONAL ACADEMY OF SCIENCES

2101 CONSTITUTION AVENUE
WASHINGTON, D.C. 20418

COMPUTER SCIENCE
    AND ENGINEERING BOARD
Project on Computer Data Banks
Alan F. Westin, Director

Project Headquarters:
Joseph Henry Building, Room 536
2100 Pennsylvania Avenue, N.W.
Phone (202) 961-1835

Dear _____:

I am delighted that we were able to arrange by telephone a visit by _____ to _____.

Let me briefly describe our Project so that you will have a better idea of the interest that we have in the system you are developing. Under the auspices of the National Academy of Sciences and Russell Sage Foundation, we are undertaking a study focusing on the issues of confidentiality and access in computerized record systems. Our Project is designed to explore the balance being sought between the information needs of organizations and protection of the privacy and due process rights of individuals.

Our primary objectives are to collect data on the process of computerization in systems containing information on persons, and to trace out the implications of this process for privacy protections. To that end, we are visiting a variety of private and governmental organizations to develop detailed pictures of information gathering, storage, sharing, and use. We have already visited organizations such as _____.

From you and others at _____, we wish to learn how computerization helps you to meet information needs at

_____ as compared with satisfaction of such needs in the precomputer environment. It is important that we discuss with you the matter of confidentiality and related issues, so as to tap the experiences, opinions, and knowledge you may have. I am pleased that you will be able to cooperate with the National Academy in this effort to bring accurate and balanced treatment to an area which has so often been the object of uninformed commentary and sensational handling in recent years.

While we realize that there are distinctive aspects in record-keeping and use in every organization, and we wish to learn about these at _____ we have identified several basic areas which we hope to explore during each site visit. I list these areas below in the hope that you will better understand our general interests in advance. I suggest the list as a partial catalogue, rather than as a rigid interview format.

1. Where a record system is now fully or partially computerized, what was the precomputer record system of the organization, what rules and practices regarding confidentiality and access prevailed, and what issues and problems arose in this environment?

2. What were the basic reasons for computerizing records in the organization and by what steps has that decision been implemented?

3. What is the layout and operation of both computerized and noncomputerized record systems containing information on individuals, and what are the major, recurring uses of this information?

4. What are the rules and operating practices, if any, relating to confidentiality and the access of individuals to their own records?

5. Have any specific problems arisen involving the issues of confidentiality or due process in the computerized record system?

6. What are your plans for the future development of information systems, especially in regard to their computer aspects? Are issues of confidentiality and/or access involved in the design or concerns for such future developments?

7. What is the thinking of executives, information system managers, and the principal information users about the relation between information needs and privacy—due-process protections within your organization? How salient are the issues of confidentiality and proper access in your organization, given its goals and specific operations?

I hope that the above list will be helpful in acquainting you with some of the areas which are of interest to us.

Let me emphasize that, while we wish to incorporate in our final report accurate accounts of the important computerized systems which are developing, and the measures being taken to ensure the confidentiality of personal data, we are prepared to abide by any necessary specifications concerning proprietary or confidential information in your system. We can treat what you tell us as "for background only," or as "for publication but not for attribution to any identified person." We can also, where necessary, describe events without identifying the specific organization or people involved.

Confidential matters derived from site visits are specifically marked and held under the National Academy of Sciences Privileged designation. Under this system, the sensitive information so identified is available only to the staff, professionals, and selected consultants on a specific need basis. Any other release or use of the information so identified requires authorization from the person or organization which originally furnished the information. This excludes from access our Advisory Group and the other members of the Computer Science and Engineering Board. The latter groups see only the documentary materials or staff write-ups which have been agreed upon between our staff and your system as appropriate for such sharing. Finally, we can provide you with a draft of any description of your organization which we wish to publish, so that factual errors or incomplete summaries can be corrected.

Our Project team mixes social and computer scientists and will include _____. We are eagerly looking forward to meeting with you.

Sincerely yours,

Typical Letter Requesting Review of Profile

NATIONAL ACADEMY OF SCIENCES

2101 CONSTITUTION AVENUE
WASHINGTON, D.C. 20418

COMPUTER SCIENCE
   AND ENGINEERING BOARD
Project on Computer Data Banks
Alan F. Westin, Director

Project Headquarters:
Joseph Henry Building, Room 536
2100 Pennsylvania Avenue, N.W.
Phone (202) 962-1835

Dear＿＿＿＿＿:

Since we visited＿＿＿＿＿, we have completed our final report. It has passed through the Academy for initial review and is now nearing publication. From the 55 organizations that we visited, we have selected fourteen to illustrate how government and private organizations are computerizing their record-keeping operations. Descriptive "profiles" of these will appear in a chapter on "The World of Computerizing Organizations."

Since we plan to use＿＿＿＿＿as one example, we want you to have the opportunity to review our write-up with the following responses in mind:

1. To correct any factual errors or suggest any interpretive mistakes we may have made.

2. To indicate whether we have, unwittingly, allowed any confidential or proprietary information to slip into this account.

3. To have you bring up to date anything significant that has changed since our site visit with regard to your organization; its computer usage; new rules, laws, issues, or practices relating to confidentiality and access matters; and your plans for the future. We would especially welcome your supplying 1970 or 1971 figures wherever these are available to update figures we obtained earlier during our visit.

4. To inform us whether any quotations that we have used from our site visits should not be directly attributed to a specific individual but only as from an official of the organization. We believe authoritative statements are best identified, but we will respect your wishes in any cases that seem particularly sensitive.

Apart from literary and copy editing, and possibly some effort at shortening, this is the version that we anticipate sending to the publisher. Please feel free to call me if you should want to discuss any aspect of this profile on the telephone.

Sincerely yours,

Index

Abbreviations, in computer records; affecting decisions, 624-66
"Abuse of the Record of Arrest Not Leading to Conviction," 388*n*
Access, right to, unimpeded by computerization, 258-59, 430-32
Access to files in precomputer era, 16-17
Access rights as area of priority for public policy, 355-72
   challenge, 370-72
   courts, possible role of in defining, 357-60
   inspection, 364-70
   legislative treatment of, 360-72
   notice, 362-64
ACE, 183-92
   See also American Council on Education
Accuracy of computerized information, 294-303
   computer improves, 298-300
   computer as source of error, 300-02
   general considerations, 294-300
   and interpretation of facts, difference between, 295
   substantive correctness, 300
   survey findings on, 433-436
Administrative Adjudication program of New York State Motor Vehicle Bureau, 69
Administrative files, as a type, 361, 364
Advisory Group, project established, xvi
ADP in Municipal Government, 88*n*

AFIPS-*Time survey*, 263, 466-67, 481-84
ALERT system of Kansas City, Mo. police department, 80-2
   challenges to, 85-8
ALPS project, of the New York State Identification and Intelligence Agency, 294
American Airlines SABRE reservations sytem, misunderstood capabilities, 269-79, 321
American Association of Motor Vehicle Administrators, 71
American Bankers Association, 113, 117
American Beliefs and Attitudes about Intelligence, ix*n*
American Civil Liberties Union, 53, 99, 126*n*, 189, 270, 358, 378*n*, 390*n*
American Council on Education, profile of computerization at, *183-92*
   Campus Unrest study, 189-91
   CIRP, 184-86
   computerization, 186-88
   confidentiality of records, 188-91
   criticisms, 189-191
   function, 183
   future activities, 193
   LINK file system, 192-93
   Office of Research, 184-85
   response of Council Research Office, 191-93
American Express card records, misunderstanding about, 275-76, 321

American Federation of Information
Processing Societies, 263*n*,
466-67, 481-84
Anderson v. Sills, 19*n*, 381*n*
Applications, software, prospects for
future development of, 328
Armor, David, 470*n*
Army surveillance of political dissi-
dents, debate over, 5, 46, 264-
65
Arrest records, FBI Identification
Division, national repository of,
48
Arthur D. Little, Inc., 325*n*
*Assault on Privacy: Computers, Data-
banks and Dossiers*, 18, 270,
275
Associated Credit Bureaus of Ameri-
ca, Inc., 131
Astin, Dr. Alexander W., 184, 192,
192*n*, 193
Atropos, 3
*Audit Report on Financial and Oper-
ating Practices, New York State
Identification and Intelligence
System*, 311
Auerbach Corp., 325*n*
Automated Law Enforcement Re-
sponse Team of Kansas City,
Mo. police, 80-2, 85-88
"Automated Police Information Sys-
tems: A Survey," 77*n*
Automatic License Plate Scanning,
systems project of NYSIIS,
294
Avirgan v. Rizzo, 381*n*
Awareness of public of computerized
record-keeping, 257, 465, 482-
84
increased, 257, 484

Baker, Bobby, 50
Baker, Michael A., xvi
Ball, SSA Commissioner Robert, 34,
34*n*

Bank of America, profile of computerization at, 113-30
access to records, individual, 124*n*.,
126-29
California Consumer Credit Reporting Act of 1970, 127
computerization history, 116-19
confidentiality issues, 122-25
customer records, 119
employee records, 119-20
ERMA, development of, 116-17
Fair Credit Reporting Act, 127-
28
future plans, 129-30
information security, 125-26
privacy aspects, 121-22
social policies, 114-15
statistics, 113-14
"third party" files, 120-21
Bank Security Act of 1970, 124*n*
Banking, computerization and, 111-
30
concentration of computers in
largest institutions, 113
prime candidates for, 112
See also Bank of America
Barber, Bernard A., xi
Barrett, James, 144, 148
Batch and on-line processing, differences between, 10-11, 13-14
Bay, Christian, 190*n*
Bayh, Senator, 361*n*
Behavioral research, computerization
and, 182-93
See also American Council on Ed-
ucation
Berger, Mark, 99
Berkeley, California, citizens' super-
visory committee in, 352-53
Bible, Senator Alan, 61
Binary number system basis for digital
computers, 8
Black Panther party, 85
Board of Citizens Access Rights, sug-
gested establishment of, 370-
72

Bockelman, Melvin, 79, 83, 84, 85
"Booking" records of local police
    departments, 76
Boruch, R. F., 192*n*
Brandeis, Justice Louis, 17
Brennan, Supreme Court Justice,
    358-59
Brenton, Myron, 4
Brim, Orville G., Jr., ix, xi, xvi
Bruce, Professor James, 173, 174
Bulletin, FBI, 54
Burdick, Senator, 390*n*
Burger, Chief Justice, 163
Bursten, Dr. Ben, 99

California Bankers Association, 125*n*.
California Consumer Credit Report-
    ing Act of 1970, 127
Campbell, Angus, xii
Cantril, A. H., 343*n*
Caravan Surveys, 467*n*
Carnegie Corp., 184
Carte Blanche card records, misun-
    derstandings about, 275-76
Carter v. Gallagher, 388*n*
Case Incident Reporting System in
    New Haven, 98-9
CATV, future development of, 329
Central file of FBI, 50
Challenge, right to, unimpeded by
    computerization, 258
    as third element of access rights,
        370-72
Challenges to established system,
    343-44
CHAMPUS, processing for by Mutual
    of Omaha, 147
Chance, K. A., 124
*Changing Values on Campus: Politi-
    cal and Personal Attitudes of
    Today's College Students*, 468*n*
Chapin v. Tynan, 164*n*, 381*n*
Circulation Associates, 72
CIRP research of ACE, 184-186

CIRS in New Haven, 98-9
Citizen's Guide to Files, publication
    of recommended, 362-3
Citizen's right to see his record as
    area of priority for public poli-
    cy, 355-72
    challenge as element of access con-
        cept, 370-72
    courts, possible role of in defining,
        357-60
    inspection as element of access
        concept, 364-70
    legislative treatment of, 360-372
    notice as element of access con-
        cept, 362-64
City Directory Division of R. L. Polk
    & Co., 157
City University of New York, 185
Civil division of FBI fingerprint and
    identification file, 49
Civil liberties
    implications of future
        technology for, 330-35
        conclusions, 334
        information sharing, tremendous
          increase in, 332
        security, 332-33
    and record-keeping, 14-20
    threat to, of automated data
        banks, 3-4
    See also Due process and record
        systems; Privacy, right to
Civil Liberties Union, 53, 99 189,
    270, 358, 378*n*, 390*n*
Civil Service Commission, Bureau of
    Personnel Investigations of, and
    computerization, 46
CJIC of Santa Clara County, 108
Clark, Attorney General Ramsey, 53,
    270
*Closed Door: The Effect of a Crim-
    inal Record on Employment
    with State and Local Public
    Agencies*, 387*n*, 388*n*
Closed file policies, attacks on, 356
Clotho, 3

Coding, in computer records, affect-
ing decisions, 264-66
Colleges, computerization in, 168-82
    See also Massachusetts Institute of
        Technology
Collier, Congressman H. R., 183n
Columbia Law Review, xi
Columbia University, xv
Commercial firms, unauthorized sale
    of information to, 19-20, 49,
    70n, 87, 308, 313, 388
Commercial organizations, computer-
    ization and, 111-67
    See also Banking, computerization
        and; Commercial reporting
        agencies; Insurance compan-
        ies, profile of computeriza-
        tion of; Mailing list industry
Commercial organizations, due-pro-
    cess rights in, 17, 20, 371
Commercial reporting agencies, com-
    puterization and, 130-41
    types, two main, 131
    See also Credit Data Corp.
Commission, national study, pro-
    posed for data-bank control, 351
Committees, standing legislative,
    need for, to protect civil liber-
    ties in increasingly computer-
    ized age, 350-54
Common-law right to privacy, 19
Communications systems, prospects
    for future development of, 329
Community Progress, Inc. of New
    Haven, 91-2
Completeness of records improved by
    computerization, 280-84
Complexity of relating data to goals
    as hindrance to data-bank de-
    velopment, 238-39
Computer Operated Planning System
    of Kansas City, Mo. Police, 88
Computer Science and Engineering
    Board of National Academy of
    Sciences, xiii, 5
Computer technology, fundamentals
    of, 7-14

Computer technology:
    See also Technology, computer
Computers, future availability of,
    328
Computerised Data Banks in Public
    Administration: Trends and
    Policy Issues, 489n
Computerizing organizations, profiles
    of, 23-214
    subjects of data collection, as
        poor source of information
        about, 26-7
    systems included, range and type
        of, 25
    topics to be investigated, check-
        list of, 25
    See also Commercial organiza-
        tions; Government organiza-
        tions; Nonprofit organiza-
        tions
Computerizing organizations, survey
    of, 407-62
Confidentiality, effects of computer-
    ization on, 241-56, 437-42
    definition of, 393, 251-56
    issues of information consolida-
        tion and data sharing, 251-
        56
    See also Privacy, effects of com-
        puterization on
Confidentiality and data sharing, re-
    commendations on, 372-78
    See also Welfare program
Confidentiality and security related,
    303, 393-4
    and future welfare reform, 313-17
    and charge card, bank records, 318
Configuration arrangements,
    prospects for future develop-
    ment of, 326-27
Confront accusers, individual's right
    to, 15
Considerations of Data Security in a
    Computer Environment, 394
Consolidated Policy Accounting
    System of Mutual of Omaha,
    146

Constitutional limits
  on record systems, 380
  on right of due process, 15-17,
    355
  on right of privacy, 17-20
  on right of inspection, 355
Constitutional Rights Subcommittee
    of US Senate, actions of, 37
Converse, Philip E., xii
Cooperative Institutional Research
    Program of ACE, 184-86
  content of inquiries, 185-86
COPPS of Kansas City Police, 88
Cornell Law Review, 388n
Correctness of information, no
    major effects of computeriza-
    tion on, 300
Counsel, individual's right to, 15
County government, databanks and,
    100-110
  functions of, 100-01
  See also Santa Clara County,
    California
Courtney, Robert E., 306
Courts, actions of, re civil liberties
    groups v. law enforcement
    agencies, 59-61
  possible role of, in defining access
    rights, 357-60
    in defining confidentiality
    protections, 372
  unwillingness to place constitu-
    tional limits on records,
    379-83
CPAS of Mutual of Omaha, 146
Creager, John A., 184
Credentials system, determines op-
    portunities in U.S., 342-43
  challenges to, 343-45
Credit Bureau of Greater New York,
    131
Credit bureaus, 130-41
  See also Commercial reporting
    agencies
Credit Data Corporation, computeri-
    zation and, 123, 125, 132-41
  current files, 135-36

Credit Data Corporation:
  development of, 132-34
  and Fair Credit Reporting Act,
    137-39
  future, 140-39
  government inquiry, 139-40
  invasion-of-privacy debate, 134-35
  services provided, current, 136-37
  statistics, 132
Crime Control Act of 1968, 77, 108
Criminal Justice Information Con-
    trol system of Santa Clara
    County, California, 108
Criminal record checks, increase in
    number of jobs requiring, 389
Criminal section of FBI fingerprint
    identification file, 49
Cusick, Paul, 173
Customs, Bureau of, and computer-
    ization, 46

Dahl, Robert, 91n
Databank, definition of, 9n, 89n,
    229
  in reality few and far between,
    235-240
Data collection, limiting of unnec-
    essary, 379-92
Data integration in one organization,
    254-55, 427-29
Data sharing
  increased feasibility of, as most
    important development in
    1970's, 342
  rules for, 372-78
  types, four, 252-55
  See also Confidentiality, recom-
    mendations on
Daunt, Jerome J., 52, 55, 63
Davis, Lou, 210, 212
Davis, Dr. Ruth, 326n
De Lay, Robert F., 166-67
"Defendant's Right of Access to Pre-
    sentence Reports," 367n
*Digital Information and the Privacy
    Problem.* 491n

DIME file in New Haven, 98
Direct Mail Advertisers Association, 165, 385
Direct-mail advertising, privacy issue and, 161-163
  recommendations for, 385-86
Direct-mail industry, computerization of, 154-67
  See also Mailing list industry
"Discrimination on the Basis of Arrest Records," 388*n*
DMAA, 165, 385
Doe v. Scott, 18*n*
"Domestic intelligence community," sharing of information in, 46
Donovan, Joseph, 70, 73
Douglas, Supreme Court Justice, 358-59
Dual Independent Map Encoding file in New Haven, 98
Due process, impact of computerization on, 256-69, 430-32
  access and challenge, right to, unimpeded by computerization, 258
  procedural, in computerized record systems, 256-59
  See also Substantive due process issues
Due process of law and record systems, 15-7
  definition, 393
  elements, three, 15
  and freedom-of-information laws, 16
  and private institutions and commercial organizations, 17
Due process rights, recommendations for improving access, 355-72
Dun and Bradstreet, 131

EAM equipment defined, 12
Eddy v. Moore, 381*n*
EDP equipment, history of, 12-14
  first generation, 13

EDP equipment:
  second generation, 13-4
  third generation, 14
Edwards, Congressman, 390*n*
Efficiency, organizational, increased due to computerization, 341
Eisenstadt v. Baird, 18*n*
"Election Time Series Analysis of Attitudes of Trust in Government," 343*n*
Emergency Civil Liberties Committee, 73
Employability and the Juvenile Arrest Record, 388*n*
Employee records at Bank of America, handling of, 119-120
Employee right-to-privacy bill, federal, 384-85
Employees of organizations maintaining files, security breaches by, 308
ERMA, development of, for Bank of America, 116
Ervin, Senator Sam, 5, 37, 86, 179, 312, 353, 384, 397, 468
Etzioni, Amitai, 190*n*
Experimentation with Human Beings: The Authority of the Investigator, Subject, Profession and State in the Human Experimentation Process, xi

Fabian, Robert, 123, 125*n*
Fair Credit Reporting Act, 127-28, 135, 137-39, 151, 257, 380*n*
Fano, Dr. Robert, 178
Fates, three, as determinants of life, 3
FBI, bank records subpoenaed by, 124*n*
  computerization and, 45-64
  criminal history records system, 57-63, 377-78, 389
  recommendation concerning, 400-02

FBI:
    criticisms, 47-8
    early computerization in, 51-3
    fingerprint and identification re-
      cation records, 48-9
    name-index file, 51
    narrative or central file, 50
    National Crime Information Cen-
      ter, 47-64
    statistics concerning, 48
    uniform crime reports, 57
      recommended changes in,
        400-402
    See also Fingerprint records of
      FBI; Law enforecment,
      federal; Narrative file of
      FBI; National Crime Infor-
      mation Center
Federal Aid to Families with De-
    pendent Children program, 358
Federal Aviation Agency, 164
*Federal Databanks, Computers and
    the Bill of Rights*, 179n
Federal funds
    encourage law enforcement sys-
      tem development, 57, 77, 98
    shortage of, as detriment to data-
      bank development, 240
Federal government computerizing
    organizations, profiles of, 29-
    64
    costs, 29
    "databanks," 30
    law enforcement, 45-64
    Social Security Administration,
      31-45
    social services, 30-45
    users, primary, 29
*Federal Statistics: Report of the
    President's Commission*, 322n,
    401n
Federal Trade Commission, 165n,
    263
Feinhandler, Sherwin, 470n
Fenwick, Russell, 118, 121, 130
Fidelifacts, 131

*Fifteenth Ward and the Great Soci-
    ety: An Encounter with a
    Modern City*, 91n
File, definition of, 9
File automation, 221-29
    meaning of, 229
    as reality, 234-35
Finance, computerization and, 111-
    130
    See also Banking, computerization
      and
Fingerprint records of FBI, 48-9
    access to, 49
    civil division, 49
    criminal section, 49
Firestone, Ira, ix
Ford Foundation, 92
Forecast, technological, elements of,
    319-35
    civil liberties implications, 330-35
    intraorganizational constraints,
      322-23
    limits on, 334-35
    organizational goals and priori-
      ties, effect of, 321-22
    prospects for 1970's, 324-30
    social and political conditions,
      323-24
    timespan, consideration of, 320
    users of computer systems, vast
      increase in, 319
Foreign nations, databank develop-
    ment in, 489-94
"Forgiveness" principle, destruction
    of by computerized record
    system, 267-68
Francis, Al, 167
Frankfurter, Justice Felix, 15
Freedom of Information Act of
    1966, 44, 164
Frost and Sullivan, 325n
Future directions in computer tech-
    nology, 317-35
*Future of Law Enforcement Statis-
    tics: A Summary View*, 401n
Futterman, Jack, 45

Gallagher, Cornelius, 50, 134, 163,
    165, 312
Gallati, Dr. Robert R. J., 312, 314n
Gallup Poll, 474
"Garbage-in-gospel-out" attitude not
    generally prevalent, 262
Genealogical Society of Mormon
    Church, 198
General Electric, 116
Gesell, Judge Gerhard, 60, 372
Giannini, A. P., 113
"GIGO effect" as creed of computer
    personnel, 300
Glass, David C., ix
Goals, organizational, important in-
    fluence of on future technol-
    ogy, 321-22
Goslin, David A., ix
Government Dossier: Survey of In-
    formation Contained in Gov-
    ernment Files, 362n
Government organizations, profiles
    of, 29-110
Greeley, Andrew, 190n
Greene v. McElroy, 15n
Gregory v. Litton Systems, Inc., 60n,
    388
Guide to Files, publication of, rec-
    ommended, 362-63
Guidelines for the Collection, Main-
    tenance and Dissemination of
    Pupil Records, x

Habeas corpus, right of, 16
Halleck, Seymour, 190n
Hanlon, Joseph, 59
Hanna, William, 39
Hansen, A. M., 148, 150
Hardware, meaning of, 12
Harris Associates, 466, 466n
Harvard University, 179n, 470, 479n
Haymarket Collective, 157n
Health, Education and Welfare, De-
    partment of, 30-1, 397, 399, 400

Health centers, computerization of,
    203-14
    See also Hospitals and health cen-
        ters
Hearings before Subcommittee on
    Constitutional Rights of the
    Committee on Judiciary, 349n
Heinig, J., 343n
Hess, 388n
Hodges, John D., Jr., 77n
Hollerith, Herman, 12
Holmes v. Church, 381n
Hooper-Holmes, 131, 152
Hoover, J. Edgar, 47
Hopes and Fears of the American
    People, 343n
Horton, Congressman Frank, 164-65
Hospital Financial Management Asso-
    iation, 204n
Hospitals and health centers, com-
    puterization of, 203-14
    legal complications, 204
    problems with, 204-05
    See also Kaiser-Permanente Med-
        ical Care program
Housekeeping functions, initial com-
    puterization for, 220-229
    growth of computerization,
        reasons for, 228-29
    high-volume file automation, 221-
        29
    increase in volume of transactions,
        table of, 224-27
    manual files still retained, certain
        number of, 222
Human experimentation, problem of,
    xi
Human Meaning of Social Change, xii

IBM, 89, 93-7, 306
IBM-New Haven project, 89-90, 94-7
Identification, Social Security num-
    ber for, 41-42, 75, 124-125,
    137, 150, 181, 189

Identification records of FBI, 48-9
Identification system, national
  establishment of, 41-45,
  396-400
Immigration and Naturalization Service, computerization in, 30
*Indicators of Social Change: Con-
  cepts and Measurements,* xii
Individual as source of privacy complaints, 446-53
  and action on privacy issues, 403-
  04
Information in files, greater use of
  through computerization, 284-
  88
Information Processing Center of
  MIT, computer centralization
  in, 171-74
Information Sciences, Inc., 119
Information sharing
  computer impact on, 51-56, 291-
  93
  tremendous increase of in future
  years, 332
*Information Systems Technology in
  State Government,* 64n
Information trust agencies, priority
  of establishment of, 400-02
Input process of computer systems,
  8-9, prospects for future development of, 325-26
Inquiries, faster handling of through
  computerization, 289-90
Inspection as second element of access rights, 364-70
Institutional record-keeping, balance
  between personal privacy and,
  x-xi
Insurance companies, 141-54
  functions of, 141-42
  See also Mutual of Omaha, profile
  of
Integrated-circuit technology characteristic of third generation
  EDP equipment, 14

*Integrated Data Bases in Public Ad-
  ministration,* 489n
Integration, data, in one organiza-
  tion, 254-55, 427-29
Intelligence files, as type, 361, 364
  and computerization, 244-45,
  275
Intelligence community, 46
Inter-Departmental Intelligence Unit
  of Justice Dept., 63n
Internal Revenue Service
  Bank records open to, 125n
  computerization in Intelligence
  Division of, 30, 244-45
  computer impact on use of data
  at, 284-86
International Association of Chiefs
  of Police, 58
International City Managers Association, 88-9
International Data Corp., 325n
Interorganizational networks, creation of, through computerization, 291-93
Interpretation of facts and accuracy
  of computerized information,
  difference between, 295
Intraorganizational constraints and
  influence on technology, 322-
  23
*Investigations Relating to Insurance,
  Job and Credit Applications: A
  Nationwide Study of Public Attitudes,* 467n
Issues regarding records, computers
  and civil liberties, setting of, 1-
  20
  computer technology, fundamentals of, 7-14
  Fates, three, ancient belief in, 3
  1960's, anxiety in, 4-5
  report, outline of, 5-7
  See also Technology, computer,
  fundamentals of

Joint Center for Urban Studies of
     Harvard and MIT, 97
Jones, Leroy, 100
Jordan, Dr. Harry C., 132
Judgments
     computer impact on, 259-64
     challenges to criteria of, 343-45
Judiciary
     role vis à vis access rights, 357-60
     unwillingness to place constitu-
          tional limits on record sys-
          tems, 379-83
"Junk mail," privacy issue and, 162-
     63
Jurisdictionwide data banks
     proposals for, 232-33
     problems in building, 235-40
     See also Santa Clara County and
          New Haven, Conn.
Jury of one's peers, individual right
     to, 16

Kafka, Franz, 359*n*
Kaiser-Permanente Medical Care pro-
     gram, 205-14
     computer development, 207-09
     confidentiality issues, medical
          records and, 211-13
     future, 213-14
     impact of computer, 209-11
     preventive medicine, emphasis
          on, 206
Kansas City, Mo. police department,
     profile of, 77-88
     administration, 77-8
     ALERT system, 80-2
     challenges to ALERT, 85-8
     civil liberties issues, 83-5
     databanks and teleprocessing,
          move to, 79-80
     future plans, 88
     LEMRAS, 82
     management evaluation of com-
          puter system, 82-3

Kansas City, Mo. police department:
     manual record-keeping and initial
          computerization, 78
     safeguards and civil liberties is-
          sues, 83-5
Katz, Jay, xi
Kaufman, Joseph, 190*n*
Kelley, Clarence M., 78-88
Kelley, Frank, 97, 98, 100
Keniston, Kenneth, 190*n*
Keyes, Thomas, 99
Kindleberger, Charles P., Jr., 96*n*
King, Martin Luther, Jr., 50
Koch, Congressman, 361*n*
Kohanek, James J., 146-54
Koppe, Bruce, 124

Lachesis, 3
Lamont, Corliss, 73, 164
*Lamont v. Commissioner of Motor
     Vehicles*, 73*n*, 164*n*, 381*n*
Landrum-Griffin Act of 1959, 17
Langdon, Don, 151
Laser communications networks,
     prospects of, in future, 330
Laser storage, erasable, as prospect
     for future, 330
Latter-Day Saints, Church of, com-
     puterization at, 194-203
     business enterprises, 195
     computerize, initial decision to,
          199-200
     current computer system, appli-
          cations of, 200
     future plans, 203
     Genealogical Society, 198
     history, 194
     Management Systems Corp., 200
     manual and computerized files,
          comparison between, 201-
          02
     record-keeping, traditional, 195-
          99

Law enforcement, federal, and computerization, 45-64
  "domestic intelligence community," sharing among, 46
  National Crime Information Center of FBI, 47-64
  "privileged" information in general, 46-7
  See also National Crime Information Center
Law enforcement, municipal, and computerization, 76-88
  See also Municipal law enforcement
Law Enforcement Assistance Administration, 57, 77, 98
"Law-enforcement intelligence subject," meaning of, 81
Law Enforcement Manpower Resources Allocation system, 82
Learson, T. Vincent, 395*n*
Lee, Mayor Richard C., 90-100
Lee, Robert S., 485, 485*n*
Legislation
  not kept pace with computers and public concern, 347
  managers' opinions on need for future, 353-58
Legislature, role of,
  in controlling use of social security number, 398-400
  in creating information trust agencies, 400-02
  in supporting access rights, 360-72
  in supporting confidentiality, 373-78
  in limiting collection of unnecessary data, 383-92
LEMRAS, 82
Lenk, K., 489*n*
LePoole, 388*n*
Letters, site-visit, 497-501
Libraries and Information Technology: A National System Challenge, 325*n*, 329*n*

LINK file system, development of, 192-93
Local government computerizing organizations, profiles of, 76-88
  See also Municipal law enforcement
Local Government Information Control, establishment of, in Santa Clara County, 103-5
  See also LOGIC
LOGIC, birth of, in Santa Clara County government, 103-05, 236
  challenges to, 105-107
  implementation of, 105
  progress in, 107-09
  timetable, 109-10
Long, Senator Russell, 373, 376-78
Louis Harris Associates, 466, 466*n*
Lumbard, Judge, 140
Lundborg, Louis B., 115
Lyons, Robert K., 90

MacPherson, Duncan, 71
Mail Preference Service of DMAA, 165-67
Mailing-list industry, profile of computerization in, 154-67
  sources of information, 155
  See also R. L. Polk & Co.
Management information system, 232*n*, 233*n*
Management Systems Corp. of Mormon Church, 200
Manual records
  as greatest security problem, 307-08
  defined, 9
  still contain most sensitive data, 249-51
  used alongside computer files, 222
Marine, Donald R., 161

Marketing Services Division of R. L.
Polk, 158
Massachusetts Institute of Technology, profile of computerization at, 169-82, 321
civil liberties concerns, within Institute, 178-79
civil liberties issues in student records, 175-77
computer development at, 171-74
confidentiality, 177-78
future, 181-82
impact of computer, 174-75
ombudsman as arbitrator, recommendation for, 181
personal records, 170-71
privacy, ad hoc committee on, 179-81
Mathias, Senator Charles, Jr., 86
Matter of Smith and Vasquez, 388*n*, 389*n*
Mayor's Game: Richard Lee of New Haven and the Politics of Change, 91*n*
McClellan, Senator, 190
Medical Information Bureau, 142, 230
Medical records, confidentiality and, 40, 74, 148-50, 176-177, 204, 211-13
individual access to, 40, 177, 212, 365-66
Medicare program as amendment to Social Security Act, computer impact of, 32-45
See also Social Security Administration
Menard v. Mitchell, 60-61, 372, 382, 389*n*
Metromedia, Inc., 165*n*
MICR, development of, 116
Midwest Research Institute, 88
"Militants, activists and mentals," file of ALERT system on, 85
Miller, Prof. Arthur R., 18*n*, 270
Miller, H. S., 387*n*, 388*n*
Miller, William Lee, 91*n*

Miller v. NY Stock Exchange, 381*n*
Mills, Sam, 68-9, 74, 75
"Minicomputers," 12
future development of, 326-27
Misunderstanding, public, about computer's impact, a case study, 269-79
Missouri Uniform Law Enforcement System, 88
Mitchell, Attorney General John, 59
Model City: A Test of American Liberalism, 91*n*
Modern Data magazine, 178
Moore, Wilbert E., xii
Morrow v. District of Columbia, 59*n*, 381*n*
Motor List Division of R. L. Polk, 158
Motor Vehicle Department, New York State, profile of computerization at, 66-75
Administrative Adjudication program, 69
administration and control, improved, 69
American Association of Motor Vehicle Administrators, participation in, 71
commercial firms, sales to, 72-5
future prospects, 75
licensing and registration, applications in, 67-70
manual records, 66-7
National Driver Registration Service, 71
parking violators, increased control over, 69-70
security and privacy concerns, 70-72
MULES, 88
Municipal government, 88-100
See also New Haven, Conn. databank for municipal government
Municipal law enforcement, computerization in, 76-88
Crime Control Act of 1968, 77

Municipal law enforcement:
  intelligence files confidential, 76
  records, three categories of, 76
  See also Kansas City, Mo. police
    department
Mutual of Omaha, profile of com-
    puterization at, 141-54
  benefit histories on tape, 147
  CHAMPUS, 147
  computerization, 145-48
  confidentiality of records, 148-50
  CPAS, 146
  federal constraints, 151-53
  future plans, 153-54
  growth in past twenty years, 143
  manual insurance records, 143-45

Nader, Ralph, 270
Naked Society, 4
Narcotics and Dangerous Drugs, Bu-
    reau of, computerization in, 46
Narrative file of FBI, 50
  confidentiality of, 50
Narrative records, difficulty of com-
    puterizing, 224, 250-251, 424-
    26
National Academy of Sciences, ix, xv,
    25, 27, 325*n*
National Association for State Infor-
    mation systems, 64*n*, 65
National Bureau of Standards, 326*n*
National Center for Health Services
    Research, 208
National Council of Churches of
    Christ, 195
National Crime Information Center
    of FBI, computerization at, 47-
    64, 81
  civil liberties discussions, early,
    53-4
  computerization, 51-53
    of criminal histories, 57-59
  criminal history file, policies for,
    61-3
  criticisms, 47-8

National Crime Information Center:
  future plans, 63-4
  Menard v. Mitchell, 60-1
  operations of, 54-5
  system safeguards, 55-7
  See also Fingerprint records of
      FBI; Narrative file of FBI
National Driver Registration Service,
    71, 291
National Goals Research Staff, xii
National Institue of Mental Health,
    189
"National numbering agency," prob-
    lem of Social Security Admin-
    istration as, 42-5
National Student Association, 188-
    89, 190
*National Survey of the Public's Atti-
    tudes Toward Computers*,
    263*n*, 460*n*
Nations, foreign, databank develop-
    ments in, 489-94
Naval Intelligence, Office of, 46
Neulinger, John, ix
New Haven, Conn., profile of data-
    bank for municipal govern-
    ment, 88-100
  CIRS, 98
  Community Progress, Inc., 91-2
  current applications, 97-100
  data processing, 92-3
  databank approach, move to, 93-4
  DIME file, 98
  future plans, 100
  IBM-New Haven project, 89-90,
    94-7
  "model city," 90-2
  organization, municipal, 92
  Re-Development Agency, 91-2
  urban reform, 91-2
New Left Notes, 189
New York State Identification and
    Intelligence System, 294, 311-
    15, 369
  ALPS project of, 294
Newman, James, 82, 87
Niblett, G. B. F., 491*n*

Nonprofit organizations, profiles of
        computerization in, 168-214
    See also American Council on Ed-
        ucation, Kaiser-Permanente
        Medical Care program; Lat-
        ter Day Saints, Church of;
        Massachusetts Institute of
        Technology
Norrgard, David L., 76*n*
Northwestern University, 192*n*
Norton, L. A., 157*n*
Notes on Security, 157*n*
Notice, as element of access right,
        362-64
NYSIIS, 294, 311-15, 369

Obey, Congressman David, 468, 475
Ombudsman as mediator, recom-
        mendation of MIT ad hoc com-
        mittee for, 181
On-line systems, and batch processing,
        differences between, 10-11
    defined, 10-11, 13-14
    and faster access to data, 289-90
    future use of, 326-27
    and growth of networks, 232,
        235, 291-3
    misunderstood capabilities of,
        269-79
*On Record: Files and Dossiers in
        American Life*, x
Opinion Research Corp., 152-53,
        467*n*
Organization for Economic Coopera-
        tion and Development, 7, 489-
        94
Organizations, problem of power of,
        over individuals, x-xi
Organizations studied in survey, se-
        lection of, 410-11
Organizations' decisions about people,
        computer coding and, 264-66
Organized Crime Intelligence Unit of
        Justice Department, 63*n*
Orwell, George, 87
Output, computer, 11

Output devices, prospects for future
        development of, 329-30

Packard, Vance, 4
"Panel research," meaning of, 182
Panos, Robert, 184, 188
Parrish, Benny Max, 404
*Parrish v. Civil Service Commission
        of Alameda County*, 404*n*
People v. Belous, 18*n*
Permanente Medical group, part of
        Kaiser-Permanente system, 206
    medical records, 211
    See also Kaiser-Permanente Med-
        ical Care program
Personnel records
    at Bank of America, 19-20, 26-27,
        284
    and privacy of federal employees,
        384-85
    of Protestant denominations, 249-
        50
*Peterson v. Idaho First National
        Bank*, 122*n*
Pipes, R., 489*n*
Pinkerton Detective Agency, 71*n*
Police departments, local, computer-
        ization and, 76-88
    See also Municipal law enforce-
        ment
Police Operational Intelligence, 157*n*
Policy, areas of priority for public;
        355-405
    citizen's right to see his record,
        355-72
    confidentiality and data sharing,
        rules for, 372-78
    other areas, 402-04
    safeguards, technological, for in-
        formation systems, 392-96
    sensitive data, trust agencies for,
        400-02
    Social Security number as univer-
        sal identifier, 396-400
    unnecessary data collection,
        limiting, 379-392

Political conditions, impact of upon future technology, 323-24

Powell, Robert, 189

Powledge, Fred, 91, 91n

Priorities, organizational, influence on future technology, 321-22

Privacy
and computers, public opinion on, 479-85
effects of computerization on, 241-56
and collection of more information, 243-51
confidentiality issues of information consolidation and data-sharing, 251-56
data-sharing rules, four types of, 252-55
evaluation and planning, increased information for, 245-46
files, two types of automation of, 246-47
minimal information possible, attempting to keep, 247-48
proprietary concept, development of, 254-55
"sensitive" information, definition of, 249-51
measures to protect, 379-92
See also Data collection unnecessary limiting of
and records, public opinion on, 466-79
right to, 17-20
common-law right to, 19
definition, 393
"right most valued by civilized men," 17

Privacy Battleground, 468n

"Privacy and Behavioral Research," xi

Privacy, Computers and You, 491n

Privacy and Freedom, ix, 18n, 242, 242n

Privacy Invaders, 4

"Privacy and the Public," 153n

Privacy and the Rights of Federal Employees, 384n

Private organizations, due process rights in, 17, 20, 371

"Privileged" information of federal law enforcement agencies, 46-7

Procedural due process in computerized record systems, 256-9
public awareness, increased, 257

Processing by computer, described, 10-11

Procheck, 63n

Profiles of computerizing organizations, 23-214
See also Computerizing organizations

Programming, computer, 11-12

Programs, meaning of, 10

Project Talent, 182

Proprietary concept about data-sharing, development of, through computerization, 254-55

Proprietary data, and security concerns, 309, 311

Prospects, technological, for future, 324-30
civil liberties implications of, 330-35
communications systems, 329
computers, availability of, 328
configuration arrangements, 326-27
input, 325-26
output, 329-30
software and data-base management, 327-28
storage, 326
system reliability, 327

Proxmire, Senator William, 135

Psychiatric records, confidentiality of, 40, 176-77, 211

Public misinformation on computer impact, a case study, 269-279

Public opinion, on privacy
    and records, 466-79
    and computers, 479-85
Public policy implications of
    computer technology, 337-
    405
    assumptions, two basic, 339-40
    priority, areas of, 355-405
    significance of findings, 341-354
    See also Policy, areas of priority
        for public; Significance of
        site-visit findings
Public trial, guarantees of, 16

"Quality Index" of R. H. Donnelley
    Corp., 155
Questionnaire for survey, content of,
    413-14

Race, as decision criterion, 145, 371,
    387-8
    problem of question about in
        SSA application, 34
Random-access devices, use of, 11
    improved as characteristic of
        third generation EDP equip-
        ment, 14
    See also On-line Systems
Realities of computerization efforts,
    233-40
    databanks few and far between,
        235-40
    file automation, here and "irre-
        versible," 234-35
Recession as detriment to databank
    development, 240
Record, definition of, 9
Record-keeping, civil liberties and,
    14-20
    See also Due process of law and
        record systems
Record-keeping, effects of compu-
    terization on, 280-315

Record-keeping:
    accuracy of information, 294-303
    complete and up-to-date records,
        280-84
    information in files, greater use
        of, 284-88
    inquiries, faster handling of, 289-
        90
    interorganizational networks,
        creation of, 291-93
    large systems, increased number
        of, 293-94
    security of information, 303-315
    See also Accuracy of computer-
        ized information
Record-keeping, initial computeriza-
    tion, reasons for, 228-29
    growth of computerization, rea-
        sons for, 228-29
    high-volume file automation, 221-
        29
    increase in volume of transactions,
        table of, 224-27
    manual files still retained, certain
        number of, 222
Re-Development Agency of New
    Haven, 91-2
Reforms, in decision making, call
    for, 343-44
Refunds, duplicate tax, eliminated by
    computerization, 193-203
Regional Law Enforcement, 76n
Religious organizations, profile of
    computerization in, 193-203
    See also Latter Day Saints
*Report of the Committee to Investi-
    gate the Effect of Police Arrest
    Records on Employment Op-
    portunities in the District of
    Columbia,* 388n
Research files as type, 182-83, 361,
    364
Respondents to survey questionnaire,
    414-16
Retail Credit Co. of Atlanta, Georgia,
    74, 131, 144, 152, 153n, 250
Retz, Gene, 151

Reuben H. Donnelley Co., 155,
    157*n*, 167
Ribicoff, Senator Abraham, 373
Richardson, Elliot, 44, 397, 397*n*
Riesman, David, 190*n*
Rise, Inc. of Los Angeles, 155*n*
R. L. Polk & Co. profile of compu-
    terization at, 72-5, 156-67
  beginnings, 156
  computerization, move to, 159-61
  divisions, three, 157-58
  future plans, 167
  Mail Preference Service, 165-67
  privacy issues and direct-mail ad-
    vertising, 161-63
  response to criticism, 165-67
  "selectivity," computer's impact
    on, 160
  tests of privacy issue, judicial and
    legislative, 164-65
Rockefeller, John D. III, Foundation,
    468-69, 468*n*, 475*n*
Roll, C. W., Jr., 343*n*
Roosevelt, President Franklin D., 31,
    36
Roper, B. R., 343*n*
Rowan v. Post Office, 162*n*
Rowe, B. C., 491*n*
Rubenstein, Dr. Eli, 190
Ruebhausen, Oscar M., xi
Russell Sage Foundation, ix
Ryan, Judge Sylvester, 139

SABRE reservations sytem of Amer-
    ican Airlines, misunderstood
    capabilities, 269-279, 321
Safeguards for information systems,
    technological, priority of de-
    velopment of, 392-96
Samuelson, E., 491*n*
Santa Clara County, California pro-
    file of computerization at
  characteristics, 101-02
  civil liberties issues, discussion of,
    105-07
  future plans, 109-10

Santa Clara County:
  LOGIC, birth of, 103-05
  progress in LOGIC system, 107-09
  record-keeping and move into
    ADP, 102
  record-keeping practices, effects
    of computerization on, 109
Santarelli, Donald E., 391*n*
Sapolsky, Karen, 470*n*
Schafer, John S., 153*n*
Schaffer, Benson, 367*n*
Schultz, D. O., 157*n*
SCOPE, 130
Scott, Basil, 66, 73
Scott, Robert H., 171-72, 174, 178,
    181
SDS, 189
SEARCH, project of, 57-8
*Search for Ability: Standardized
    Testing in Social Perspective*,
    ix
"Second-chance" tradition, destruc-
    tion of, by computerized re-
    cord system, 267-68
Secret Service, computerization and,
    46, 47
Security
  of computerized information,
    303-15
  case history of gap between
    security goals and organ-
    ization performance,
    311-15
  employees of organizations
    maintaining files, in-
    volved in breaches of,
    306-09
  findings, general, in site-visits,
    304-05
  in future years, 333
  increasing difficulty of, 333
  manual records, greatest in-
    cidence of security
    breach in, 307-08
  as priority for public policy,
    392-96
  in service bureaus, 310-11

Security:
  of computerized information: sur-
    vey of safeguards in use of
    record systems, 322-33,
    441-44
Security investigations, at M.I.T., 175-
  76, 180
Self-incrimination, individual's privilege against, 16
Sensitive data, establishment of information trust agencies to
  handle, 400-02
"Sensitive" personal information, explanation of, 249-51
  most still in manual records, 249-
    51, 424-26
Service bureaus, security of computerized information and,
  310-11
  increased use of in future, 330
Shared central databank
  in actual existence, 233-37
  manual versions, 230-31
  meaning of, 229-30
  proposals for, 231-32
Sharing of data as most important
  technological advance in
  1970's, 342
Sheel, Karl, 102, 106
Sheldon, Eleanor, Bernert, xii
Sherrill, Robert, 270
Shorthand, in computer records, and
  decisions about people, 264-66
Significance of site-visit findings,
  341-54
  in context of growing protest and
    challenge, 343-47
Site-visit findings from 55 systems,
  215-315
  assumptions underlying, 217-220
  See also Realities of computeri-
    zation effects
Site visits to computerizing organi-
  zations, 23-214
  research procedures, 23-28
  See also Computerizing organi-
    zations

Smith, Bruce, 200
Smith, M. Brewster, 190*n*
"Social Attitudes and the Computer
  Revolution," 485*n*
Social factors, specification of per-
  tinent in forecasting computer
  technology, 320-21, 323-24
Social indicators, problem of development of, xii
Social Security Administration, profile of, 31-45
  access rights, 39-42
  computer's impact at, 35-6
  confidentiality of files, 36-9
  data processing within, 33-4
  files, current, 34-5
  future, 45
  identification, number for, 42
  information in files, personal, 32-
    33
  "national numbering agency,"
    dealing with issue of, 42-
    45
  statistics, 34
Social Security number as universal
  identifier, 396-400
Social services agency, federal, profile of, 30-45
  "welfare" programs, two types
    of, 31
Software, meaning of, 11-12
Software and data-base management,
  prospects for future development of, 327
Software problems as detriment to
  databank development, 239
Sorensen, Robert A., 106
Sparer, E., 388*n*
Speer, William, 176, 177
Spock v. District of Columbia,
  389*n*
Standard Analytical Services, Inc.,
  146*n*
Stanford University, 116
State regulatory agencies, comput-
  erization and, 64-75
  statistics, 64-65

State regulatory agencies:
 units, eleven, 65
 See also Motor Vehicle Bureau,
  New York State
Statistical data, computer encourages
  sharing of, 441-42
Stone, Attorney General Harlan, 47
Storage, computer prospects for
  future development of, 326
Storage in computers, 9-10
 "databank," meaning of, 9*n*
 file, definition of, 9
 record, definition of, 9
Substantive due process issues, 259-64
 coding and organizational decisions, 264-66
 "print-out," charge of reliance on
  in judgments, 259-64
 unforgiving record systems, creation of, 267-68
Sullivan, Paul E., 115
Supervisory agencies for computer
  databanks, suggestion concerning, 351
Surveillance, 346
 by U.S. Army on civilians, 46,
  264-65
Survey of managerial opinion on
  impact of computers in record-
  keeping, 407-62
 objectives and methods, 409-17
 presentation of data, 416-17
 questionnaire content, 413-14
 respondents, 414-16
 results and their interpretation,
  417-58
 summary, 458-62
Survey of public opinion literature
  on privacy and computers,
  465-85
Sutton, Willie, 125
Syrett, George Jr., 67
System for Electronic Analysis and
  Retrieval of Criminal Histories,
  57
System reliability, prospects for future development of, 327

Taggert, Thomas, 129
Talbot, Allan R., 91*n*
Tarver v. Smith, 358*n*
*Task Force on Science and Techno-
  logy*, 387*n*
Taviss, Irene, 470*n*, 479*n*
Technical problems in software as
  detriment to databank development, 239
Technology, computer, fundamentals
  of, 7-14
 history of, 12-14
 input, 8-9
 output, 11
 processing, 10-11
 programming, 11-12
 storage, 9-10
 not "thinking" machine, 7-8
 See also EDP equipment, history
  of, Storage in computers
Telecommunications facilities, third
  generation EDP equipment
  characterized by, 14
"The Next (and Last?) Generation,"
  325*n*
Thomas, U., 489*n*
Time, Inc., 263*n*
Time-sharing computer facilities, increased use of in future, 330
*Toward Central Government Com-
  puter Policies*, 489*n*
Trans World Airways, 272
Transactions, faster handling of
  through computerization,
  289-90
 record, table of increases in,
  224-27
Transistors as basic elements of second generation EDP hardware,
  13-14
Transportation Institute, 468
Travelers Research Corp, 97
Trends in computerizing personal
  records, 217-40
 See also Personal records, trends
  in
Trial, 359*n*

Trust agencies, special, for sensitive data, establishment of, 400-02
TRW-Credit Data Corp., 123, 125, 132-41
See also Credit Data Corp.
Tunney, Senator John, 125n
Turning, Walter, 92, 95, 99

UMIS, of New Haven, Conn., 90, 97, 233n, 236
Un-American Activities Committee, 188
Unforgiving record systems, criticism of computer-created, 267-68
United Nations Commission on Social Development, xii
United of Omaha, 146
See also Mutual of Omaha
Universal identifier, Social Security number as, 42-5, 396-400
Universities, computerization in, 167-82
See also Massachusetts Institute of Technology
University of California, 115, 179n
University of Michigan, 270, 343n
University of Missouri, 85
University of Wisconsin, 179n
Unwanted mail, problem of, 161-67
See also R. L. Polk & Co
Up-to-date records, more possible by computerization, 280-84
Urban Management Information System of New Haven, Conn., 90, 97, 233n, 236
Urban and Regional Information Systems Association, 96
U.S. v. Davey, 140n, 381n
U.S. v. Golembiewski, 55n
U.S. v. Kalish, 59n, 381n
U. S. v. McLeod, 59n, 381n
U.S. v. Rickenbacker, 19n, 381n
U.S. v. Vuitch, 18n
Users of computer systems
early naïveté of, 228-29

Users of computer systems:
era of "users Lib," 235
vast increase in, 319

Vacuum-tube elements basis of first generation EDP hardware, 13
Van Brunt, Dr. Edmund, 209
Vandermate, George, 107
Veterans Administration, 164

Waldie, Jerome, 163
Weaver, HUD Secretary Robert, 92
Weizenbaum, Prof. Joseph, 179
Welcome Newcomer, 165n
"Welfare" programs of federal social services agencies, 31
Welfare reform program, suggested revision of, 373-77
civil liberties implications, 376-78
enforcement perspective, 374-76
work requirements, 374
Westin, Alan F., ix, xii, xv, xvi, xvii, 18n, 342n
Wheeler, Stanton, x
Wheeler v. Goodman, 59n
Whisenand, Paul M., 77n
Who Governs? Democracy and Power in an American City, 91n
Wichita Falls, Texas, Data Access Advisory Board in, 352
Wiesner, Dr. Jerome, 178-79
Wilson, Logan, 184, 190
Withington, F. G., 325n
Work requirements of proposed welfare programs, 374

Yale University, x, 91
Yankelovich, Inc., 468n
Younger, Sir Kenneth, 419n

Zeisel, Hans, 401n
Zipf, A. R., 116-17